Bergsonian Philosophy and Thomism

THE COLLECTED WORKS OF JACQUES MARITAIN
Volume 1

Honorary Editor-in-Chief

Theodore M. Hesburgh, C.S.C.

Founder

Ralph McInerny

Editors

John O'Callaghan

John Hittinger   Alice Ramos

Acknowledgments

To a grant from George Strake and the Strake Foundation for support of this series.

Bergsonian Philosophy and Thomism

JACQUES MARITAIN

Translated by
Mabelle L. Andison

in collaboration with
J. Gordon Andison

Presented by
Ralph McInerny

University of Notre Dame Press
Notre Dame, Indiana

Published by the University of Notre Dame Press
Notre Dame, IN 46556
www.undpress.nd.edu

Manufactured in the United States of America.

Library of Congress Cataloging-in-Publication Data

Maritain, Jacques, 1882–1973.
  [Philosophie bergsonienne. English]
  Bergsonian philosophy and Thomism / Jacques Maritain ;
translated by Mabelle L. Andison in collaboration with J. Gordon Andison ;
presented by Ralph McInerny.
    p. cm. — (The collected works of Jacques Maritain ; v. 1)
  Originally published: New York : Philosophical Library, c1955. With new introd.
  Includes bibliographical references and index.
  ISBN-13: 978-0-268-02152-8 (cloth : alk. paper)
  ISBN-10: 0-268-02152-x (cloth : alk. paper)
1. Bergson, Henri, 1859–1941. I. Title.
  B2430.B43M373   2007
  194—dc22

                                                2006102638

∞ *The paper in this book meets the guidelines for permanence and durability of the Committee
on Production Guidelines for Book Longevity of the Council on Library Resources*

CONTENTS

FIRST PART

THE DOCUMENTS IN THE CASE

FIRST SECTION
GENERAL ASPECTS OF BERGSONISM

SECOND SECTION
CRITICAL EXAMINATION OF THE PHILOSOPHY OF BERGSON

INTRODUCTION

"Read Bergson. I have criticized him a lot, but read Bergson!" Thus Jacques Maritain spoke to Yves Floucat in 1960. Misgivings about the severity of his criticisms of Henri Bergson in his first published book, *La Philosophie Bergsonienne,* were already expressed in the second edition. However profound Jacques Maritain's disagreements with Bergson might be, he could never forget the decisive role the philosopher had played in saving himself and his fiancée Raïssa from the despair induced in them by the philosophy taught in the Sorbonne at the turn of the century.

In her memoirs, written during their war-time exile in New York, Raïssa recounted in the unforgettable pages that bear the heading "In the Jardin des Plantes" the crisis the young couple had reached. Their cultural milieu, the ambience of the Sorbonne, was materialist and could not provide any answer to the most fundamental question of all: What is the meaning of life? Raïssa and Jacques did not see any reason to go on living if indeed there was no reason for living at all. This despairing gloom first began to lift when they were taken to the Collège de France by Charles Péguy to follow the Friday afternoon lectures of Bergson. Here, the possibility of metaphysics, of something transcending the material, was opened up to them in a way that, years later, both Jacques and Raïssa were still effusive in describing.

No doubt it was precisely the profound impact that Bergson had on him that was the basis for Jacques's personal need to attack him when Jacques saw that a thinker who had once been so great a boon became an obstacle to the truth he had found in Saint Thomas Aquinas. But at those lectures in the Collège de France, Péguy, Ernest Psichari, Raïssa, and Jacques sat spellbound. The book before you, in its first version, was perhaps necessary to exorcize the defects of Bergson's philosophy as they were revealed to the eye of one now schooled in Thomism. But it was only right that, this being done, Jacques should return to Bergson and moderate his criticism in the long preface to the second edition.

The vagaries of reputation in philosophy are a story unto themselves. There was a time when the writings of Henri Bergson were a constant point of reference. This is no longer so. It would be ironic if Bergson became known to present-day readers only through such a massive criticism as that Maritain leveled in his first book. When he wrote it, Maritain was taking on a superstar of the times, whose reputation seemed assured and who could not have been mortally damaged even by so thorough a critique as that found in *La Philosophie Bergsonienne.* Maritain would be the first to urge the reader to go to Bergson's own writings in order to appraise what is said of them in this book. Of course, not all of Bergson's major works had appeared when Maritain wrote this book. But Maritain could assume a thorough knowledge of his opponent on the part of the reader. As he said to Floucat, *"Lisez Bergson!"*

Maritain's own reputation has known its ups and downs. When the Jacques Maritain Center was founded at the University of Notre Dame in 1957, under the triumvirate of Rev. Leo R. Ward, C.S.C., Frank Keegan, and Joseph Evans, it was envisaged as the eventual repository of Maritain's papers. Raïssa died in 1960, in France, to which they had returned for treatment, and from that point on, the center of gravity of Jacques Maritain's life returned to his native land. The more than dozen years of life left him came to be divided between Toulouse and the Little Brothers of Jesus, an order in which Jacques would take the three vows of religion in 1971, and the chateau at Kolbsheim where he was the honored guest of the Gruneliuses. It was there that Raïssa lay buried and where Jacques would lie beside her after his death in 1973. He was no longer a household word in his native land, perhaps, but Kolbsheim fittingly became the repository of his papers; there, under the capable administration of Réné Mougel, the Centre d'Etudes Jacques et Raïssa Maritain laid the groundwork for the renaissance of interest in Maritain in which it continues to play the major role.

Since his death, the reputation of Jacques Maritain has been recovering from the dip it took with the appearance of *The Peasant of the Garonne,* his mordant look at what some were making of Vatican II. The prescience of those misgivings has long been clear. Meanwhile, new societies devoted to the thought of Maritain have sprung up: in Kolbsheim, of course, but also in Rome, in Latin America, in Canada, and in the United States. John Paul II cited Jacques Maritain by name in his 1998 encyclical *Fides et Ratio* as a model of the continuing effort to effect a *modus vivendi* between faith and reason. Young Catholic intellectuals are finding inspiration in the motto Jacques Maritain took from John of St. Thomas, *Philosophandum in fide:* One should philosophize in the ambience of the faith.

This Notre Dame edition faithfully reproduces the translation of Mabelle L. Andison in collaboration with J. Gordon Andison published by the Philosophical Library in 1955.

Ralph McInerny
The Jacques Maritain Center
University of Notre Dame

FOREWORD TO THE ENGLISH TRANSLATION

La Philosophie Bergsonienne was my first book; it was published forty years ago when I was young, and did not hesitate to rush in where angels feared to tread.

In the *Preface to the Second Edition* I tried to make clear the meaning of the book and to atone for its violence. Explain myself as I may, however, I am still afraid of possible misunderstanding, and it is not without serious misgivings that I have authorized the English translation which is now being published. The picture it offers of Bergsonian philosophy is necessarily incomplete, since some late works by Bergson—especially his important treatise on *The Two Sources of Morality and Religion*—had not yet appeared when I wrote my Essays. The fact that my own philosophical exposition is interwoven with religious and theological concerns was quite understandable at the time, given the intellectual situation in France and the purpose of my book. Here and now it may appear as something bizarre and unfamiliar, and is liable to mislead some people as to the real significance—philosophical, not theological—of my life work.

I nevertheless yielded to the request of the *Philosophical Library* on the ground that, after all, this early work (which constitutes the first and largest part of the present volume) is probably a fair-to-middling account of basic Thomistic philosophy and, first and foremost, that despite its deficiencies it still has historical interest for those who are concerned with the movement of ideas at the beginning of this century. But I beg the reader to take into consideration the above indications.

It would perhaps be well to explain the composition of the book in translation. The *First Part* comprises all of the work known as *La Philosophie Bergsonienne,* with some changes in the titles of the sections, and a few cuts in the text. The *Second Part*—an *Essay of Appreciation*—though much shorter, is important to the volume as a whole, because it represents the later stage of my thought on the subject, and thus makes up for the harshness of my former criticism. This Second Part is taken from *Ransoming the Time;* the two chapters of which it is composed were translated by Mr. Harry Lorin Binsse. For the privilege of using them here I should like to thank Charles Scribner's Sons.

Except for these two chapters, the translation of the entire book is the work of Professor and Mrs. Gordon Andison. I extend my sincerest thanks to them for the exceedingly careful and thoughtful manner in which they have performed their task. I also thank the publisher for his patience and courtesy.

J. M.

Princeton, N.J.
January 1954

PREFACE TO THE SECOND EDITION OF
LA PHILOSOPHIE BERGSONIENNE

BERGSONISM AND METAPHYSICS

I

This book, now being re-published, first appeared toward the end of the year 1913 and has long been out of print. It consists of three studies which, while differing in point of view, deal each from a particular angle with Bergsonian thought as a whole. Thus in the first edition we had a series of lectures given in April and May, 1913, at the Catholic Institute in Paris under the title *la Philosophie de M. Bergson et la philosophie chrétienne;* then an article on *l'Évolutionnisme bergsonien* which first appeared in the *Revue de Philosophie* (in the number of September–October 1911) and finally an article which appeared in the *Revue thomiste* (July–August 1912), entitled *Les deux bergsonismes.* In this new edition it has seemed advisable to put the essay on *l'Évolutionnisme bergsonien* first in order of sequence since that is where it belongs chronologically. As for the text, it has undergone only those modifications which a lapse of fifteen years has rendered indispensable, modifications about which I should like to give a few explanations.

It is indeed a painful ordeal and melancholy task for an author to reread and re-state as best he may the matter of a book from which he is separated by a long interval of time. This is the first book I ever wrote; and however one may wish to judge its value, it happens that it has a place in the history of ideas in France in this early part of a new century. It was one of the first manifestations, along lines of lay thinking, of that rebirth of Thomism toward which, in the sacred order, eminent thinkers had been working since the time of Leo XIII and the encyclical *Aeterni Patris.* That is why I have been so anxious to maintain its characteristic underlying movement.

I shall not seek to minimize its shortcomings. This does not mean that I consider the doctrinal positions it defends as being any less well-founded today: on the contrary I maintain every one of them whether they concern the criticism of Bergsonian philosophy or the doctrines of Saint Thomas; and it is evident that if such were not the case, I should not now be re-publishing this work. For I have no taste for relativism in matters intellectual, and I do not believe truth to be a function of time. It is indeed a cause for satisfaction on my part to discover that thanks to God,—and whatever may be the weaknesses of the work in other respects,—I have had to make no important modification in substance or doctrine, merely a few precisions and completions here and there, certain accentuations given with greater firmness and nicety, and in two Chapters [*Man* and *Freedom*], some important elucidations on the theory of memory and the theory of liberty.

What makes the reading of the early text somewhat painful to me today is the youthful turgidity, the uncompromising bombast of its style. Here they are then, these pages written only for the sake of the pure and simple truth, and which we took to be transparent to the light of the object alone. The mood of the moment also appears in their style:—their style! It is no business of the philosopher to have a style—it is not for him to give way to his feelings. This particular philosopher nevertheless managed somehow to clothe in a garment which dates the truths he was recalling, to involve them in the transitory, to imprint on them the trace of time. With all the respect and gratitude he never ceased to pay to Bergson, he permitted himself to use, albeit in the very just criticism he was making of Bergson's doctrines, in the just and necessary nay the salutary conflict he was provoking between Bergsonian thought and that of Thomas Aquinas, language at times so imperious, so lacking in deference, that through his brashness he not only ran the risk of scandalizing certain timid minds, but what is more, prejudicing well-intentioned minds against the indispensable revision of values he was proposing. All of which refers to nothing more than the *tone* of the book, but everyone knows how important tone can be in works of the mind.

I do not wish to imply that the tone of this book was entirely bad,—why speak with calumny of oneself? One's neighbour is there to do it for one, and only too well. A tone which takes liberties in dealing with the wisdom of the times, a tone of certitude in affirming what is certain, is nothing that will ever give me cause for regret. What I do regret is having given way more than once, carried along as it were by the movement and rhythm of the exposition, to that sort of insistence and euphoria which is always a danger, as Charles Du Bos[1] pointed out in a recent book, for a mind only too happy to be right. I do not say it was pride: I was spared that temptation. It was clearly evident that it was not I who was right but the Doctor whose disciple I had become, and all the age-long genealogy of wisdom whose beneficent *magisterium* he brings to those who listen to him. No, it was a more subtle danger. I was not then aware that if one can never be too right, it is nevertheless so great a privilege, and so undeserved, that it should always make one feel apologetic, —a form of politeness we owe to truth. Christ, when He taught, proclaimed aloud the divine truth; that truth should be shouted from the house-tops. Human truths require in the telling a voice more modestly pitched. If the de-

---

[1] Charles Du Bos, *Le Dialogue avec André Gide*, Paris, Au Sans Pareil, 1929.

cisiveness of the affirmation should correspond to the certitude of the proof, the modulation should be proportioned to the difficulties of the search. The immense advantage of a *via disciplinae* which transmits taught truths to us and enables us to grasp them in their state of fulfilment and objective completion as it were, should not be turned to underestimating and disparaging the sort of native vigour and active freshness with which, in its nascent state, the most hesitant truth *invented* (or re-invented) by a thinking brain reaches us, even though tainted with possibly serious errors. It was my duty to criticize as I did the conception of the Divinity which the philosophy of pure movement suggests. Perfect moderation would have required to be shown, even more specifically than I have done, how the powerlessness to establish divine transcendence which must be denounced in this conception springs not so much from a deliberate complacency, but rather from the failure of a metaphysics condemned by its internal logic to succumb in spite of itself to pantheism. It would also have required to be expressed, to a greater degree than I have been successful in doing, the profoundly human interest of the inner movement which led a philosopher nourished in the pure "scientistic" and "experimentalistic" tradition of the age of Auguste Comte and the steam engine to an idea of a creative God, however deficient that idea might have been.

And lastly, the most serious reproach I felt obliged to direct against my work was that it allowed the philosophical controversy to take on, at times, an almost partisan tone: a clumsiness in wording, I hope, rather than an error in thought, for that very thing whose fundamental opposition to Bergsonian principles of philosophy I was affirming, I knew to be of all things the one which recoils most from even the appearance of a *party*, that catholic wisdom which is offended and betrayed by any particularization.

God does not need our services, yet He wishes us to serve Him. He had an ark of acacia wood built unto Himself covered with gold; He employed in the work the art of the cleverest craftsmen. While He is having it transported on an ox-cart from Cariathiarim to Jerusalem the cart leans a little to one side and Oza steadies the ark with his hand: he falls dead because he has touched the ark of God. "And David was troubled because the Lord had struck down Oza: And he feared God at that time."[1] Blessed be self-knowledge when it comes, for it purifies with its taste of death a zeal too keen, placed youngheartedly, with the heart of a novice, at the service of truth.

Christianity, as I have often said, does not make things easier; it does not facilitate art and, in a certain sense, it does not facilitate philosophy. If it is facility we seek, we might better become a pumpkin or a melon (the melon Descartes dreamed about in his warm little room). It is easier to be a stone than a shrub, a shrub than a bird, a bird than a man, a businessman than a poet or a philosopher, a poet or a philosopher than a Christian, a poet and a

[1] *Paralip.*, [*Chronicles*] I, xiii, 11-12.

Christian or a philosopher and a Christian than a Christian poet or a Christian philosopher. What greater encumbrance, what greater folly can there be for a philosopher, than to add to his speculative task and to the problem of knowing, the preoccupations of the fate of truth in souls, or of the future of a perishable culture, and a helpless pity for the hearts that God seeks? *Stultitia gentibus,* that is the folly we are commanded to choose. We prefer Plotinus surrounded by the orphans he had adopted to Descartes and Spinoza entrenched in their prudence and their apparent detachment from human things (apparent, I say, for they were burning with desire for the success of their god). And we have before us a greater model than Plotinus. To subordinate speculation to no matter what temporal result is to betray as a pragmatist, a saducee of the intelligence, a politician would betray; and it is also to betray, as a pharisee of the intelligence, to make of speculation an absolute end in itself; then it withers on the stalk; and he who thought himself a priest of metaphysics, before an empty tabernacle offers incense in reality only to himself. If speculation is good by itself, and an end in itself, like art, neither the one nor the other can be the ultimate end for him who thinks or who works; he must suspend them from the very Principle "from which are suspended heaven and all nature," and which is called Love and Charity,—and which it is better for us here below to love than to know. A disciple of the Angelic Doctor may incur many well-deserved reproaches through his own infirmity; because his master gives him some intelligence of the order of life I just mentioned, at least he will avoid, as between his will whose law is love and his virtue as a philosopher whose law is knowing, making one bend before the other. He knows furthermore that in advancing along the road, the Christian limps as he runs. He prefers to go forward thus, like Jacob, rather than remain ensconced in history or in bookish formulas, like some self-satisfied doctors. What matters is to be true to the rule of the spirit, and whatever one's aim in heaven may be, never to deflect the pure exigencies of science and reason. For philosophy as for art, it is simply a question of strength.

No deflecting or swerving of the thought, no involuntary deviation from the philosophical line, induced supposedly by religious preoccupations or an instinct for controversy, no, none of these have I discovered in my *Philosophie bergsonienne* in reading over the text of the first edition. But it is of the general tone of the work that I am speaking. And there only too often have I found, especially in the lectures of 1913, those irritating defects already mentioned, which resulted mainly from a lack of skill in endeavoring to smooth away in men's minds powerful obstacles in the way of the true.

While maintaining, as I said above, the general underlying *movement* of the work (and it is precisely on account of that movement that it had, at a given moment, a certain effect) I have been anxious to correct as far as possible the defects to which I refer. The result of this revision is that the work now being published is not quite either the one I wrote seventeen years ago, or the one, I like to think more complete and more closely-knit, that I should write today. Let us say that it corresponds roughly to the book I should like today to have written then. Thanks to these corrections, thanks also to certain other amendments intended to increase the propriety as well as the exactness of the terms, I hope this work will render durable service; I should be happy if there might be found in it not only criticism of erroneous philosophical principles, but also an exact synthesis, not too technical, but accessible without vulgarization, in short a correct primer of the main metaphysical positions of the Angel of the School.

My studies have been blamed for not criticizing Bergsonism *from within,* for constantly contrasting it with another doctrine, and for combatting a philosophical enquiry in the process of becoming, with the help of a rigourously systematized doctrine. This reproach fails to appreciate my real purpose which was precisely to recall that there are criteria of truth independent of the inner movement of a thought in the process of formation, and to turn men's minds toward the powerfully coherent but indefinitely progressive doctrine of Saint Thomas Aquinas, as toward the sole philosophy exclusively commanded by *what is.* The constant comparison thus instituted between Bergsonism and Thomism certainly lacks literary attractiveness. In making a frontal attack on the complacent prejudice which maintains that philosophical doctrines are incommensurable universes each justified in itself, and on that other prejudice according to which the truths thought by the ancients have become unthinkable to ourselves because we have changed and because we no longer kill with arrows but with gases; and further, in coupling with the criticism of a doctrine conforming perfectly with the peculiarities of an age and best adapted to please an intellectuality refined in its exercise and feeble in its power of adhesion to being, fond of movement and of images,—in coupling with the criticism of this doctrine the analysis (of necessity succinct if not at times elementary—and how necessarily so) of a lasting doctrine which demands of intellect its innate resources of spontaneity and decision, yet which has fallen into discredit through schoolroom habits of long standing and pedagogical rust, I placed myself voluntarily and from the very outset at a decided disadvantage. But no matter! The important thing was, in present-day language, to get a message through; and in spite of everything, it did get through.

And finally, it was not *a priori,* as has sometimes been alleged, or in the name of Thomistic authority that my critique of Bergsonian philosophy was made. No,—it was based upon reasons that anyone can verify; it does not ask the reader to take Saint Thomas's word for anything,—on the contrary it claims to incite him to reflect upon Saint Thomas by way of Bergson; it offers him the Thomistic doctrine as an answer to the difficulties with which, as he may already have noticed, contemporary thought is vainly struggling; and in what is a purely philosophical discussion it refers solely to the two authentic sources of any philosophy: experience and intelligence. To these two sources, of course, when the relations of Bergsonism to the Catholic faith are being examined, the nature of things necessitates the addition of a third, by which I mean the very principles of that faith. And that no doubt is what has thrown a number of people off the scent. However, no confusion follows in reality from this; if, in order to answer questions at once distinct and joined, (the value of a philosophy taken in itself, the value of that philosophy in relation to revealed truths), if, I say, the two distinct lights of reason and faith do come into play, they intercross without being altered in themselves and at each moment the discrimination is perfectly clear between the purely philosophical consideration and the philosophico-theological one.

But what a danger there is of being misunderstood in thus joining these two considerations, what a risk of creating a reputation for fanaticism, of losing face before the assembly of this world's sages and before that dear Sorbonne where you were nourished! Unavailing arguments, these. The only consideration that might have given me pause was the risk of speaking a language too harsh for those who might be moving toward faith through Bergsonism. Even today as I publish this second edition I feel a certain apprehension on this point, yet I know my task is only to speak the truth as I see it. This sort of philosophico-theological consideration had moreover become indispensable as a result of the modernist crisis and also because of the application of Bergsonism attempted by certain people (and in what mode!) to religious and dogmatic matters. It also echoed a personal experience whose significance seemed to me to have a general application.

II

It was in 1908—while I was deliberating, in the country around Heidelberg, whether I could reconcile the Bergsonian critique of the concept and the formulas of revealed dogma, that the irreducible conflict between the "conceptual" pronouncements of the religious faith which had recently opened my eyes, and the philosophical doctrine for which I had conceived such a passion during my years as a student and to which I was indebted for being freed from materialistic idols, appeared to me as one of those only too certain facts which the soul, once it has begun to admit them, knows immediately it will never escape. The effort, unobtrusively pursued for months, to bring about a conciliation which was the supreme object of my desire ended abruptly in this unimpeachable conclusion. The choice had to be made, and obviously this choice could only be in favour of the Infallible, confessing therefore that all the philosophical toil which had been my delight was to be begun again.

Since God gives us, in concepts and conceptual propositions (which reach us dripping with the blood of martyrs—in the days of Arianism men knew how to die for the sake of an iota) truths transcendent and inaccessible to our reason, the very truth of His divine life, that abyss which is His, it is because the concept is not a mere practical instrument incapable in itself of transmitting the real to our mind, whose only use is in artificially breaking up ineffable continuities, leaving the absolute to escape like water through a sieve. Thanks to analogical intellection, that natural marvel of lightness and strength which, thrown across the abyss, makes it possible for our knowledge to attain the infinite, the concept divinely elaborated in the dogmatic formula, contains but does not limit, and causes to descend in us, in an enigmatic and mirrored but altogether true manner the very mystery of the Deity which pronounces Itself eternally in the Uncreated Word, and which has been told in time and in human language by the Incarnate Word. We must therefore conclude that there was at the outset of the Bergsonian assault against carnal reason some fundamental misconception; the concept was made the normal vehicle of rationalism,—therein lies the crucial error; the affirmation of the ontological value of the intelligence and of its statements was confused with the helplessness of a sterile intellect eager to submit all things to its own level. That much I learned in too certain a fashion ever to forget it. If all that is desired is to seek a compromise one can always arrive at conciliations in words, at diplomatic appeasements: those who have understood the real antinomy will never accept them. Nor was I at that moment familiar with the works of Saint Thomas. As far as I was concerned it was upon the indestructible verity of the objects of faith that philosophical reflection rested in its effort to restore the natural ordination of the intellect to being, and to recognize the ontological genuineness of the work of reason. In thus completely accepting, without quibble or reserve, the authentic reality value of our human instruments of cognition I was already a Thomist without being aware of it. When a few months later I came upon the *Summa theologica* its luminous flood was to find no opposing obstacles in me.

The present, as it passes, changes its colour; the mere fact that it becomes the past and is no longer continued in the duration joining it to the new present we are in, except through certain of the virtual rays with which it was charged,—a single bundle of which became, so to speak, actualized in the course of that duration,—means that it has become extinguished in respect of all the other rays of futurity which remained merely virtual in it yet which constituted an integral part of its vitality of the moment, and might have won out in the contest of possibilities. Not only has the past ceased to be, but in addition,—because in the continuity of time it has no existence *separated* from the future,—one can say that when seen by spirits the flux prolonging it causes what it was to vary constantly; its value will not finally have become fixed until, at the end of time, it has been most completely stripped of the colour and life it had for a single moment. We need not therefore feel astonished that we cannot keep intact in the full vitality of a moment now past and gone a bit of history still near to us. For those who did not know it, even for those who did, it is impossible adequately to appreciate in 1929 what the spiritual situation was in the years of "modernism."

It was the period in which many young priests spoke of nothing but becoming and immanence, of the evolutive transformation of the expressions of faith, of the prismatization of the ineffable through dogmatic formulae ever provisional and deficient, of the evils of all abstract knowledge, of the inability of "conceptual" or "notional" reason to establish the supreme natural truths, of the idolatrous, superstitious (and above all outmoded) character of the principle of contradiction. A courageous generation intellectually unarmed, which felt the weight of an imminent catastrophe pressing down upon it, was feverishly seeking in pragmatism a means of regaining somehow or other the realities of life of which it had been deprived by an all-too-attentive education. For this generation there was no salvation, no organ of truth except in action. To look down upon the intellect was considered to be the beginning of wisdom, and became axiomatic.

Bergsonian philosophy, more or less well understood, which alone appeared in this desert of intellectuality as a lofty demand for the claims of metaphysics, seemed destined to provide these "cultural" predispositions with the form and animating principle they were seeking. A more and more consistent link bound the Bergsonian criticism of intellect to a religious revival in danger of being contaminated by modernist anti-intellectualism. This was the knot which had to be cut.

By nature, religion and philosophy are made to give one another mutual aid and support. It happens, through the fault of the human subject, that the one can harm the other and vitiate its development. There is nothing quite so dangerous for a philosopher and a philosophy as the religious exploitation sometimes too eagerly undertaken as a result of a mistaken and imprudent zeal. Descartes cherished the ambition to introduce his philosophy into the schools and the religious orders; he succeeded in having Cartesianism condemned. Bergson, though never obsessed by any such ambition, is not the only one who has experienced the disadvantage of finding himself with disciples in religious seminaries and of being *utilised* by apologists and theoreticians of dogma, miracle and belief. During the period I have referred to there were many among those whose judgment on the question of the moment was commanded more than anything else by considerations of persons or of spiritual *tactics* if I may so express it, who were indignant that someone should, in the name of Thomas Aquinas, direct a severe criticism against Bergsonism, hated as it was by the rationalists and the official representatives of atheistic science.

They were not only forgetting the primacy of truth and that the *magis amica* of Aristotle (Aristotle again!) is the sole spiritual tactic worthy of the mind,—but also that in cutting all doctrinal links between Bergsonian philosophy and the sacred realm, in destroying the hopes professed by some of renewing Catholicism by its aid, the true physiognomy of Bergsonism in the profane order was being restored. For it is there that its future lies, whatever its intrinsic value may be.

Need I add that in formulating without the slightest attenuation my objections to Bergsonian philosophy (in fact the harshness I have attempted to mitigate in the present edition is an evidence of that uncompromising wrench which I had to make on my own account, and which left its mark in me), my criticism always remained foreign to that passion for disparagement of which there have been, then and since, several examples? Having so obviously become a peacemaker all along the line did I not in this second edition have also to modify the expressions I used at that time with reference to Mr. Benda? Finally, in the third section of the work, I carefully tried to bring out the invaluable presentiments and the fundamentally correct views, the salutary metaphysical *directions* which seemed to me to be contained not, certainly, in the philosophical principles of *Bergsonism of fact,* but in the spiritual tendencies of *Bergsonism of intention.* Someone recently wrote: "Universal mobilism would be innocuous if it were only a verbal exaggeration of the following Thomist proposition: being is dynamogenic; there are no 'things' in the sense of dead things, of possibly inert things; being is 'tension'; and, in the supreme Being, it is therefore perfect tension, that is to say, full possession of what is manifested in His work through a 'continuity of shooting out.'" "I am not ignorant," the same author said, "of the difficulties of such a transcription, but I do not believe they are insurmountable; by carrying to the absolute Bergsonian *action, vital impulse, creative evolution,*—an operation which, as we know, de-essences them,—we can get back to pure Act."[1] I am the more inclined to accept this viewpoint as I myself had already proposed it seventeen years ago. But it seems indispensable to add: 1) that a *de-essenced* philosophy ceases to be itself, and 2) that as long as it keeps its metaphysical principles, which make it what it is, a philosophy cannot be *de-essenced.* Hence, properly speaking,—for grace completes nature and baptism has never *de-essenced* the baptized,—Bergsonism can never be "baptized,"[2] as the eminent author from whom we have taken these lines seems to hope, unless it is a question not of Bergsonism of fact, but only—and in the very exact sense in which we have defined it—Bergsonism of intention.

This distinction between the *two Bergsonisms* is always necessary. If it permits one to do justice to the great Bergsonian labour and to the intentions

[1] A. D. Sertillanges, *Nouvelles littéraires,* December 15, 1928.
[2] *Ibid.*

animating it, it also permits one to avoid the troublesome "confusionism" and, strictly speaking, the *departures from truth* to which so human and natural a desire for sympathy and superficial effusion sometimes lead. Reading in a literary weekly to which the Nobel prize had revealed the topical value of pure duration a letter in which a Carmelite nun, who appeared to know Bergson only through Jacques Chevalier's book, was justly extolling the intellectual loyalty of the philosopher, but with perhaps less discernment his way of "proving the reality of intuition,"—which deserved, we are told, "all the gratitude of the contemplatives,"*—I thought that the re-editing of my critical studies, harsh but true, was decidedly opportune. How much happier I should be could I hold the same opinion as everyone else! Alas, this good fortune is reserved for a few historians. For my part, I must be resigned to making myself disagreeable to everyone by recalling, now here, now there, norms which do not change. New errors succeed the old; with time, the old ones take on an air of respectability which affords them new opportunities; we must be on the watch in all directions.

Not that in my opinion Thomistic philosophy should limit itself to a defensive and critical function. On the contrary, I believe that its possibilities of invention and of progressive synthesis are inexhaustible, and that it is called upon not only to refute errors but also and especially to get to the very bottom of the problems which assail modern thought on all sides. I must confess, in this connection, that certain serious-minded people have seriously misunderstood the meaning of my critique of Bergsonism. Where Albert Thibaudet perceives the reaction of strong intellectual routines to a completely new philosophy, a more sensitive psychological approach would have enabled him to see in a young philosopher accustomed to Bergsonian stock formulae, an entirely new and correspondingly enthusiastic discovery of those famous routines still fresh with dew, and themselves newer even than the dawn. That Bergson "did not use his thought to think of what had already been thought,"—no, that is not what I regretted then, or what I regret today. "It is the very act of this philosophy," Thibaudet writes, "to keep itself and the mind from being carried down the slope of the ready-made and of scholasticism."[1] If this were so, no one would be less scholastic or more Bergsonian than Saint Thomas Aquinas. "'Scholasticism,'" we read further, "suits the Church as plain-chant suits the church service."[2] No! But rather as human speech is suitable in the liturgy and the sermon (and in the street as well). "It requires the positing at its base of a revealed truth, namely, that God has made man in His image and His likeness."[3] *Primo,* this revealed truth,

* *Nouvelles littéraires,* December 15, 1928.
[1] Albert Thibaudet, *Le Bergsonisme,* II, p. 234.
[2] *Ibid.,* p. 235.
[3] *Ibid.,* p. 236.

insofar as it affirms that all perfection and in particular intelligence and free-dom, is a participated similitude of subsisting Life,—is also a rational truth; *secundo,* if scholastic theology bases itself on revealed truths, like all theology, scholastic philosophy, like all philosophy, bases itself only on the natural light. Thomism, Thibaudet continues, constitutes "a philosophy eminently proper to the vocational training of the clergy, who cling to it for reasons somewhat analogous to those which bind the profession of medicine to a materialistic scientism. To exercise these trades is to have neither the time nor the inclina-tion to doubt, and these philosophies give to the one a provision of spiritual certitudes, to the other a stock of practical certitudes, by means of which one may easily spend his life profitably practising his profession."[4] Thibaudet for-gets that the vocation of the clergy is to lead men to the primary Truth; it is a transcendental vocation. As to that of the Thomists, it is to contemplate the transcendentals and to apply the principle of contradiction through the length and breadth of experience. Moreover, if he knew the clergy better he would pay greater tribute to its freedom of mind; he would know too how slight is the desire of a respectable number of its members to encumber them-selves with a supply of Thomistic certitudes. Modern systems are less cumber-some to carry around. In reality, if the renaissance of Thomistic philosophy has any meaning, it is that this philosophy is not a philosophy of the vestry but a philosophy of the open air; it draws all its strength from what is most natural in man: sense and reason, and the Church recommends it so insistently only because, having among us the deposit of divine Truth, she considers the health of our reason to be worth the most careful supervision.

Need I add that I have never had any illusions as to the degree of *success* so demanding a philosophy may encounter? So it is that Providence, whose law seems to be a divine pragmatism,—(the saints call it a madness of love)— does not seem to take any very immediate interest in the recognition of sane metaphysics among men. At least it contents itself in this domain—probably because it is not a question here of election to eternal life—with the smallest number of the chosen. Saint Thomas's struggles against the pseudo-Augus-tinians and the Averroïsts will have to be taken up again and again.

III

I have several times remarked in my book that if one were to transfer to intellectual perception properly so-called,—which takes place by means of abstraction, and whose object is being,—certain of the values and privileges that Bergson attributes to "intuition," the Bergsonian critique of intellect would find itself as it were automatically rectified, and instead of ruining our natural power of attaining the true, would be directed only against the wrong

[4] *Ibid.*

use of it. That is one of the traits that should be emphasized with regard to *Bergsonism of intention.* Does real Bergsonism allow of a similar transposition? To admit this would be to regard Bergsonian philosophy as a sort of metaphysical plasmodium, without any axis of internal organization. However attached it may be to becoming, this philosophy has, on the contrary, an axis and a direction that are exceptionally well-defined. I consider, in taking my stand against it, that I am dealing more honourably and with greater fairness toward it than certain Catholic disciples whose spineless eclecticism, applied to the reconciliation of Bergsonian intuition with *philosophia perennis,* runs the risk of "de-essencing" both of them and proposes a Bergsonism made so acceptable that it becomes almost non-existent. To be sure, Bergson is free to formulate, as several great philosophers have done, a *second philosophy.* He can recast his doctrine in a new synthesis and substantially transform it. And this transformation might bring it closer to the eternal metaphysics. No one desires this more than I. But until this has been accomplished we can call "Bergsonism" only the doctrine enunciated up to the present in his works. And no one, not even he, can change the intrinsic meaning and internal logic of the principles which specify this doctrine.

It happens that one of the obvious signs most characteristic of Bergsonism, I mean the intellect-intuition opposition, has, at least with regard to the vocables chosen, depended in no small measure in Bergson upon a certain contingency. Bergson, in fact, as I have pointed out in my studies and as Jacques Chevalier confirms,[1] hesitated a moment before naming *intellect* and *intuition* the two powers of knowing that he opposes to one another. And he himself, as a philosopher, has and practises too profound a love for intellect not to suffer in spite of everything from the reputation for anti-intellectualism he has brought upon himself. Alas, he it is who has made it inevitable. For although he may have hesitated, he has nevertheless chosen; and how decisively! And so it cannot here be a simple question of words, and one would have to be rather ingenuous to suppose that if Bergson,—in order to designate this so-called faculty which breaks up and immobilizes, which is adapted to matter alone and which collects external views without penetrating the intimate nature of things,—had chosen another name than that of intellect his metaphysics of knowledge would at once have become the metaphysics of the *philosophia perennis.* In reality, behind and conditioning the choice we are discussing was a whole long theoretical elaboration, a whole series of assumptions concerning the very nature and value of human intellect and of ideas. And that is what is important.

Bergsonian philosophy here, as its most favourable interpreters must recognize, is closely dependent, as far as its results (or prejudices) are concerned,

---

[1] At least as far as the choice of the word 'intuition' is concerned. *Nouvelles littéraires,* December 15, 1928.

upon modern tradition. It is in terms of Taine and Spencer and more profoundly of Kant, and still more profoundly of Descartes that it has taken shape
and is to be understood. Bergson got from Taine the idea of a naturally
mechanistic intellect, from Spencer the idea of an intellect engendered according to certain needs and certain demands of evolution and concerned with
linking phenomenon with phenomenon. He has worked on the notion, received from the old Kantian stock, of the concept as an empty form, and on
the one inherited from Descartes of the idea as a mental picture interposed
between the real and the mind. It is against this intellect that he is fighting.
Of course;—and such considerations explain many traits of the Bergsonian
theory of intellect and intuition; they do not justify it. For if Bergson has re-
acted against certain consequences of modern gnoseology he has done so in
accepting its premises. He was called upon to restore the true nature of intellect: he has tried to surpass it. In order to forge a better instrument he had
the pretension, supported by age-long errors whose subversive value he made
so admirably evident, of abandoning intellect to a consubstantial materialism
and to the domination, to the fascination of inert matter. Nothing can here
temper the opposition Bergsonism merits; it is a question of a basic decision
with regard to the whole of philosophy.

In the genesis of Bergsonian thought the theory of intellect and of intuition
has no doubt held a far less central place than the elucidation of the meaning
of *duration*. But in fact, the Bergsonian notions of duration and intuition are
strictly correlative; one cannot subsist without the other. Let us recall the
text where Bergson himself gives us important information on the history of
his thought. "In my opinion," he wrote to Harold Höffding, "any résumé of
my views will distort them as a whole and thereby expose them to a host of objections if it does not place itself at the outset and does not constantly return to
what I consider the very centre of my doctrine: the intuition of duration. The
representation of a multiplicity of 'reciprocal penetration,' quite different
from numerical multiplicity,—the representation of a heterogeneous, qualitative, creative duration,—is the point from which I started and to which I
have constantly returned. It requires a very great effort on the part of the
mind, the breaking-down of many frameworks, something like a new method
of thinking (for the immediate is far from being the easiest thing to perceive); but once one has arrived at this representation and possesses it in its
simple form (which must not be confused with a recomposition by concepts),
one feels obliged to shift the point of view one has of reality; one sees that the
greatest difficulties arise from the fact that philosophers have always placed
time and space on the same line: most of these difficulties diminish or fade
away. The theory of intuition, upon which you insist much more than on that
of duration, did not become clear to me for some time after the latter: it derives from it and can only be understood through it [. . .]. This intuition [. . .]

no doubt admits a series of successive planes; but on the last plane, the main one, it is the intuition of duration."* We see clearly here that Bergsonian duration and intuition cannot be considered independently of one another. We also see that Heidegger has a partially inexact idea when he connects the Bergsonian theory of duration with a critique of the Aristotelian theory of time.† Things happened otherwise, I believe. Proceeding first of all from a meditation on modern science and physics, and occasioned perhaps by the study of the arguments of the Eleatic philosophers against motion,[1] Bergson's central—and, to the extent that it was a genuine *intellectual intuition,* infallible —discovery was that real time *is not*[2] the spatialized time of our physics: and nothing is truer, for the physicist's times are mathematical entities constructed upon complexes of spatio-temporal measurements and founded no doubt on real time, but which are not this time; real time is physical, not mathematical. To this truth however something else is immediately added: taking for granted—and in this Heidegger is probably right—the identity of the spatialized time of our physics and Aristotelian time (as if the concrete continuity of succession in movement, numbered by the mind but essentially impermanent, were not the exact opposite of a spatial representation),[8] for

---

* Letter to Harald Höffding, reprinted in the appendix to the French translation of Höffding's book, *La Philosophie de Bergson,* Paris, Alcan, 1916, pp. 160–161.

† Heidegger, *Sein und Zeit,* Halle, 1927, pp. 432–433, note; cf. p. 26.

[1] "It was at the end of a course of lectures given to his pupils at the *lycée* [of Clermont, where he taught from 1883 to 1888] on the argument of the Eleatic philosophers, that the main idea of his doctrine took shape." Joseph Desaymard, *La pensée d'Henri Bergson,* Paris, 1912, p. 11. Cf. Jacques Chevalier, *Bergson,* pp. 50–51.

[2] Speaking of the central intuition from which great philosophical doctrines proceed and of the intermediary "image" between the absolute simplicity of that intuition and the complexity of its conceptual translations, Bergson writes: "What first of all characterizes this image is the power of *negation* it possesses . . . Faced with currently accepted ideas, theses which seemed evident, affirmations which had up to that time passed as scientific, it whispers into the philosopher's ear the word: *Impossible!* Impossible, even though the facts and the reasons would appear to invite you to think it possible and real and certain. Impossible, because a certain experience, confused perhaps but decisive, speaks to you through my voice, because it is incompatible with the facts cited and the reasons given, and because hence these facts must have been badly observed, these reasonings false. . . . Later [the philosopher] may vary his affirmations; he will not vary in what he denies. And if he varies in what he affirms, it will still be in virtue of the power of negation immanent in the intuition or in its image." (*Philosophical Intuition,* in *Creative Mind,* pp. 129–130.) [*L'Intuition philosophique,* Rev. de Mét. et de Mor., 1911, pp. 810–811. Published separately in 1928, Paris, Helleu et Sargent.]

[8] There remains, in Aristotle's conception, this trace of kinship between time and extension, that time also—but in an indirect and derived way—has to do with the order of quantity, and thus presupposes matter. While for Bergson, (real) time is essentially and exclusively qualitative and has to do above all with the mind. In reality, however, in order that time be irreducible to extension it is not at all necessary to make it qualitative and spiritual, to take it from its metaphysical state bordering on non-being and to confuse it with what endures in it.

To go more closely into the relation of time to quantity certain precisions concerning the nature of time may be useful. Time is something of movement, it is not movement itself, it is its duration or its continuation of existence,—that is to say, as nothing of movement as such is permanent,—the uninterrupted flux of its impermanence. This flux is an ontological con-

Bergson, condemnation of the first automatically involved condemnation of the second. Conversely one might say that the idea of substance and the idea of real time, and the idea of psychic flowing and multiplicity have been indissolubly fused in the idea (but it is no longer an idea) or rather in the intuition (but this time Bergsonian and unthinkable) of Bergsonian Duration. But even that has been possible only in the absence of a system of certitudes concerning the value of rational knowledge, which might have opposed it; and

---

tinuum whose parts (parts of the uninterrupted variation of an impermanent existence) are not distinct in act: or in other words it is a potential plurality of parts (but ontological or existential, not geometrical) constituting a unity, and therefore numerable. Continuous and divisible and numerable like the movement whose duration it is, and by reason of movement which is itself continuous and divisible and numerable by reason of the spatial continuum in which movement takes place, time (like movement) is thus a *quantity* only *per accidens* or rather *per posterius*, by derivation, *in quantum quantitatis divisionem ab aliquo priori sortitur.* (Saint Thomas Aquinas, *in Metaph. Arist.,* lib. V, lect. 15, Cathala ed., n. 985.)

When we say that time is a *number,* it is important to understand that this number is not only a concrete number, but the number of a continuum of (impermanent) existence, not of a mass or a spatial magnitude (quantity properly so-called): a number which presupposes, as a prerequisite, extension and matter, but which by no means includes extension in its formal constitutive, and which in itself (for the unity which numbers is homogeneous to the thing numbered) is measured by times, by fluxes of impermanent existence, not by portions of space. All that is necessary to know and appreciate time is a memory "retaining" the flow of sensitive life: animals measure time without spatio-temporal instruments. It is solely because focal points in space alone furnish our senses with sufficiently precise and socially utilizable means of measurement that we use measures in space,—with the help of astronomical positions or of clocks,—as *signs* of the measure of time. Time is thus measured by us with the help of conventional units, only indirectly, *per accidens* and *per posterius.* If it is true that the whole universe is "a machine for marking out time," the measure nature uses for numbering time remains unknown to us.

On the other hand, if in itself time is independent of our mind (*sicut possunt esse sensibilia sensu non existente, ita possunt esse numerabilia et numerus, non existente numerante*), however, because it has no permanent being in things and has existence in act outside of the soul according only to its indivisible (according to the present instant, which does not endure), it exists, like movement, completely and perfectly, only in the soul which retains its parts. Cf. Saint Thomas, *in Phys. Arist.,* lib. IV, lect. 17 and 23.

And finally, real and physical time is irreversible like the movement itself of the whole universe, and of the universe of life and the human universe which endure in it. The past remains not in time, but in what endures and insofar as it has modified what endures in time.

Putting into concrete form with the great lyricism of the Presocratics a conception of the world which would resolve philosophically into Saint Thomas's conception, Paul Claudel has admirably expressed this idea of time in the language of the senses. "Thus Time is not only the perpetual starting afresh of the day, the month and the year, it is the craftsman of something real which each second increases, the *Past,*—what has once received existence. All things must be in order that they may no longer be, that they may give place to the subsequent which they summon. The past is an incantation of the thing to come, its necessary generating difference, the ever-increasing sum of future conditions [. . .]. The present minute differs from all other minutes in that it is not the border of the same quantity of past. It does not explain the same past, it does not imply the same future. I continue more than the grandsire from whom I have sprung. Each time we breathe the world is as new as it was at that first mouthful of air which made up the first man's first breath [. . .]. Through Time, everything that will be has the means of being in order no longer to be. Time is the *Invitation to die,* the invitation to every sentence to decompose into the explanatory and total harmony, to consummate the word of adoration in the ear of *Sigé* the Abyss." (Paul Claudel, *Connaissance du Temps.*)

especially, whereas psychological introspection was to endeavor to verify the duration thus discovered, critical reflection was inevitably to be applied to justifying the *new method of thinking* linked with this duration in such a way that the theory of intuition, though it emerged later, was nevertheless to react in turn on the philosophical theory of this same duration. If a certain critique of the intellectual process and of analysis had not developed simultaneously, the experience of lived duration would without any doubt have given rise in the philosopher to a different conceptualization, the Bergsonian doctrine of duration would not have been what it has.

*   *   *   *   *

If one tried hastily to schematize a long philosophical evolution, one might say that Descartes, re-discovering this great fact (upon which Thomists never tire of insisting): that thought, immanent to itself, attains its object inside itself,—but understanding it in a thoroughly materialized fashion,—has bequeathed to modern philosophy the pseudo-axiom that the direct object of thought is itself or its ideas. He admitted an intuition that was intellectual (and even conceived on an angelist type, since it gave us exhaustively the nature of substance, corporal or spiritual), but this intuition attained at first and immediately only thought itself, the first object of intellection, and the representations, innate in thought, of those "atoms of intelligibility" he called *simple natures*. At the same time he considered the understanding to be purely passive, and this completely passivist conception of knowledge—which in him expressed mainly a deficiency, the non-investigation of the proper mystery of intellectual apprehension—was to reach its lowest and most characteristic level in the sensualism and empiricism of the eighteenth century. What Kant in his turn re-discovered was the great fact of the activity of the mind in cognition. He understood that cognition is entirely the work of the mind; he likewise discerned how much construction, how much internal fabrication this work involves. But he too,—understanding these things in a totally material way, and in other respects attached to the Cartesian prejudice that thought attains immediately only its representations and that if there is anything supra-sensible in it and known to it, it cannot have received and taken it from things,—as a result, makes of that element of construction and fabrication, in reality wholly secondary and instrumental, the whole of the mind's activity consequently conceived on the type of activities *ad extra* that we observe in the world of bodies. The sole object of cognition as such is therefore the world itself of representations; the thing in itself which duplicates them henceforth evades the grasp of the intellect, affirmations about it are possible only by mode of belief, as postulates of moral action. Anything that is suprasensible in the knowing mind is exclusively its own structure, or in other words, its *a priori* forms. The concept is only an empty form imposed upon the matter of sensibility (thanks to the 'planes of cleavage,' if one may use the expression, which the schemata of imagination produce in this matter) by the *a priori* functions of judgment, and its sole rôle is to unify and synthesize the matter—to organize it—under universal and necessary laws. The only kind of intuition is sensible intuition, whose empirical content has from the beginning a mathematical character resulting from the *a priori* forms of space and time. It is the content of this sensible intuition that fills the concept, and consequently all knowledge stops at experience,—not at the crude experience of the senses but at experience elaborated and rationalized, at that heaven of phenomena which revolves around the human mind and whose demiurge it is. Bergson, we are told, tried to do what several great philosophers had already tried their hands at,—to shatter this heaven-idol in which modern thought was encaged; he wanted to pierce through this arch of appearances to the real itself, to regain possession of the real and of the spiritual real. Nothing is truer, and it is what constitutes the strength and the merit of Bergsonism of intention. But *how* has he carried on this undertaking?

Precisely by granting Kant's essential presupposition, by admitting with him that abstraction never makes us see anything, that in itself the concept is empty, unsuited to communicate the real to us,—a simple form expressing not the *a priori* Kantian functions but the practical attitudes of our fabricating mind and the habits of materiality;—by maintaining then that by itself the intellect, modelled on corporeity, can, from the moment it ceases to manipulate matter mathematically, only enclose us in a world of mechanistic illusions; and by demanding next the means of an evasion into the real, from an intuition which transcends the intellect and which will plunge—like the sense, and much more so—into the pure concrete as such.

Consequently, if in the order of intention is given an impulse, which can lead to an authentic realism, in the order of doctrine the proposed cure is, in truth, worse than the disease. On the one hand philosophical intuition is sought outside of and above the normal functions of the intellect. It is called a *supra-intellectual* intuition.[1] Beyond the concept and even by turning against it the direction of thought, above and beyond all the abstractive and the properly rational that the activity of human intelligence inevitably includes, an immediate knowledge, an intuition of the real, which is spirit, is the

---

1 *Creative Evolution*, p. 360.—"You are perfectly right," Bergson wrote to Jacques Chevalier, "in saying that all the philosophy I set forth beginning with my first *Essay* states, contrary to Kant, the possibility of a supra-sensible intuition. Taking the word 'intelligence' in the very wide sense that Kant gives it, I could call 'intellectual' the intuition of which I speak. But I should prefer to speak of it as "supra-intellectual," because I believed it necessary to restrict the meaning of the word "intelligence," and because I reserve this name for the discursive faculties of the mind as a whole, originally destined to think matter. Intuition bears upon the spirit." (Letter [April 28, 1920] published in Chevalier's book, *Bergson*, Paris, Plon, 1926, p. 296.)

"specific instrument"* of philosophy. "Intuition bears upon the spirit."† In other words, a direct and supra-conceptual grasp of the nature of spirit, an immediate and concrete perception of the metaphysical universe, fugitive as it is said to be and contrary to the natural bent of the intellect, is the sole organ proportionate with philosophical knowledge to the extent that this knowledge rises above matter. However purified it may be in a Bergson and a Biran this philosophical ambition to "penetrate experimentally into the beyond"‡ brings us back in some way to that false notion of metaphysics which old Kant (from the time of the *"Dreams of a Ghost-seer"* on) had in mind for denying the possibility of metaphysics as a science, and which furnished an excuse for his attacks. In any case a fundamental verity is destroyed: one considers false that humble and magnanimous avowal, the point of departure of all metaphysics, that if each one of us perceives experimentally the *fact* of his own and singular spiritual activity, the existence of his soul, of his freedom, nevertheless it is only by analogy (by analogy with sensible being known first) that we can know in its essential determinations the *nature* of these things and still more by analogy that we can raise ourselves philosophically to the purely spiritual world, and to the Divinity, which cannot be grasped in itself immediately by any created mind either angel or man, with his natural strength alone.

On the other hand no matter how much Bergsonian intuition is presented to us as "supra-intellectual" or "ultra-intellectual"[1] we still must recognize that in point of fact, in reality, it can be only *infra-intellectual*. (I take as being known what intellect is.) An intuition which demands a sort of violent recovering, by an effort contrary to our nature, of the instinctive virtualities spread along the course of zoological evolution; (if Newman used the expression *instinct of the mind* it was in a very different sense; Bergson's texts are clear,—it is instinct as it differs from intellect that intuition, "almost extinct" in us,[2] must join;) an intuition "which prolongs, develops and transposes into reflection what instinct remains in man,"[3] which plunges us into

---

* Letter to Harald Höffding, in Höffding, *la Philosophie de Bergson*, French translation, p. 159.

† Letter from Bergson to Chevalier, quoted above.

‡ This is the expression used by Bergson himself with regard to Maine de Biran, *Rapport sur le concours pour le prix Bordin, comptes-rendus de l'Acad. des Sc. morales et polit.*, Paris, Picard, 1906, t. I, p. 156.—The philosopher, moreover, immediately qualifies his use of the word: ". . . the idea of penetration experimentally into the beyond, or at least of arriving at its threshold, taking internal observation as a guide." I am quite willing to concede this *at least*, but "penetrating experimentally into the beyond" is quite another thing. And to the extent that it yields to this ambition Bergson accords a place to metaphysics.

Internal observation is very definitely an instrument of knowledge, and one which can orient us in the direction of metaphysical truth; but in no way can it constitute metaphysical knowledge itself.

[1] *Creative Evolution*, p. 360.

[2] *Ibid.*, p. 267.

[3] Letter to Harald Höffding (quoted above), p. 163.

concrete perception in order to deepen and widen it, an intuition which is a dilatation by an effort of will inserted into it, of the perception of the senses and of consciousness,[1] a painful effort in which "turning back upon itself and twisting on itself, the faculty of *seeing*" is henceforth to be "one with the act of *willing*,"[2]—no, only on paper will it ever be made into an "intellectual" or a "supra-intellectual intuition."[3] Intellect is there only to sharpen the sense, to communicate the colour of the mind, the lucidity and subtlety of the intellective operation, to an astonishing labour of the whole being in which all the sensible, instinctive and tendential dynamism strives to be *possessed* by the object, and which can only mimic true intellection.

In short, the first effect of the remedy Bergson proposes for the Kantian disease is to mutilate and dispossess intelligence, if it is true that the latter's absolutely primordial activity is to *see* in depth and that its primary object is being. Bergson's followers should understand that no dialectical artifice can exonerate their philosophy from such a reproach. It is not enough to say that Bergson has in view only the conceptual intellect,[4] as though in addition to the

[1] *The Perception of Change*, in *Creative Mind*, p. 158. "But suppose that instead of trying to rise above our perception of things we were to plunge into it for the purpose of deepening and widening it. Suppose that we were to insert our will into it, and that this will, expanding, were to expand our vision of things. We should obtain this time a philosophy where nothing in the data of the senses or the consciousness would be sacrificed . . ."

[2] *Creative Evolution*, p. 237.

[3] If one brings this "intuition" back to its true proportions,—by getting rid of the exaggerated systematization that Bergson subjects it to, and the character contrary to nature that he attributes to it (precisely because he wants to make a metaphysical instrument of it), and the far too important part that, according to him, sense perception and instinct have in it,—one finds oneself facing an effort of the whole being which normally has its place either in the *creative invention of the artist* or in the psychological application to a certain *internal observation*. This effort remains intellectual but, because it is a question of penetrating the contingent singular, the intelligence in it is "pushed out of doors," into the domain peculiar to sense. The error he makes is in looking there for the "specific instrument" of philosophy.

For Saint Thomas, the faculty of *seeing and that* of *willing*, far from being foreign to one another, mutually envelop and contain one another; but they remain essentially distinct. The will always intervenes in the order of *exercise*, and to *apply* the faculties of knowledge to their object with greater or less force. And further, in an immense human domain, not philosophical but ethical and aesthetic, the will intervenes also in the order of *specification*, to determine the very texture of knowledge. The fact remains that in the elaboration of philosophical and metaphysical knowledge (whether it is a question of moral philosophy or speculative philosophy), the dispositions of the will have, of themselves, no specificative part to play.

Let us add that the two-fold movement of experience and criticism by which the *moralist*, in the sense that this word has assumed in French literature, tries to discover human reality proper in himself and in the works of the mind,—belongs of itself, not to the philosophical domain but to the domain of the *practical science* of moral activity; that is why the dispositions of the will with regard to the goals of the human being play an essential part in it.

[4] Jacques Chevalier goes so far as to suggest (*op. cit.*, p. 277[2]) that what Bergson means by *intellect* would correspond rather to what the scholastics designate as *cogitativa* or *ratio particularis*, that is to say, to the highest of our sensitive faculties (in the animal called *aestimativa*). It is unfortunate for this interpretation that what Bergson calls intellect should be characterized by abstraction and "formal knowledge," the universal concept, conceptual analysis, reasoning properly so-called, etc., all of which are things that the scholastics rightfully refuse to the *ratio*

intellect which uses concepts, judges, affirms and denies, there were in us another intellect which knows without ideas, another faculty of thinking of which their master moreover, and quite wisely, has never spoken. What we are discussing is the intellect you call conceptual, it is abstraction, it is the value of knowledge by ideas. The answer that should have been given against Kant is that intellect sees by conceiving, and conceives only to see. Its operation does not consist in subsuming a sensible content beneath an empty form,— nor in cutting out the real according to ready-made forms. In an inner word whose content escapes the eye and the touch and transcends in itself all order of sensation, but has greater density and fullness the more purely intelligible is the sound it gives out,—the intellect attains reality itself brought to the level of our mind. In short, if we call intuition a direct knowledge of what is,[1] there is indeed a philosophical intuition, but it is in the concept and by the concept that this particular intuition, which is intellectual intuition, intellection itself, takes place.

*　*　*　*　*

All great philosophers have recognized the existence of and necessity for an intuition from which their wisdom is suspended. It is on the nature of this intuition that they are divided: as much, to tell the truth, as on the nature of the human being, which Aristotle alone was able to contemplate with quiet glance as an animal endowed with reason. The genuine and nourishing intuition of human knowledge and of philosophy is not an intellectual angelistic intuition reserved for the wise like the Platonist intuition of separate Ideas or Spinoza's knowledge of the third genus; nor an intellectual angelistic intuition accessible to all, like the Cartesian intuition of thought and of clear ideas; nor a supra-individual intellectual intuition like the Hegelian communion of the universal spirit with itself; nor a supra-intellectual intuition continuing the intellect and transcending all sense experience like the ecstasy of Plotinus; nor a "supra-intellectual" intuition running counter to intellect and plunging into sense experience, like the folding back by which, in Schopenhauer, the will becomes conscious of itself; or like the Bergsonian intuition of duration. It is a *human intellectual intuition,* the intellection of being which, suprasensi-

---

particularis. What may be conceded to Chevalier is that a nominalist conception of the intelligence will always tend to confuse it with a sort of *ratio particularis,* and, in the eyes of the scholastics, that is precisely a fundamental error.

[1] In the scholastic vocabulary, an "intuitive" knowledge bears upon a *singular* and *physically present* object (this is the case with the intuition of sense). This is not the meaning that *we* give to the word 'intuition'; in such a case a simple indication should suffice to reassure those who are particularly fond of dictionary definitions. See *infra,* p. 150, n. 2. Let us add that the word *direct* knowledge may signify either *without an intermediary object first known* (for example, the apprehension of the intelligible realities proportionate to our intelligence), or *which does not result from a reasoning* (the perception of first principles, for example).

ble in itself, is directly grasped in the sensible in which it is immanent, and pursued into the pure spiritual analogically attained,—an intellection at first rudimentary, and naturally progressive, like everything human, and due to the essentially human process (too human, like everything human) of the abstraction of intelligibles. As Hamelin rightly pointed out, intuition plays a capital rôle in Aristotle's philosophy; this is particularly evident in the Aristotelian theory of first principles, and of those primitive intelligible articulations that we scholastics call *per se primo et secundo modo,* and that a modern would call *a priori* notional syntheses. But this intuition is at the very humble level of the animal endowed with reason, and though it is true that —in virtue of a dynamism also profoundly human, of which Aristotle's philosophy itself gives evidence in aspiring to surpass itself—it naturally tends to perfect itself in a superior intuition which would bear upon the transcendent individual Living Being on which depends the whole of nature, nevertheless all human means, all philosophical effort must avow itself powerless to attain such a vision.

Saint Thomas Aquinas insists, in his turn and even more strongly, both on the essentially intuitive nature of intellect as such and on the limitations proper to human intellectual intuition. Let us not forget, however, (and the readers of Rousselot might find it useful to bear this in mind), that when the Angelic Doctor thus points out the inferiority of knowledge by abstraction and by discursive reasoning it is in order to show the imperfection of human intellect in comparison with pure intelligences,—"the human intellect is at the lowest degree in the order of intellects, *infimus in ordine intellectuum,* and the farthest removed from the perfection of the sovereign Intellect" (I^a, 79, 2),—not to credit us with some intellectual intuition other than the one proper to us, or to demand of some supra-intellectual intuition that it compensate, in the very order of philosophical cognition, for the infirmity of our concepts, or to deprive the latter of the intuitive light without which they would not be formed. For Saint Thomas, human intellect,—which following its natural bent ascends to the great common verities,—knows only by filling itself with immaterial words or concepts and its natural means of progress in knowledge is the rational movement which, continually taking in fresh supplies of experience, leads it from the intellection of principles to the intellection of conclusions.

Thus man has an intuition as animal, sense intuition, and an intuition as reasonable, the intellectual intuition we are discussing. The latter is the very act of the life of the intellect in him, an immaterial life incomparably more *life* than organic life, and the natural peak of immanent activity.

Descartes was right in thinking that intellect attains its object within itself, but this object is first of all (for the sense, from which we derive everything, orients us originally toward the outside, and spiritual introversion is, in us, only a *returning* from the outside to the inside) the extramental real, the being in which we bathe, transferred to the bosom of the mind: so that our intellective operation does not end in our thought itself and in our representations, but attains in us being itself independent of us, born in us again—in the vitality of the *verbum cordis*—in a better way than in itself, in matter. And Kant was right in affirming in opposition to the empiricists the sovereign activity of the mind; his error lies in not having seen the supreme immanence, in other words, the properly spiritual character of this activity. The essence of such an activity is not to produce but to *become* or to *be,* in virtue of oneself, infinitely above and beyond simple existence in one's own nature: so that becoming thus by intellection that which is not us, knowledge does not only issue complete from the knowing mind; at the same time it issues complete from the object known. It is so true that what formally constitutes intellection is a certain doubling of existence, or rather if I may say so, an active *superexistence,* peculiar to spiritual natures,—that at the supreme summit of things where all perfection is fulfilled in the Pure Act, the being of God in its own nature is, without any distinction, even simply virtual, the divine intellection itself by which God knows Himself,—Himself, and secondarily all the rest in Himself. There we have in the pure state the vital immanence of intellection. And this vitality is no doubt also productive, it is fecund: in the exhaustive intuition of self by self natural to angels it is in an internally produced word in which all its substance is immaterially proffered in the state of intellection in act that the created spirit knows itself; and in the increate Intellection a consubstantial Word is engendered, *Sapientia genita.* But it is in virtue of the vital immanence of the act of intelligence that this internal procession occurs, and in deity it takes place through pure superabundance, as a manifestation of the generosity essential to Intellect and to God.

If our abstract concept is far removed from the perfection of the word of pure intelligences,—and by how much more from that of the Word itself,— it retains, however, its indestructible similitude, it remains a living fruit of the knowing mind. But its function is not only to manifest; it is there above all to make good the indigence of an intellect originally empty and purely potential,—*tabula rasa,*—and to make present in it, raised to the highest degree of intelligible actuation, the thing known. Here intervenes that constructive and organizing action, fabricating if you wish, which Kant took to be the essential activity of the mind. What is meant, of course, is a vital and spiritual fabricating in which, much better than in vegetative auto-construction, each part expresses the whole. Just as our intellect, before vitally and by itself becoming the thing known, requires an indispensable moment of passivity with regard to the latter (since it *receives* it from the senses, again, it is true, in virtue of its own efficacious light which from the sensible causes the intelligible to surge up), so our immaterial word, because it is drawn from things, is abstract. Because it is abstract it proliferates by multiplying, grasps the real only by crumbling it into a plurality of objects of thought. It thereby demands composition and division, discursive movement and, beginning with something already known, the unceasing generation of new mental constructions. All these traits are also the mark peculiar to the specific inferiority of our intellect, the misfortune peculiar to a spirit which is a soul and which is nourished by a body. They are, in our intellect, a sort of impression left by the materiality out of which it emerges, while its intuitivity is the vestige of the Spirit from which it descends. Let us beware, however, of supposing one can separate this intuitivity from this rationality, intellection from concept, pure intellective immanence from production of ideas! It is the capital sin not only of Kantian formalism but also of Bergsonian mobilism thus to break asunder what is one, to rip apart the life of the intellect. A Thomas Aquinas, who conversed with angels, accepted his condition, piously honoured the humble instruments attaching to his origin as a man. We must detest Manichean idealism which, in condemning the humility of our nature, at the same time destroys any sublimity in it. It is one and the same activity in us, essentially immanent and virtually productive, that engenders concept and perceives what is, that perceives in conceiving and conceives in perceiving. It conceives in order to perceive; it abstracts, it enunciates, it reasons in order to perceive. All, in it, that is elaboration and disposition of ideas is regulated by intellection and is a *means* of intellection.

Thus on the one hand the object, considered in what it is, remains intact, all the arrangements it undergoes in us affect only its mode of existing in an intellect which indeed surpasses the whole order of the material universe, but which is the feeblest of all minds,—in short, they concern the manner in which we conceive, not the truth of what is conceived. And it is not an innate suprasensible structure or *a priori* form which occupies the immateriality of our intellect,—it is a suprasensible object brought there from without and disengaged from the sensible, thanks to that abstraction which Kant never understood. On the other hand all this conceptual machinery is at the service of intellection and lives by it alone. This machinery is alive with the very life of the intelligence, like it is immaterial, is immanent to it, and the intellect, at least as long as it does not weaken or doze off, handles with a divine energy this inner world of notions supremely plastic in the sense that nothing foreign to intellection binds it, and supremely hard in the sense that the necessities of intelligible being measure it every instant. With its insatiable hunger for reality, the intellect ceaselessly travels over the whole extent of exterior and interior experience, the whole extent of already acquired truths, in a perpetual *hunt for essences,* as Aristotle said. All concepts and ideal constructions which it produces in itself are only designed to serve *this sense of being* which is its most deeply-rooted characteristic and to obtain an intuitive discernment which is its very act, the act of this "conceptual" intellect that Bergson so heavily indicts.

It is true this essential life of the intellect is, in us, constantly threatened. The very machinery it creates for itself runs more risk of dulling it the more it develops, and of intellect above all must it be said, according to a characteristically Bergsonian formula, that life must always defend itself against the mechanisms it has itself set up: separated from intellection, the whole apparatus of concepts (but then they are no longer concepts, they are words, and extinct words) is no more than a material mechanism, so many dry bones. It is the old conflict between technique and inspiration. That is how the scholastics perish. We may denounce this evil as much as we like! Intellection alone can recover from it; it remains accidental to intellect.

Nor am I forgetting that there is much more in the life of the intellect than in what philosophers generally think of it. They often strangely fail to understand this life, passing over all that the mind, brought back upon itself by reflection on its acts, can learn of itself,—nay!—ignoring the essential spirituality of logic (because they materialize the concept by confusing it with the word, and the word itself by detaching it from the movement of thought),—neglecting especially—to the advantage of conceptual organization (*coacervatio specierum*), which in them must be carried to the maximum of perfection though it still has only an instrumental and material rôle—the more deepseated energies and spontaneities of intellect, particularly those dispositions and vital tendencies which, developing in it, dynamically regulate it with regard to this or that object and which we call *habitus*.

In scientific or philosophical knowledge itself the rules for ordering concepts apply not to the order of discovery (*via inventionis*) but to the order of verification (*via judicii*);—these rules concern the firmness or stability of a conclusion already supposed to be found. Invention depends on laws more hidden, and more individualized as well, and more incommunicable, and sometimes it derives less from the principles one brings into play than from a goal to which one tends without knowing it. In the incomparable moments of *intellectual discovery,* in which, capturing for the first time in the seemingly infinite breadth of its possibilities of expansion a living intelligible reality, we feel the spiritual word which renders it present to us well up and fasten itself in our very core, we know what the intuitive power of intellect is and that it exerts itself through concept. Such moments leave us the solemn recollection of all birth, and what is born in us then, is born for always. Nothing replaces these perceptions, no discursive reasoning can furnish a substitute; we grasp not a word but the reality most tangible to the mind and most perfectly experienced, when we grasp the self-evidence of primary truths, where one intelligible object is immediately articulated with another, in the saturating and spontaneous plenitude of a necessity which issues forth sometimes for all men (when they are objects visible to everyone), sometimes only "for the sages." Thus are born in us metaphysical intuitions which bear not upon the pure spiritual, but on the transcendentals, on analogous intelligibles (of which the pure spiritual is the supreme analogue). Whoever does not see that *act is limited only by its potentiality,* or that *all that is by participation presupposes what is by itself,* no reasoning will ever convince—although reasoning can, by helping the mind better to grasp the ideas in play, lead him to see. At the heart of any great philosophical system there is likewise, as Bergson has pointed out in a celebrated passage, a very simple yet inexhaustible vision or insight which at a given moment filled the mind with certitude;—true, the mind can fuse it with errors, but in itself it never deceives. And I say that never more than at this very moment of insight was the mind more formed by, and filled with, an inner word or concept: a concept that words and formulae will never have finished elaborating.

Any important progress in the sciences of nature depends on *intellectual discoveries* of such a kind; here they have particular characteristics because they are in a much closer relationship with experience and a whole vast stock of observations. Nothing shows with greater evidence the vitality, the intuitive energies of the power of abstracting. It is a question of calling forth a brand new Word, never yet conceived, from the dark yet fecund waters which have poured into the soul through the sluice-gates of the senses. Intellect gropes its way, strives, waits; it seeks a gift which will come to it from its nature. It must retain everything it knows about things, and forget what it knows about the ideas it has already learned (especially philosophical ideas), plunge into a bath of active forgetting, render soluble and virtual and bring to a state of confused vital tension its acquired experience, sympathize with the real as it would in mimicking it. Beneath its inner active light, at some unforeseeable moment of decisive emotion, the coveted idea will be born. It is an idea, and that is why, although it has so many traits in common with Bergsonian intuition, this intuition is not at all Bergsonian intuition. It is an intellectual intuition which proceeds from the power of abstraction, is accomplished through and in a concept, and comes to fruition in a definition. The fact remains that if the descriptions Bergson gives of his intuition find analogies in reality, it would seem to be especially in this scientific intuition. And in order to call the attention of philosophers to the mystery of the *hunt for definitions,* especially with those particularities this hunt involves in the realm of natural sciences, (which for the last four centuries has been preparing a new field of investigation for philosophers), perhaps the untenable excesses of the metaphysics of Duration were necessary just as the error of Plato and of the metaphysics of Ideas had been necessary in order to teach philosophers the eternal necessities.

As for the scientists, they—the biologists at least—are less concerned over

Bergsonian philosophy than over the methodological ideas it conveys,—ideas which are all the more likely to hold their interest as this philosophy seems progressively to descend from metaphysics, hoped for and announced with the *Essay*, to psychology with *Matter and Memory*, and finally with *Creative Evolution*, to biology itself. In every country today we see the sciences of life throw off the rationalist and mechanistic yoke, and strive to understand the irreducible originality of their object. It is not surprising that Bergsonian philosophy helps them in many cases, and that the most profound action of Bergsonism and the least dangerous (for the work of experimentation tends automatically to re-establish at least *in actu exercito*, the value of concepts and of rational analysis), thus exerts itself in the scientific domain. From this point of view it is rather interesting to note in present-day science a network of disparate philosophical influences,—whether they come from Bergson, from the phenomenologists, or from a renascent Aristotelianism,—by which the scientist profits without worrying about the incompatibility of principles. Among the men of science with whom we are most in sympathy, if certain of them have received much from Aristotle and from Thomas Aquinas, it happens that some are greatly indebted to Bergsonism,—just as in another sphere several of our friends have been led by it right up to a spiritual threshold which they have crossed without it. It would grieve me if for any of them my critique of Bergsonian philosophy seemed to imply that I was forgetting these accidental virtues which I have, on the contrary, always been careful to recognize. Bergsonian influences unfortunately have other aspects which it is too easy to see in the properly philosophical realm. They encourage, in various parts of Europe, a pseudo-intuitivism sickening in its facility, and the vital impulses of thinkers who hastily discover outdated profundities. One wonders if the important renewal toward which the biological, psychological and sociological sciences are striving,—and which everywhere (save in France perhaps, where old-fashioned conceptions still survive) is definitely moving away from mechanicism, but not always avoiding a certain irrationalist festering,—would not run the risk of resulting either in a sort of pseudo-vitalist disorganization, or in a sort of mechanistic reaction, if it did not allow itself to be informed by a sane metaphysical entelechy.

But let us get back to our subject. If in the order of scientific and philosophical knowledge philosophers too often fail to recognize the vital and spiritual activity of intellect, what can be said of those vast regions of knowledge, some inferior others superior to philosophy, in which the verifications of science do not come into play? It is there that the immense majority of men have their opinions, their certitudes, and some a wisdom that philosophy envies. A good workman does better work with a poor tool than a mediocre workman does with a perfect instrument. How many naturally vigorous intellects go more directly to the truth with a rudimentary rational equipment than many a doctor with his logic! What they know they have divined. The poet divines by an instinct of the mind. The prudent man is instructed in another way,—he judges by consulting his virtue. The great common wisdom of the people, like the experience of old men, abounds in undemonstrable certitudes due to an immediate practical perception which Aristotle[1] and Saint Thomas[2] tell us to respect as we would axioms. The man accustomed to live in himself is capable of metaphysical experiences which enable him to grasp in their concrete application certain transcendent verities and which, although they are not exactly metaphysics, offer the metaphysician useful objects of reflection. Great faithfulness in seeking in everything one's own human truth, familiarizing the soul with what is spiritual, finally imposes upon it the practical confession of the true God. All these forms of knowledge, which depend upon the rectifications of the acting subject and on an affective and practical connaturality, fall within an order inferior to philosophy. Or we might even say they are the philosophy of those who do not philosophize at all. (The reproach that must especially be directed against Blondel's system is that it claims to set up as a philosophy and a doctrine an essentially infra-scientific mode of knowing, at the same time adding a bit of supra-philosophical cognition so that what happens is simply the suppression, —in favour of this spurious succedaneum,—of all the middle ground, which is philosophy itself.) Above philosophy, finally, the wisdom of the saints, which is supernatural, experiences divine things in the darkness of faith, in virtue of infused love which makes them one single spirit with God. All of this is what rationalism and a certain philosophical idolatry of learned notions fail to recognize. But the internal word of the intellect, the concept, is not absent from any of these sorts of knowledge. All the regulating of knowing does not take place in them through concepts as in science,[3] whose proper characteristic it is to be delivered from the crutches of the affections and inclinations of the subject and to regulate itself purely on the object as such, and therefore by concepts as formal means, because it is concepts which intelligibly present the object. Nevertheless, in the whole domain we have called infra-scientific, concepts are there, and more than that they are very actively working, the various subjective aids and the different kinds of divination we have mentioned always having the effect of stirring and welding thought. And if in contemplation they are silent and are surpassed, there must be admitted in the soul the presence of some habitual word,—however indistinct and confused,—which in this case is not the formal means of cognition, and

---

[1] Aristotle, *Nic. Eth.*, VI, 11, 1143 *b* 11–14.

[2] Saint Thomas Aquinas, *Sum. theol.*, I–II, 95, 2, *ad* 4.

[3] At the dictation of the experiment in the case of experimental sciences, where verification takes place in the sense.

which love prostrates, and of which mystical experience knows nothing, but which meets the conditions nature assigns to our intellect in order that it may find itself in act.*

*   *   *   *   *

The philosopher is inclined to reduce all concepts to the technically formulated concept,—a product more or less lofty in abstraction, but always rectified and purified,—of science and philosophy. There could be no greater error. The learned concept is a point of completion; it emerges from a world of spontaneous concepts which analysis distinguishes from phantasms and isolates, but which in the psychological concrete are all dripping with the sensible and entangled in images. What is more, before attaining its finished formation our mental word, as Saint Thomas pointed out,[1] passes through a series of successive determinations and differentiations. First of all it is formless, scarcely discernible, as for example when we have as we are apt to say "an idea that we cannot yet express." Finally it is by forming a second concept,—a reflex concept,—that we become aware of the concept by which we think things. The concept, moreover, did not appear in wise men's doctrines until philosophy became aware of itself and reached the age of discretion. Socrates did not invent the concept; he discovered it. In order to discern within us that by which the known object is *formed* in us the power of abstraction and reflection had itself to be *formed*. But therefore, born in philosophical and socratic soil, the idea of the concept was to find itself as though saturated with philosophy and with logic, and was henceforth to bear, not in itself certainly, but in the halo of associative images for which names are responsible, some noble and cumbersome memory of immobile Exemplars and Platonist Forms.

Why should we be surprised if this idea is lacking, as it were, in certain great realms of thought—in Indian thought in particular? If, in the few suggestive pages he recently devoted to *La spécificité de la psychologie indienne*,[2] Masson-Oursel seems, at least in my opinion, to give that specificity a too irreducible meaning, it is perhaps because he himself, in spite of everything, has not sufficiently respected it, for he attributes to Indian thought, more than he had intended, something like a philosophy properly so-called. I am careful here not to encroach on the domain of the orientalists; I merely accept their data and reflect thereon. But I may certainly be allowed to remark that all movement, and in particular all thought movement, is specifically determined by its goal; thus especially by the goal pursued did Aristotle dis-

---

* Cf. my study *Expérience mystique et philosophie*, Revue de Philosophie, November–December, 1926.

[1] *Comment. in Joann.*, I, 1.

[2] École pratique des hautes études, the section of religious sciences, year-book for 1928–1929.

tinguish between speculative intellect and practical intellect.[1] It seems that a good many things would become more intelligible if, instead of regarding the ordering of Indian thought toward a certain aim of deliverance as being the result of a certain conception of mind, one were on the contrary to regard the latter in terms of the former.[2] What I believe should be pointed out here as the foremost and most profound characteristic is precisely that from the very beginning, I mean from the fifth century B.C., India did not take knowledge itself as its goal, and that all its speculation is an ascetic discipline having deliverance as its avowed or virtual aim. The practical concern for a certain spiritual purification or, to come back to an essential distinction of Cajetan's, the conformity to a certain *direction* of our inner life, and not the conformity to the *being* of things, is consequently the principal norm of this thought. And precisely because it has not formulated any scientific knowledge or philosophy properly so-called,[3] which would have played a precipitating rôle, it was in the appearance of a philosophy, it was as substitute or succedaneum of a *Weltanschauung* (for one is always philosophizing), that the conceptu-

---

[1] I am not speaking here of the final goal to which we order the *exercise* of our act of knowing and which cannot, without a sort of idolatry, be knowledge itself. I am speaking of the end which intervenes in the *specification* of this act, which intrinsically affects its nature.

A practical goal (in the broadest sense of the word, comprising in practice eternal salvation itself) can affect the object insofar as the object is in itself *something to be done* (moral acts, for instance), the mind however, continuing to approach this object speculatively, that is to say, in order to *know* it, according to the nature of things. In this sense theology, for Saint Thomas, while being a speculative wisdom, is *eminenter practica* and treats of human acts according to how they must be directed toward their ultimate goal.

But the practical goal may even affect *the very mode* of approaching the object, which it is no longer a matter of knowing according to what is, but of *positing in being, of realising,* in accordance with the right direction of what is to be done. We then have practical intellectuality in the strictest sense, such as, according to Aristotle and Saint Thomas Aquinas, we find either in "practical science" and in art, or in prudence.

In my opinion, it is the rule of that particular intellectuality which, with regard to the deliverance to be obtained, and in keeping with the exclusively religious ordination of Indian thought, commands for that thought speculation itself.

[2] Without, of course, forgetting that here as elsewhere, and more than elsewhere, *causae ad invicem sunt causae.* The Indian conception of deliverance (cessation of transmigration) will be itself a function of the Indian conception of mind and duration.

[3] I hope the reader will be good enough to take these expressions in the most formal sense. By philosophy properly so-called I mean a wisdom which approaches things *modo speculativo* only, in the order of pure knowledge, and having for its sole rule conformity with what things are. I do not claim that India has had no philosophy, which would be absurd; but that its philosophy was not a philosophy properly so-called in the sense I have just indicated;—but was rather the philosophical conceptualization of the work of realization of deliverance, of the ascetic effort toward salvation by the liberation from the conditions of human nature.

Let me add (and this perhaps is the most serious objection one could make to the work of Masson-Oursel quoted in these pages) that it is no doubt unwise to attempt to characterize at the same time modes of thinking as different as the Brahmanic and Buddhistic modes of thinking. However, the remarks suggested here in a necessarily schematic form, perhaps enable us to understand how it was precisely in the form of the Buddhist heresy that the dehiscence of Hindu thought was to take place, soon followed, moreover, by the philosophical reaction of the Vedanta.

alization of an immense effort of the intellect took place—an effort originally directed not toward knowledge pursued for its own sake, but exclusively toward salvation: a mirage of philosophy all the more apt to delude us as it identifies itself, especially in Brahmanic orthodoxy, with admirable metaphysical divinations, and which induces us to attach a directly philosophical meaning to theories that have originally a purely anagogical and cathartic meaning; a pragmatism lived but transcendent, in the very heaven of intellectuality. For a meditation which does not seek to know what perception is for example, but to know how we must use perception to purify ourselves of desire, nothing is more normal than to say that "one has the perceptions one deserves; in any case those which the persistent influence of our preceding thoughts fashions in the present moment of our thought." The philosophical (pseudo-philosophical) transcription is: "What we take for an object is only the residue of our experiences."[1] For a meditation which does not aim at knowing the nature of things, but at freeing itself from human nature, nothing is more natural than to retain of the object only the result of our act, of the imaginative functions only an "orthopraxy" designed to make us masters of our representations, of action only its physical as it were fructification as merit or demerit, of mind only its creative spontaneity,[2] of knowledge itself only the liberation from oneself, and a "realization" which will de-essence the sage. We can understand then how India has *dispensed with ideas*,[3]—has not known concept. Its philosophy has never been sufficiently *formed* to see it. We can understand why "metaphysics, there" did "not need essences."[4] There, the goal has never been metaphysical *knowledge* properly so-called; metaphysical thought, however lofty, has never gained its autonomy, has always remained an outboard appendage in the effort toward sanctity to which it claimed to lead and to suffice. "Λόγοι, *veritates aeternae* of the Mediterranean world, celestial decrees, innate ideas as the Chinese conceived them remained foreign to the Indians. Once again they claimed to surpass existence, not to harmonize it."[5] They did not seek to conquer intelligibly the world man lives in, and in

---

[1] Paul Masson-Oursel, *op. cit.*, p. 4.

[2] "If the European mind has conceived of itself as a mirror, the Indian mind has conceived of itself as a lantern." (*Ibid.*, p. 13.) With regard to the European mind, with which I am slightly acquainted, this generalization seems to me somewhat rash. In Aristotle in any case the European mind was conceived *both* as a lantern (*intellectus agens,* which abstracts) and as a mirror (*intellectus possibilis,* which knows),—but as a living mirror and itself active.

[3] *Ibid.*, p. 6. "It was rather late in elaborating a logic of extension and comprehension, perhaps under the direct or indirect influence of Aristotle; its indigenous logic rested on other principles. In the Sanscrit philosophical vocabulary, rich as it is, none of the terms designating the intellectual operation which decomposes (prefix vi-) or the one which combines (prefix sam-) corresponds to 'concept,' or implies induction or deduction, analysis or synthesis, with the peripatetic meaning of these notions. One may join, construct, without generalizing; one may dissociate, dissolve, as an acid would, without passing from the more to the less general."

[4] *Ibid.*, p. 6.

[5] *Ibid.*, p. 7.

which in fact these essences are contained, these λόγοι germinate, and where rule those eternal truths that intellection discovers in forming ideas.

It is not that the human mind is irreducibly different on the banks of the Ganges from what it is on the shores of the Mediterranean: it was oriented here and there toward different finalities.—Nor is it that reason is a Greek fiction: India was attached to a work for which she had no need to draw Minerva from the forehead of her gods. Neither is it that in fact she has never used the concept; theories and schools, *darshanas* she has had: but she was content with the concept in its least differentiated state. The mere fact that she thought meant that she used the mental word, but she left it or desired it as formless as possible; in this sense, but only in this sense, can one say that her tragedy has been to want Intellectuality without the Word. Disdaining the human word, good enough for the Greeks, being ignorant of the divine Word, revealed to the sons of Abraham, Isaac and Jacob, she has suspended her soul to an eternal Wisdom which is not the increate Logos,—to a human wisdom which is not reason. And as there is no other wisdom than these, either she has followed them without knowing them, or she has declined from wisdom. Bearing heroic testimony to the postulations of the spirit in us she has chosen at all costs to transcend human nature and reason. And why? unless because man aspires of himself to the superhuman and because, unhappy in his own nature, he seeks to escape from it and enter into another. Here so many "efforts against nature that we can scarcely suspect," and which for the Brahman or the Buddhist are "current experience, traditional usage,"[1] have as their limit,—and how much more powerful and inexorable even than in the Alexandrines,—a beleaguering, a denaturizing of man at the touch of pure spirit, the kiss of the Angel. One therefore will not waste time in distinguishing the sensible from the intelligible, notion from intention; all this has a common empirical origin; one will have to apply oneself to it only to surpass it. And of contemplation itself, for which formlessness and *dissolvi* are not sufficient, whose whole is *esse tecum,* one will have realized only the negative,—with such courage that it is impossible to believe that sometimes grace's ways of compensating (for we know that God disguises Himself), or sometimes other influences less pure, do not nourish the soul in secret. But of itself the goal toward which one aspires, loss of self in the absolute of the Vedanta, or in the Buddhist nirvana, if indeed it is other than a pure annihilation,[2] is also something quite different from union with a divine Thou where all love is consummated; in it the mind wholly exhausts itself in an eternal projection.

Bergson has not, like Schopenhauer, sought to learn from the Hindus (his contact with the Orient was established through Plotinus). But the similari-

[1] *Ibid.,* p. 14.
[2] Cf. Louis de la Vallée Poussin, *Le Nirvăna,* Paris, Beauchesne.

ties between his doctrine and certain aspects, if not always of the great tradition of the Vedantas, at least of that characteristic heresy of Indian thought, Buddhist meditation, are only the more remarkable, however superficial such comparisons no doubt remain. A thought which believes it can dispense with concepts or transcend them, and is not concerned with distinguishing between idea and image, which attributes to the ideas it forms a value which, after all, is merely nominalist and which demands of an effort contrary to nature the concentration by which one enters into spiritual reality,—the idea of a sort of universal consciousness in which waves of perception propagate and intercross, where being is regarded as a transitory residuum of becoming and of action, memory conceived as the mind itself subsisting on its acts and as a past which endures,—all of these features at first glance suggest Bergsonian conceptions. One may nevertheless wonder whether speculation would stand to gain by returning to a state of non-formation from which once upon a time in Greece it was lucky enough to escape. It should also be noted—and this renders the Bergsonian positions particularly untenable,—that if Brahman and Buddhist intellectual disciplines received their whole direction from an original ordination not to knowing but to a flight out of experience, Bergsonism on the contrary claims to dig in the bed of experimental science, lead to a knowledge, and be a philosophy properly so-called.

Philosophy requires a word, and a perfectly and scientifically *formed* word. Philosophical wisdom is the perfect work of reason, *perfectum opus rationis*. That is why it refuses for its work proper any other rule than that of the object, any other light than evidence. That is why it demands such a critical elaboration, so rigorous an ordination of its conceptual forms. These, because they are pure, appear anaemic to man. They are neither for his traffickings nor for his play; they are not measured to his prudence, or even to those inchoations of wisdom he receives from works and days and which are worth more to him than many a system. They are for the loftiest knowledge (in the natural order, at least) and for the most difficult. Concepts are not the life of philosophy;—that life is intellect and intellection; nevertheless it passes through them and uses them indispensably. Thanks to them and to their apprehension of being, it attains in direct line (but by the properties which manifest it), the suprasensible immanent in the sensible; and, by analogical refraction, the suprasensible separated from the sensible,—the pure spiritual. It obtains, about the spiritual world and about God, certitudes in themselves firmer and more perfect than mathematical certitudes. By dint of logic it holds being in its grasp. It is only too easy to declare that if the positive part of Bergsonism is "provisional," the Bergsonian critique of mechanistic errors is purely and simply just and definitive. No! Things are not as simple as all that. In this Bergsonian critique of mechanism there is also the Bergsonian critique of intellect and concept, and this, which consists in short in abolishing the proper value of abstraction, destroys philosophical knowledge as it destroys all speculative certitude acquired by strictly rational means. As to Bergsonian intuition, it leads to movement without a mobile, the past which subsists and the substantiality of change.

*   *   *   *   *

Intellectualism, anti-intellectualism,—to be absolutely exact one should use these words only to designate two opposing errors. It is improperly and through reaction against the contemporary anti-intellectualist current that the thought of Saint Thomas has sometimes been called intellectualist (it has been done in the present work); others in so designating it tended to displace its centre of gravity and in a way to transfer it into conditions of intellect in the pure state. The best way of designating it, in reality, would be rather as critical realism. Intellectualism which realizes abstractions or scorns experience or makes of the real a pure object which human intellect completely exhausts is no better than anti-intellectualism.

Bergsonians have reproached their adversaries for having given way, in calling Bergsonism an anti-intellectualist philosophy, to outrageous simplifications. No less outrageous is the simplification which claims that in employing this vocable one is quite plainly reproaching Bergson with having tried to philosophize without intelligence, yes, and even to "de-cerebrate" his unhappy disciples. Thus to deplore the lack of intelligence of the "intellectualists" is too easy a pleasure. Thibaudet is right in pointing out that "the Bergsonism of pure instinct, Bergsonism as the enemy of thought, dada-Bergsonism, is a caricature about as exact as the Socrates of the *Clouds* when he measures a flea's jump, or the Rousseau of the *Philosophers* when Palissot makes him appear on the stage walking on all fours."[1] But if misunderstandings of this kind are always possible, I am quite sure I have not laid myself open to them, even in my harshest expressions. I know that "the clearest impression Bergson's exposition gives us is that of intelligence," that "the light of his thought is indeed the light of intellectualist philosophers (Plato excepted), from Aristotle to Spinoza and Leibnitz," that "it lacks warmth as much as the *Ethics*" (I should say more than the *Ethics*) "or as the *New Essays*" and that "there is nothing less pathetic than that *pathetic philosophy* denounced by Benda."[2] Need I add that the elegance of the arabesque, and a sort of mathematical acuity seem to characterize an intellectuality in it quite definitely purified of any contamination of pathos. I know too that for Bergson intellect attains "something of the absolute" in the mathematical knowledge of matter, and that it is a power for research opened on to an unlimited field, in short, that

[1] Albert Thibaudet, *Le Bergsonisme*, t. II, p. 101.
[2] *Ibid.*

"intellect occupies a large part in his doctrine";* that for him "the philosopher is a freedman liberated from intellect, but a freedman in the Roman sense; he remains within the family circle and almost in the house of the intelligence."† . . . But if being an intellectual does not oblige one to be an intellectualist, neither does it hinder one from being an anti-intellectualist. One misjudges intellect when one admits that it really knows matter only, that it seeks but that another finds, that all it has is *a share* (and what a share) in the knowledge of philosophical truth. One shatters in reality the philosophical instrument when one claims to exorcize from philosophy abstraction which is the proper mode of human intellection, when one affirms that in order to philosophize one must push intellect out of doors, and put oneself back into the original impulse from which intellect and instinct have dissociated themselves,—finally, that logic, like geometry, is "rigorously applicable"[1] to matter alone. The philosopher is not a freedman liberated from intellect, nor is he its slave. Intelligence is freedom. He is not a god of intellect, for our nature is "in bondage in too many respects."[2] He is a freedman by virtue of intellect (and one who is constantly freeing himself, because his work is never finished), he is a self-freeing, a self-liberating, a making-self-free by intellect. In calling Bergson's philosophy anti-intellectualist I am not claiming that he has in view the annihilation of intellect; I do claim that the conception he forms of it deprives it of its nature and of the function for which it exists in us.

I understand full well that his design was much less to institute a theory of knowledge than to criticize one method, in order to substitute for it another method—and to do so by the very movement of his research, as Diogenes did by walking. In that, there may have been some contingency in imposing the name "intellect" on the disapproved manner of operating, which one might equally well have imputed to "fabricating imagination" or to "spatializing analysis," for example. But, as we have already seen, profound necessities, immanent in Bergsonian thought in its most individual aspect, have in reality suggested such a designation. Anti-intellectualism is not only an apparent sign, it is an essential characteristic of that thought.

Any method of cognition presupposes a metaphysics of knowledge; and in Bergson more than in anyone else, because he would not elaborate for its own sake such a metaphysics, which remains entirely implied and inviscerated in the method employed, it is from the latter that one must seek the former. Why then in Bergsonian formulae does the word 'intellect' constantly slip over from the mode of functioning (by mechanistic reconstruction or breaking-up retrospection) to the faculty, and from the faculty to the mode of

* *Ibid.*, p. 35.
† *Ibid.*, p. 101.
[1] *Creative Evolution*, p. 161.
[2] Aristotle, *Metaph.*, lib. I, c. 2, 982 *b* 29.

functioning, unless it is because this mode of functioning expresses the nature of the faculty, because the criticism of the intellect-method-for-allowing-the-real-to-escape-and-for-satisfying-itself-by-geometrizing-life anastomoses and intermingles, becomes identified from the outset with a criticism, less explicit and correspondingly more corrosive, of intellect as a faculty. Considering its natural bent, this latter is characterized according to Bergson, by an essential incapacity to understand life, by the negation of all veritable novelty in becoming, by the spatialization of the spiritual, etc.

And so Bergson's method, if one refrains from decanting or transposing it and if one takes it as it is—whole, integrated to the totality of its results, such as it directs and vivifies the main structure of Bergsonism—Bergson's method, I say, is one of the most powerful solvents of the laws of the intellect philosophy has yet invented. Because the continuous duration of life baffles any logic and cannot be bothered with the principle of non-contradiction, "the method necessitated by this density proper to things of the soul cannot be anything but completely 'irrational.' "* One of the merits of Vladimir Jankélévitch, in one of the best expositions that have been made of Bergsonism from Bergson's own point of view, is that he does not leave the reader any doubt on this important point.

In the study just referred to, one so favourable to Bergsonian philosophy, we find many a remarkable verification of the propositions put forward here against that philosophy. In particular we find in it what I consider to be one of the fundamental procedures of Bergsonism. Bergsonism quite rightly denounces a vicious method of analysis, but only to impute it to the essential demands of rational knowledge. It discovers or restores, in the field of psychological observation, some very precious truths,—and need I repeat that it is certainly not against them that my criticism is directed. Strictly limited in this respect, it is against the Bergsonian philosophy of nature and against Bergsonian metaphysics that my whole criticism is brought to bear.—But from the beginning these psychological truths which as such originate in a marvellously acute introspection, are clothed, inextricably enveloped in, errors of an essentially philosophical or metaphysical order—errors due precisely to an effort contrary to nature to *reduce* rationality or to twist it out of shape. All the examples proposed by Jankélévitch (organic totalities, the learning of a living language,[1] the effort of intellection, freedom, teleology) abound in apt psychological remarks which do not demand an upsetting or a twisting of our faculties but only (if it is true that in this order of knowledge our judgments should all be modelled on the sense)[2] an exact insertion of the intellective ef-

---

* Vladimir Jankélévitch, *Prolégomènes au Bergsonisme;* Rev. de Mét. et de Mor., October–December, 1928, p. 42.

[1] Let us point out here, in defence of "grammars," that their object is not to teach us (practically) to speak a language, but to make the structure of that language known (speculatively).

[2] Cf. Saint Thomas Aquinas, *in Boet. de Trinitate,* q. 6, a. 2.

fort into the experience of the inner sense. But everywhere, at the same time, it is taken as an established fact that the *explanation* which satisfies the intelligence mechanizes the real and substitutes for the vital processes posthumous refabrications effected with illusory elements, without perceiving that such mechanistic reconstructions (such "retrospective schemes")—which are, if you wish, "the intellectualist sin *par excellence*"—are precisely the contrary of a satisfactory *explanation,* deceive and irritate the intellect and are the object of very distinct reprobation on the part of an authentically rational knowledge. Everywhere, finally, we meet this postulate, revived from old Empedocles, that things should be in knowledge as they are in themselves and that "one really understands movement and action only by moving and acting,"[1]— "as, following the aphorism of Empedocles, like is knowable only to like, so life, one might say, is knowable only to life, [. . .] there is only one good way of demonstrating possible freedom and that is to will and to act,"[2]—which is, for reason, the most radical confession of helplessness, because it amounts to saying that to know truly would be to live and not to know, or even that the more one knows the less one understands: "The tragedy of the mind consists in this, that our knowledge of objects obstructs, so to speak, our intimate and central comprehension of them."[3] The effect of such a metaphysics is therefore to implicate the correct observations we have mentioned in general interpretations of a surprisingly arbitrary kind (be the credit he gives "the philosophy of life" ever so great, a man who has once *chosen* in his life will never admit that one *"deliberates after having resolved"*),[4] and once the bounds of pure psychology are passed, to lure the mind into a psychologism perniciously carried to the absolute.

If, as already mentioned, the method of the "philosophy of life" leads finally to the affirmation that change is substance itself and thus to the destruction of the principle of contradiction, the Bergsonian critique of intelligence or rational method is consummated in that famous critique of the ideas of

[1] Vladimir Jankélévitch, article quoted, p. 464.

[2] *Ibid.,* p. 465.

[3] *Ibid.,* p. 473.

[4] *Ibid.,* p. 458. In italics in the text. "Everything takes place then as though the momentary hesitations were, in a sense, merely an unconscious bit of make-believe we indulge in so that we may be right with the intellect and retrospectively legitimize a decision which, at bottom, was made well in advance in our minds. [. . .] There is confusion between our real conduct and an ideal scenario that we construct after the event." It is true that at the moment of our choice we are not in a state of perfect neutrality (like the famous scales of the determinists), but on the contrary are pulled by profound tendencies whose roots may go back to our most distant past; it is also very true that the justifications we constantly make to ourselves for our conduct in terms of the imaginary social setting interposed between us and ourselves, constantly give place to those retrospective illusions in self-knowledge pointed out by Max Scheler. But if there is an immediate datum of consciousness, it is the control we exercise over the practical judgment which enables us to emerge from the state of indetermination, and which can be pronounced *against* everything that desire preformed within us.

nothingness and of disorder and of the principle of finality which rejects as radically as possible any effort to penetrate the world intelligibly. As I have pointed out in my studies on the subject, the history of philosophy presents few so artistically devised attempts at suicide. This critique amounts, in a word, to challenging the very first division of being into necessary being and contingent being, and to replacing the being of things which could have not been by an auto-creative becoming which is neither necessary since it is free, nor contingent since it postulates no reason outside itself. The aseity of pure change thus crowns the substantiality of this same change, and if one is still thinking in terms of intelligence, one is forced to declare that they both constitute one and the same primary absurdity at the heart of things. Bergson sees in finalism only an upside-down mechanism;[1] for him finality as intelligence conceives it signifies that before being made, that which was made was already ready-made in the state of a pre-established plan. It has been rightly pointed out[2] that such a critique may have some bearing against the Leibnitzian conception of virtuality which is only a hindered act, it has no effect against the Aristotelian conception of potentiality which is irreducible and which, as very potentiality, is ordinated to the act. Nothing ready-made here, but rather the reality of potentiality and of its aspiration, which is itself, toward what it not yet is—and the reality of becoming. To suppress finality is not only to suppress efficiency and all causality, but also to suppress all potentiality in things, to say that they are their action and to make of substance, with Spinoza, or of change, with Bergson, pure Act. And here we are, back again, at the aseity of change.

Malum ut in pluribus in specie humana—in relation to knowing this fundamental adage signifies that if, in philosophy, it follows the inclination of *the easiest,* our intellect, because it is turned in the direction of the senses and the imagination, will go toward materialistic pseudo-explanations. We may say that therein lies a permanent temptation toward illusion. But to follow this inclination is precisely for it to abandon itself. To be sure it does not exhaustively understand the things of life and of the spirit any more than it does anything in the world. Yet its instinctive and spontaneous activity, before it thinks of being learned, brings it into accord with life rather than with geometry, with animism rather than with mechanism. Materialism is the barbaric state of learned reason.[3] And when this reason becomes adult and when, turning toward the reality of life and the reality of the spirit, it en-

---

[1] *Creative Evolution,* p. 39.

[2] R. Dalbiez, *le Transformisme et la Philosophie,* in *Le Transformisme,* first book of Phil. de la Nature, Paris, Vrin, 1927, p. 211.

[3] "It would be difficult," writes Bergson (*Creative Evolution,* p. X), "to cite a biological discovery due to pure reasoning." I should think so! But the state of pure reasoning is not the state connatural to human intelligence. It is the to-and-fro movement between experience and reasoning that reflects the most natural play of our intellect.

genders in itself Words fashioned to their measure, it is capable of knowing them, of entering into their density. *Fehlt, leider! nur das geistige Band?*[1] Like the Bergsonians, Mephistopheles leaves man only a blighted reason. Who takes life *in his hand* holds only disjointed parts, but *in the intellect* the spiritual bond is not lacking. Where the philosophy of duration is content with a metaphor: "Nature has had no more trouble in making an eye than I have in lifting my hand,"[2] Aristotle, elaborating the notion of formal cause and substantial act, and the notion of immanent activity, enables us to raise ourselves to a proper knowledge of the organism. It is a philosophical knowledge that his realism proposes to us, but a sober one which consists in acquiring the understanding of a mystery; whereas anti-intellectualism (which cannot find in any nature or essence—either of the object known, or of the subject knowing—any principle of auto-limitation) plunges into an infinite plenitude in order to relive it all, and tends to awaken that metaphysical arbitrary which, in Schelling's time, discredited vitalism and the philosophy of nature.

IV

I readily admit, as I have said before, that in these critical studies of Bergsonism I have considerd its doctrinal significance more than its genesis. My purpose was not so much to try to relive Bergson's thought as to try to test its truth. Neither did I undertake to study all the aspects and all the virtualities of Bergsonism. My attention was directed essentially to its metaphysical value.

It was certainly my right and even my duty to do so. It must be noted however that my perspective was consequently no longer Bergson's. It had been possible to believe for a moment that he would undertake to construct a metaphysics; all he sought to do was to introduce us to the subject. Many of his listeners at the Collège de France, because he had awakened in them a desire for metaphysics, expected him to give them one. They were disappointed. Today, much better than twenty years ago, we can see that Bergsonian philosophy never completely acknowledged to itself the metaphysics it enveloped and which it could have brought to light. It has remained much more closely riveted to positive science and more dependent upon it, much more *scien-*

---

[1] M. Jankélévitch has placed as the epigraph to his *Prolégomènes au bergsonisme* these lines of Mephistopheles to the Student:

> *Wer was Lebendig's will erkennen und beschreiben*
> *Sucht erst den Geist herauszutreiben;*
> *Dann hat er die Teile in seiner Hand,*
> *Fehlt, leider! nur das geistige Band.*

[2] *Creative Evolution*, p. 91.

tistic itself than its sharp reaction against scientistic metaphysics led one to suppose. In his desire to free metaphysics from the arbitrariness of transitory systems, Bergson trusted in the possibility of a philosophical method "closely traced upon (internal and external) experience," and one which "does not permit the enunciation of a conclusion which in the least exceeds the empirical considerations upon which it is based."[1] Which, strictly speaking, amounts to denying the autonomy of metaphysics as a science. Resolved to remain absolutely faithful to the method thus defined and no doubt noticing the lack (for there are none) of the *experiences* which would have been necessary for arriving at metaphysics along this road, one may even wonder whether, as a result of the internal incompossibilities of his empirical metaphysics, he was not brought by his methodological probity itself progressively to renounce the metaphysical only to fall back more and more upon the empirical.

Was there then some injustice in *too directly* confronting Bergsonian thought with a deliberately metaphysical thought like that of Aristotle and Saint Thomas? All I can concede here is that perhaps (and without making any change in substance) I should now propose my criticisms somewhat differently. But the urgency of such a confrontation was all the greater because a metaphysics, even though implicit, is no less real and active, efficacious and insidious. Thus it is, as was pointed out above, that although Bergson's critique of the concept relates especially to a certain scientific use of the concept, what it actually does is touch to the quick the concept itself and intellect itself. *Carentia boni debiti!* The most serious objection one must raise here against Bergsonism is that it was not daring enough, that in the very exercise of philosophy it failed to recognize the power of intellect and of philosophy and that it recoiled from any recognition of the autonomy of metaphysical knowledge.

The first chapter of *Matter and Memory* clearly shows that Bergson thought he could get along without choosing between the idealist and the realist conception of knowledge and, leaving this problem to be disputed by the metaphysicians, that he could proceed as though it were merely a question of two styles or two vocabularies where the only thing demanded of each is to be coherent. If, however, he had treated the problem of knowledge for itself as should be done, he might perhaps have been forced to give up his nominalism and entirely recast his critique of intellect. Perhaps too, he would have been led to rediscover *intentional being* (as happened in the case of Husserl, following Brentano), which would no doubt have brought about essential changes in his theory of memory and duration (for the two questions are closely allied, as I have more explicitly indicated in this second edition). A metaphysics unafraid of existing for its own sake or of having recourse to

---

[1] Letter to de Tonquédec (June 12, 1911). *Études*, February 20, 1912, p. 515.

the proper intelligible means of a supra-experimental discipline might perhaps have enabled him to arrive at the true meaning of the invaluable observations in his *Essay* on the transcendence of the psychic in relation to
quantitative number, or to save in the light of reason that feeling for the ir-
reversibility of time, for the unforeseeableness, the incessant novelty of concrete becoming, which in him as in the pluralist philosophers deserves so
much attention and respect.

But allow me to dwell for a moment on this last point. As has been justly
pointed out, chance, which is the intersection of independent causal series, is
defined "by pluralism, and not by unforeseeableness, as is sometimes believed.
If one takes the positions and initial speeds of two bodies, it is obviously easy
to foresee their meeting. Shall we say therefore that it is not a thing of chance?
This would be to forget the pluralism of the initial data."[1] Likewise, it is by
the dominating indifference of the will with regard to any particular good
proposed as such by the intellect, not by unforeseeableness, that freedom is defined. The question of the foreseeableness of free acts and of the contingent
or fortuitous events which occur in nature is, however, worth going into.
In both cases this foreseeableness must be denied, but for totally different reasons. The free act is *by its very essence* absolutely unforeseeable because the
cause from which it comes is not predetermined to produce it. The contingent
event and the fortuitous event result either from a cause determined by nature
to an effect but which can be prevented, or from the meeting of several causal
series none of which is determined on its own account to produce it. Of themselves these events do not resist calculation or foreseeing. *Actually,* however,
if one considers, not a case simplified and isolated by the mind, like the one
considered above, but nature as a whole and the concrete events which depend upon universal interaction, one sees that in order to calculate ahead of
time with scientific certitude a contingent or fortuitous event, one would be
obliged, beginning with the initial state of all the cosmic elements—a state
supposed to be known—to trace, without dropping the slightest stitch, the
individual history of all the actions which will cross one another in the universe and which might concur in the production or prevention of this event—
which is, properly speaking, not so much calculating in advance (that is to
say, passing by way of a law which dispenses with an infinity of particular
facts), as following in advance, in all the multiplicity of its singular determinations, the historical unfolding of universal duration, exhausting the productivity of nature. Such a foreseeing presupposes an exhaustive comprehension of the whole being of things, and as a result surpasses the power of any
created intellect. That is why Saint Thomas teaches that Angels have not
naturally the certain, (but have only conjectural) knowledge of contingent
futures. As to the uncreated Intellect, it does not calculate in advance—to tell

[1] R. Dalbiez, *op. cit.,* p. 179.

the truth it does not foresee—it *sees* in the absolute simplicity of its act; because for it all is present. And thus, in actual fact, there is no intellect—either human, or angelic, or divine[1]—which has by a previously-made calculation the knowledge of all singular events—because such a calculation is in no way conformable to the natural desire of intellect as such.

Whereupon we shall perhaps ask with Gabriel Marcel, who is quite right in putting to the philosophers this embarrassing question: how are we to account for the fact of prophecy? If it is a question of prophecy properly so-called, of divine origin, the Thomists will answer that moments of time, although succeeding one another in time, are all present at once in their physical reality, as terms of creative action, to the eternity which, wholly without succession, from on high measures and contains them. "In that today of God," said Saint Peter Damian, "that day is still immobile in which this world was born; and no less present already is the day when it will be judged."[2] It is in this eternal present that the prophet sees. If it is a question of the pseudo-prophesying of mediums and clairvoyants, the answer is much more doubtful. For my part, and naturally assuming well-established facts, I think some contact with the world of pure intelligences must in this case be admitted. Without mentioning the divine revelations they receive, these intelligences can, much better than man and much more frequently, conjecture with certitude. Let us also remember that they know in a participation of creative Ideas the things of the here-below as they come into existence, and each of their acts of cognition is an immobile instant which endures and with which there co-exists a certain flowing of our time. Hence it seems (I hazard this hypothesis) that they must know our time as through *quanta* or pulsations of duration if I may say so, in such a way that in the limits of each one of these slices of time, the whole sequence is there for them in one single glance.

* * * * *

Are we to believe that the whole ambition of Bergsonian thought is limited to an attempt to act upon science, to propose new objects to it, to bring it to the consideration of the organic and the spiritual, to snatch it away from the idols of mechanicism? The implicit but very active metaphysics of Bergsonism goes much further.

[1] Of course, God Who knows the totality of the causes which may provoke and the causes which may hinder the contingent event, knows a particular one not only in its being proper but in the whole texture of its causes. But it is not by a *calculation* that He has this knowledge, it is by the intuition of His essence and His creative causality, in which He knows all. Cf. Saint Thomas Aquinas, *Sum. contra Gent.*, I, 66, 67, 68.

As to the event not only contingent but free, it can be known with certitude only according to its presentiality, since the totality of created causes leaves it indeterminate in advance. Cf. Aristotle, *Perihermeneias*, chap. IX, lect. 13 and 14 of Saint Thomas.

[2] Saint Peter Damian, ep. IV *de Omnipotentia*, chap. 6. Cf. John of Saint Thomas, *Curs. theol.*, q. X. I. P., disp. ix, a. 3, n. 14.

Intellectus supra tempus. Metaphysics was constituted from the beginning as transcendent to time; it was born when the intelligence of philosophers raised its head above the flood of succession. From the world of existence, from the flux of the particular and the contingent, it then brought out and as it were isolated before the mind objects of thought which only exist immersed in singularity and in history—natures, essences, laws: the loci of intelligible necessities upon which rests the stability of knowledge. These natures or essences which, as Spir pointed out concerning the principles of reason, far from being a simple sublimation of the empirical, first disconcert so to speak the sensible imagery in which the mind verifies them, are a stumbling-block for modern thought, and stir up in us philosophers a sort of sore point. In the metaphysical heaven to which analogy transports essences, the mind sees and handles them, discovers their articulations. But below man and human things, although it necessarily affirms them, it discerns them very badly. Modern science, in order to constitute itself, had to eliminate them from its most formal weft along with all the properly philosophical notions bound up with them, leaving them in the scientist's mind in the state of a latent substructure, indispensable as a psychological *point d'appui* but without any epistemological right or value. It took the innocence of youth and the imprudent daring of an intellect happy in having come into its own to speak of them to readers of this day and age in the tone used in this book. Today I should no doubt adopt another mode of exposition. Analysing the world of our objects in the manner of Whitehead or the German phenomenologists (who find in their language a *Wesen* less shocking than our word *essence*) we should rediscover them under names charged with a less weighty past. And as a matter of fact it might be advantageous to renovate, on this point, the traditional analyses, and by showing that the intellect cannot dispense with recognizing in the real what we might call knots of intelligibility, thinkable interiorities, or densities of being, to try to restore to the noun οὐσία, out of courtesy toward our contemporaries, a little of the colouring of its hey-day.

Whatever such considerations may be worth, the day that the physico-mathematical method made possible the establishment of a science of phenomena *as such,* on condition that intelligibility be renounced so to speak, I mean on condition that we resolve concepts in *measurable sense-data* only, and reduce the rôle of the ontological to the construction of "explanatory" beings of reason (*êtres de raison*) to support a weft of legalities and mathematical formalities unifying phenomena—on that day it can be said that the mind re-installed itself in time. It took it three centuries and the Kantian revolution to become aware of this fact. What then is to become of metaphysics? If it is faithful to itself and to what is, it will transcend the science of phenomena as it transcends time, and by the same token will recognize that this science, because it consists in an *empiriological* or *empirio-mathematical* analysis of the real, is both autonomous with regard to the ontological or metempirical analyses which the philosopher makes, and in contact with philosophy (which interprets it according to its own light)—but does not itself contain, hidden within it, a philosophy. But if one denies metaphysics this transcendence and this personality with regard to science, yet even so desires to establish a metaphysics, one must seek it, not above the world proper of the mathematization of the sensible, but in its depths. That, it seems, is a point of view common to a good many contemporary thinkers. Otherwise why should Brunschvicg, for example, make philosophy, which for him is spirit itself, so wretchedly dependent upon science and upon its history? Thus the whole question between them and us comes back to knowing whether the order proper or the object proper of wisdom is transcendent or immanent to the object proper of science. In the latter case one will have to seek—(and that is quite illusory indeed)—one will have to seek *underneath* the physico-mathematical weft a substance, a metaphysical stuff with which, without knowing it, the physico-mathematical knowledge of nature is presumably pregnant.

But where is this knowledge installed, if not in the fluent itself? What is it striving to organize in its formulae if not the relational stabilities it isolates in the very by-flowing of sensible becoming? Bergson's stroke of genius was to see that if the science of phenomena itself envelops and dissimulates in its proper order and its formal object a metaphysical stuff, this stuff can only be time. It is into time that we must *plunge* if we want to find a knowledge which will have as its direct term not the necessary and the universal, but the very flux of the singular and the contingent, pure movement considered as the very substance of things: which presupposes, as Bergson perfectly well saw, the total surpassing of the concept and a total inversion of the natural movement of the intellect. In this same time in which physics is installed without wishing to consider it in its reality (for physics is content with its mathematical substitute) and which it translates into spatial symbols and which mechanicism suppresses, metaphysics will seize the absolute itself, which is invention and creation. Much more fundamentally dependent on modern physics than the immanent Cause of Spinoza which "substantified" the mechanistic explanations of a science of phenomena still in its youth, and the victim of a much more profound prestige, Bergsonian Duration realizes in metaphysics the very soul of empiricism or of pure experimentalism of which this science has become conscious as it progressed and with which it approaches the real in order to explain it. The last pages of *Creative Evolution* are eminently significant in this regard. "It seems then that, parallel to this [modern] physics, a second kind of knowledge ought to have grown up [. . .] It is within becoming that it would have transported us by an effort of sympathy. [. . .] If [this knowledge] succeeds it is reality itself that it will hold in a firm and final embrace."[1] "An experience of this kind is not a non-temporal experience. It only seeks, beyond the spatialized time in which we believe we see continual rearrangements between the parts, that concrete duration in which a radical recasting of the whole is always going on."[2] "The more we reflect on it, the more we shall find that this conception of metaphysics is that which modern science suggests."[3] "So understood, philosophy is not only the turning of the mind homeward, the coincidence of human consciousness with the living principle whence it emanates, a contact with the creative effort. It is the study of becoming in general, it is true evolutionism and consequently the true continuation of science."[4] In short and properly speaking, metaphysics consists in "seeing in time a progressive growth of the absolute";[5] it is summed up in the affirmation that *time is creative*. But if what is, is, this metaphysics is only a dream.

What is in time, Aristotle taught, grows old and fades away; the fact that there is *something new* is not to be imputed to time, but to the active causes in play in nature. "However, generation like corruption takes place in time; that is why some attributed to time the generation of things, and the acquisition of knowledge, and all progress of that sort, saying that time goes of itself to wisdom, because the generation of knowledge takes place in time. But a certain philosopher, by the name of Paro, and of the sect of the Pythagorians, affirmed quite the contrary, namely that time is repugnant in itself to wisdom, because through the passing of time comes forgetfulness. And in this he has spoken with greater exactitude: because time has in itself more affinity with destruction than with production; for it is the number of change; and of itself, changing, considered as changing, means rather destruction and corruption (it is to depart from what one was), and means only by accident production of being: what change brings in fact of being or new disposition, does not come from change as such, but as it involves finiteness and completion; and this it gets from the tendency of the active cause, which moves to a determined end."[6] In short, from the very fact that it is essentially linked to matter, time goes of its own inclination toward dissolution, not toward invention, and all progress is, metaphysically, an effort of redress against time. The fact that it was not ignorant of this fundamental law, this sort of metaphysical entropy, did not mean that ancient wisdom failed to recognize to what extent real novelty, growth, progress are to be found in concrete duration, especially in vital and spiritual duration. But it distinguished between time itself and what endures in time, that is to say, substantial reality with its activities and its mutations, an all the more active reality because it has more life and immanence. Nor did the ancients think, as Bergson believes, that

---

[1] *Creative Evolution*, pp. 342–343.   [2] *Ibid.*, p. 363.
[3] *Ibid.*, p. 343.   [4] *Ibid.*, p. 370.   [5] *Ibid.*, p. 344.
[6] Saint Thomas Aquinas, *in Phys. Arist.*, lib. IV, c. xiii, lect. 22.

"the duration of a thing manifests only the degradation of its essence."[1] On the contrary, for them the duration of a thing was the very *existence* of that thing, insofar as it continues in time. And if things, from the point of view of the mode of existing itself, have a better existence in the intellect of God where they are God Himself, than in themselves, nevertheless, Saint Thomas explains,[2] from the point of view of what they are it is better for them to exist in their proper nature and in time, for then they are more truly what they are. Aristotle and Saint Thomas would agree with Bergson in reproaching mechanicism for suppressing time and movement, and therefore "nature" as a whole,[3] and in pointing out that our modern science, by the very fact that it takes a wholly mathematical view of the physical real, neglects time in its reality (which is of the physical, not mathematical order) only to substitute for it *entia rationis* (creations of the mind) based upon spatio-temporal measures. But for them this physical reality of time and movement implies an irreducible potentiality, by reason of which it has a lower (transcendental) degree of being than the causes in act upon which it depends.

Jankélévitch is right in relating the metaphysics of Duration to the negation of the *possible* included in the Bergsonian critique of the idea of nothingness,[4] and in noting here as does Thibaudet,[5] an echo of Spinoza, to whose intuitions "Bergson himself has perhaps not rendered full justice."[6] "What geometrical entities prepare us to understand," Jankélévitch continues, "is, in Léon Brunschvicg's words,[7] 'the universe of a science which refuses to allow itself to be led into the shadows of virtuality, which brings everything into light and into act' . . . Equations and figures, we might add, like life, offer us an infinite plenitude; nowhere does logic admit the slightest vacuum, the slightest rarefaction of existence, or those gradations in 'perfection' which make possible our dissolving doubts (aporias). Now, pseudo-philosophers need a vacuum of this kind to sanction the superstition of finality . . . The

---

1 *Creative Evolution*, p. 343.

2 *Sum. theol.*, I, 18, 4, ad 3.

3 Aristotle, *Phys.*, III, 1, 200 *b* 14–15.

4 The author makes a reference on this point to Bergson's Address at the Oxford meeting of 1920. (Cf. *Revue de Métaphysique et de Morale*, 1921, pp. 100–103.) He justly regrets the fact that these characteristic pages are so little known. It is also to be regretted that the two lectures given at Oxford on *The Perception of Change* (see *Creative Mind*, pp. 153–186), should be only too rarely quoted by Bergsonians themselves. These lectures and this address reveal a good many of the secrets of Bergsonian metaphysics.

5 Albert Thibaudet, *Le Bergsonisme*, t. I, p. 138.

6 V. Jankélévitch, article quoted, pp. 485–486.

7 *Le Progrès de la Conscience dans la philosophie occidentale*, 1927, t. II, p. 687.—Note that there is virtuality even in geometrical beings, for in them a logical distinction (a virtual distinction) subsists between nature and properties, so that the intelligibility of their nature is in itself (and not only for us) the reason for the intelligibility of the properties. Furthermore, far from having an *infinite* plenitude, each of these beings *is not* what the others are. If there is no finality in the geometrical world, it is because in it there is neither action nor efficient causality.

moment the shadow of the possible invades the universe, engendering the optical illusion of finality, disorder and indifference, we get the idea that perhaps things could have been other than they are,"[3] and this idea gives rise in us to the "fanatic's" wonderment as he looks upon the spectacle of the world.

Would Bergson approve without further reservation the anti-finalist fanaticism of Spinoza? What remains in any case is that, not seeing that if real possibility or potentiality is not simple logical non-impossibility, neither is it "a virtual or ideal pre-existence,"[4]—in short, confusing potentiality with some prevented or diminished act, he is of the opinion that the possible, if it preceded the actual, would in itself be something "representable in advance,"[5] an "image of tomorrow" contained in our actual present although we do not manage to grasp it:[6]—all of which is contrary to the true idea of potentiality. In order to save not only the absolute unforeseeableness of free acts and the relative unforeseeableness of contingent events in the course of nature, but also a so-called "radical unforeseeableness" of every moment in the universe, he will therefore affirm: "The illusion consists in believing that there is *less* in the possible than in the real and that therefore the possibility of things precedes their existence. [. . .] Leaving out of account closed systems subject to purely mathematical laws, isolable because duration has no effect upon them, and considering concrete reality as a whole or simply the world of life, all the more the world of consciousness, we find that there is *more* and not *less* in the possibility of each successive state than in its reality. For the possible implies the real and in addition an act of the mind which throws its image back into the past once it has happened."[1] A future work *will have been* possible, but at present it *is* not so. "As reality creates itself, unforeseeable and new, its image is reflected behind it into the indefinite past; thus it finds itself to have been possible since the beginning of time: but it is at this precise moment that it begins to have been always possible, and that is why I say that its possibility, which never precedes its reality, *will have preceded* it once the reality has appeared. The possible is therefore the mirage of the present in the past." It is an illusion "natural to the human mind and immanent to most philosophers" to believe "that the possible is anterior to its realization and obtains it by a reinforcement of itself, by the *acquisition* of existence, in short, by the addition of something. One might as well believe that man in the flesh results from the materialization of his image seen in a mirror. [. . .] Let us resign ourselves then to speaking of radical un-

---

[3] V. Jankélévitch, article quoted, p. 486.

[4] H. Bergson, in R. Lenoir, an account of the Oxford meeting, *Revue de Métaph. et de Mor.*, 1921, p. 102.

[5] *Ibid.*, p. 101.　　　　[6] *Ibid.*, p. 102.　　　　[1] *Ibid.*, p. 101.

foreseeableness and of realities which are not at all realizations of possibles."* It is impossible more absolutely to declare that all is in act at the same time that all is becoming.

Here the fundamental error, as we indicated above, bears upon the nature of the *possible,* which is regarded as a second rate *actual,* and which consequently, unless one denies becoming, can only be ideal and retrospectively expressed in the future perfect. In reality, in change, what happens at a certain moment did not exist at all in the preceding stage as an already-happened-not-yet-manifested. What will be is in no way already realized under any form whatever. However, what the subject becomes, not being a simple extrinsic denomination, must affect the subject in its being: but cannot affect it according to what it already is (I mean in act), because what it already is, it is,—it does not become it. The new qualification therefore affects the subject and is drawn from it according to a sort of ontological reserve or fecundity which is *absolutely irreducible to being in act,* and which, no doubt, actuality invests on all sides and sustains in being, but which in itself is absolutely non-actual, non-realized, pure determinability, in a word—potentiality. And if it is true that the possible is known after the event, once realization is accomplished, it is precisely because potentiality, being nothing of what one can enunciate, for all one can enunciate is in act, being purely *ad actum,* is knowable only through act. It is the very hall-mark of the created, of what can grow up, acquire or undergo, of what can change, of what depends upon something else, to be subject in its inmost self to this metaphysical cleavage which is abolished only in subsistant Being itself, which can become nothing because it is everything supereminently. In all that is not God, reality is the realization of a possible. For Bergson, on the contrary, things no doubt were not what they become, but before becoming it they were already all they could be. From the very fact that they are actual they pass on to another actuality—the fact that they are is sufficient to enable them to become something else. Here we are faced with a "new method of thinking" which consists in substituting fully and in everything the verb *to change* for the verb *to be.* An affirmation of *pure actuality* not of Parmenidean being, or of Spinozist substance, but of movement itself and of becoming—"there is," as has with good reason been said,[1] "only one transposition to make to get from the impassive universe of Spinoza to the qualified universe of Bergson."

That Bergson intended to direct the criticism of "dogmatic metaphysics" which we find in certain pages of *Creative Evolution* especially against "the ineffectual god of modern agnosticism"[2] I willingly concede to Jacques Chevalier. I also know that Bergson *does not want* to be a pantheist and that cer-

---

* *Ibid.,* pp. 102, 103.
[1] V. Jankélévitch, article quoted above, p. 487.
[2] *Les Lettres,* June 1920, p. 182.

tain profound inclinations which cause him to seek in all things qualities and discontinuities, freedom and creation, orient him in the exact opposite direction from classical pantheism. But from the outset and by virtue of its most intimate structure it is absolutely beyond the power of his metaphysics to establish a *real and essential* distinction between God and the world.* For it, everything is pure act, pure act in a state of perpetual increase, radical remelting and spurting of novelty; which tempers deification by radical contradiction: nothing other than the sphere of Parmenides, turned river and mobility.

Neither *does* Bergson *want* there to be between man and animal merely a difference of degree. He affirms between them a "sudden leap," a difference "of nature."[1] And no doubt the distance "from the closed to the open," from the "limited to the unlimited"[2] (the human brain giving the choice, unlike the animal brain, among an indefinite number of triggers) suffices to mark in the order of experimental sciences a "distinction of nature," but in that order the word "nature" has only an empiriological significance. And in the metaphysical order, the presence, admitted by the philosopher, of a veritable though inchoate intellect in animals, in the vertebrates in particular, and the production of man through the spontaneity of a vital impulse common to the whole universe of organisms, actually destroys this distinction of nature. And finally Bergson *does not want* to reduce freedom to simple spontaneity—

---

* "This problem [of God]," wrote Bergson in his letter to Höffding, "I have not really approached in my works; I believe it to be inseparable from moral problems, in the study of which I have been absorbed for some years past; and the few lines of *Creative Evolution* to which you allude were put there only as a note for future work." (Letter to Harald Höffding, in the appendix to Höffding's *La Philosophie de Bergson*, Fr. translation, p. 159.) In the last few pages of *Une nouvelle Philosophie*, on the occasion of which Bergson wrote to the author: ". . . Nowhere does that sympathy appear more clearly than in your last pages, where you indicate in a few words the possibility of subsequent developments of the doctrine. Were I to deal with the subject I should say exactly what you have said." (*Une Philosophie Nouvelle*, Paris, 1912, preface, 9 v.) Edouard Le Roy likewise sets out to show that on the subject of the religious and moral problem the Bergsonian doctrine is open to unforeseeable developments which, far from being deduced from results already acquired, will suppose intervention of new data, new points of view and new intuitions. That is quite true. But the question is not to foresee what will be, or would be, or might have been the contour of the moral and religious edifice set up by Bergson, it is to know what its foundations are worth. It is to know whether these new problems will force Bergson to break, not "with the *conclusions* of his earlier studies" (Le Roy, *op. cit.*, p. 205), but with the essential principle of his whole philosophy, that is, with his metaphysical conception of duration. If so, we shall have a *second philosophy* which will deny the first. If not, the pantheism of the doctrine *cannot be* really overcome because the logic of principles always prevails. One cannot refuse the critic the right to see in the note for future work put into *Creative Evolution* or *Introduction to Metaphysics* anticipated confirmations of the metaphysical impossibility. Neither can one oblige him to close his eyes to those applications of Bergsonian principles to the religious problem which have been attempted by certain disciples lacking the discretion of the master, and by Edouard Le Roy himself in the all-too-significant pages of *Comment se pose le problème de Dieu (Rev. de Mét. et de Mor.*, March and July 1907).

[1] *Creative Evolution*, pp. 182, 185. Cf. *L'Énergie spirituelle*, p. 21.

[2] *Creative Evolution*, p. 263.

he affirms the freedom of human will; and this simple affirmation of freedom has had for many a liberating virtue. But if one notices the profoundly irrational character of the freedom thus proclaimed, if one realizes that what we must see in it is only an eminent case of that gushing proper to life, which for the metaphysics of Duration constitutes the substance of concrete time, it is difficult not to subscribe to this judgment of one of the most recent interpreters of Bergsonism: "Necessity means plenitude, in Bergson as in Spinoza, and freedom is nothing but the central destiny of the self as prisoner of its own riches."[3] And Thibaudet in turn concludes: "We must agree (as I take it that Bergson does), to call human spontaneity freedom, because it concerns a greater intensity of being than animal spontaneity and covers a vaster field of consciousness."[4]

Does science at least stand to gain from this metaphysics which thinks itself called by science and which buries itself in time? Experimental science requires of the metaphysician not that he discover in the bosom of that flux to which it applies its methods of analysis a creative absolute which, to be attained, would require a complete reversal of scientific intelligence; what it does require is that it be freed itself from the obsession of mechanicist or rationalist metaphysics (and it is in this, but only in this, that it will have been able to receive from Bergsonism a definite historical service); and that it be linked (but here it has nothing more to hope for from Bergsonism) to a correctly established ontology and critique of knowledge, which will justify both its instinctive realism and its consciousness of the limitations and the precariousness of human knowledge. And finally, experimental science requires that the metaphysician set free (by placing it in a more highly and more firmly rational scientific light than its own) the substructure of philosophical ideas which sustain it implicitly in the mind of the scientist, without having the right of admission into science itself.

As to spirituality, toward which are oriented all the intentions of Bergsonian thought, it must be maintained, against the onslaught of a good many doubtful mysticisms, that it is not to be sought in time—neither in the instant, nor in the flux, nor in the concentration of time—but in the intemporal. If already the imperfect spirituality of art and poetry sometimes seizes in time itself snatches of the intemporal, and if the purely rational spirituality of logic and of metaphysics already dominates time, spirituality in the full force of the word (for in the eyes of *spiritualis homo* reason can still be called sense, to such an extent does it draw everything from sense), itself dominating the firmament of poetry and the firmament of abstraction, dominates time still more, and leads to a certain participation of subsisting eternity. There, in that true firmament of contemplation, which is naked like the cross and which

[3] V. Jankélévitch, art. quoted, p. 488.
[4] Albert Thibaudet, *op. cit.*, t. I, p. 244.

like it adheres to God, every concept and every distinct notion is surpassed, but only because love and its infused gifts have become, in a supernatural light which is "like a ray of darkness for our intellect,"[1] the very means of a knowledge which exceeds all sentiment. Many voices cry on all sides, spirit, spirit—as others cry: *templum Domini, templum Domini, templum Domini est.*[2] And it is the flesh that answers. The philosopher clasps his wisdom to his bosom, it is all contained therein. The Christian has his wisdom hidden in another, it does not belong to him;—he is dead and more living than anything which lives in this world, holding to a life which is the Life, to a spirit which is the Spirit, and which leads him where It wills. The best a philosopher can do is to humble philosophy before the wisdom of the saints.

May 1929.

P.S. [for the reprint of the French second edition in 1947]. *To humble philosophy before the wisdom of the saints is in the last analysis what Bergson himself has done in the* Two Sources. *Thus has been completed the admirable curve of the movement of his thought, and an incomparable philosophical adventure in which the purest impulse of spirituality, and a constant fidelity to the light, have made the philosopher transcend his own system of concepts.*

On the last developments of Bergsonian philosophy I have attempted to add a number of precisions in the first two chapters of De Bergson à Thomas d'Aquin.[3] *Of my first book, I have explained above that I regret its excessively severe and often unjust tone; but that I believe the doctrinal substance still to be sound. If it is to be taken as a witness of the historical moment for which it had significance, one must of course preserve its tartness. With the exception of a few slight corrections in style, this reprinting follows the text of the second edition. But I do not wish to allow it to leave the press without invoking here, with veneration, the memory of my first teacher, and without manifesting my gratitude for the tokens of friendship which, in spite of the criticisms I formulated against his ideas, he was kind enough to give me in the years before his death. There is no sweetness equal to that of such a friendship regained. Nor can I refrain from mentioning that to the anxious hope expressed in the last pages of this book, the great solitary and noble search pursued by Bergson throughout his life has responded in a way that marvellously fulfilled it.*

August 1947.

[1] An expression from the pseudo-Denys, quoted by Saint John of the Cross, *Vive Flamme*, st. III, line 3, sec. x, Ger., II, p. 455.

[2] Jeremias, VII, 4.

[3] These two chapters make up the Second Part of the present English volume.

FIRST PART

THE DOCUMENTS IN THE CASE

FIRST SECTION

GENERAL ASPECTS OF BERGSONISM

(And yet) there is only one truth.
(*Creative Evolution*, pg. 238.)

Chapter One

THE PHILOSOPHY OF INTUITION

The final alternative of modern thought

The usual starting-point of modern metaphysical systems, especially since Kant, is the *a priori* opposition of subject and object, of the knower and the known, which must first be presented to one another and whose relations must then be suitably regulated. The modern philosopher, being dominator and legislator by right of birth, places himself from the outset above things and above himself, then, casting his sovereign glance over the whole, undertakes to decide, as he chooses, whether the object will be resolved into the subject or the subject into the object, or whether both will result from a third term. He does not perceive that *if* it is perfectly permissible for those who, from the beginning, put their trust in knowledge, to ask it next how it proceeds and what its real object is, on the other hand it is self-contradictory to question, from the very outset, the relation of the faculty of knowing to reality and then to determine this relation by means of the very faculty one holds in doubt. The problem thus posited is absurd, not because knowledge is asked to know itself, but because this is asked of a knowledge from which, by hypothesis, one should accept nothing (since whether or not it speaks the truth is not known); and because, in addition, it has been rendered incapable of speaking the truth (since it has not yet been allowed to know anything and has been kept enchained). Thus the solution necessarily belongs to the realm of fantasy, not of science, whether the philosopher starts out in grandiose fashion in the absolute by "positing" what he will, or whether he undertakes to reconstruct in his own way the universe and the mind.

On the other hand, for whoever insists on being "modern," and believes that the era of freedom began with Descartes, the development of philosophy in the last three centuries ends in a truly tragic alternative. While metaphysics, obstinately intent on deducing evidence, vainly seeks its equilibrium, passes from system to system and finally proclaims its total helplessness, positive science alone—and by that we mean the physico-mathematical knowledge of matter—imposing itself upon the world by the extraordinary abundance of its actual results and by its utilitarian applications, appears to be possessed of the rules of truth. The only philosophy which seems to rest on tested principles is the philosophy which that physico-mathematical knowledge has in tow, and which is a mere automatic generalization of it. Moreover, this mechanistic philosophy lays open claim to sovereignty, declares itself ready to explain everything by certain infinitesimal beginnings taken from matter or from sense experience, and treats with the conqueror's scorn the timorous little vestiges of spiritualism which some distinguished minds try to set up against it, begging the favor of a few conclusions, after having capitulated on all the principles. That, then, is the last word of intelligence! If one aspires to the absolute and refuses to be satisfied with half-measures, there remains only the choice between two doctrines: either radical mechanism, the abandoning of all that makes thought worthy of being thought; or radical skepticism, which is intellectual despair and the abandoning of thought.

There might indeed be one last resource. If it were possible to demonstrate that alongside our ordinary knowledge, above intelligence, there exists another mode of knowledge, a faculty more intuitive and closer to the absolute—if it were possible to lay hands on that faculty and force it to reveal the secret of reality, could one not then break out of the absurd circle indicated above and the dilemma just mentioned; either by determining, thanks to that superior knowledge, the true relation of subject and object, and so passing sentence on intellect and certitude; or by agreeing that intelligence leads inevitably to mechanism, but maintaining that a higher faculty makes us "transcend" mechanism and introduces us into the absolute? At the same time philosophy could take pride in remaining truly modern, since it would have found a *new basis* for human thought—an indispensable minimum for any self-respecting doctrine. In any case, this way out is the very last. This is so true that all those among the moderns who have tried to save the truth of the spirit have had more or less recourse to this solution: it is already present in one form or another in Jacobi as well as in his great adversary Schelling. But it is assuredly Bergson who has most completely formulated it in giving it all the advantages of a method, no longer logical or ideal, but "experimental" and "positive,"—hence the name of *new positivism* by which he sometimes designates his doctrine,—and all the attraction of an innovation rich in hopes which promises to reconcile the eternal aspirations of thought with the demands of the physical sciences.

* * * * *

Duration[1]

Metaphysics, here again, begins with psychology. If the philosopher, once and for all renouncing any preconceived idea, any bias toward analytical ex-

[1] See *infra*, pages 172–178.

planation, tries, by a powerful effort of introspection, to grasp the intimate reality of his psychological life, he first sees the images that external objects outline upon the surface of his soul gradually fade away; he finds himself faced with thoughts, affections, memories that follow one another without interruption, and which seek only an opportunity—a question raised by external perception or by the intellect—to group themselves as it were around a fixed point and to take on an order with regard to one another by limiting one another distinctly. But if, instead of that, the philosopher energetically pursues his inner effort, he sees the contours of these various "states of consciousness" progressively fade away; if he fixes his glance on one of them, he isolates and immobilizes it; but let him concentrate his attention on his conscious life itself and all these states melt into one another, no one of them at any time remains the same. It is an indistinct and moving surge, a flux, a stream of more or less frequent vibrations all of which respond to and penetrate one another, an elusive but none the less real flow, a continuity of becoming. At this moment the philosopher feels that he is touching the very bottom of reality; nothing further separates him from himself; he knows himself in the incommunicable depths of his personality; the *intimate sense*, suitably forced or dilated, thus has what traditional philosophy calls the *essence* of the soul perceived in itself and by itself. No idea can express this, nor any reasoning lead to it. One can at most attempt to suggest it by images, symbols less misleading than ideas, or by fluid, moving concepts quite different from those we ordinarily use, and which make us know the soul as "a certain restlessness of life," and life as a "tendency to act on inert matter."[1]

This reality which the philosopher, by an exceptional tension of his will and his consciousness, succeeds in knowing on the fringes of the unconscious, with a knowledge impossible to fix indeed, a fading knowledge, Bergson calls *duration* or concrete time. I perceive myself enduring, I am, I am duration, that is the beginning of philosophy.—I think, therefore I am; therefore I am thought, Descartes had reasoned. It is not a question here of reasoning, the three terms are given simultaneously by a unique experience of inner sense, an experience *sui generis* that each one can renew according to his dispositions, but which in itself will always remain individual and incommunicable. The physical and natural sciences can no longer pride themselves on being the only experimental ones. Metaphysics is much more experimental than they.

Duration, which constitutes the very stuff of our self, is also the substance of all things. Everything around us changes, all is movement, and movement, if we try to know it in itself, by transporting ourselves through an effort of

---

[1] *Creative Evolution* (trans. by Arthur Mitchell, Henry Holt & Co., 1911), p. 98; *Introduction a la Métaphysique* (*Revue de Mét. et de Mor.*, January 1903, pp. 9–15, 27, 31).

intellectual sympathy to the interior of the mobile, reveals a nature similar to our duration. At first glance beings of nature present themselves to our eyes as distinct and in some respects immobile objects, but immediately science, pulverizing our qualitative perceptions into a multitude of vibrations of all sorts, and reducing the whole of reality to mutations of energy, warns us that the material world resolves itself into a universal interaction where we still find,—if we try to perceive things in their intrinsic activity by attuning our life so to speak to theirs and by fusing our mind with them—a duration like the duration we perceived in ourselves, more qualitative than science says, but diluted this time, relaxed, resembling almost a pure repetition. Thus time, the flow of becoming, change, is reality itself.

The intellectual operation by which we grasp ourselves in becoming, and through which we make contact with the essence of things by transporting ourselves within them, Bergson calls *intuition*. Intuition does not reason, does not discourse, does not compose nor does it divide. Because it is consciousness itself folding back upon duration, and because duration is the living basis wherein all things communicate, it makes us actually coincide with the object known, or rather felt, or even better, lived; it assimilates us to its most intimate reality in a transcendant and inexpressible experience: "This intuition attains the absolute."[1]

Concept and practice[2]

But we were not born to speculate in the absolute, we were made to act. *Prius vivere.* A purely theoretical knowledge which would make us fuse with nature would be of no use to us, and because it would adapt our duration to the very rhythm of the duration of things, it would dissolve all our activity and make us, properly speaking, *waste our time,* or dissipate our substance. Hence the necessity for a knowledge relative to ourselves, that is to say, to our practice.

This practical or symbolic knowledge begins with external perception. Our perception would extend *de jure* to matter as a whole, whose becoming we should thus live. It is limited in fact to certain aspects of things, offering us the outline of our possible action on them, and toward that end *isolating* first what interests our action (so that the first function of perception is not to cause us to know certain things—since by right all is known,—but to cause us to ignore all the rest, so that all the rest may remain unconscious), *immobilizing* next, by concentrating in one single representation millions of intuitive virtual representations, the things thus cut out of the universal flux.

If perception, by a certain power of condensing becoming and distinguishing (or rather inventing) resemblances which are not given in the real but

1 *Introduction à la Métaphysique* (*Rev. de Mét. et de Mor.,* January 1903), p. 20.
2 See *infra*, Second Section, Chapter VII.

which express only an identical possibility of action of the subject on the object, constructs, so to speak, the individualities of the external world, so concept,—which after all is only a name heralding a whole condensation of memories, something like the banner of a battalion about to attack,—constructs, by a perfectly similar process, the generalities upon which our intellect works. Its essential characteristic is fixity. Because of that it is always at our disposal, we can manipulate it as we wish: social and communicable by nature, it lends itself marvellously to language, which in return confers upon it an extraordinary variety of combination and adaptation. It is the instrument *par excellence* of the action of humanity upon matter, the inexhaustible currency which for us replaces reality. The universal is nothing in things, it is only an external sign, the sign of an identical practical attitude taken by the subject with regard to the object.

Now it happens that being made to act, we do not merely act, we claim to know in a disinterested fashion. A strange ambition, which probably comes from the fact that, having succeeded too well in our effort to impose our contingency on matter, we have at our disposal unforeseen leisure, a sum of available energy which we use then in reflection; a deceptive ambition, though not altogether illusory, which gives us nobility but which makes of us, as it were, strangers wretchedly alone in a world where everything is made for brute force and for action.

Our first movement, when we wish to philosophize, is to apply to speculation the processes of knowledge that are natural to us, that is to say, which were created by our practice and for it. The knowledge which results from this will necessarily be artificial, convenient perhaps, but of a certainty inexact: that, for Bergson, is *analysis*. Faced with a new object presented to our minds, this knowledge does not seek to transport itself into it in order to unite itself with its uncommunicable reality, for this would oblige us to make for each thing a knowledge *to order,* and what is more, fading, as we said above. No; like external perception, which is a first analysis, it proceeds by putting questions, so to speak, to the object; is it this? or that? or again that? all these 'thises' and 'thats' being merely so much *already known.* Thus it tries on that object all sorts of ready-made clothing, and by dint of trying, will finally end by dressing it up in bits and pieces; or else, according to another of Bergson's comparisons, it takes a multitude of external views of it, and by moving all around it, will manage to rebuild an image of the object from all these views taken from without, an image that is probably convenient in practice, but one in which the simple reality that accounts for the unity and peculiarity of the object will be precisely absent. The image thus obtained will in fact be composed of distinct elements, dissociable at will, since it is with them that it will have been fabricated; but these elements will be parts of the symbol, and not parts of the real which, properly, has no parts.

Furthermore analysis, being in conformity with action which always proceeds by *yes* and *no*, will no doubt define the object by *yeas* and by *nays*, yet the reality which, Bergson avers, is never either yes or no, will always escape it. This, then, is how we represent to ourselves, instead of movement itself which is simple and indecomposable, the multitude of points, that is to say, the multitude of positions, or virtual immobilities, through which it has passed, thus substituting for movement (action in the making) the line traversed, (the thing *already-made*). This again is why we always conceive time in the form of space, and why we can more or less easily force all things to fit into our framework, but only on condition that we empty all things of their proper reality.

Hence the apparent triumph of mechanicism, and hence also all the difficulties of philosophy, the inevitable antinomies, the insoluble problems.

Intuition as philosophical method[1]

Of another kind would be our knowledge could it proceed by intuition, not by analysis. In that case the problems which have so long tormented human thought would solve themselves or rather vanish, for we should perceive that there was no occasion to raise them. And modern philosophy could send both the materialists and the spiritualists packing, the former because they take their poor artificial constructions for reality, the latter because, accepting the principles of the former, they try to make intuitive truths conform to them, truths that are stripped by analysis not only of their life but of their true significance, and which are, because they originate in intuition, nevertheless incompatible with the systems into which they are supposed to fit.

Bergson thus gives us a key with which we can easily open all those cages in which philosophy holds truth captive. . . . And yet because the operation is so easy it is astonishing that so scrupulous a philosopher as Bergson, and one who knows better than anyone else that the *finest things are difficult*, did not suspect that such great facility was probably the sign of a great illusion. Be that as it may, by applying the process of discrimination described above to the various classical problems Bergson was able to formulate, both in his early works[2] and his courses at the Collège de France, not only a remarkably efficacious criticism of pseudo-scientific theories and claims but also a great

---

[1] See below, on intuition, pages 147–171, on human personality, on the soul and the body, on memory, on external perception: Second Section, chap. X; on liberty: Second Section, chap. XI.

[2] Cf. especially the *Essai sur les Données immédiates de la Conscience* (1889) (*Time and Free Will*); *Matière et Mémoire* (1897) *Matter and Memory*; *Introduction à la Métaphysique* (Revue de Métaphysique et de Morale, January 1903, pp. 1–36) *Introduction to Metaphysics* in *Creative Mind*; *Le paralogisme psycho-physiologique* (Report read at the Congress of philosophy at Geneva in 1904 and published in the Revue de Métaphysique et de Morale, November 1904. [Reproduced in *l'Énergie spirituelle*, Paris, 1919, under the title: *Le cerveau et la pensée, une illusion philosophique.*])

many new solutions which, although inacceptable in the last analysis, do nevertheless attract minds by their powerful spiritualist *intention* and by the observations, ingenious or profound, with which they are studded.—The problem of personality is solved because the self is a living and continually changing duration, whereas neither the states of consciousness with which some undertake to compose it as though with so many atoms, nor the amorphous, "empty" and "rigid" substance which others imagine in order to weld these states, can be anything but symbol and fiction; in that way associationism is refuted, and spiritualism in its common forms is transcended. The relations of the soul and the body are explained, soul and body making up but one single whole because they are one same continuity of duration; soul and body being distinct because that living duration with its innumerable virtualities which is our soul makes use of corporal mechanisms which it has itself set up as it would of an instrument to assure its independence in the universe. Thus psycho-physiological parallelism is refuted, and this visible body no longer appears to be anything more than a small part of ourselves, indispensable but made for use, the sharp point by which we insert our action into becoming. Solved is the problem of memory, because our past is preserved integrally, being our very substance, and because there is thus no need to search in the brain for some chest in which to store our memories. Solved also the problem of freedom, because the various motives, whose disagreement we imagine, have only an artificial existence, as the symbolism of space, introduced everywhere, alone permits us to isolate and number the states of consciousness, which in reality are one single and ever-new flux. Consequently, action once accomplished is easily explained by its motives, but the motives themselves are only what we make them, and so the contingency of our actions remains radical. Solved is the problem of external perception, (posited by modern psychologists in so absurd a manner), for if it is true that we plunge into a becoming which by itself is consciousness in the diffused state, and that perception comes into being, as we have said before, through a sort of choice operated by our action, it is no longer necessary to explain how purely quantitative changes transmitted to a purely material organ and from there to the brain, are suddenly transformed by the touch of a magic wand into sensible representations. In short the basis of the mechanistic doctrine,—the idea that a universal mathematics could embrace all that makes up the world and that things are bound together in such a way that "an intelligence which, for a given instant, knew all the forces with which nature is animated and the respective situation of the beings composing it, if it were vast enough to submit these data to Analysis, would embrace in a single formula the movements of the largest bodies in the universe and those of the slightest atom: for it, nothing would be uncertain and the future like the past would lie before its eyes,"[1]—such an idea is reduced to nothingness by the affirmation of time as absolute reality, as living becoming, the indefatigable inventor of the new.

Considering what we have thus far set forth of Bergson's doctrines, one might give them a certain meaning which (I regret to be obliged to put it in these terms) would be misrepresentative. The terms used by a philosopher—by a modern philosopher—can in fact be taken in two different ways; either by their content, their particular significance, or by the use the philosopher makes of them, that is by the *tendency,* not systematic but, as it were, moral, of the thoughts into which these terms enter as elements. If therefore the reader is more spontaneous than reflective, and if the content of the terms be ever so vague and fleeting, it is to the second means of interpretation that he will instinctively have recourse. Consequently, by *duration,* what will he understand if not *essence?* By *intuition* what, if not *perception of essence?* By: *everything is in the process of being made,* what will he understand if not: *becoming is real,* that is to say: *all is not given in act?* By *analysis artificially constructs what it believes it knows,* what will he understand if not: *the knowledge of being and causes extends infinitely beyond mathematical analysis?* Thus, by a strange effect of the intellect's instinct for self-preservation, the reader will involuntarily transpose Bergsonian theses into the rudiments of scholastic theses, and so will plant in his soul the first desires for the great Thomist light. Coming out of the exhausting darkness of materialistic relativism, the simple affirmation that the absolute is knowable is a first liberation of the mind, and the appetite for truth which without the slightest doubt animates Bergson's teaching, will seem of itself to bear toward the regions of light.

This state of mind, however, as is obvious enough, is quite provisory and illogical, since it consists in thinking something other than what is said. And if such were the only meaning of Bergsonian theses, they should first be formulated in different language, then corrected on a number of essential points, and finally articulated to traditional philosophy. No; to the extent that these theses claim to be original they must lead to another system, they must produce new fruit. And although it is not impossible to judge them in themselves, we shall know them more easily by this fruit. For Bergson the real signifies time, intuition is the coincidence, lived and felt, of the subject and the object; geometrical analysis, the universal process of the intellect. If therefore the very stuff of things is change and movement, if the very essence of intelligence is symbol and artifice, it will indeed be necessary the moment one wishes to systematize,—that is, to know in a coherent and complete way,—to explain the world and life through the impulse of an absolutely universal evolution, and to present intelligence as an accidental product of that evolu-

[1] Laplace, *Introduction à la théorie analytique des probabilités;* quoted by Bergson, *Creative Evolution* (tr. Mitchell), p. 38.

tion. Any philosophy is obliged to systematize, just as anything must tend toward its end; and the philosophies of intuition attempt to escape that law only in order to systematize the more boldly. So those disciples of Bergson's who welcomed *Creative Evolution* with some astonishment, if not disappointment, have only their own inconsistency to blame.

Chapter Two

BERGSONIAN EVOLUTIONISM

A double genesis

Human intelligence, if evolutionist explanations extend to its very essence, can be but a product of evolution, that is to say, a particular instrument fabricated by evolution for particular needs in particular conditions and for certain particularly evolved beings; and consequently, not only the manner of our knowing but the very act and object of our knowledge can relate only to a part of the evolved, and evolutive becoming in its entirety infinitely exceeds them. But how are we to place ourselves before the beginning of the intellect? Only Bergson's philosophy, which has at its disposal an intuition anterior and superior to the intellect and a duration which can give being to any reality, can make us see the genesis of the material universe and the genesis of the intellect, and present us with origins really different from the present state.

To engender matter and engender mind is the duty of Bergson's philosophy. In order to do this, "one must take things by storm; one must thrust intelligence outside (itself) (i.e. in the fluidity of intuition) by an act of will"[1] so that "reabsorbed into its principle," it may thus "go back through its genesis in reverse."[2] The undertaking is "more modest" than one might at first think. It cannot in fact "be achieved in one stroke; it is necessarily collective and progressive. It consists in an interchange of impressions which, correcting and adding to each other, will end by expanding the humanity in us and making it transcend itself."[3] In short, *the moment has come to attempt a genesis of intellect at the same time as a genesis of material bodies.*[4] It is all very well to be witty at the expense of the ontology of the ancients, with its ambition to know essences! We the moderns, on Bergson's advice, shall throw

[1] *Creative Evolution*, p. 193.
[2] *Ibid.*, p. 191.
[3] *Ibid.*, p. 192. (Translator's note: Mitchell's translation does not follow the original text at this point.)
[4] *Ibid.*, p. 186. The italics are mine.

74

ourselves into the water without knowing how to swim,* into the primitive waters where the world came into being.

And like a good swimmer who delights in the waves,

we shall transcendentally enjoy living our own genesis and the genesis of all things. To whom then, in very truth, shall we not compare ourselves? *Quando praeparabat coelos, aderam ...*

The Genesis of Bodies

For Bergson, the *theory of knowledge* and the *theory of life* are inseparable, they illuminate one another and should both result from an identical investigation of the nature of evolution. We shall, however, for the clarity of the exposition, try to summarize separately what Bergson teaches us of the genesis of bodies and what he reveals of the genesis of intellect.

In Bergsonian perspectives the problem of creation, like most problems, is one which should never have been raised and which might better be left to fade away. Since the substance of things is a really active duration, and since this duration whose nature we test within ourselves signifies continuity of change, the uninterrupted production of new actions, of original situations, of unforeseeable inventions, in short, perpetual growth and incessant creation, —it is no longer necessary to ask oneself whether the universe was created in one stroke or whether it exists in its own right. It is creating itself, that's all. To say that a *thing* creates itself would be contradictory, the thing being only a solidification of becoming brought about by the understanding; there are no created *things* and no creating *being*. "But that action"—pure, extra-spatial action—"increases as it goes on, that it creates in the measure of its progress, is what each one of us observes when he watches himself act."[1] Thus "the idea or creation becomes clearer, *for it is merged in that of growth*,"[2] but of an always new growth, radically unforeseeable. "Creation thus conceived is not a mystery; we experience it within ourselves when we act freely."[3] And in that sense, "the creation of a world is a free act."[4]

Let us fuse into one nature what we perceive of ourselves when we get farthest away from intellectuality: that is, consciousness not turned inward upon itself but tensed in action (i.e. supra-consciousness), an instinctive and spontaneous will, an impulse which will affirm itself in contingent acts. We can thus form an idea of the principle of evolution, which is "a continuity of shooting out. God, thus defined, has nothing of the 'ready-made'; He is un-

* *Ibid.*, p. 193.
[1] *Ibid.*, p. 249.
[2] *Ibid.*, pp. 240–241. The italics are mine.
[3] *Ibid.*, p. 248.
[4] *Ibid.*, p. 247.

ceasing Life, Action, Freedom."[5] He is the centre from whence worlds shoot out "like showers of sparks from a rocket."

In each of these worlds there are two things to consider: matter and life. The movement of an arm being raised and then falling again, a gesture making itself and then unmaking itself, that is creation,—and the creator and the created. The gesture unmaking itself, the downward movement, the fatigue of a creation which renounces itself and subsides,—that is matter. But in the very midst of this fall, something of the original impulse subsists, something continues the gesture making itself, the upward movement, the creative activity: that is life, a unique impulse which, passing through generations, seeks, so to speak, to retard the fall of matter, utilizing the energy of matter in order continually to create the new and to release contingency. The problem of matter does not arise, for matter as such has no reality of its own; it is only a *minus,* a lack. In fact it is only the inversion, or what amounts to the same thing, the interruption of creative movement; as Carnot's principle points out, it is proceeding toward the homogeneous and the pure repetition of elementary shocks, that is to say, toward the minimum of activity or of reality. Posit therefore the creative movement, then interrupt it, you automatically have matter; posit the tremendous tension of the creative impulse, then interrupt it, relax it, you find you automatically have extension, and thus you engender space, which is nothing but the ideal limit of the falling movement of matter. But, at the same time, you get the indefinite complication of the elements distinguishable in this relaxing reality, and thus you engender the geometric order, which is only the relaxing of the vital and creative order. All this represents nothing positive; all we have is a "deficiency of will."[1]

While matter tends, without ever attaining it, toward perfect spatiality which would consist in a "perfect externality of the parts in relation to one another"[2] and toward de-individualization, in such a way that the sole material object that can be isolated is the solar system as a whole, a movement in an opposite direction crosses it and runs counter to it. Here we have truly positive reality, the continuation of the creative impulse, the *vital impulse.* Life is first of all a "tendency to act on inert matter" and to obtain from it the means of affirming by action the liberty of the creative will. "The impetus of life . . . consists in short in a need of creation. It cannot create absolutely, because it is confronted with matter, that is to say with the movement that is the inverse of its own. But it seizes upon this matter, which is necessity itself, and strives to introduce into it the largest possible amount of indetermination and liberty."[3]

[5] *Ibid.,* p. 248. That God is Love, Bergson was to affirm in *Les Deux Sources* (Note from the 3rd ed.).

[1] *Ibid.,* p. 209.   [2] *Ibid.,* p. 203.   [3] *Ibid.,* p. 251.

Let all forms of life, all tendencies, all psychic modalities that the universality of living beings presents to us be dissolved in one original impulse and we shall have some idea of the "immensity of potentiality"* and the prodigious concentration of the vital impulse in the origin of its effort. Starting from nothing, so to speak, forced, in the small masses of scarcely-differentiated protoplasm which were first formed and which doubtless resembled—with the "tremendous internal push"[1] of the vital impulse in addition—the amoeba of today, forced to "shuffle humbly along" with the physico-chemical forces, life developed gradually,—by dissociation of the complementary tendencies it contained from the beginning and thanks to an extraordinary multitude of wholly contingent inventions, and after thousands of various attempts, of successes, of setbacks, of checks and of progress,—two great divergent series; the vegetable series, occupied especially in accumulating solar energy; and the animal series, occupied especially with expending that energy in movements; both these series being themselves divided into a number of divergent series which in turn branch off indefinitely. Bergson describes at length this "creation that goes on forever in virtue of an initial movement"[2] and goes beyond both Darwinism and Lamarckism, as well as any theory which would seek to make evolution the realization of a preconceived plan. He also shows us that as life is a psychological reality, and that as the psychic, which by nature transcends unity and multiplicity, is both multiple unity and one multiplicity, the vital impulse, called upon by the matter to which it communicates, to choose either unity or multiplicity, "leaps from one to the other indefinitely,"[3] and thus tends of itself on the one hand toward association, on the other to individuality, which although nowhere fully realized is essentially sought after by life. So each living organism forms a naturally closed system and must be compared not to a definite material object (artificially cut out of the whole), but rather "to the totality of the material universe."[4] Life, contrary to matter which tends toward necessity and spatiality, advances toward intensive unity and freedom. But why is this so, unless because life seeks first of all to introduce contingency into the world and because these closed systems are, above all, centres of contingent action?

Life and *Consciousness* have almost the same meaning for Bergson; they are, by essence, an exigency of creation; consciousness is "synonymous with invention and freedom."[5] Consciousness therefore is everywhere proportionate to the power of choice at the disposal of the living being, and to say that the vital impulse tends to "*liberate consciousness*" is to say that it tends to assure the living being an unlimited power of choice. It is a question of "creating, with matter, which is necessity itself, an instrument of freedom, of making a

---

* *Ibid.*, p. 258.
[1] *Ibid.*, p. 99.
[2] *Ibid.*, p. 105.
[3] *Ibid.*, p. 261.
[4] *Ibid.*, p. 15.
[5] *Ibid.*, p. 264.

machine which should triumph over mechanism, and of using the determinism of nature to pass through the meshes of the net which this very determinism had spread."[2] Now the vegetable world and the animal world everywhere show us the lamentable failure of this enterprise,[3] consciousness everywhere "remaining captive to the mechanism it had set up," and even among the superior animals, adding only with great difficulty some "free" activity to the routine of the habits of the species. "In man, and in man alone, does consciousness set itself free."[4] The brain of man is a machine which, instead of engaging the attention of its driver, allows him to let his attention wander and to think of something else.[5] It can set up an indefinite number of mechanisms from which consciousness may choose. And because man's power of choice is thus unlimited, whereas that of animals is, on the contrary, limited, there is, says Bergson, a difference in nature between man and animals. In man life has achieved "a unique and exceptional success." This success could very well have not taken place; even supposing this success, man might have been entirely different from what he is both as to body and mind, since he is only a product of evolution and since, as such, he bears inscribed in his nature the immense multitude of accidental variations invented along the way by evolution. Nevertheless, once man has been produced, one may say that he answers the essential search of life and that he is, if we dare to use such a word, even with all its necessary restrictions, the very goal of evolution.

The genesis of intelligence

The effort of consciousness to free itself therefore succeeded in that privileged vertebrate called man, at least as far as consciousness signifies *free action*. But the word 'consciousness' has another meaning,—true, a secondary one for Bergson,—the meaning *knowledge*. Did life also succeed from this point of view? No; it must have left the essential by the wayside to the extent that if metaphysics could not, by an effort contrary to nature, go back and pick up these abandoned virtualities, we should have absolutely to give up knowing anything but geometry and physics, give up all superior truth.[1] And thus we are brought to the second genesis made by the new philosophy, to the genesis of intelligence.

This genesis can be told in a few lines: the essential function of intelligence for Bergson is to bind like to like, and to know facts which repeat themselves. Now, the more we detach ourselves from the external, the more we bring our self to coincide with itself, the more we feel a living duration in which noth-

[2] *Ibid.,* p. 264.
[3] *Ibid.,* p. 129. ". . . failure seems the rule, success exceptional and always imperfect."
[4] *Ibid.,* pp. 264, 265.
[5] *Ibid.,* p. 184.
[1] *Ibid.,* p. xii.

ing is repeated, "where the past, always in progress, is endlessly enlarged with an absolutely new present"; and at the same time, the more we absorb intellectuality in going beyond it. Our consciousness, at this moment, is our very life. What then constitutes our intelligence, if not a *minus,* a lack, a distension of that life concentrated in effort? As matter results simply from a deficiency of the creative impulse, so intelligence results from a deficiency of this same impulse: *"It is the same inversion of the same movement which creates at once the intellectuality of mind and the materiality of things."**

At the same time, therefore, that the vital impulse was creating by its ramifications the thousands of living species, in one of which it succeeded in liberating life, the psychic factor immanent to that impulse, fascinated by the necessity of acting upon matter, was relaxing into intelligence; but if intelligence is its distension, where did it remain concentrated? Bergson answers: in the *spirit.* "The spirit overflows the intellect," the intellect is a "special function of the spirit, essentially turned toward inert matter."[1] Let us make no mistake: spirit here can signify only that sort of Schopenhauerian and supraconscious will which presumably makes up our personality. Bergson may call it anything he likes because any name will suit, but against it the name of *spirit,* in its true sense, absolutely rebels.

How then did evolution produce human intelligence, and what are the characteristics of intelligence from this point of view? In proportion to its growth life has spread out, as we have already said, in divergent series, and has reached the point where it has split its original virtualities into three great complementary tendencies (and not hierarchized tendencies, as Aristotle maintained): torpor (or vegetative life), instinct (or sensible life), intelligence (or reasoning life). The first made the plants, the second the insects, the third the vertebrates (for, to Bergson, it is not to man, but to the totality of vertebrates that intelligence is given), but by the very fact that they are complementary, each of these tendencies necessarily carries with it something of the two others, as a reminder of the primordial and essential unity of life. On the other hand animals are characterized by mobility; they are consequently under obligation to act upon inert matter. Now life has invented two methods of acting upon inert matter. In order to act, we must have instruments. The first method therefore consists in "using and even [in] constructing organized instruments"[2] (the very parts of the animal are the tools it employs); it is instinct, whose most complete development is presented to us by the hymenoptera; in instinct everything happens as though the animal had innate knowledge both of the organized instrument it uses and of the object on which its action has to bear, that is, of certain determinate *things.* This knowledge, by

* *Ibid.,* p. 206.
[1] *Ibid.,* p. 206.
[2] *Ibid.,* p. 142.

that very fact, is limited, but within its limits it is perfect; almost unconscious, because in it representation is constantly inhibited by action; it is a sympathy, a simple intuition, "(*lived* rather than *represented*), which is probably like what we call divining sympathy,"[1] and which as a result it is impossible to translate in terms of intelligence. And because it bears essentially on life (the instrument employed being an organ of the animal and the object of action another animal, like the cricket for the sphex, etc.), this sympathy "if it could extend its object and also reflect upon itself, would give us the key to vital operations."[2]

The second method on the contrary consists in "making and using unorganized instruments,"[3] tools properly so-called, with which one will act upon inert matter. That, in very truth, is intellect. Intellect is "the faculty of manufacturing artificial objects, especially tools to make tools, and of indefinitely varying [their] manufacture."[4] All its characteristics derive from this definition. Having to manufacture tools that are indefinitely varied in order to be able to act upon anything whatsoever, if, like instinct, it has a certain innate knowledge, this knowledge will not bear upon determinate things, but upon *relations,* (relation of attribute to subject, of cause to effect, etc.), on empty *forms,* where it will be able to introduce anything it likes; and because it aims at manufacturing tools with inert matter, the intellect "has for its chief object the unorganized solid,"[5] "of the discontinuous alone does (the intellect) form a clear idea,"[6] "of immobility alone";[7] it is "characterized by the unlimited power of decomposing according to any law and of recomposing according to any system,"[8] and finally by a "natural inability to comprehend life."[9] Such are the principles of intelligence, thus it has been created little by little throughout the whole of animality, and has suddenly affirmed itself with an extreme power when the impulse of consciousness jumped abruptly from animal to man. Being the faculty of *analysis,* as we have already described it according to Bergson, it is in this way that, fashioned by action on matter and attracted by it, "fascinated by the contemplation of inert matter,"[10] it has followed, as we said above, the road of materiality. Why therefore is it surprising

---

[1] *Ibid.,* p. 175.

[2] *Ibid.* It seems useless to point out: 1) that instinct supposes, in fact, an innate knowledge (furnished by the "estimative,") a knowledge strictly limited to the accidental, to the *hic et nunc* and incapable of penetrating to the essence, incapable by nature of giving us the key to any reality; 2) that it is false that instinctive knowledge should bear essentially on other living things, (instincts of nidification, of migration, etc.).

[3] *Creative Evolution,* p. 138.

[4] *Ibid.,* p. 139.

[5] *Ibid.,* p. 153.

[6] *Ibid.,* p. 154.

[7] *Ibid.,* p. 155.

[8] *Ibid.,* p. 157.

[9] *Ibid.,* p. 165.

[10] *Ibid.,* p. 161.

that being absolutely formed according to matter it finds itself fully prepared to know it? It follows up and completes in an ideal space the very movement of matter toward extension. "Geometry and logic are strictly applicable to matter," but outside this domain reality follows other laws.

We are thus reduced to the melancholy conclusion that: "There are things that intelligence alone is able to seek but which, by itself, it will never find. These things instinct alone could find, but it will never seek them."[2]

Fortunately, nature has not made pure understandings. Evolution has been able to cut intelligence out from the fluidity of life only on condition that it allows it to bathe in a nebulosity of intuition, of "instinct which has become disinterested and self-conscious." Man is not made for knowing, he is made for acting, his real name is *homo faber,* not *homo sapiens,*[3] and in him "intuition is (in fact) almost completely sacrificed to intellect."[4] Yet intuition is there, and when the desire to know surges up in him man will be able, through a painful effort in which "turning back on itself and twisting upon itself, the faculty of *seeing* is made one with the act of *willing,*"[5] to dilate and link up his vanishing intuitions, to enter into intimate contact with reality, and led by the new philosophy, to fuse once more with the ocean of life in which he is immersed.

Metaphysics and mathematical science

Having now reached the end of our investigation, it seems that we have successfully surmounted the two great difficulties that modern philosophy comes up against, and which we stated at the beginning of this study. On the one hand in fact we have, by a double genesis of matter and intelligence, determined the connection between subject and object and shown how they adapt themselves to one another; and this without a vicious circle, since it is both by means of a knowledge different from intelligence, truly co-extensive to the real, by means of intuition, and by assuming at the beginning of things a reality different from the reality actually given, that we arrived at this result.

On the other hand we have by that very fact the means of judging, amicably and to the satisfaction of both parties, the old quarrel between "scientific" mechanicism and metaphysics. Let us emphasize this point. As there are two movements of reality, the creative impulse and matter, as there are two modes of knowledge, instinct or intuition and intelligence, so there are two orders in the world and the mind, the vital order and the geometric order. The first is identical with the indivision of creative duration, the second is simply the relaxation and distension of the first. Matter and intellect, both resulting from

2 *Ibid.,* p. 151.
3 *Ibid.,* p. 139.
4 *Ibid.,* p. 267.
5 *Ibid.,* p. 237.

one and the same inversion of the vital movement, tend equally toward the geometric order. It follows that intellect insofar as it knows matter, it follows that physics, considering its general form and not the detail of its realization, actually touch the absolute. No definite system of mathematical laws is at the base of nature, but *mathematics in general,* which is nothing *positive,* which represents simply the direction in which matter falls, is essential to matter and gives it what it needs to fit into our framework. Matter is ballasted with geometry; "like one of those little cork dolls with feet of lead,"[*] it will always fall back, no matter how we take it, into one of our mathematical frames. It follows that "none [of the particular laws of the physical world], taken separately has any objective reality,"[1] that our science in its particular and determined form is contingent, relative to the variables it has arbitrarily chosen; and that, nevertheless, insofar as it bespeaks in general a relation to the mathematical order, our science attains the absolute.[2]

According to Bergson, the part of contingency that modern science includes comes in the last analysis from the fact that, having, contrary to ancient physics, related to time as an independent variable the different changes it is studying, nevertheless because of the very nature of the understanding, it can retain of time only its spatial substitute, the line traversed. Thus it is forced to neglect invention, the very reality of time, and that is why it remains approximative; yet, as this reality of time, this continuous invention tends in matter to a minimum, it follows that in physics our science keeps close to reality. But as soon as it studies life, as soon as it becomes interested in biology, in psychology, or in metaphysics it is condemned, if it keeps to the same method, to a pseudo-knowledge radically inadequate. Here we must change our method and have recourse to intuition. It alone here attains the absolute. We shall then superimpose on science a true knowledge of life and duration; we shall settle ourselves at the heart of becoming, we shall see that "substance" is change, is flowing concrete time, and we shall replace on their true foundation, upon intuition, the great theses of metaphysics. Need we add that this work will presuppose a subordination but not an ousting of dialectics. Dialectics,—"which is only a relaxation of intuition,"[3]—is necessary in order to put intuition to the test, to refract it in concepts and to communicate it. So the philosopher, possessing but for an instant a vanishing intuition, will grasp

---

[*] *Ibid.,* p. 219.

[1] *Ibid.,* p. 218.

[2] *Ibid.,* p. 208.—It is even solely because the mathematical order has no positive reality that mathematical physics can succeed: "If the mathematical order were a positive thing, if there were, immanent in matter, laws comparable to those of our codes, the success of our science would have in it something of the miraculous. What chances should we have indeed of finding the standard of nature and of isolating exactly, in order to determine their reciprocal relations, the very variables which nature has presumably chosen?" (*Ibid.,* p. 219.)

[3] *Ibid.,* p. 238.

in it an impulse which he will then develop by dialectics, only to make contact later, by means of a new intuition, with the real, correcting the results of his preceding dialectic and beginning a new one and so on. He will therefore manage to make these two efforts in opposite directions collaborate, a dialectic without intuition being only an empty mechanism, an intuition untried by dialectics being, as Bergson himself has said, only an empty dream.

Chapter Three

BEING IN ITSELF AND CONTINGENT BEING
THE IDEA OF NOTHINGNESS

It seems that every reader of *Creative Evolution* must infallibly propound the question: if the impulse of becoming explains everything, has it no cause itself? Does creative evolution tell us why the world in which it is deployed exists, and what is the reason for the evident order which reigns in this world, especially the reason for the internal harmony without which living beings would not be? Similar questions torment the reader's mind, and make his adherence to the system very insecure. Bergson foresaw them. He does not hide from us the fact that they exist at the basis of all great systems which the history of thought brings before us. But they are only illusion. To make clear the nature of this illusion there are, therefore, three theses devoted to *nothingness,* to *disorder* and to *organic finality,* which are definitely, against the wish of the philosopher himself, one of the most specious snares that philosophy ever set for human reason, to turn it from its Principle.

The question: Why does the universe exist? What is the cause of the world? should not be asked, Bergson tells us. In view of the extreme subtlety of his argumentation,[1] I shall take the liberty of condensing it into a certain number of closely-linked theses and answer them in order.

1. Any man who has "scarcely begun to philosophize" asks himself why he exists, why the universe exists, and if he "refers the universe to a Principle immanent or transcendent that supports it or creates it," asks "why this Principle exists," why something exists, why there is being.

If one accepts this "agonizing problem" one can only answer with Spinoza: being, which is at the bottom of everything, is the cause of itself, meaning a purely logical being eternal by itself like any logical principle or any essence; such a being in fact seems the only one capable of "vanquishing non-existence." It "posits itself throughout eternity as logic posits itself." But then we shall have to abandon all efficient causality and all freedom in things, both

[1] *Creative Evolution*, pp. 275–299.

of which will proceed from this principle just as propositions flow from an axiom.

The positing of this problem implies the supposition that nothingness is before being, that being is "spread upon nothingness as on a carpet," either that nothingness preceded being in time, or that it will eternally serve as its "substratum or receptacle." If this supposition is absurd, the positing of the problem will also be absurd.

2. As a matter of fact, the idea of absolute nothingness, the idea of the nothingness of all being[1] is a *pseudo-idea* which we never really *think* as such. This is the reason why:

a) An idea really thought has a content. It represents something,—otherwise it is simply a word. What are we thinking about then when we think the idea of nothingness?

Take any particular thing. Let us suppress it, cut it off from being by thought; then extend that operation to one thing after another, to everything, in short; we shall have the idea of absolute nothingness. Yes; but if the mechanism by which we thus construct this idea were to imply contradiction, that idea would be unthinkable, as much as the idea of a square circle. Now, psychological analysis informs us on this point. It shows us that to think nothingness of a certain thing is to posit the reality of another thing, and that consequently to think absolute nothingness, the nothingness of everything, implies contradiction.

b) For, to think the nothingness or non-existence of a reality is to think *the substitution of another reality for that particular reality*. The proof Bergson gives of that thesis admits three degrees.

Negation has no power to create ideas (negative ideas), for a negative judgment "this table is not white," "the object A does not exist," consists in warning an eventual interlocutor that for a certain affirmative proposition (for instance: "this table is white," "the object A exists"), must be substituted *another affirmative proposition* (for instance: "this table has a certain colour *x*," "actual reality excludes the object A as incompatible with it"), and in that there is only positive and nothing negative.

Moreover we cannot think an object, as Kant definitively showed in his critique of the ontological argument, without thinking it as existing. To say that the object A does not exist or to think that object as non-existent, "cannot therefore consist in withdrawing from the idea of that object the idea of the attribute existence," but can only consist in thinking that another reality with which it is incompatible supplants it. By that reality the object is then

---

[1] In this whole discussion it is a question of the 'nothingness' of *all* being from the point of view of extension (negation of all beings), not from the point of view of comprehension (the negation of all that makes the being of this or that thing).

expelled from actual existence and *ipso facto* thrown back into purely possible existence; so that the simple possibility or "the unreality of a thing consists in its expulsion by others."

The fact is that, in a word, we never think except in terms of the plenum. A thing can disappear only on condition that another take its place, therefore what is, what one perceives, what one effectively thinks, is the "presence of the former object in a new place, or that of a new object in the old." So that an understanding which would be nothing but understanding, that is, one on which external reality would purely and simply be inscribed, would not even have the idea of negation. It "would express only what is and what is perceived; now what is and what is perceived is the *presence* of one thing or of another, never the *absence* of anything whatever,"[1] it is not the negation of a reality, it is the substitution of one positive reality for another.

c) How does it happen then that we do not state what we have in our minds, namely the existence of the replacing reality, but that we are content to deny the existence of the replaced reality?—Because of the fact that something *is added* to the intellectual representation, an element that is extra-intellectual, either the disappointment of not finding what one expected to find, or the desire, pedagogic or social in nature, to correct or to forestall a possible error on the part of someone else.[2] This affective or social element causes us to fasten our attention only on the replaced reality, in which alone we are interested; and because of it we express the substitution thought by us only in function of its first half (the replaced reality, of which we say that it is not) while the second half (the replacing reality) is left in indetermination. Negation therefore owes its specific character to the intrusion of an element foreign to the intelligence. Consequently, it cannot give birth to any veritable idea.

Conclusion: What we think in the idea of the nothingness (of a certain thing) is reality (the reality of something else), but under a form different from our ordinary thought and one which is due only to extra-intellectual elements. It is therefore absurd to extend the idea of nothingness to the uni-

---

[1] "A being unendowed with memory or prevision would not use the words "void" or "nought" (p. 281).

"Give knowledge back its exclusively scientific or philosophical character, suppose in other words that reality comes itself to inscribe itself on a mind that cares only for things and is not interested in persons; we shall affirm that such or such a thing is, we shall never affirm that a thing is not." (p. 291.)

"Suppose language fallen into disuse, society dissolved, *every intellectual initiative,* every faculty of self-reflection and of self-judgment *atrophied in man,* [. . .] The intellect will still affirm, in implicit terms [. . .] But this passive intelligence, mechanically keeping step with experience, neither anticipating nor following the course of the real, would have no wish to deny. It could not receive an imprint of negation . . ." (p. 292; the italics are mine.)

[2] "Suppress all interest, all feeling, and there is nothing left but the flowing reality, together with the ever-renewed knowledge that it impresses on us of its present state." (p. 295.)

versality of things; absolute nothingness is a pseudo-idea, a word which covers nothing thinkable.

3. Still, because our action is always aimed at satisfying a desire, that is to say, always goes from an absence to a presence, and because on the other hand we improperly carry the proceedings of practice over into speculation, we hypostasize this negation that the extra-intellectual elements made us formulate; we believe that in things as in our actions the vacuum precedes the plenum, nothingness precedes existence. In short, extending to the whole the same pseudo-intellectual procedure, we think "that before things, or at least beneath things, there is nothingness," that nothingness, "conceived as an absence of everything, is pre-existent to all things by right, if not in fact."

But if absolute nothingness is unthinkable, one can no longer say that nothingness is before being, or that things have to "traverse nothingness" to get to existence.

Nor should one ask oneself the reason for the being of things. In reality, being, which is at the bottom of everything, being pure and simple (we mean *duration* or "concrete time") posits itself by itself. It is not a purely logical being like Spinoza's: it is the very being of what becomes; things are because they are, becoming has its *raison d'être* in itself.

Now here is the reply this argumentation calls for according to my way of thinking:

1. From the very beginning of the discussion there has been a confusion of two problems, one of which is legitimate and necessary, the other absurd. It is absurd to seek a cause for God's being, it is legitimate and necessary to seek a cause for the world's being. Out of these two problems is made a single pseudo-problem: why is there being?

In fact, being which is being according to its whole self and in which essence and existence are one, cannot have any cause. On the other hand, being which is participated and in which essence and existence are distinct, absolutely needs to have a cause;[1] and this cause, far from being posited "at the bottom of everything" like a principle in logic, exists necessarily above everything like a boundless plenitude of perfect life whose being transcends infinitely the being of things and is designated by the same word *being* only in virtue of an *analogy*. If from the outset there is confusion between God's Being, whose richness transcends all thought, and the being common to all things, which is the most general and consequently the poorest of entities, we have an *a priori* positing of pantheism. One is then obliged to choose between Spinozism and Bergsonism.

But the problem does not present itself thus. It is evident that, absolutely

---

[1] Cf. *Summa theol.*, Iᵃ, q. 44, a. 1, *ad* 1. "Ex hoc, quod aliquid per participationem est ens, sequitur quod sit causatum ab alio [. . .] sed quia esse causatum non est de ratione entis simpliciter, propter hoc invenitur aliquid ens non causatum."

speaking, being comes before nothingness, in reality as well as in knowledge; yet to affirm that a certain being is "preceded by nothingness," either in the sense that its essence does not comprise existence, or in the secondary sense that it has not always existed, in no way contradicts the above-mentioned principle since in this case what one is in fact positing is the existence of another being which will be the reason for that being and which will precede its nothingness. There is then no occasion to ask oneself why Being is Being, but there is reason for asking oneself if *such and such being* is Being by itself, and if not, why it has being; in other words, one should ask oneself if the universe has being by itself or if it participates in being, and in the latter case, one should find the reason for its being in a principle which is itself being by essence. This question is primordial and inescapable. As has just been said, it in no way implies that nothingness is before being, but only that it is not true that in each thing *to exist* is identical with *to be this*, which is evident since there are things which cease to exist.—Yet, it implies that to think the nothingness of the universe[1] (to think that the universe does not exist) is perfectly possible in itself. But as the nothingness of the universe is not the nothingness of all being it in no way implies the idea of the nothingness of all being or of absolute nothingness. The critique could stop there without following Bergson any further.

Nevertheless we might say that in the demonstration of the existence of God, especially in the *tertia via,* the idea of absolute nothingness does come in, since we rely upon the principle: "if at a moment nothing is then eternally nothing will be." Moreover and especially, the manner in which Bergson tries to establish that the idea of absolute nothingness is contradictory destroys the true nature of the idea of nothingness and signifies, in reality, that *the contingent exists by itself.* We shall therefore have to examine this argumentation more closely.

2. We deny then that the idea of nothingness is a pseudo-idea.

a) By the content of an idea is meant an object that the intellect can contemplate in it. Now the idea of nothingness or of non-being has indeed a content: it is quite simply the content of the idea of being, but this content is here affected by negation; any negative idea is in the same position in rela-

---

[1] Not only can the nothingness of any created being be thought, but also the nothingness of any created truth. Saint Thomas clearly shows that if (for the mind which knows the existence of God and what first Truth is), "non potest intelligi simpliciter veritatem non esse," "potest tamen intelligi nullam veritatem creatam esse, sicut et potest intelligi nullam creaturam esse. Intellectus enim potest intelligere se non esse, et se non intelligere, quamvis non intelligat sine hoc quod sit vel intelligat: non enim oportet quod quidquid intellectus intelligendo habet, intelligendo intelligat, quia non semper reflectitur supra seipsum; et ideo non est inconveniens, si veritatem creatam, sine qua non potest intelligere, intelligat non esse." Saint Thomas Aquinas, *De Verit.,* q. 1, a. 5, *ad* 5.

tion to the positive idea it presupposes.[1] The negation is understood from the sign which affects the content of the idea, not from the content itself, and it is the negative sign which is proper to the negative idea, not the content, which is that of the positive idea. It is therefore just as illusory to seek in the idea of nothingness a content negative in itself, which is proper to it, as to seek in the negative number, minus 3 for example, an absolute value proper to it and negative in itself. Bergson's error lies in trying to find such a content in the idea of nothingness.[2] Since this content does not exist, psychological analysis will invent one which thereafter will be easily shown to be fictitious, and thus a great deal of subtlety will have been expended in vain.

This is not the proper place for psychological analysis. It is by logical analysis that the idea of "square circle" is proved to be false; there is no need to have recourse to the mechanism of its formation. Proceeding through psychology and ending up at logic one deduces an obvious datum (that which a certain idea gives us) from obscure data (what the psychological genesis of such an idea is), and if the philosopher makes some error in the process he will want to persuade us that we think something else than what we think—a rather astonishing claim in a philosophy of immediate experience! The idea of absolute nothingness is not formed by progressive extension. As soon as we have the idea of being, we immediately form the idea of nonbeing.

It therefore follows that the idea of the nothingness of a being presupposes only the idea of that being, and not at all the idea of another being which is substituted for it.

A negative judgment presupposes an eventual positive judgment, but it supposes only that and the activity of the mind. It is true that in general another positive judgment can replace the one that is denied, but this is a state of fact which derives from the constitution of things and which remains entirely external to our thought. Negative judgment in no way implies either determinately or indeterminately that other positive judgment. Furthermore, there are cases when this replacing judgment does not exist; if I say: "This man has no children," I am certainly not thinking that he has other things than children; and even if I say: "Before the world was," I am certainly not thinking: "When actual reality excluded the world as incompatible with it!"

To say, moreover, that we do not think any object without thinking it as existing, means simply that we do not form any idea without implicitly affecting it with the sign of existence (*possible,* either in things or only in the mind). And our negative ideas themselves, including the idea of nothingness,

---

[1] "Ex hoc ipso quod cognoscitur res, cognoscitur privatio rei; unde utrumque cognoscitur per praesentiam formae in intellectu." *De Verit.,* q. 2, a. 15, ad 3.

[2] This is so true that he begins by seeking to find out what the *image* of nothingness is, an image which *a priori* is quite impossible!

are in this category. To have the idea of non-being is to conceive non-being and posit it before one's mind, assuredly not as being able to exist in itself, but as capable of being thought, of existing in our mind (*ens rationis*). Before the content of our positive idea *being,* we have simply placed the negative sign.

If Bergson denies the possibility of this intellectual act, the reason is, it seems to me, that he mistakes thinking an existing (ideally existing) object for thinking *that an object really exists.*[1] Hence it appears to him that real existence is an attribute included in all the objects that we think and that the reason for the simple possibility or unreality of one object is only in the actual reality of all the others. But this is in fact committing the fault of which the ontological argument is justly accused, and concluding—this time for all objects of thought—from ideal existence to real existence.

And furthermore, for him,—the passages quoted above show clearly—understanding which is only understanding without any admixture of affection or practical interest, is only a merely passive power of recording external events; now it is quite evident that the non-existence of something cannot be recorded. If, therefore, such an understanding nevertheless produces a negative idea or judgment, it can do so only because it has recorded the existence of something other than what it expected and because an extraneous element has come from without to prevent it from simply expressing this substitution. One might nevertheless ask oneself how this understanding, which cannot record an inexistent thing, can record an indeterminate thing as, according to Bergson, is the second half of the substitution in the negative judgment? In reality the understanding as such is active, it is not a prisoner of sense perception, and any idea, positive or negative, results from a *dictio verbi* and supposes the fundamental activity of the intellect. There is no nothingness, Bergson as much as tells us, except for a mind capable of thinking. Granted,—and there is no (known) being except for a similar mind.

c) That is why there is no need to seek any extra-intellectual element in negation. It is the activity of the mind which produces it; and all the effective or social elements which are easily found as external motives for our intellectual operations are no more of its essence than of the essence of affirmation.

The activity of the mind can then produce a veritable idea, and this is the case for the idea of nothingness. What the idea of nothingness expresses is the pure and simple non-existence of a being, not the existence of another being. Hence it follows that the idea of absolute nothingness is not contradictory.

---

[1] This confusion of conception (simple apprehension) and judgment is one of the great causes of error most prevalent in modern philosophy. It often seems to imply (and here in particular) a confusion between intellectual perception, which disregards actual existence, and sense perception (which implies the actual existence of the object).

3. It is sufficient clearly to understand this *idea* of nothingness; as a result we can never make of nothingness a *thing* which is to being a sort of "carpet," or "substratum," or "receptacle." Neither can it be said that, speaking absolutely, nothingness precedes being: absolute nothingness (the nothingness of *all being*) which can quite legitimately be *conceived,* cannot even be *affirmed* without contradiction.[1] As to relative nothingness (the nothingness of *this* or *that being*), it can readily be affirmed but it always presupposes a being which comes before it either to give total being to what, in an absolute sense, was not, as in creation; or to give a certain being to what was not in a certain manner, as in movement.

From the principle, in itself true, that being comes before nothingness Bergson therefore draws a false conclusion, namely that nothingness cannot precede *any being,* as if because, speaking absolutely, cause comes before effect, one should conclude that *no cause* comes after an effect (of another cause). And from this reason, in itself false, that absolute nothingness is impossible to think, Bergson draws a true conclusion, namely that being comes before nothingness.

But we say this precisely because the idea of nothingness is a valid idea, and because it is immediately seen, through the principle of non-contradiction, that being cannot come from nothingness; and because of this we understand that there would be no universe without God the Creator, nor any participated being without cause, nor any movement without a mover.

For Bergson, on the contrary, the idea of nothingness is wholly relative to practice and in reality only posits being; we do nothing but affirm, and the act of existing is an attribute of all the objects that we think. There is therefore no need to distinguish being by itself and participated being; everything is absolute being, as Parmenides claimed, only we turn the absolute being of Parmenides upside down by affirming that *things which pass need*

---

[1] At least insofar as by a second act, thought, reflecting back upon itself, necessarily sees that the proposition by which it affirms that nothing exists, exists itself. If one considers only this proposition itself and the relation of the predicate to the subject, one cannot say that the proposition "nothing exists," "no (thinkable) being exists," is *impossible, contradictory* in the very notions with which we form it: in order to do so it would be necessary for exercised existence to be a part of our idea of a (thinkable) being, and not one of our ideas makes us see exercised existence in the constitutive of an essence. (Cf. Cajetan, in I^{am}, q. 2, a. 1, *ad* 2.) The contrary is the case only in the conditions of beatific vision where, seeing the divine essence itself and in itself (not in an idea), we shall see that it cannot exist. (Cf. *de Veritate,* q. 10, a. 12).

These considerations are radically opposed both to Bergson's argumentation against the idea of nothingness and to any attempt to demonstrate *a priori,* or starting from notions alone, the existence of God (whether it be after the fashion of Descartes, or Leibnitz, or of the Kant of 1762.)

In order to forestall any misunderstanding we might add that the formula (non-contradictory in its wording, *in terminis,*—unless it be reflexively with respect to the act of the one who states it) "Nothing exists," must not be confused with the formula (contradictory *in terminis*) "Nonbeing exists."

no cause of their being. Bergson has no other way of avoiding classical pantheism than by impugning not only the notion of nothingness but above
all the notion of being,—which boils down in fact to falling back again into
the shadows of the essential non-distinction between God and things, for it
is necessarily a failure to take into account divine transcendence.[1] If one puts
a Principle "at the bottom of things" (not in virtue of the law of causality,
but because one comes into contact, through intuition, with a series of more
and more concentrated durations which one tries to follow to the end),
this "Principle of creation" immanent to things and source of things will
not be *Being through itself, necessary Being,* by opposition to the *participated
being* that things have,—it will be *becoming, moving, changing* like them, but
only to the highest degree of contraction and concentration. In reality, this
Principle is no more God than the things which come from Him; no matter
how enormous and tense one imagines it to be, it is, like them, fundamentally
indigent.

And so, once one *thinks* Bergsonian images, once there comes into the
mind the light of the idea of being, the idea the intellect cannot do without,
we see that if ancient pantheism absorbed participated being in Being by essence and transformed things into God and into divine eternity, now it is
Being by essence which is absorbed in participated being, it is God Who is
reduced to becoming and to time. Parmenides claimed to break the world
against the principle of non-contradiction. Bergson's world claims to break
the principle of non-contradiction. The world still holds. And so does the
principle of non-contradiction.

[1] Bergson, in two letters to de Tonquédec, tried to show that his doctrine, far from being
pantheistic, is "the refutation of pantheism and monism in general."—It is certainly so in the
philosopher's intention. But taken in itself and in its internal logic, if it is diametrically opposed
to the monism of *Spinoza,* it tends by itself,—whether one thinks it rationally or whether, being
content with images, one refuses reason and its distinctions,—toward another sort of monism. To
establish "the impossibility of nothingness" (1st Letter to Father de Tonquédec, *Études,* February 12, 1912, p. 515), is not simply to "show that something has always existed" (*ibid.,* p. 516),
it is to show that it is *unthinkable* that something has not always existed; that, therefore, is
denying the radical contingency of being as our intellect discerns it in things. Bergson's argument "does not in any way say that what has always existed is the world itself, and the rest of
the book explicitly says the contrary" (*ibid.,* p. 516). But certainly it is not claimed that Bergson
identifies purely and simply God and the world, the "source" and one of the "impulses" or
"currents" coming from it; it is claimed that in his doctrine they are not distinct absolutely,
really and essentially, and that each "impulse" or "current" can, in a word, appear in it only as
a sort of ontological *continuation* of the creative "source." See below, pp. 196–203.

Chapter Four

THE ORDER OF THE WORLD
AND ORGANIC FINALITY

We shall dwell less upon the two theories of disorder and organic finality, which rest upon a principle analogous to the principle of the theory of nothingness. In the first,[1] Bergson admits that there are two essentially different orders, the vital or willed order, relating to a certain simple and unforeseeable creation (example: a symphony by Beethoven), and the geometric or automatic order relating to a certain complicated grouping of necessary things (example: astronomical phenomena). As we have already said in discussing matter the simple interruption of the first order gives rise to the second; and to deny one of these two orders is to posit the other (thus we say that a room is "in disorder" because we were expecting the first order and we find the second, that is the automatic arrangement of efficient causes; and we imagine chaos as a "disorder," substituting in the universe, for the second order, that is, for the actual mechanism of causes and effects, the first order, that is a series of arbitrary arrangements decreed by our will). Hence it follows that the idea of disorder is also a pseudo-idea (quite as much as the idea of a language which would be neither poetry nor prose), and that it is absurd to ask oneself why there is order either in things if one is a realist or in the mind if one is an idealist; at once natural philosophy for the realists and the theory of knowledge for the idealists are marvellously simplified.

To this we can reply as follows. In the first place, assuming the existence of these two orders bound to one another by the relation Bergson mentions, the idea of disorder and the question: why the order in things? are nonetheless legitimate and even necessary. Because two species are opposed like two contraries within the same genus, it by no means follows that the negation of the genus cannot be thought; and if M. Jourdain,[2] after his lesson in philosophy, came to the conclusion that since what is not poetry is prose and what

---

[1] *Creative Evolution*, pp. 216–236.
[2] In Molière's *Le Bourgeois Gentilhomme*.

is not prose is poetry, and since in order to speak prose one has only not to speak in verse, then the idea of an absence of language is a pseudo-idea and the question: "why do men speak?", an absurd question, he would be reaching a very bad conclusion. In other words, if the second order is only the interruption of the first, one can and one should always ask why the first exists, —and therefore the two. In fact, Bergson thinks that the first order being immanent to the creative impulse posits itself just as this impulse does; but we have just seen in speaking of nothingness, what this thesis is worth.

Moreover, he omits the proper nature of the idea of order, to which may be added the ideas of free will or of automatic necessity as accidental characteristics, but which they cannot constitute: order is not only a satisfaction of our thought, nor an agreement between subject and object.[1] Order betokens by essence a certain measure of multiplicity by unity, and a certain proportion of means to end, which in things is the invincible imprint of an intelligence. That is why there are not two orders; the order of the course of the stars and the order of a symphony are one and the same order which reveals, in one as well as in the other, intelligence; the disorder of an untidy room and the disorder of chaos as Bergson imagines it, are one and the same disorder, which in one as in the other denotes a certain absence of intelligence. Bergson's first order, the willed order, is order only because the will presupposes the intellect, and his second order, automatic order, is order only because the efficient causes, in no matter how formless a world, would never begin to be efficient, to act, if they were not directed toward an end,[2] and if thereby they did not imply some manifestation of the intellect.

In reality, if absolute disorder is thinkable (not imaginable), it is nevertheless impossible ever to affirm it; for the concept of order—once diversity is assumed—follows the concept of unity and there is unity to the extent that there is being, so that no being is absolutely without unity and, as a result, without order. So it is that in positing a nature one posits at the same time a certain order, as in positing the circle one posits the order of propositions which derive from its essence, nature and order both having their principle in the divine Intelligence which is the cause of every being.

But to this order which flows from the nature of each being taken separately is, in fact, added another, which comes from the fact that the various beings in the world have opposing inclinations and tend to destroy one another; so that if the good of the whole is always and the good of particular

---

[1] *Creative Evolution*, p. 223. "Reality is *ordered* to the exact extent that it satisfies our thought. Order is therefore a certain accord between subject and object."

[2] Saint Thomas, *Contra Gent.*, I, III, c. ii. (On the principle of finality, see R. Garrigou-Lagrange, *Revue thomiste*, July–September and October–December 1921: Roland Dalbiez, *le Transformisme et la Philosophie*, in *le Transformisme*, Paris, Vrin, 1927; and chapter iv of the new edition of *Antimoderne*.)

species most frequently obtained, it is because the Intelligence of God ordains these beings to one another and because His Providence governs them.[1]

From the first order, were it possible to imagine it as existing without the second, could only result for the whole an immense confusion, such as there would be in an orchestra where each instrument played a different composition at the same time. But in reality it is at the same time and by the same stroke that these two orders come into existence, for it is in consideration of the perfection of the whole, not only that its harmonious organization was given to the universe, but also that the natures which go to make it up were chosen among the possible. Thus the order of created things is as gratuitous as their being. And this order is so essential to creation that in everything, Saint Thomas tells us,[2] it is the vestige of the Holy Ghost insofar as He is Love, and that the universe as a whole, having implied, from the moment it began to be, a distinction of parts,[3] has manifested order from the beginning; then there was less order, there was not disorder. In modern times philosophy has made itself so petty by dint of looking at itself and turning away from the reality of divine works, that all it cares henceforth to know about order is "how science is possible"[4] and how our physics succeeds. But our science is infinitely surpassed by the supple and living order that creates the beauty and prosperity of the world and by which "creatures act upon one another, are made in the resemblance of one another, and are the goal of one another."[5] This order could have not been; common sense rightly sees in it "a kind of grace,"[6] and if it is absurd to try to explain it by the "principle of conditions of existence"—which assumes it in reality—or by other materialist fantasies, it is just as absurd to claim that it is explained by its very existence and that it has no need of cause.

With regard to the organizing activity peculiar to life,[7] which no one can in fact deny, Bergson easily shows that it eludes all attempts at mechanistic explanation but he adds that it "transcends" finality also, because the doctrine of finality has the radical disadvantage of proceeding, like mechanicism, with *ready-made* elements and of imagining the organism as a collection of machine parts cleverly integrated by some internal artisan, or like an innumerable society of small workmen led by a whole hierarchy of overseers; a conception which he criticizes for its artificial and anthropomorphic character.

[1] Cf. *De Veritate*, q. 5, art. 2.
[2] *Summa theol.*, Iᵃ, q. 45, a. 7.
[3] *Ibid.*, 2. 66, a. 1.
[4] *Creative Evolution*, p. 231.
[5] *Sum. theol.*, Iᵃ, q. 47, a. 3, *ad* 3 (ms. 138 of the Monte-Cassino; as footnote in the Leonine edition).
[6] *Creative Evolution*, p. 95.
[7] *Ibid.*, pp. 37–53; 84–97.

We willingly agree with the criticism; what Bergson is criticizing here is in fact only the shadow of true finality, an entirely mechanical finality, the only one which can subsist,—and that with great difficulty,—in a philosophy which, since Descartes, bases nature on purely quantitative and mathematical principles. In reality, the activity of life toward an end is fundamentally distinct from the activity toward an end of an artisan making a machine. The latter arranges in order elements *already existing* in a certain accidental whole, but for the living, to live is to be, to the point that a hand cut off can no longer be called a hand except in an improper sense,[2] and the elements one distinguishes in the living *do not exist* as such before their organization into a substantial whole; the vital principle therefore does not resemble the waterworks engineer who sets a ready-made machine going or even who makes it from various materials:[3] it is a principle of being and existing and a principle of intrinsic activity.

It is true that in this conception of the organism the soul is regarded as the *substantial form* of the living body. Rather than return to so ancient a doctrine, one moreover incompatible with naturalistic transformism, of a so-called "scientific" kind,[4] Bergson has recourse to the *vital impulse* to account for organic finality. Organization results, in his opinion, from the sole encounter of two simple and as has already been explained, inverse movements,—the movement of life, or of the creative impulse, and the movement of matter,—and from the *modus vivendi* resulting from such an encounter. The relation of vision to the eye, for example, is comparable *to the relation of an arm thrust into iron filings to the arrangement of the particles which would result from this movement.* The vital impulse, solely by the production of simple acts like that of seeing, would therefore arrange matter organically; one could thus readily understand how, according to the intensity and the perfection of this simple act, material organization seems more or less complicated, but is always complete and adapted to the function, whether it be, for example, the most rudimentary eye or one as complex as the human eye. One could also understand how, on absolutely divergent lines of evolution, life has given birth

---

[2] Aristotle, *De Anima*, I, II, c. 1, 412b 14, 21; *Metaph.*, I, VII, c. 11, 1036b 32.

[3] Cf. Descartes, *Tractatus de Homine*, II, 16.

[4] I mean, with any form of transformism implying (like Darwinism and Lamarkism, and like Bergsonian evolutionism), that an historical process in which the laws of corporal nature alone are involved, causes the succession of organisms to pass through a series of different (philosophical) species. That a (philosophical) species branches out in the course of time into a plurality of varied forms (taxonomical species),—or that the action of a cause superior to sensible nature, using the organisms as instruments, makes them pass through a series of different (philosophical) species, or in other words makes them educe from the potentiality of matter, in the generation of a living being, a specific form higher than the engendering one,—is not incompatible with the philosophical doctrine of the soul as *substantial form*.

to extraordinarily analogous organs, such as the eye of the molluscs and the eye of the vertebrates.

Let us however closely examine the comparison just made: how can one help but see that here it is a question of a *trace* left in *a passive medium* (the iron filings) by a thing already organized (the arm) and set in action with an end in view (the movement to accomplish)? No finalist, no matter what Bergson says, will, in this case, try to explain the disposition of the iron filings by supposing elementary actions exerted by these particles on one another and a general plan presiding over these actions; one might as well attribute to the intention of an artist the regular disposition of prints left on the ground by an animal in flight! But neither will anyone take it that one can compare to a process of this kind the organization of living bodies. Like everything that truly manifests finality this organization does, in fact, result from the combination of several partial causes (and not from the presence of a passive medium) producing by their proper activity an *effect* to which they are all ordered (instead of receiving the imprint from another active cause); in other words, whoever says organization says distinction of real parts positively concurring with a view to a certain end; and a theory which sees in these parts only the negative expression or the hollow imprint of a simple act, destroys the very reason for the organization; furthermore, Bergson's doctrine makes matter a simple cause of resistance to the vital activity in the living body without there being, even in plant life, unity of operation between matter and life. It supposes that the act of vision precedes the eye by right, and this form of dualism in turn destroys the very notion of the living body; finally, not to mention other insurmountable difficulties,[1] this theory,—invented to explain a hypothesis, namely, how a ("phylogenetic") evolution due to a blind thrust would have produced at all degrees of life organs always complete although more or less complicated,—makes inexplicable a fact of experience, namely, how "ontogenetic" evolution produces (I mean in a vital manner, not by the play of any mechanism) organs, the eye for example,

---

[1] How, for example, does the vital impulse retrace its steps, how does it begin over again a new point of departure, on the one hand at each new generation, on the other hand in many cases of regeneration or of "regulation"? How, in general, are we to make an evolutive conception which reduces life to an impulse, a course, a romantic cavalcade without specific limit and predetermined end, agree with the scrupulously careful, stable and regular harmony which characterizes life everywhere, in its organization as well as in its functioning and in the operations of the instinct? All this harmony can be, for Bergsonism, only fabricated mechanisms or imprints left by life: but this active harmony is life itself and can only be explained by the unity of the specific substantial form. Without this specific form organization has no *raison d'être*. The finality and harmony which characterize life are conditioned by the stable limits of the species (I am speaking of the *philosophical* species, which need not coincide with the taxonomic species and which is probably much broader); if these limits are done away with, it disappears. *Qui faciunt in finitatem (quoad speciem) naturae viventis,* we might say from this point of view, *auferunt naturam vitae.*

which at first are only incomplete rudiments and which are perfected little by little *before being able to function*: the materiality of the organ is here in advance of the simple act which it only "explains negatively"!—So therefore, even supposing to be intelligible the hypotheses and principles indicated above, one must conclude that they destroy organization instead of explaining it; and it is in vain that one insists, against all likelihood, on making of vision not the final cause but a sort of efficient cause of the visual apparatus.

All modern discussions on the finality of organism would gain much in clarity were formal cause and final cause properly distinguished. Once formal cause is denied, we see in the living being nothing more than a dust of efficient causes, and if mechanicism appears to be radically incapable of explaining the harmony of these causes, finalism, in turn, can do nothing but invoke a kind of vital sprite entrusted with the direction of the play of efficient causes and itself supplied with an extraordinary knowledge of the ends to be attained. As Bergson rightly points out, we then suppose that "nature works like a human artisan, in assembling parts," and forget that "life does not proceed by the association and addition of elements, but by dissociation and division."[1] But he himself seems to think that if there is no *assembling of parts,* it is because in reality *there are no parts,* and he substitutes for the organizing work of nature the incomprehensible efficient activity of an "impulse" which "automatically"[2] moulds itself in matter. He is nearer than he thinks to the theories he is combatting, since between the matter and the principle of life he cannot establish any substantial unity, and he only replaces the little intelligent sprites and the dust of causes of the "vitalists" by a big blind demon struggling in a jelly ballasted with geometry.

If, on the contrary, we admit with the scholastics the existence of prime matter, a principle of pure receptivity which *cannot be* without form, and the existence of substantial form, a principle of being and activity which in the non-living and the living other than man, *cannot be* without matter, so that the compound of those two alone is *a being,* both mechanicism and pseudo-finalism are avoided, and finality's true nature is restored to it. For we can say, along with Bergson, that "finality is external or it is nothing at all,"[3] if by this we mean (the final cause acting only according as it is represented in knowledge and desired by the appetite or the will)—that where there is no knowledge, as in inorganic bodies and in plant life, the agent that tends toward an end is directed toward it by another agent, by an intelligent cause, as the arrow is directed toward the target by the archer. From whence it follows that one cannot admit an "internal finality" in the sense of a direct action of the

---

[1] *Creative Evolution,* p. 88.
[2] *Ibid.,* p. 91.
[3] *Ibid.,* p. 41.

final cause in natures deprived of knowledge. From this point of view, while man acts toward ends known as ends, and thus directs himself toward his end, while the animal acts toward ends which are doubtless known but not as such, and thus is directed toward its end by another, inorganic bodies and the living bodies of plant life are all equally directed by another toward an end which they do not know so that "all irrational nature is to God what the instrument is to the principal agent."*

There is then no difference, from the point of view of their relation to the final cause, between inorganic bodies and organisms. It is from the point of view of the mode of being and the mode of attaining their end, that is, from the point of view of the formal cause, that they differ. The first, as a matter of fact, receive their being from the outset; the second which, according to the scholastic definition, *move themselves,* give themselves the complement of their being, and so their immanent activity must be directed toward the perfection of the substantial whole they constitute: in this sense, one can indeed speak of internal finality. But they both act only in virtue of the forces and inclinations they have received from God, and to Him alone must be ascribed the intention of the end as well as the wisdom manifest in its execution. In short, what God puts into beings is not an impression which necessitates them by violence or compulsion, as is the case for the arrow launched by the archer and for the products of our art, but their very nature,[1] so that there is in them a *natural appetite* for their end, either in order to preserve themselves in existence and to develop, or to pour out beyond themselves the good they possess, or to perfect themselves by producing changes in other beings,[2] and that in short *omnia appetunt divinam similitudinem quasi ultimum finem.* Here again we may say with Bergson, that life (and nature in general) is not expressible "in terms of (*human*) ideas," and that it is more than "the realization of a (*human*) idea conceived or conceivable in advance,"[3] not in the sense that we cannot form an exact idea of it, but in the totally different sense that its intimate operation is not comparable to the realization of a human idea according to a human programme, precisely because all our operations are exerted upon already existing material, on which we impose an accidental form, while life acts in virtue of the substantial form actuating prime matter. Nevertheless, from the fact that this operation exceeds all our imaginings, from the fact that it does not take place through an *assembling* of pre-existing parts, and that not only is the work wondrous in itself, but wondrous also the manner in which it is accomplished, we can but find still another reason

---

* Saint Thomas, *Summa theol.,* Iᵃ IIᵃᵉ, q. i, a. 2.
[1] *Summa theol.,* Iᵃ, q. 103, a. 1, *ad* 3.
[2] Cf. Kleutgen, *Philos. Scol.,* t. III, p. 496.
[3] *Creative Evolution,* pp. 223–224.

to "admire," we see with all the more evidence the necessity for recognizing an Intelligence as principle of Creation, which is already, being the first of the divine works, *magnum pietatis opus.*

Shall we now try, no matter how difficult it may be to reason on images, to characterize in general Bergson's doctrine on the order of nature? It seems as though Bergson wished above all to explain things by dispensing with finality properly so-called, that is with intelligence, or rather by retaining as much finality as possible while sacrificing intelligence. He does not claim like the mechanists that order comes spontaneously out of disorder, but he denies the idea of disorder and puts into purely efficient impulsion, into the *vis a tergo* of his vital impulse, as much finality as he can: life, consciousness, appetite, effort, unity prodigiously rich in tendencies, exigence of creation,—everything in short save intelligence. Now, all this is utterly useless without the intellect. If we suppress intelligence *nothing* of finality remains. That is perfectly evident since the end, the final cause as such, acts (*before* being attained or realized) to determine the efficient cause, and as a result can act only as *known* by an intellect (and willed consequently by a will). That is why any attempt to find a mean between finality and chance, and to philosophize with *impulses, tendencies, directions,* etc., while excluding any *goal* pursued and explaining things by a purely efficient impulsion, is foredoomed to contradiction and to failure.[1]

And as a matter of fact the vital impulse, for example, is characterized only in terms of intelligence, terms united contradictorily, it is true. If there is a *vital order,* either in works of art, or in works of life, it is because intelligence is implicitly assumed. If the intelligence in which the goal pursued is represented is not in the creative movement, then it is before that movement,— and that is just where Bergson places it: I mean to say in the very mind of the philosopher, which judges that the vital impulse "proceeds to vision" or to "the liberation of consciousness," or to other goals, and which, as a result, imparts to that impulse a determined direction. Without this original act of intelligence, the vital impulse would never take off, its activity not being determined toward anything. If there is an *organization,* the "simple act" which creates an organ must certainly be ordered to a definite goal and also, since the life of each living thing implies the harmony of numerous functions, there must be an order between the aforesaid simple acts; and this always supposes an intelligence, that of the philosopher for want of any other. Even so, in spite of that, as we have seen, Bergsonian evolutionism can furnish us with only the shadow of organization.

[1] Cf. *Creative Evolution,* pp. 102–105.

Finally, insofar as the *order of matter*[1] is concerned, the latter can be only disorder (if it is true, as we have stated, that disorder is not a pseudo-idea), since it is the simple suppression of the "vital" order which is order itself. Bergson tells us[2] that in listening to a poem, then relaxing our attention, we pass from one order to the other, first attentive to the thoughts expressed, then in a dreamy abandon considering nothing more than the disposition of the syllables and the interweaving of the letters. But, either these elements were already ordered, as is the case in the example,—contrary to the hypothesis, moreover,—or else it is we who capriciously imagine in them some order or other, and that is still intelligence. In fact, this relapsing matter, this disintegrating reality cannot even tend toward a mathematical disposition which implies not only extension, but a certain form and a certain order in extension; it is only an amorphous medium out of which our intellect cuts anything it wishes, and the order of matter henceforth depends only on mere idealism (an untenable thesis in a doctrine which posits the objective existence of external reality in living bodies!).—Some philosophy other than the philosophy of duration and intuition is needed to bring metaphysics and physics into accord, by showing the objective reality of *order* in things, and by re-linking that order to the creative Intellect.

[1] With regard to the mathematical order of matter, the only one considered here by Bergson, the fact that number is really at the base of nature—*omnia in mensura et numero et pondere disposuisti*—does not constitute, as has been supposed (in somewhat too paradoxical a manner) in *Creative Evolution* (see above, *supra*, p. 82, n. 3), an obstacle to the success of physico-mathematics; this latter, in fact, not pursuing the discovery of causes in themselves but only as they lend themselves to the translation of events into a certain system of numerical relations, does not need to "find the standard of nature" or the variables "chosen by her." Nature chooses her unities arbitrarily, and is engaged above all in seeking the *functions* between variable magnitudes, not the *causes* of phenomena, so that if, behind this mathematical net to which she can add new meshes indefinitely, and which alone is her proper formal object, she tries to imagine causes, principles, natures, causal laws properly so-called, she can only imagine hypotheses, whose convenience alone (not whose truth) she can appreciate; in that, she contains an element of contingency. For the same reason, physico-mathematical science,—the only science in which, according to Bergson, we made contact with the absolute through our intellect,—leaves us in reality quite ignorant of the constitutive principles of things.

[2] *Creative Evolution*, p. 209.

Chapter Five

BERGSONIAN EVOLUTIONISM AND THE INTELLECT

Bergson's original insight

We believe that Bergsonism originated in a singularly clear and profound view of a certain evil and a certain error, which are at the very bottom of modern philosophy: the evil is the pride in and perversion of an intellect which has been separated from its principles and given up to matter; the error is mechanicism and mathematicism, the reduction of everything to quantity and the consequent abolition of all life and all real movement in the world. But once having discovered this evil, instead of working back to principles Bergson has continued in the same direction as modern thought; granting in accord with the modern error that perverted intellect is the Intellect, and that the fictitious being (purely logical or purely mathematical) of the mechanistic theories is Being, he has abandoned intelligence and abandoned being, replacing the first by an extra-intellectual intuition and the second by movement. Thus the remedy is worse than the evil, but it is still true that modern philosophy is incapable of answering Bergsonism, and that Thomistic philosophy alone has the means of refuting it.

Analysis and the Intellect

If we read what Bergson says about the intellect and analysis, deliberately modifying his thought and taking his words to apply, not to the intellect but to a certain use of reason, not to analysis but to a certain method of analysis, then everything takes on a perfectly correct meaning. Instead of a misunderstanding of the intellectual light we have nothing more than an admirably firm and precise criticism of materialistic intellect and mechanistic analysis. Then it can indeed be said that this intellect knows only the immobile and the discontinuous, that it understands nothing of life, that it artificially breaks up the real into parts, that it substitutes for reality fictitious elements chosen from the *already known,* and that thus, seeking facility not truth, and emptying all things of their proper reality, it can only apply itself to the quantitative and geometrical elements to which it wishes to reduce everything. *Corruptio op-*

timi pessima. It is just and good that in order to witness against such an intellect we should call upon instinct and sentiment, the heart's desires and the will's demands, the divinations of art and even practical experience. If powers which, to the extent that they manifest the laws of life and bear upon the real, contain, to be sure, a capacity for truth but are not ordered to truth as to their peculiar good, are to save (because what exists refuses to perish), vital truths which are imperiled by reason which is out of alignment, then the imposture of the latter will only stand out more clearly. One is right in proving the reality of movement by walking. But if one were to start from there systematically to make the intellect subordinate to sentiment or to action, one would reverse the order upon which everything rests and correct an error of fact by an error of principle.

In reality, Bergson's critique does not deal with a faculty but rather with a state of mind; what he distrusts is not the intellect, it is reason reduced to its material functioning, *mechanically discursive reason.*[1] It is the ineffectual method of those who call themselves positivists and for whom anything that is not sensible and mechanically measurable is devoid of meaning, any science which does not break down its object into machine-like parts, a mythological speculation. But how could Bergson confuse the intellect with this disgraceful caricature? The palpable proof that what he is talking about is only a pseudo-intellect and a pseudo-analysis is that the results they furnish have nothing necessary about them, and they are given the title of science in a futile attempt to dazzle the ignorant; true and pure science has nothing to do with them. If Bergson's view of the intellect were true we should always have to tend toward mechanicism whenever we exerted our faculty of knowing in a natural way. Now, during all of classical antiquity and the Middle Ages the reigning philosophy was inspired not by mechanics but by life; and scholastic metaphysics formulated in a purely rational mode doctrines that were most opposed to mechanicism. Finally, far from ending inevitably in mechanicism, reason has no trouble in refuting it. For that beautiful creature the human intellect, doubtless very fallible but made for truth, Bergson mistook an abortion begotten by the sensualism of the Renaissance and the pride of the Reformation, brought up in an 18th century physics laboratory by mathematicians, philosophers and doctors, and deified by Robespierre.

Bergson assures us that if we raise our arms we have inwardly the simple perception of this movement, but that the *concept* of the movement means nothing to us but a series of positions successively passed through, or of virtual rests, in short, a recomposition of that simple act by means of exterior views. Who will believe this to be the concept or idea of movement, and that when we think "movement" we think "succession of states of rest"? We have

[1] Cf. my study *La Science moderne et la Raison,* Revue de Philosophie, June 1910 [reproduced in *Antimoderne,* chap. I].

no need either to circle about the mobile or to place ourselves within it to know what movement is; it is enough that our intellect forms for itself an idea made to measure. It is a simple perception, true enough, but an intellectual perception. False analysis consists precisely in replacing this idea of movement by the idea of successive states of rest. And if from the beginning the *idea* is confused with the *false analysis* the criticism will be easy but will miss its mark.

Bergsonian criticism *a priori* deprives the intellect of its own life and its essential activity, of its power to form ideas and of the intuitive light of first principles; it therefore lays itself open to attack. Bergson will doubtless be right against the wholly passive intellect of the Cartesians and the sensualists, with its innate ideas or its generalized images; but he will have said nothing about true intellect. Let us for the moment recall what the scholastics teach about *abstraction:* how the "formative intellect" (*intellectus agens*) throws its light upon the images provided by external perception, which are the very form of the object transferred into the sense, and freed but not from individuating material notes; how, not in virtue of a generalization or a comparison, but by its proper and natural activity this intellect abstracts from these images thus illuminated the intelligible similitude that they contain potentially, the immaterial form which, received as *"impressed* species" by immaterial intelligence, is only so to speak the object itself immaterialized; how thus informed by the *impressed* species, the "to-be-formed intellect" (*intellectus possibilis*) then *conceives* and produces, in an eminently vital reaction, the *"expressed* species," word of the spirit, common fruit of the intellect and its object, in which the intellect perceives the object: *in quantum dicit verbum anima cognoscit objectum;*[1] a simple, irreducible, active, spontaneous perception that may well be called intuitive[2] for it truly puts us in communication with the real, but which is, however, in this first operation of the mind where "the intellect is never false,"[3] only the indispensable preparation for true knowledge. This latter in fact takes place only in the judgment.

It is true that because of the weakness of the intellectual light within us our understanding is a discursive understanding; but this very fact implies that since our knowledge goes from potentiality to act, from the imperfect to the perfect and thus from the general to the particular, abstraction gives us in the most universal and simple ideas and *par excellence* in the idea of being a knowledge which gushes forth of itself, on the occasion of our primary experiences, in judgments in immediate conformity with the real; judgments

---

[1] On this doctrine see Saint Thomas, *De Veritate,* q. 4, a. 2; *Sum. theol.,* I, q. 34, a. 1; *Sum. contra Gent.,* lib. IV, c. 11.

[2] The word 'intuitive' is taken here in the wide sense that it has in the moderns. See *infra,* p. 150, n. 2, and *Réflexions sur l'Intelligence* (2nd ed., Appendix II).

[3] Cf. Saint Thomas, *Summa theol.,* Iª, q. 85, a. 6.

doubtless very general but also very evident and certain, such as the principle of identity and the other first principles, primordial intuitions without which no true enunciation would be possible. Reasoning consists in bringing the secondary propositions back to these original intuitions and in coming down again from these intuitions to conclusions. This does not mean that all other truths are contained in the principles as though in a chest since, on the contrary, experience is necessary for the formation of all our concepts; but it means that the secondary propositions are to be seen in the *light* of the first principles and that all along the course of reasoning the propositions communicate to one another that light which is evidence, up to the final conclusion. Then, at the end of the search the intellect knows again by a vital act, by a *dictio verbi;* it grasps the real by a *"simple perception"* expressed in a judgment (*secunda mentis operatio*) and one which restores to unity the at-least-virtual complexity discovered in the object. The end of science is thus to arrive at the *proper* knowledge of essences,[1] that is, in modern terms, to make for each thing a garment ordered for it alone.[2]

When, after that, we are told that for intellectualist philosophy "to think consists in going from concepts to things"[3] and "in forcing the real into a pre-existing framework at our disposal,"[4] the *thinking* referred to is obviously not the same as genuine thought; here it can be a question only of mutilated intellect.

For the scholastics, therefore, understanding unites both "intuition" and discourse in the same appetite for being and in the same harmonious activity; the first is found at the beginning in definitions and principles, and at the end in the intellectual perception of conclusions; the second, uniting ideas according to their proper articulations, transmits evidence from judgment to judg-

---

[1] "Intellectus noster singularia [directe] non cognoscens, *propriam habet cognitionem de rebus, cognoscens eas secundum proprias rationes speciei;* unde etsi etiam intellectus divinus singularia non cognosceret, nihilominus posset de rebus propriam cognitionem habere." Saint Thomas, *de Verit.*, q. 2, a. 4, *ad* 1.

[2] Let us recall that the scholastics were so scrupulous in their definitions that they regarded as imperfect the "physical" definitions ("man is a being composed of a body and an intellectual soul"), in which each part of the definition is said only of a part of the object, and that they stressed only "metaphysical" definitions ("man is a rational animal") in which the parts of the definition can each be said of the whole object;—definitions which thus manifest the object. (Cf. Saint Thomas, *Summa theol.*, I^a, q. 85, a. 5, *ad* 3.—Suarez, *Metaph. Disp.*, disp. vi, sect. 9.)

[3] *Introduction to Metaphysics* (*Rev. de Mét. et de Mor.*, January 1903, p. 16), in *Creative Mind*, p. 208.

[4] *Creative Evolution*, p. 48. The criticism Bergson here makes of Plato seems quite unjust. Doubtless the theory of Ideas is inacceptable, but they have nothing of a "pre-existing framework" about them. In any case it is a strange abuse to make Aristotle and the philosophers of his school pay the penalty for Platonism on the precise point on which they refuted it. So likewise is it, to claim that for Aristotle vegetative life, sensible life and rational life are three successive degrees of a same developing tendency. (*Ibid.*, p. 142.)

ment, all the way to conclusion. *Discursus rationis semper incipit ab intellectu et terminatur ad intellectum.*[5]

But if this is so Bergson's critique is itself an example of defective analysis. It artificially separates "intuition" from reason, takes away from the first its intellectual character and from the second its light. Limited to the pseudo-analysis of the sciolists it is decisive. But transformed into a theory of knowledge it yields only disappointment.

If from this point of view one rereads the passages of *Creative Evolution* we have tried to sum up above,[6] one will doubtless wonder how it is possible that intellectual knowledge differs only in degree from sense knowledge while contrary to sense knowledge it is abstract, universal and bears on the very *being* of things; how the power to fabricate tools (otherwise known as art or industry) can define intelligence, whereas this power itself already pre-supposes the value of intelligence and its principles; how one can *a priori* know relations without terms that are related; whether first principles bespeak such relations, or whether they do not rather rest on the knowledge of "things" (not particular things it is true, but universal) such as the transcendentals; what is a form into which anything whatever can enter; what good would a knowledge be that decomposes and re-composes according to any law whatever; and finally, how it happens that if intelligence is fascinated by matter and made for geometry it should have awaited Kepler, Newton and others in order to study matter mathematically, and that it should have been clumsy enough to think things with all those unfortunate ideas of another age, which are so repellant to mechanistic explanations that Mr. Levy-Bruhl is forced to go in search of their origin among wonderfully mystical savages and that Mr. Le Dantec is obliged, in order to write his books in peace, to invent at every instant a new language.

The concept

In the critique we like to make nowadays of concept and language the fact that our intellectual knowledge is limited is often taken as an evidence that this knowledge is false; that savours of too great haste. Certainly, the concept cannot replace sensation or sentiment and has never claimed to do so; a good deal of the oratory concerning the *ineffability* of the real has no other meaning however. On the other hand, we have no *science* of the singular; matter and potentiality are not known in themselves precisely because our knowledge bears upon things as they are (in act), and not as they are not, or as they are only in potency; that, moreover, in no way prevents the intellect from knowing potentiality in relation to act, matter in relation to form; as to movement,

---

[5] Saint Thomas, *Sum. theol.*, IIa–IIae, q. 8, a. 1, *ad* 2.
[6] See *supra*, pp. 80–81.

the intellect knows it as the passage from potentiality to act; and that is a true knowledge which has nothing in common with the "cinematographical"[1] procedure described by Bergson. In fine, it is through the intellect, clearly in the deductive sciences, through signs and "blindly" in the inductive sciences that we know the specific nature of singular things,—and through return or "reflection" on the senses (which genuine spiritualism is careful not to despise) we know their very singularity. In all that, it is only a question of a limitation; and certainly our intellect suffers here below far more serious limitations since except by analogy we do not understand spiritual natures! But that is neither fault nor error.

How could one fail to see that in explaining the concept by the necessities of practical experience and in saying that it is simply the sign of an identity of attitude in the face of an object one is contradicting the very evidence itself, since one is taking away the universal not only from things but even from the mind, in which we very well know, however, that the universal is *thought?* —The concept is reproached for its fixity, its immobility, but this reproach is in great need of precise definition. Is it meant that since reality is submitted to change and to becoming, ideas which do not themselves change could not make it known? In that case it seems that we are misled by the principle of the old philosophers that *like knows like,* and that we are forgetting that the similitude of the object is found in the intelligence *secundum modum recipientis;* as though the soul should be, as Empedocles would have it, fire in order to know fire, earth to know earth, in short, mobile in order to know movement and material to know matter, when it is its very immateriality which permits it to receive within itself the forms of all other things. Or is it meant, on the contrary, that our ideas falsify the real because they represent essences and immutable relations, whereas everything is in a continual flux and *it is impossible to touch the same water in a flowing river twice?* In that case, if we refuse to answer with Saint Thomas[2] that it is not true that everything is movement; that all movement, on the contrary, supposes something immobile; that essences cannot change; that "even for things mutable and changing, there are immutable relations that do not change; thus it is that even if Socrates is not always sitting down, it remains no less immutably true that when he is seated he does not change place; so that nothing prevents us from having an immutable science bearing even upon mutable things,"— then we shall have to confess in effect that thinking is indeed lying; any proposition expressed will be false of itself since the flux of the real will have run out before any judgment can have been brought upon it; but therefore Bergson will no longer be able to say either that "movement is indivisible" or that "time is real" or that "intuition attains the absolute"; in general, no one

[1] *Creative Evolution*, p. 306.
[2] *Summa theol.*, I^a, q. 84, a. 1, *ad* 3.

will be able to express any principle whatsoever and the philosopher will be condemned to perpetual silence.

Of course "pure reasoning"* is worth nothing without common sense; but common sense is not "quite a different thing" from reasoning, it is only the healthiness of reason, the lively perception of first principles and of the intelligible realities drawn from experience,—it is the very life of logic.

Intuition

If the concept and the intellect Bergsonian philosophy speaks of are only a pseudo-concept and a pseudo-intellect, intuition, with which it strives to save the truth, has only an apparent resemblance to the intellective perception recognized by the scholastic teaching. Assuredly there is something in common between Bergson's intuition and this perception,—I mean the union of the known and the knowing. But the essential difference is that according to Saint Thomas this union takes place *secundum modum cognoscentis,* and that according to Bergson it would take place *secundum modum cogniti.* When Bergson insists upon the superiority of purely intuitive knowledge,[1] no one can contradict him; at most one could add that if our knowledge is discursive by nature and therefore inferior, it is not therefore false, and that in any case it would be useless for us to try to transcend ourselves to play the angel. But what then is, according to the Angelic Doctor, the intuition of the angels? Material objects act in no way upon the mind of the angel; it is through an intelligible species imprinted by God in his understanding that the angel knows immediately and non-discursively the essence and properties of things. In the case of the angel and in the case of man the object, even material, is immaterially known in an immaterial intellect; and this intellect possesses the truth as its own, that is to say not only does it speak truly but it even knows it speaks truly, which implies judgment.[2]

For Bergson on the contrary intuition surpasses intelligence absolutely, it is incommensurable with the idea and coincides with the object itself. This intuition therefore wills to give us infinitely more than the intellectual perception of which the scholastics speak; instead of ending inwardly in a mental word pronounced in the mind, instead of admitting the limitations which come in man, from the fact that he draws his knowledge from material things and from the fact that the singular eludes human knowledge, it claims to end in a fusion of the mind in the thing, it transports us into the object

---

* *Creative Evolution,* p. 161.

[1] Cf. *The Perception of Change* (Lectures given at the University of Oxford, 1911), in *Creative Mind,* pp. 155–156.

[2] *Summa theol.,* I*, q. 16, a. 2.

and identifies us by an intense and even painful effort of sympathy[1] with what is unique, inexpressible, incommunicable in the thing, I mean with matter itself—which, united to form, makes the singularity of the thing. But at the same time this intuition gives us infinitely less than the intellectual perception of the scholastics: properly speaking it deprives us of the truth. As long as truth is in our mind only as it is in the sense, or as it is in each true thing, "that is to say, which has truly the nature or the form it should have, in which sense we say of bread, gold, water, that they are true,"[2] truth is neither our possession nor our perfection; we do not possess it as truth. In order to do so it must be in us as *thing known,* and this supposes that there is in us an intelligible similitude of the thing (and a judgment). Now, Bergson's intuition is a lived identification of the mind and the thing in its *real* being (and not in its *intentional being,* which Bergson cannot admit). Although supra-intellectual in the intention of Bergson, it reduces itself in reality to the sensible order since it is an experience of the very materiality of the thing and it does not even possess what the sense possesses, an intrapsychic likeness of the object. With such an intuition we do not give light to things, we seek in them a contact which changes us into them. We do not possess things, we are possessed by them; we do not intellectualize matter, we materialize the mind. Bergson is right in assimilating his intuition to instinct; like instinct it is blind, and it is only because of a desperate effort of the will that it does not lose itself in unconsciousness.

That at least is what intuition would be if it were a special faculty opposed to intelligence. In reality, it seems clear that the intuition Bergson describes is composed of quite diverse elements artificially gathered together; analyzing it, we should doubtless discover, joined to intellectual perception properly so-called, the activity of that sensible faculty the scholastics call *estimative* in animals, *cogitative* in men, which is none other than instinct inferring from the particular to the particular; then a sort of experimental knowledge, which proceeds by conformity to the inner inclinations of the subject and which is "a manner of judging that is affective or instinctive, or by inclination,—"[3] as the virtuous man judges of virtue instinctively, being himself according to Aristotle, the rule and measure of human acts,—a very precious knowledge for the estimation of particular cases as well as for practical skill and for discovery, but which cannot replace intelligence and still less contra-

[1] "If metaphysics is possible it can only be (a laborious, even painful) effort to re-ascend the slope natural to the work of thought, to place oneself immediately, through a dilation of the mind, in the thing one is studying." (*Revue de Métaphysique et de Morale:* January 1903, pp. 21–22.) *Introduction to Metaphysics,* in *Creative Mind,* p. 216.

[2] Th. Pègues, *Commentaire français littéral à la Somme théologique,* t. I, vol. 2, p. 174 (Iª, q. 16, a. 2).

[3] *Summa theol.,* Iª, q. 1, a. 7 *ad* 3.

dict it; then again the kind of *sensible sympathy* which, for the artist, takes the place of the impossible intellection of the singular and which he needs in order to express in matter his model or his idea, and which is wholly turned toward artistic *operation,* not toward speculation;—finally, a share of natural mysticism which would make this intuition akin to the ecstasy of Plotinus.

And now,—that intuition as Bergson describes it does not exist as a special function of the mind will be shown by the following remark.[1] All those errors that this intuition claims to refute, reason refutes; thus it is that Aristotle did not need this intuition in order to refute Zeno of Elea and to show that Achilles can overtake the tortoise because, as Saint Thomas says, of the *continuity of movement.*[2] From another angle all truths claimed to be established by this intuition, reason establishes,—and without any admixture of error. But if Bergsonian intuition were truly a special and indispensable faculty it would of absolute necessity have to denounce errors irrefutable by reason and reveal truths undemonstrable to reason! Now that is not the case and intelligence knows the true without any need of it. The philosopher who relies upon it as upon a true faculty of knowledge surrenders in reality to the divinations of his sensibility, to which the vicinity of intelligence can give a surprising acuity; he will henceforth attempt to think with images, he will be able to express himself only by sensible similitudes, he will be led by it into an imaginary world.

It is time to ask ourselves whether or not in the Bergsonian theory of the intellect and intuition the truth subsists. There is no doubt as to Bergson's intention; it is to attain truth that he philosophizes, and it is truth which gives to intuition its whole value:—*there is only one truth*[3] and this truth is

---

[1] It could also without any difficulty be shown directly: either, in fact, Bergsonian intuition is an operation of the entire soul acting by itself, which is impossible, for no created substance can act by itself, not being its action (cf. *Summa theol.,* I[a], q. 77, a. 1); or else it is the operation of a special faculty having as object the nature of things. But in that case the faculty of intuition becomes one with intelligence, since intellect has precisely as its object the nature of things and since the faculties are distinguished according to their objects.

[2] "How," asks Bergson, "could the moving object *be* in a point of its trajectory passage? It *passes through,* or in other terms, it *could be there.*" ("The Perception of Change," *Creative Mind,* p. 168.)

That is saying, very exactly, that it *is there in posse* and therefore that movement is divisible *in posse.* "Mobile autem infinitatem mediorum locorum non consumit, nisi per continuitatem motus: quia sicut loca media sunt infinita in potentia, ita et in motu continuo est accipere infinita quaedam in potentia. Si ergo motus non sit continuus, omnes partes motus erunt numeratae in actu. Si ergo mobile quodcumque moveatur motu non continuo, sequitur, quod vel non transeat omnia media, vel quod actu numeret media infinita, quod est impossibile." *Summa theol.,* I[a], q. 53, a. 2.

[3] *Creative Evolution,* p. 238.

speculatively knowable (although in an evanescent way). In this he is essentially to be distinguished from the pragmatists, although they refer to him as though he were their master. But does he in fact succeed in preserving the knowledge of the truth? At first glance it seems that intuition in its purity being inexpressible, and conceptual knowledge being entirely artificial everywhere but in mathematical physics, truth must necessarily escape us or at least take flight in a desert of silence. But Bergson on the contrary makes every effort to unite this intuition and this concept, which he has violently separated. "It is not enough to cut out, one must also sew up." He then establishes a sort of continuity of movement between intuition and logic, the latter being only the "relaxation" of the former. On the one hand, as we have already seen, dialectics has need of intuition in order to progress with certainty; on the other, intuition must be expressed and verified by dialectics. On the one hand the philosopher must assemble all the results of positive science before getting on with his act of intuition,[1] on the other, intuition, a vanishing thing if left to itself, can and must be expressed or rather suggested by representations that are more supple and fluid than ordinary concepts;[2] and thus intuition and conceptual knowledge are no longer opposed except in order to support one another. But is this accord legitimate? If intuition attains the absolute and if the concept is only a ready-made frame should we not be shocked to see this concept prove and verify this intuition? In reality, an intuition which needs a concept to be assured that it is not a hollow dream and a concept which has need of an intuition to assure itself that it is not an empty word can never verify one another. Each of these two halves of knowledge has its own peculiar principles. If none of these principles guarantee certainty and if there is no common evidence to act as final criterion, knowledge is forever uncertain, intuition and dialectics are two blind men leading one another.

The one, furthermore, inevitably leads thought to affirm that being comes before becoming, that all movement assumes a mobile, and every mobile a mover. The other discovers that action increases and creates itself as it advances, that "duration is continuous creation," that movement is self-sufficient, that it is posited by itself, that the same engenders the other, that movement has no need of mobile and consequently of mover,[3] in short, that reality follows a law quite contrary to the principles of identity, of sufficient reason, of causality, of substance, etc. Is there continuity between this intuition and this dialectic and can one go from one to the other by a simple relaxation?

[1] *Introduction to Metaphysics* (*Rev. de Mét. et de Mor.*, January 1903, p. 36); in *Creative Mind*, p. 217.

[2] *Ibid.*, *Creative Mind*, p. 198.

[3] Cf. "The Perception of Change," *Creative Mind*, p. 173; *Creative Evolution*, pp. 214, 240, 247–248, 301, 341–344.

No, there is a complete inversion. No sooner will the philosopher have left his intuition to enter upon dialectics than he will do exactly the opposite to what he did in intuition; no sooner will he leave his dialectics to plunge again into intuition, than he will do the exact opposite of what he was doing in dialectics. If intuition makes him take a step forward dialectics will make him take the same step backwards; with the best will in the world, with all the dilatations, distensions and approximations he likes, he will never advance. The method described by Bergson therefore remains imaginary and impossible to put into practice, unless we replace his intuition with true intellectual perception, which is in natural continuity with reasoning.

Let us nevertheless grant what Bergson asks. Let us grant that intuition can be continued in dialectics. It is a necessary postulate of the Bergsonian system; for as long as the philosopher has not yet succeeded in suggesting the truth to his auditors by means of a harp or an oboe he will have to express it or rather suggest it in words, and language is already dialectics. Under these conditions, what can be the relation of a proposition expressing a philosophical truth,—for example, "man is endowed with free will,"—to reality? When it merges with the inexpressible experience which gave it birth it will touch the absolute. But once one has left this experience behind one will go from intuition to the intellectual content of the proposition, or to the *concept;* and this concept will be wholly external, it will more or less symbolize intuition and consequently suggest it more or less well, but in itself it will never *express* it. Otherwise one would have to say that an intuition manifests itself in a concept and this would make of intuition an act of intelligence.

Let us add that the intellect is subject to becoming and evolution. Consequently, either the proposition corresponding to a truth of intuition, the notional formula, will itself change: the construction of concepts "man is endowed with free will" will become out-of-date, an act of assenting "so it is" can no longer bear upon it, that is to say that it will no longer be true, and that in order to correspond to the same intuition one will have to deny tomorrow what one had affirmed today; or else the proposition itself will not change any more than the intuition which brought it into being,—we shall continue to say "man is endowed with free will," but giving this proposition another intellectual content (as though the intellectual content of a proposition were not inseparable from it), in short, thinking something else than what we are enunciating. In both cases one will have torn truth from the mind; one will leave man with nothing but words.

It is truth itself which without wishing to we jeopardize when we declare that the intellect "has been formed by an uninterrupted progress along a line which ascends through the vertebrate series up to man,"[1] that it is "a lantern

---

[1] *Creative Evolution,* Introduction, p. ix.

glimmering in a tunnel,"[2] that it has been "fashioned" by "the evolution of life,"[3] that it is "relative to the needs of action."[4]

Truth

God is subsisting Truth. "Truth, in fact, is found in the intellect insofar as it seizes the thing as it is, and in things insofar as they have a being which can be adapted to the intellect. Now it is in God that this is found in the highest degree. For His being is not only in conformity with His act of intellection; it is that act itself. And His act of intellection is the measure and the cause of all other being and of each other act of intellection. And He is Himself His being and His act of intellection. In such a way that not only is the Truth in Him, but He is also the Truth itself, sovereign and primary."[5]—The truth is in the intellect before it is in things, that is why the truth of things depends on their relation to the divine Intellect, and consists in the fact that things are in conformity with their principle which is this Intellect. Eternally they are, by their reasons or their ideas, in that Intellect where all is life. And in the pure intelligences, to whom God communicates the knowledge of things before creating things, they exist by their intelligible similitudes, before existing in themselves. It is so much in their nature to be capable of being communicated to an intelligence that they receive being because they are first known of God and that they are in the minds of angels before having received being. This intelligibility of things is the imprint in them of the divine light, the imprint of the Archetypal Word. —But *our* intellect must be regulated on things. The truth of *our* intellect consists in the fact that it conforms to things. These, in their created being, are only potentially intelligible because of the matter in which their form is received; they therefore await, so to speak, a light which makes them luminous in act. It is the formative intellect (*intellectus agens*) which performs this function, for by virtue of it sense images are rendered capable of supplying intelligible notions through the act of abstraction. And now, what is this formative intellect, the intellectual light within us, if not a "participated likeness of the increate light, in which are contained the eternal reasons"?[1] *Signatum est super nos lumen vultus tui;* it is by the imprint of the divine light within us, by the imprint of the Illuminating Word, that all things are shown to us.

The primary cause of all truth, the corner-stone of all certainty is therefore He Who lightens every man that cometh into this world, He Who does not

[2] *Ibid.,* p. x.
[3] *Ibid.,* p. 29.
[4] *Ibid.,* p. 152.
[5] Saint Thomas, *Summa theol.,* I^a, q. 16, a. 5.
[1] *Ibid.,* I^a, q. 84, a. 5.

admit the *yea* and the *nay*, but in Whom all is *yea: Dei enim Filius Jesus Christus non fuit* EST *et* NON, *sed* EST *in illo fuit.**

The human soul is doubtless the last of the intellectual substances for it has to be united with a body to know things; it has as proportionate object only the natures immersed in the sensible. It knows the spiritual natures only by analogy; and our intellect, according to Aristotle's expression taken over by the "intellectualism" of the scholastics, is to the most luminous truths,— the glimpse of a tiny particle of which gives it so much joy,—what the eye of the owl is to the light of the sun. It is, however, ordered to being itself. From however low it may take off, it moves nevertheless from the first in the light, and only rests when it has "seized upon intelligible being":† and far from having a wholly external view of things, in the intact immateriality of its nature it becomes everything it knows: *anima fit quodammodo omnia.* We are not "walled in" as the descendants of Descartes claim,‡ we communicate on the contrary with the being of things, but with the intelligible being, by the intellect, in a light which comes from God. Whereas an "intuition" which would make us coincide with matter would lose us in the darkness, the intellect has a better grasp of truth, which is its own good, the farther it gets away from matter; and if grace is present to complete nature, this movement has its end only in heaven, in the beatific vision of increate light.

To err on the subject of the intellect, Saint Thomas tells us, is the most unfortunate of all errors;[1] and if it is true that Bergsonian philosophy is mistaken about the intellect, all the other errors we might blame it for will have their origin in that one.

It is not true that all "intellectualist" philosophy must abolish, as does radical mechanicism, the reality of time, of movement, of becoming, and all contingency in the world. What Bergson says in favour of his *duration* proves after all only the irreducible reality of movement, of becoming and of causal activity; but if his criticism is effective against mechanicism, how can it be effective against a doctrine which is based precisely on the irreducible reality of becoming, which sees in movement "whose essence," the scholastics said, "consists in a certain passing,"[2] the distinctive character of our world; which affirms that "whenever there is change, something real is born or perishes";[3]

---

* Saint Paul, II *Corinth.*, 1, 19. [Cf. Garrigou-Lagrange, *La première donnée de l'intelligence* (*Mélanges thomistes*, 1923, p. 216). In the order of invention, which is analytical and ascendant, the primary datum of intellect is being, apprehended in sensible things, and with it the principle of contradiction. But in the synthetic and descending order which assigns the supreme reasons, *in via judicii*, the fundamental truth is the *ego sum qui sum* of subsisting Being itself.]

† Cf. Rousselot, *L'Intellectualisme de saint Thomas.*

‡ A. Binet, *L'Ame et le corps*, p. 23.

[1] *De unitate intellectus*, in princ.: "Inter alios autem errores indecentior videtur esse error, quo circa intellectum erratur, per quem nati sumus devitatis erroribus cognoscere veritatem."

[2] Opusc. (apocryphal). *De Instantibus*, cap. 1.

[3] Kleutgen, *op. cit.*, III, 466.

and which gives created causes so real an activity that in its eyes the world is the scene of veritable substantial destructions and generations, by means of which bodies in mutual reaction cause another body to pass from non-being to being, by *educing* its form from the potentiality of matter? Malebranche, that strange Oratorian whose heart palpitated at the reading of a treatise by Descartes, was shocked at this last theory which, he thought, would confer upon creatures a creative virtue; that is false, for the substantial form is not a being, properly speaking, and the new substance, which alone is properly a being, is not produced from nothing, but from pre-existing matter.* This shows, nevertheless, how far the scholastics were from claiming that "everything is given," that "everything repeats itself," that "nothing new ever takes place in the world"; how opposed they were to any foolish dream of "universal mathematics." But far from abandoning reason because of this, they could rationally account for becoming and change because they made use of the principle of potency and act, discovered by Aristotle's genius. If this principle is abandoned, and if it is postulated that everything exists in act, human knowledge will always be powerless before nature; it will succeed only in mathematics, and philosophy will indefinitely repeat Democritus or Heraclitus.

Instead of distinguishing being in act and being in potency, the metaphysics of Bergson abandons being to the mechanists, as it had already handed over the intellect to them; and this is natural since being is the formal object of the intellect. It declares that "there are changes, . . . but change has no need of a support. There are movements, . . . but movement does not imply a mobile."[1] Change is self-sufficient, it is the thing itself.[2] Change is substance.[3] Such, in fact, is certainly the fundamental proposition of the doctrine. It is a pure contradiction,—or else the idea of being must also be a pseudo-idea! Thus one tears being away from reality as one had torn truth from intelligence, and destroys the very principle and the permanent object of all our knowledge,—one denies the intuition *par excellence*.

The initial error of the Bergsonian philosophy seems to consist in the socalled intuition of duration which introspection supposedly gives us; in reality, we do not know ourselves by our essence, but only by our acts and operations, and pure and simple psychological observation, artificially separated

* Saint Thomas, *Quaest. disp. de pot.*, q. 3, a. 8.—Like all movement, substantial transformation requires something mobile, a foundation which does not change. But this foundation, here, is not properly speaking a being, it is *prime matter*, an absolutely formless principle of receptivity, which never exists separately, which is not an *object* given in itself. In this sense only can one say with Bergson that all movement does not "presuppose necessarily invariable *objects* which move." ("The Perception of Change," p. 173.)

[1] "The Perception of Change," p. 173.
[2] *Ibid.*
[3] *Ibid.*, pp. 175, 183, 184. Cf. *infra*, pp. 175–178.

from intelligence, cannot procure the principle of metaphysics; the more or less continuous "stream of consciousness" revealed to us by inner sense is not at all our essence, it is only its "phenomenal" manifestation. As to time, it is certainly a flux, but we are not this flux, and Bergsonian "duration" unites on the faith of a sense experience which cannot reveal to us our substance two absolutely different things: the thing which endures, that is, which perseveres in being, and time, which measures that duration. As Descartes confused the substance of bodies with extension, so Bergson confuses it with time.

But there is another error of which we have already spoken: the one which consists in rejecting the intellect because of the faults that many commit in its name: that is to say, abandoning a principle in order to save a result. The service we owe to truth is, however, to keep principles, even to the last iota. If madmen misuse their intellect and if the world forgets the truth, the truth is still beautiful, the intelligence is still master, the Light which lightens every man that cometh into this world knows no dimming.

Bergson had a profound and vivid insight into the vanity of materialist or positivist rationalism and the way that so barren and proud a doctrine offends the beauty and richness of life. One can well believe that the desire for truth and the very instinct of his mind led him to desire above all an entirely different philosophy, a philosophy of the absolute and the real, of life and movement, of quality, of freedom; a metaphysics founded on experience; a truly disinterested philosophy free from the cares of practical application, despising nothing of what is, shaping its concepts to reality, and capable of the highest knowledge without, however, violating common sense. This philosophy exists, dark perhaps,[a] but more beautiful than tongue can tell; it is Thomistic philosophy. Bergson, it seems, did not know it, the French University being in the habit of skipping boldly on from the Alexandrines to Descartes, over the *shadows of the Middle Ages,* leaving those she trains,—she who knows everything,—in an inviolate ignorance of Thomistic doctrine.[1] Pursuing his solitary way, Bergson thought he had found in duration and intuition the foundations of the true philosophy, and it was in a philosophy of pure becoming that he logically ended.

(a) "I am black, but comely" . . . (*Cant.,* I, 5).

[1] Since these lines were written we have been able to note an important change in the mental habits of the University. Thanks to Etienne Gilson, to whose works I am glad to pay tribute here, it discovered, eight or nine years ago, mediaeval culture and philosophy; it will doubtless not be long in thinking that it alone can speak of them according to the proper method.

SECOND SECTION

CRITICAL EXAMINATION OF THE PHILOSOPHY OF BERGSON

Chapter Six

THE BERGSONIAN DOCTRINE

I.—HOW THE PHILOSOPHICAL PROBLEM MUST HAVE PRESENTED ITSELF FOR BERGSON

Bergson has the great merit of having for a long time struggled alone (alone in the French University) against the so-called positive materialism and against the Kantian relativism which were dividing the academic world between them, and I still remember the tone of reprobation with which one of our masters in the Sorbonne, now dead, condemned the "Judeo-Alexandrine mysticism" and, to put it bluntly, the *clericalism* of this admirer of Plotinus.

Others, taking an opposite view, thank him for having freed them from the heavy yoke of atheism, for having re-awakened their soul, and for having renewed the sources of life within them.[1] In fact, not only does his influence seem to have determined among many young people a movement of respect and sympathy for Christianity, but it is also the source of several returns or conversions to the true faith. And assuredly, those he has extricated from scientism, from Spencerism, from sociologism and other modern fetishisms, from the systematic negation and the dogmatic scepticism in which French youth has long been penned up, those he has pulled from that intellectual hell inhabited only by chaos, owe him, in all fairness, their profound gratitude.

Let us imagine a young thinker casting his eyes over the vast plains of what is called *modern culture,* especially on the fields made fertile by philosophy; the spectacle, it must be acknowledged, could not have been very encouraging twenty-five or thirty years ago,—not to mention the present. In the direction of metaphysics, a desert arid as one could wish, broken here and there by impenetrable bush; in the direction of natural philosophy, immense terrains too well-watered, on the contrary, bog-lands covered over by the residual waters of science, and annexed by the pioneers of progress.

[1] See for example the answer given by E. J. Lotte to the *Enquête* opened by the *Revue de la Jeunesse,* and reproduced in the *Bulletin des Professeurs catholiques de l'Université,* January 20, 1913.

Taine, Spencer, Darwin, Berthelot, Büchner, etc., were the masters. The whole effort of modern philosophy ended in mathematism or universal mechanicism and in that venerable mixture of materialism and scepticism called scientific or positive outlook. I say deliberately: the whole effort of modern philosophy, for the state of mind of which I speak, which would have made Descartes blush, nevertheless has its source in the Cartesian reform. It is the ultimate product of the "rationalist" method, that is, of the claim of reason to set itself up as the supreme ruler of truth—which leads, finally, to reducing all things to the notions we find within ourselves through the minimum of experimental contact with reality, that is, to mathematical and geometrical notions. Toward this state of mind also converged the Cartesian cosmology which explained the universe by extension and movement, and the sensualist systems of the eighteenth century, and again—indirectly—the marvellous progress of the sciences of matter from the time of Galileo, Newton and Lavoisier; and, last of all, the influence of Kant and Auguste Comte, whose conveniently agnostic conclusions alone were retained. Thus the absolute was unknowable, there was no other reality for us but the phenomenon, that is to say, appearance and accident; the superior had its whole being and its whole reason in the inferior from which it sprang spontaneously; everything happened as though God did not exist, man had no soul, free will was an illusion incompatible with scientific determinism, and the world was one day to be taken apart by scientists like a big mechanical toy.

Such ideas, if they had been formulated by a somewhat consistent metaphysics and expounded systematically, would have manifested their own weakness. What made them infinitely dangerous for intelligence was, on the contrary, their very philosophical poverty. Not resting upon any consciously-perceived metaphysical principle, not being connected with any definite doctrine, they thereby eluded refutation. Spread far and wide, diffused in everybody's mind, turning up on every street corner, they were finally considered the necessary product of civilization and regarded almost as being self-evident. What is more, they presented themselves as being at once the indispensable postulates and the brilliant conclusions of the sciences of nature; so that atheism and science had been successfully welded together, and materialism, generally despised in its systematic form by the very ones who helped to spread it, appeared, in spite of everything, as the only possible philosophy of positive science.

And now, what did philosophers—when they did not follow the trend—have to propose in defence of the intellect? Nothing but the constantly-repeated attempts of an *a priori* metaphysics more or less spiritualist and more or less pantheist, deprived of all communication with science, condemned ever since Descartes's *Cogito* and Kant's *Critique* vainly to seek its fulcrum (*point d'appui*) in the thinking ego, and to exhaust itself in the most painful and useless efforts to have the object coming out from the subject.

There are under such conditions grounds for believing that Bergson, before protesting against pseudo-scientific materialism, had probably first experienced the fascination of modern science and that *mechanistic intoxication* he once mentioned in speaking of Spencer. There is a rather curious indication of it in the fact that one of his early works is a text-book edition of the *De Natura Rerum*.[1] But my intention is not to attempt here to reconstruct the *history* of Bergson's thought; it is only to determine the chief *logical* articulations of his doctrine. From this point of view it seems that when he came to face it, the philosophical problem must have presented itself in the following manner: Are materialist mechanicism and agnostic relativism, which claim to annex the positive sciences, the last word of philosophy? And is it not possible to discover, equi-distant from materialism and rhetorical or *a priori* spiritualism, a philosophy which attains the absolute, the absolute truth, and which thus restores the great spiritualist theses, without however contradicting in any way the acquisitions of science, and keeping constant contact with experience?—These questions may seem elementary. But precisely because they are elementary, they are fundamental. And we are bound to confess that the philosophy issuing from Descartes and Kant is not capable of solving them satisfactorily.

II.—BERGSON'S SOLUTION OF THE PROBLEM

And so Bergson, to find the solution, digs down to the very first principles of human knowledge. His intention is to question everything, and if not to discover the secret, hitherto unknown to all, of the knowledge of the true and the false, at least to find a method of philosophizing that no one has as yet deliberately practised.—That method is *Intuition,* as opposed to *Analysis* or intellectual knowledge. It leads Bergson to proclaim as sole reality *Duration* or change, as opposed to being.

Analysis (or the exercise of reason)

Let us first give a few examples of *analysis* in the Bergsonian sense.

a) Let us consider two points separated by an interval of space; reason tells us that space is infinitely divisible; it follows, so it seems, that between these two points there is an infinity of other points; and the conclusion is that, supposing the first point in movement toward the second, it can never reach it as there will never be an end to its enumeration of the infinity of points that separate it from the second point. Thus it is that Achilles will never manage

---

[1] *Extraits de Lucrèce, précédés d'une étude sur la poésie, la philosophie, la physique, le texte et la langue de Lucrèce,* by Henri Bergson, former student at the École Normale Supérieure, professor 'agrégé' of philosophy at the lycée in Angers. Paris, Delagrave, 1884.

to overtake the tortoise, the space separating him from that peaceful animal diminishing constantly without ever becoming completely nil. According to Bergson, no philosopher has yet managed satisfactorily to refute Zeno of Elea on this point.

b) Now take a point determined by its relation to two co-ordinate axes. If this point changes place in the plane, the relations in question will vary, and from the mathematical point of view, it is this variation alone which defines the movement of the point.

The point moves, it goes from a position A to a position A′; this means simply that the abscissa *x* and the ordinate *y* acquire, say, a value twice as great.—If now, instead of supposing that the point in question moves from a position A toward a position A′, we suppose on the contrary, that it is the system of axes which is moving in the opposite direction over an equal space, the result will be absolutely the same, the abscissa *x* and the ordinate *y* will have acquired a value twice as great. The variation of the relations of the point to the two axes, that variation which defines the movement, will be absolutely identical in both cases. Hence the conclusion that movement is something entirely relative which is judged only by comparison, or again, to use Descartes's words, that the "transport" (that is to say, the movement) "is reciprocal,"[1] and that "all that is real in moving bodies, in virtue of which we say that they move, is also found in those touching them, although we consider them as being at rest";[2] in other words, there is in an object which changes place in relation to another, no reality independent of the mind permitting us to affirm that the one is moving and the other is at rest. That is the doctrine of the *relativity of movement.*

c) Let us go on now to another order of ideas. If we consider the will in its relation to motives, it seems to us that the will is attracted in opposite directions by motives of more or less great intensity acting upon it as forces on a mobile. From which it clearly follows, it seems, that free will is an illusion, the strongest motive necessarily pulling the will as the heaviest weight necessarily tips the scales.

d) In the same way, analysing our psychological life in the manner of David Hume and John Stuart Mill, and seeing in it only phenomena following one upon the other, one will declare that everything boils down, in us, to states of consciousness bound to one another by the laws of association, just as material atoms, for the natural philosophy of the close of the eighteenth century, were joined to one another by certain laws of attraction, which were only one particular case of the great law of universal attraction. That is the psychological doctrine of *associationism.*

[1] *Principes,* II, 29.
[2] *Ibid.,* II, 30.

These few examples, which are all paralogisms or sophisms, show us what, according to Bergson, is the process of knowledge he calls *analysis*. It is a vicious method which proceeds by false breaking up into parts, by false analysis; it is a bad way of reasoning, a very general and very frequent sophistic procedure.

But this sophistic procedure becomes, under Bergson's gaze, rational analysis in its essence, the universal procedure of intellectual knowledge, the sole method that intellect and reason left to themselves and functioning naturally use in the face of reality.[1] *Analysis,* otherwise known as the normal exercise of reason, consists then, according to him, in taking a certain number of external views of reality, which furnish us symbolic elements, signs convenient to manipulate, capable of *replacing* for us the real. Working next on these elements, we work on parts of our symbolic representation, not on parts of the real; placing these elements in juxtaposition, we give ourselves an artificially-composed image, we do not give ourselves reality; *analysis,* in other terms the normal exercise of reason, allows reality to escape as a net allows water to run out through its meshes. As the examples we have given show, it ends in theses which are logically established,—according to Bergson,—and convenient for language and scientific work, but quite erroneous as far as reality is concerned.

To take for reality the results of this analysis is the great illusion of philosophy. And let us note the following point, which is essential: this illusion, short of an effort against nature by which we violently set our knowledge up again by pushing the intellect out-of-doors, as Bergson says, this illusion is almost inevitable, since analysis is the *natural procedure* of the intellect. Left to itself intellect will inevitably lean toward the erroneous theses which are the result of analysis; thus it is that mechanicism, mathematism, and, to speak plainly, materialism is the natural bent of the human intellect: not of the intellect *when it lets itself go* (that we would grant), but of the intellect as such. Thus according to Bergson, in a discussion, any defender of free will, for example,— and it would be the same for any other metaphysical truth,—is condemned in advance, even though in the right, to be reduced to silence by his adversary.

Intellect

How does it happen that such a strange fatality is attached to the exercise of reason? It is because man is not made for knowing, because human intellect is not made for truth.[2] Man is made to fabricate: *homo faber,* Bergson tells us, and not *homo sapiens.* Intellect is a faculty directed toward practice. Now, as the practice of man consists essentially in acting upon inert matter

---

[1] Cf. *Introduction à la Métaphysique* (*Revue de Métaphysique et de Morale,* January 1903). [*Introduction to Metaphysics* in *Creative Mind.*]

[2] Cf. *Creative Evolution,* pp. 139–165.

and manipulating solids, the human intellect will be essentially geometric, it will transform everything it touches into immobile and artificially cut-out things, into solids juxtaposed in space; thus there will be innate adaptation between intellect and matter; when it is a question of doing geometry or even physics, and especially of handling blocks of stone and beams, or inventing instruments, "making tools to make tools," the intellect will be about its own business. But when it is a question of knowing the nature of things, and particularly the things of life, and above all the things of the soul, the intellect will manifest its radical incompetence; *fascinated by matter,* by space and by geometry, it will everywhere introduce artificial frameworks, posit inexistent problems, and insolently demand that its questions be answered by *yes* or *no*; in short, left to itself and to logic, it will lead infallibly to error.

The Concept

For Bergson this practical, pragmatic character of human knowledge is already discernible in external perception. But it appears to him pre-eminently in the concept, in the general idea, the favorite victim of the new philosophy. For Bergson, the abstract and general idea is not of a higher order or nature than the sensible image, it is even inferior to it, it is a diminution of it; it is only *this or that one of our concrete perceptions elaborated, whittled down, subtilized,*[2] arbitrarily chosen to represent the real and associated with a word. Thus the concept, being abstract in the above sense, allows everything essential in reality—reality which is above all original and individual, with the wealth of a thousand nuances—to escape. Always identical with itself, it immobilizes, it brutally solidifies reality, which it deprives of its life and its movement. Distinct from other concepts, it artificially cuts out and breaks up reality, the continuity of which it simply disregards. The concept is a wholly utilitarian sign corresponding to the various practical attitudes we need to take toward objects and to the various conveniences of language, but not at all to the nature of things. No matter how much we juxtapose, divide and arrange concepts, we shall no more succeed in expressing the irreducible, inexpressible and supple simplicity of the real than in expressing the living unity of the model by juxtaposing photographs taken from different points. It is not astonishing that in working solely with concepts linked together by reasoning, discursive understanding—when it is concerned with truth and not with making tools —should arrive at complete failure.

Intuition

Let us now put aside logic and reasoning and try to grasp the real, this time not by an idea and with the help of intellectual knowledge, but directly in itself, through a sort of living sympathy which makes us coincide with it, or

---

[2] "The Perception of Change," in *Creative Mind,* p. 157.

rather, to call things by their name, by a dilation[1] of perception and through an effort of our whole soul to transform us into the object, to 'play' it, to enter into it, as an actor plays a character and assumes it. And then, armed with this vehement desire to go beyond the intellect, let us return to the various examples we used in connection with analysis, but this time beginning with the last one.

First of all, is there any reality more intimate to us than ourselves?—Yes, doubtless, there is one; it is the divine reality, infinitely transcendent and distant from us in its nature, but absolutely immanent by its action, it is God present in our innermost depths by the immediate contact of His virtue, by His universal causality which gives us being and action, present also by His grace in those animated by the supernatural life. . . . But let us return to Bergsonian philosophy. This philosophy admits that we can, by a sufficient dilation of our intimate sense (self-consciousness), perceive immediately in its essentials that reality which is ourselves and make a *felt* contact with what traditional philosophy calls our substance. Going down thus into the very depths of our consciousness, we succeed, by an intense and even "painful"[2] effort, in grasping ourselves on the edge of the unconscious. What we seize there, with a knowledge lived and incommunicable, cannot be translated into either concepts or propositions. Only sensible metaphors can suggest to others what we have perceived, helping someone else to make the same metaphysical effort. It will then be said that the essence and basic reality of ourselves is a continual flux, a current, a river which is being constantly swelled by an incessantly-created *new,* a flowing of vital vibrations in a more or less hurried rhythm, a change always taking place without ever being accomplished, in short, what Bergsonian philosophy calls a duration, a concrete and living duration. This leaves us far from the phenomenalism and psychological atomism of English philosophy. But we are also far from the *substance* of traditional philosophy, a substance which, for Bergson as well as for Taine, is only an empty medium, an imaginary framework in which to put phenomena,—in a word, a scholastic entity.

Attacking by the same method the problem of free will, we shall grasp our action as the original expression, absolutely new at each instant and therefore unforeseeable, of "the uninterrupted change that each of us calls *me.*"[3] We then see that our motives, far from causing our action to be this or that, are themselves only what we make them, and we establish by the same token, human liberty, so it seems.

Finally, projecting ourselves into the interior of a body in motion, we grasp this moving as an irreducible reality—and what is more, Bergson says, as a

[1] *Ibid.,* p. 158.
[2] *Revue de Métaphysique et de Morale,* January 1903, p. 21.
[3] "The Perception of Change," *Creative Mind,* p. 172.

self-sufficient reality, which exists by itself,—knowing perfectly well through the most commonplace experience, feeling clearly that, if our position in space changes with relation to a goal, but at the same time we are running, are out-of-breath and perspiring, it is certainly we ourselves who are in motion, and not the goal; knowing perfectly well also, according to Bergson, feeling clearly that each of our steps is an *indivisible* act and that since, therefore, movement is not subject to the laws of the space underlying it, Achilles will have no metaphysical difficulty in overtaking the tortoise.

Judging Bergsonian intuition by these few examples, one might see in it simply what in psychology we call introspection, inner observation, swollen by the interpretations of a vigorous and subtle imagination, and regarded, thanks to the most surprising abdication of intellect and reason, as yielding to us, in its "immediate data" such as they are (that is to say, in the operations, accidents or phenomena upon which it bears directly and in the first place), the intimate nature or the substance of things,—a procedure which, if it were applied to the external senses, would consist in declaring, for example, that the substance of a tree or an animal is the coloured spot or image our eye gives us.*

But for Bergson, intuition is a simple and absolutely original act, *sui generis,* an experimental knowledge which projects us into the object and makes us coincide with reality in its very depth. This intuition, according to Bergson, is related to animal instinct much more than to reason, and it goes so far beyond intellect that it cannot be adequately expressed in a concept. Having a purely speculative end, whereas everything in us is ordered to practice, it demands of us an effort contrary to nature.[1] But the philosopher who consents thus to "do violence to" his mind,[2] to twist it back on itself,[3] and to leap suddenly in a sort of metaphysical ecstasy into the heart of the real, will be re-warded by the enjoyment of the truth and the possession of the absolu . Borne along by the real, he will pass halfway between scientific or pseudo-scientific materialism and classical spiritualism, which are like two eternally opposed and equally erroneous halves of that cursed conceptual *analysis,* which is incapable of grasping *duration.*

---

* Is it not also under the guise of "immediate data" that Bergson speaks, in the early chapters of *Matter and Memory*, of the corporal world as of a collection of *images*, objective at that? Without seeing that the real way of remaining faithful to *immediate data* is to say that in the operation or the phenomenon apprehended by the sense or by consciousness the intellect immediately perceives (that) the thing or the operating agent (exists): that is why substance is said to be *sensible by accident.*

[1] Cf. *Introduction à la Métaphysique,* pp. 19, 26, 27, and Bergson's courses at the Collège de France.

[2] *Ibid.,* p. 27. "The mind must do itself violence . . ."

[3] *Creative Evolution,* p. 237. "It needs that, turning back on itself and twisting on itself, the faculty of *seeing* should be made to be one with the act of *willing.*"

Duration

What, for the philosophy of Saint Thomas and for any sane metaphysics, is the real object of intellectual knowledge, what is it the aim of intelligence to attain and possess?—It is *being.* Intelligence is satisfied only when it has seized the constitutive being, the essence of what it wants to know.

Being is what is most common; that is, in all that we can know, to whatever class of objects we address ourselves, *being is there*; (but not being *in the same sense* for all things, for substance and accident, for God and the created, because the notion of being is, as we say, an *analogous* notion, like all "transcendental" notions). Being is what is simplest, that is, one cannot reduce being to any other reality; in short, it is the very goal and reason of knowledge. Can we have any other aim, when we seek to know, than to put our mind in conformity with the being of the object, otherwise expressed, to arrive at the *truth, adaequatio rei et intellectus?* I stoutly defy anyone to give, in any other way, to the word 'knowledge' the slightest intelligible meaning. That is why it can be said that the idea of being, the transcendental *par excellence,* is the objective light of all our knowledge. In this idea of being the intellect grasps intuitively, that is immediately and without discourse, the first principles of reason:—the principle of identity or of non-contradiction, which tells us that a being cannot, at the same time and in the same respect, be and not be;—the principle of sufficient reason, which tells us that all that is, has the means of being, i.e., has what is necessary and what suffices in order that it may be, and be what it is;—the principle of causality, which tells us that all that begins to be, or all that is of contingent existence, has a *cause*;—the principle of finality, which tells us that no agent would begin to act were it not determined to a certain end, and that all order presupposes an organizer;—the principle of substance which tells us that there is no change without a thing which changes, no reality which has its being or existence in something else without a reality whose concern it is to have being or existence in itself.

And now what is the object of Bergsonian *intuition,* and what does it give us as the essence and foundation of reality? It is precisely *duration.* This Duration, fully knowable to intuition alone, and inexpressible in conceptual terms, has nothing in common with mathematical time, with the time of the ideal world of physics, with measurable time, which in reality is only space, for the physicist, a person held in little esteem in Bergsonian philosophy, persists in confusing time with the straight line by which he pictures it graphically;—mathematical time is a symbol that is merely relative, external to the real, not biting into the stuff of things, so to speak. On the contrary, Bergsonian Duration is the very stuff of things: which does not signify that it is a *substance,* a *thing* which endures. Far be it from me to utter such an intellectualist interpretation! There are no things, there is only the *in the making.*

Duration, concrete and real time, is pure change, that is to say, change without anything which changes; it is an activity without substratum; a creation without thing created and without thing which creates; a flux, a flowing constantly adding to itself, swelling as it advances, without however being something which flows and swells. To endure is, therefore, to change, but without there being any substratum to this change, and without there being in this change states which succeed one another, without the past ceasing to exist, as is ordinarily believed, in order to give place to the present; on the contrary, the past is preserved of itself and remains, "becomes identical with the present and continuously creates with it [. . .] something absolutely new."*

In order to understand this metaphysical discovery of true Duration, it is evidently necessary to have recourse to the intuition which transcends intelligence. To give an intelligible gloss of Bergsonian formulas, to claim that everything is reduced to imagining a snow-ball rolling down hill, getting larger as it goes, then to deny both the snow and the ball and everything that is not pure rolling and enlarging, would be, certainly, one of those rank incomprehensions only too frequently found in intellectualists. No, things are more subtle and more difficult, at least in the beginning. Do violence to your reason by intuition, go back up the natural slope of the intellect, turn your mind about, to plunge it into the singular and the concrete; by a prolonged effort in which all your faculties, especially the imaginative faculties, collaborate in a concerted tension of your whole being, take contact, sympathize, identify yourself with movement. Once this operation of mental transformation is accomplished, the veil will suddenly be rent: intuition will have pushed intellect out of doors, and you will feel, you will perceive as on the wing: 1) that change is self-sufficient, that is to say that for a thing which is moved there is no need for a mover: "omne quod movetur *non* ab alio movetur"; 2) that in pure change there is change without a thing which changes, movement without a mobile; 3) that the real is only change, or in other words that change is substance.[1] And you can never afterwards understand another language, to such a degree is a certain intensity of philosophical effort capable of fixing the mind in an irreformable vision.

The three theses we have just enunciated are the most evident metaphysical result of the philosophy of intuition. One does not need long practice in ontology in order to realize that they ruin the first principles upon which rest all human knowledge and all human language; they are nothing but illusions due to the breaking up and the artificial reconstructions accomplished by reason. Henceforth, we must believe that by the very fact that a thing is, it becomes something else; and that what happens has no *cause*.[2]

* "The Perception of Change," *Creative Mind*, p. 185.
[1] *Ibid.*, pp. 173–176.
[2] Cf. *Creative Evolution*, p. 56. The principle that the same causes produce the same effects is,

For Bergsonian philosophy, Aristotle and Plato are the source of all the trouble. They based the knowledge of reality on intelligence and ideas and, as a result, could only neglect becoming and movement, reconstituted with great difficulty by means of the kaleidoscope and the cinematograph.[3] But beyond these philosophers, victims of concept and language, the source of the trouble is in the very nature of the human mind; for Aristotelian metaphysics is *the natural metaphysics of human intellect,* as Bergson, not without a great deal of irony, says;[4] and if such metaphysics is illusory, it is because we have within us from birth, as a natural heritage, a principle of radical illusion.

And now, if we return to the problem formulated at the beginning of this chapter, we shall see with what simplicity the metaphysical discoveries of Bergsonism allow its solution. To mechanicism and materialism we shall abandon the Intellect and Being, and we shall grant that the exercise of the intellect and the philosophy of being naturally lead to these doctrines. But at the same time we shall posit that the exercise of the intellect and the philosophy of being naturally lead to error in metaphysics, so that mechanicism and materialism will, by that very fact, be eliminated. Nevertheless (and this should satisfy science reconciled with philosophy), the intellect will find its place in the physico-mathematical study of matter,—but only there! Everywhere else, the intellect is a master of error. It is therefore from intuition that we shall ask the truth. The new philosophy, thus transcending the intellect, and living by intuitive sympathy the very genesis and essence of the real, that is to say Duration or change, will go beyond both materialism and classical spiritualism, will institute the true metaphysics which will be *integral experience,*[1] and will restore, by a thoroughly positive method, the great theses which traditional philosophy had divined, but had not been able to establish: the existence of God, and perhaps even a creating God, the existence of a soul distinct from the body and perhaps even its immortality, the liberty of man and perhaps even his distinction from the animals deprived of reason.

III. THE CONSEQUENCES OF THE BERGSONIAN SOLUTION

Such are the principles of the Bergsonian solution. Let us look briefly at their consequences.

A duration concentrated, stretched, tightened, intensified to the point of

---

Bergson explains, the principle of mechanistic error. But it does not occur to him to point out that this principle is only a *determination* of the principle of causality which, if it is inapplicable to free beings, necessarily applies to all others (without on that account involving mechanicism in any way). It is the principle of causality itself that Bergson thus condemns.

[3] *Creative Evolution,* pp. 299–328 (especially page 306).

[4] *Ibid.,* p. 326.

[1] *Introduction to Metaphysics, Creative Mind,* p. 237.

becoming a "living and consequently still moving eternity, in which our duration would find itself like vibrations in light, and which would be the concretion of all duration as materiality is its dispersion,"[1] in short, a *centre of gushing,* is what God could be in Bergson's eyes. From this living centre gush forth, then, the worlds which are like so many creative impulses. Our own world is a tired world, in it the creative gesture is falling back, weary, upon itself; this falling, this return, this relaxation, this abandon of creation is matter, which is like the shower of sparks falling from a rocket; but up through this reality unmade comes again a reality being made,—the *vital impulse,* a continuation of the original creative gesture, the impulse which produces life and the evolution of the living; this impulse, which contains within it, in the beginning, all the virtualities and all the energies distributed in the living species, and which is, above all, something psychic, something like consciousness, seeks to deploy, not that it is directed toward an end, but because it is pressed on by a blind impulsion, by a *vis a tergo* which hurls it forward. Attached—for no very well-known reason—to matter whose downward movement opposes its movement of ascension, it seeks to retard the fall of matter and succeeds for the length of time a living being endures; then it passes into another living thing which will wear itself out in its turn, and thus it goes from generation to generation.

Forced in its humble beginnings to make shift with matter, life, which has gradually opened out in the thousand divergent branches of the great organic tree, seeks above all to liberate consciousness, spontaneity, creative action. But at the price of how many sacrifices! It loses on one point what it gains on another; and finally, after having invented plants, insects and vertebrates, it finds itself drawn along by the weight of matter, a prisoner of the mechanisms it has itself set up. In a single living being, in man, it has succeeded in fabricating a machine—the human brain—which gives consciousness the necessary leisure to have an activity proper to it, and which permits it to produce free acts. Thus man differs fundamentally from the animals, because "the number of mechanisms that [his brain] can set up, and consequently the choice that it gives as to which among them shall be released, is unlimited."[2] Man is free because his action is not limited by a definite number of cerebral mechanisms but can, because of the indetermination of the human cerebral machine, surge up without hindrance from the depths of his consciousness. Finally, the energy of the vital impulse is so great that this impulse is capable, after having rushed from generation to generation, after having jumped from plant life to animality and to humanity, of "beating down every resistance and clearing many an obstacle, perhaps even death."[3]

[1] *Ibid.,* p. 221.
[2] *Creative Evolution,* p. 263.
[3] *Ibid.,* p. 271.

Still, if the vital impulse has by chance achieved such success in man it was not, if I dare borrow a word from Hindu evolutionism, without having passed through many avatars; it was at the price of an enormous number of riches that it was forced to sacrifice in the course of the slow production of the human being, and which it has only been able to place in other living things, and especially, alas, at the cost of true and pure knowledge of the real which would have had no chance of succeeding except on the side of *instinct,* which characterizes the insects. Man is therefore a privileged being, a privileged vertebrate, but as king of nature he is certainly an uncrowned king. Far from being at the summit of material creation, he is placed rather on the side, all askew; a success obtained by all manner of more or less happy ricochets. His intelligence, of which he is so proud, is only an instrument made for practice and fabricated by evolution, a "lantern glimmering in a tunnel."[1]

Bergson thoroughly explains the genesis of this lantern, for one of his intentions pursued in *Creative Evolution* is to show us the *genesis of the intellect* and the *genesis of matter.* Both result from one identical process, from an identical inversion or interruption of the creative effort of Duration, in such a way that things go toward *materiality* and we go toward *intellectuality* in virtue of the same tendency to extension, to the exteriorization of parts in relation to one another, to passivity, in virtue of the same fall. That is the explanation of this innate adaptation between intellect and matter which constitutes as we have seen earlier the main argument that Bergsonian philosophy puts up in opposition to the claims of mechanicism and materialism, and which shows both the impossibility of any intellectualist metaphysics and the legitimacy of mathematical physics.

We shall be content with this generalized sketch of the Bergsonian system. We can now foresee without difficulty the main lines of the criticism that we shall present of this system.

[1] *Ibid.,* p. x.

Chapter Seven

THE CRITIQUE OF INTELLECT

The most apparent characteristic of Bergson's philosophy, the label under which it reaches the public and the name by which it attracts so many sympathetic responses is *anti-intellectualism*. And, as a matter of fact, as we have already seen, the *critique of intellect* is at the very threshold of the temple of intuition. This criticism will be the subject of the present chapter, and in treating it we shall use the three principal divisions previously indicated: *analysis* or the normal exercise of reason; the concept; the very nature and the so-called genesis of the intellectual faculty.

I.—ANALYSIS

If we recall what was said in the previous chapter with regard to *analysis*, one essential remark forces itself on our attention: the Bergsonian doctrine of intellect is valid only if *analysis* naturally leads to error and, preferably, to an error of a mechanistic nature. Now, for Bergson, this *analysis* is only the exercise of logic and reason left to themselves, that is to say, not corrected at every instant by incessant appeals to intuition. Let us see therefore whether reason leads naturally to error, whether it is incapable of establishing the truth by its own forces; and to do so let us first go back to the *examples* we have already used. We shall find that on these different points philosophical *reason* has long recognized truth without it being at all necessary to plunge by intuition into the gulfs of the real, in order to grasp there, on the fringe of the unconscious, the fleeting absolute. And much more, we shall find that *intuition* has not been able to preserve from serious errors the answers it inspired Bergson to make.

a) Do we wish to defend against Zeno of Elea the reality of movement? The Aristotelian distinction between being in potency and being in act removes any difficulty. Mathematical space, like any continuum, is in potency divisible to infinity. It is not infinitely divided in act; so that, between two points, there is, if you wish, an infinity of points *in potency,* that is to say, if you undertake to divide the space which separates these two points, you can continue that operation without ever stopping; but there is not an infinity of points *in act,* that is, if you do not undertake the division just mentioned, but if, on the contrary, you go from one of these points to the other, you will not meet these divisions, these divisions in infinite multitude which you would expect all ready-made, as Zeno falsely supposed. No, as long as you do not make these divisions, or do not mark these points, there are no divisions, there are no points. Now Zeno's whole argumentation rests on the hypothesis that between two points there is an infinity of points in act and that thus the distance which separates these two points might indeed become smaller and smaller, but will never be nil. Once this hypothesis is recognized as false the whole argument breaks down: the point in motion has no need to pass through an infinity of intermediate points in order to reach the second point, for the very good reason that this infinity of intermediate points does not exist. Thus it is that our *reason* affirms, quite as well as our senses, that Achilles must overtake and pass the tortoise.

But how does Bergson answer Zeno of Elea? By declaring, in the name of intuition, that movement,—each of Achilles' steps for example,—*is indivisible*: "All real change is an indivisible change."[1] UNDIVIDED, doubtless, but INDIVISIBLE, no! Indivisible signifies: *that which cannot* be divided. Now movement CAN always be divided: could not Achilles, wherever he takes one step, take two or three or four, did he so desire? . . . Bergson answers: But then, that would not be the same step, it would not be the same act! Who denies it? Certainly, if an apple is divided into two halves, it is no longer the same apple. Does that prove that it was not divisible? For a philosopher to be able to say: "I *feel* it [our motion] *undivided* and must *declare* it *indivisible,*"[2] it is to be supposed that the use of intuition leads to a strangely imprecise use of words.

b) Shall we now deal with our second example, the philosophical theory of the "relativity" or better still the *reciprocity* of movement? There is no need to call upon intuition to recognize that this theory rests upon a confusion of philosophy with mathematics. Mathematics are quite within their right in defining movement as the simple variation of the relations of a point to two coordinate axes, and more generally, as the variation of the position of one point with relation to another, so that the word 'motion' has no mathematical significance outside of this purely relative variation, and one can, with as much truth, consider this point as in motion in relation to that point supposedly immobile, or inversely that point as in motion in relation to this point. Mathematics are within their right in proceeding thus because they are concerned only with *quantity,* disregarding *being* itself as well as efficient and final cause; so that what they call movement is not in short movement in its

---

[1] "The Perception of Change," in *Creative Mind,* p. 172.
[2] *Ibid.,* p. 168. The italics are mine.

reality but only movement in its consequences or its reaction, so to speak, on quantity; or, if you wish, the quantitative translation of movement. But philosophy, as far as it is concerned, studies things in their being and in their causes, in their reality. It is the pure real which is its proper object. It is therefore absurd for philosophy to accept from mathematics the definition of movement and to give up examining on its own account the nature of movement. Is it not evident, moreover, that movement, change, that is, the passing of a being to a new state, or a new being, should constitute, like being itself, an *"absolute"* reality, I mean a reality *independent of the mind?* This certainly does not hinder local movement from necessarily implying a variation in the spatial relations of the mobile to surrounding bodies.

c) Our third example dealt with the relations of the will and motives. We shall come back to this question in connection with the theory of free will. Let us note here simply that to say, in Bergson's sense, that our motives are only what we make them is but to say that our states of consciousness are our own, and all the more ours as they integrate themselves more with the original act by which our self is expressed; they are consequently nothing apart from us without the substance in which they have their being, and so, if one wishes to speak Bergson's language, they are only what our native constitution, and our individual history, and our actual dispositions, and the continual progress of our inner discourse *make them.* The scholastics insisted precisely on that continuity of the course of our representations, on this progress of deliberation, which the will has the power to suspend at any given moment, thus causing this or that one of our practical judgments, this or that one of our "motives," to be the *last* practical judgment, the *last* motive retained, the one which will be followed by action. But the question is to know whether the will is *free* when it thus intervenes! Yes, answers Saint Thomas, the will is free because man's will is made for the sovereign Good, for the universal and absolute good to which it tends necessarily and which *alone,* consequently, is capable of *determining* it; while all the goods which our intellect can present to us here below are only partial and finite goods incapable therefore—radically incapable,—of determining our will to this action rather than that; therefore the will must determine *itself;* and it is precisely this active and dominating indeterminacy of the will with respect to all created goods which is freedom.

But intuition did not show Bergson that. In the belief that he is establishing the free will of man, he is really only establishing our *spontaneity,* an attribute that we share with *all* living beings, and which in no way distinguishes us from animals deprived of reason.

d) And lastly, in our fourth example, it was a question of the associationist or phenomenalist theory, which claims to reduce all the life of the soul to phenomena of consciousness or to mental states, psychological atoms as it were, agglomerated to one another in more or less unstable groupings by virtue of the laws of association. Here again an exact analysis is sufficient to re-establish the truth, without it being necessary to have recourse to the soundings of intuition.

It is quite true that when we observe ourselves, going back over our acts by this privilege of perfect immanence, of return, of the seizure of self by self which is proper to spiritual activity, our consciousness perceives as its primary and direct object only, phenomena, or, to use more precise language, perceives as its primary and direct object only our operations, that is to say, accidents. But, by the very fact that it perceives the operation of the agent, the consciousness also perceives the agent that operates, and so it perceives *through acts,* but in an intuitive and spontaneous manner, at least *the existence* of our individual substance.

And reason, which affirms as one of its first principles that there are no accidents without substance, and the factual datum of our personal identity, which implies necessarily the substantiality of our being, demonstrate with evidence that we are something other than our operations, something other than phenomena strung together. Traditional metaphysics is here, as always, in full accord with common sense.

The cause of the error into which the associationists have fallen, as it is easy to see in David Hume for example, is precisely that they do not wish to use either the intellect or logic; but that they confine themselves, by the effect of a wholly artificial exclusivism, to what is shown by an inner observation *separated from the exercise, even the quite spontaneous exercise of the intellect;* excluding the intellect they reject not only what is proved by reason but also what is immediately perceived by the intellect, the "immediate data" of intellectual consciousness; they only believe what their intimate sense sees or touches immediately, that is, they carry over into psychology the materialistic blindness of those philosophers who, as Plato says, "embrace with their hands the stones and trees, and clutch at all such objects, maintaining that that alone exists which is accessible to the senses."[1]

But it is important to note that Bergson, while opposing the associationists, accepts the same false postulate as those philosophers; he also denies the intellect the knowledge of our basic reality, either the intuitive knowledge of the existence of our self, or the rational knowledge of its nature. Consequently, no matter how much he claims, contrary to the phenomenalists, that our essential reality is something quite different from associated states of consciousness, the fact remains that as he insists on knowing this reality only by *intuition,* by the inner sense suitably dilated, he absolutely denies it the substantiality which intelligence alone is capable of perceiving as such. More logical than the phenomenalists whose states of consciousness and psychic atoms are

[1] *Sophist,* 246 A.

pulverized substance, he totally excludes substance from our self—as really as it is possible to do while continuing to think and speak,—and replaces it by change without anything that changes; then substance and accidents, thing in itself and phenomena disappear together; nothing remains but a nothing which changes.

I hope that these rather long but necessary explanations have made it clearly understood that the intellect is capable of establishing the theses of the *philosophia perennis* without recourse to Bergsonian intuition, and even with much more solidity and purity than that disappointing intuition; it will have been seen whether it is true that philosophical analysis and the normal exercise of reason infallibly end in the negation of movement, of liberty, of personality, and in general, in mechanistic or materialist error. *This argument, in fact, is a veritable experimental refutation of the Bergsonian theory of the intellect and analysis.*

Moreover, widening the question a little, let us admit that one must be singularly forgetful of the history of human thought, or must strangely overestimate the sorry brilliance of modern materialism, to claim that the "natural metaphysics of the human intellect" is characterized by the incomprehension of life and movement,[1] that it is fascinated by the contemplation of inert matter,[2] and that it tends of itself to a geometric and materialist conception of reality, to a sort of universal mathematics. Is not the philosophy of Aristotle and Saint Thomas, as well as the philosophy of being, a philosophy of life, of movement, of becoming, so much so that the doctrine of potency and act which dominates the whole of it has sprung from the intellectual apprehension of movement; so much so that this philosophy has been blamed for being inspired too much by concepts taken from the things of life, and for giving too large a place to the *spontaneous* and the effective production of the *new* in the universe; so much so that its most profound analyses deal with change, in its eyes the essential characteristic of our world, and that it presents us all created things in their tendency toward their final end, as an immensely varied impulse,—but an ordered, measured impulse, worthy of creative Intelligence,—toward the ineffable source of every good and perfect gift?

Bergson, in short, has fallen into the trap prepared by the materialist sciolists. By dint of crying out, through the laboratories' din, or from the bosom of a superabundant and redoubtable bibliography: we are the science! we are the intellect! they have succeeded in making people believe that in fact they were the modern result, that is to say, the ultimate and definitive result of human reason. Bergson has then confused an accidentally mutilated and blinded intellect with the beautiful and precious intelligence that God gave man in order to make him in His image; he has confused a *wrong use* of analysis—

[1] Cf. *Creative Evolution*, pp. 155, 165.
[2] *Ibid.*, p. 161.

the examples we have presented give ample evidence of this—with the essence of analysis, with the natural exercise of reason. So that to restore truth it would be necessary to reduce his theory of analysis to the following thesis: a certain way of using reason, namely the mechanical exercise of reasoning without the light of intelligence, without fidelity to first principles, without the inner and living tendency toward the possession of the real, that abnormal and vicious way of using reason which brings all things down to the measure of pre-established notional mechanisms, is a general cause of error, and especially the general cause of modern materialist error. But by thus reducing the Bergsonian thesis to a very just but very simple methodological remark, we deprive it of much of its metaphysical originality . . .

This observation, let it be noted, puts us in possession of a sort of key, if I may say so, which can render appreciable service to persons eager to indulge in the exegesis of Bergsonism: I mean, one will most often find in the works of Bergsonians a uniform critical procedure which consists in pointing out first either the unfortunate manner in which many people make use of an instrument, or the difficulty its use involves, and next in declaring that this instrument is not worth anything, or that it has some other destination than the one for which it is made.

It is this procedure—as we have just seen—which is at the bottom of the Bergsonian critique of reason.

Let us now recall the description Bergson gives of what he calls *analysis*, that is, of the normal exercise of reason.[1] Is it true that reason, when it analyzes a thing in order to discover its constitutive elements, only gives us, in the name of elements or principles, external views of that thing, photographs taken from outside, symbols juxtaposed, etc.? Not at all. A *wrongly conducted* analysis supplies false elements, *inexistent* elements, and consequently ends in an *erroneous* notion of the object; that is true. But Bergson tells us that *all* analysis carried out by reason, even well-conducted, can only give us views taken from without, elements *exterior* to the real, elements or parts of our representation, not parts of the real. It seems that in this one is the victim of the imagination, consequently of space. No doubt photographic negatives are exterior to the object photographed. But what does this metaphor signify? Does it mean that in us ideas, the intellectual determinations by which we know the elements of a thing, are "exterior" to the thing analyzed, and of another order? Certainly the idea, which makes something known, is of another order than the thing known, it is not a part or an element of that thing; we have no difficulty in granting that. But that is not what the Bergsonian metaphor claims to demonstrate: it is a matter of making us believe that *in themselves* the elements to which analysis leads and which are known by our

---

[1] "Introduction to Metaphysics," *Creative Mind*, pp. 187–218. Cf. *Creative Evolution*, pp. 299–307.

ideas are of another order than the thing analyzed, "exterior" to it. Here the photographic negatives are no longer of use, for it is a question not of the photography, but of what is photographed. Is the Parthenon exterior to Athens, not a part of Athens but only a "symbolic fragment," because a photographic image of the Parthenon which we look at in Paris, for example, is exterior to Athens? Because the idea is "exterior" to the object, is the element of the object known by this idea also "exterior" to the object?

In Bergson's eyes, to recognize in a whole, by analysis, distinct parts or elements or principles (physical or metaphysical), is to claim that the whole does not exist as such, and that the being of the whole is nothing but the being of *isolated* parts "in juxtaposition" or joined together. This latter way of looking at it is not analysis at all, but a pure absurdity,—only too frequent, moreover,—for if the parts exist as isolated parts, *are* in fact isolated, they cannot at the same time be really joined together, concur in the unity of the whole. To the extent that the whole has unity, to that extent it has being *as a whole:* not only is there more in water than in hydrogen and oxygen taken separately (and ideally joined), but there is more in a society of fifty men than in fifty isolated individuals (and ideally joined), and there is more in a city of five hundred houses than in five hundred houses isolated (and ideally joined). There is something in *six* other than what is in *three and three.* Bergson's critique tells against the absurd metaphysics which denies either the *unity* of substance or of essence of *essential wholes,* or the *reality* of the relations between distinct substances forming an *accidental whole;* it does not in any way tell against analysis itself.

II.—THE CONCEPT

The accusations brought against the concept will also have to be dropped.[1] It is just as sensible to accuse the concept of immobilizing the real because itself does not change, as to claim that the concept 'quadruped,' for example, alters and deforms reality because it has not, itself, four feet. Doubtless the concept of change does not itself change; but it is not meant to change! For precisely if it set about changing it would then cease to correspond to reality. The error into which Bergson's philosophy falls here is a very old error, which made the early Greek philosophers, Empedocles for example, believe that the soul must be *materially* all that it knows, fire to know fire, earth to know earth, etc.[2] We know, in fact, that the soul becomes what it knows: *but while keeping its nature;* and what makes knowledge, is exactly the fact that the object known is in the subject knowing according to the mode of the sub-

---

[1] "Introduction to Metaphysics," *Creative Mind,* pp. 195–199; 208–209. *Creative Evolution,* pp. 151–163, 314–330. *Matter and Memory,* pp. 202–212; and the (unpublished) courses given by Bergson at the Collège de France in 1902–1904.

[2] Aristotle, *De Anima,* I, 2. 404 *b* 9–15. Sextus math., I, 303.

ject knowing, that is, for intellectual knowledge, according to the immateriality of the intellect.

The same observation should be made for the so-called *breaking up* imputed to the concept, whose essential vice is said to be not only that of immobilizing but also of cutting up the real into artificially-distinct things. Scholastic philosophy takes care not to confuse the mode by which *we know* an object with the mode in which the object known *is,* and it establishes that we can know in a composite way and by means of a certain multiplicity of concepts, a reality which is, in itself, simple. In this case our intellect, while it has a composite knowledge, does not tell us *that* the object known[1] is itself composite; quite the contrary, it tells us that the object known is simple. Is there a more famous application of this doctrine than the complex procedure by which we raise ourselves to the knowledge of God, the supremely One?

It is true that the accusations made against the concept can be understood in an entirely different way. Conceptual knowledge will no longer be accused of being composite—as to its mode of being in us—when it bears upon a simple reality; it will now be accused of telling us *that there are* in the world distinct things and *that* the universe is composite, that a stone is not a man or a fruit, that substance is not accident, that will is not intellect, that grace is not nature, and to borrow an example from Bergson, that there is a real distinction between "a glass of water, the water, the sugar and the process of the sugar's dissolving in the water."[2] In the same way intellectual knowledge will no longer be accused of having a concept of movement which itself does not move; it will now be reproached for telling us *that* all is not movement in the world and *that* movement presupposes a subject which, as such, does not change, and *that* even for mutable things there are immutable relations: that, for example, if Socrates grows old he still nevertheless, remains Socrates, and that if Socrates is now seated, now standing up, it remains immutably true nevertheless that when Socrates is seated he does not change place. Such reproaches, one can easily see, would lead a philosophy consistent with itself to a complete skepticism,—since they call into doubt things that we perceive with *evidence,* and make all knowledge impossible,—and to a sheer monism, since they suppose that all things are only one and the same essential reality and a same becoming.

And now why does the concept thus break up and immobilize the real? Because, says Bergson, it only reflects, so to speak, the practical attitudes it suits us to take with regard to objects, because it is, for us, a signal of action much more than a means of knowledge. As though our practical attitudes were not relatively very restricted in number, while the things known by

---

[1] Cf. Saint Thomas, *Summa theol.,* Iᵃ, q. 13, a. 12, *ad* 3.
[2] Cf. *Creative Evolution,* pp. 10, 339–340. Cf. pp. 213–217.

our concepts are infinite in number! As though, above all, our practical attitudes were not determined *first* by the *knowledge* of things, and as though our action could succeed other than by being based upon the *truth* first grasped by intelligence!

At the base of the Bergsonian critique of the concept there is simply a radical *nominalism* and *empiricism*. For Bergsonian philosophy the idea or the concept is nothing more than an imaginative schema, wavering continually between pure recollection and the "word pronounced," or than one of our sensible perceptions, impoverished, thinned down, drained of colour as much as possible, set apart for a practical use and attached to a name.[1] There is, therefore, no difference of *order* or *nature* between intellectual knowledge and sensible knowledge, between the idea and the sensation or image, and consequently our entire knowledge derives from sensibility alone, from the faculty of feeling and imagining. Here we have a further general remark to use in the exposition of Bergsonism. Bergsonism regularly confuses imagination and thought. As a result, and in the first place, when it criticizes the intelligence it is really addressing imagination taken as intelligence. Thus it is that it accuses thought of seeing all things in space, which applies only to imagination, whose incessant activity moreover always underlies the work of the intellect; thus it is that it imagines that what we call substance is only an empty framework, a rigid support, an inert medium in which we place accidents like cubes in a box; thus it is that it mistakes the natural divisions which thought recognizes in being, for a so-called artificial breaking up effected in the sensible continuum, in this uninterrupted flux of sensations in which physical reality consists according to the Bergsonians, and which for them is the occasion of such bitter regret when they think that before being unhappy philosophers waving in their tunnel the lantern of the intellect they enjoyed, unfortunately without being aware of it, the pure perception of the real,—in that very infancy when their reason, with its carving propensity, had not yet awakened. But alas, one cannot always remain an infant at the breast, or even constantly keep in one's heart those precious impressions experienced, as Le Roy says, "in a wild race at high speed," when one abandons oneself "without looking ahead to the strange charm of change, to the delicious intoxication of becoming."[2]

But in the second place, when Bergsonism claims to find a means of knowing that is superior to intelligence, or to what it takes to be intelligence and which is only imagination, it can only address itself again to sensibility and imagination which it then seeks to extend, to swell, to dilate to the very es-

---

[1] Cf. *The Perception of Change, Creative Mind*, p. 172; *Matter and Memory*, pp. 206–211. See also below, Chap. V.

[2] *Revue de Métaphysique et de Morale*, 1899, p. 413.

sence of things, and which thus denatured can lead it only to the great vanity of pure change.

Let us conclude that we shall have to give up the Bergsonian criticism of the concept, as well as the Bergsonian theory of analysis, give up the idea that in the formation of concepts, in what is called the first operation of the mind, the intellect deceives us.

III.—INTELLECT

We come now to our last point, to the genesis of intellect as described in *Creative Evolution*.

It is indeed evident that the hypothetical reconstruction of the *history* of a thing is based upon some *knowledge* of the nature of the thing in question: thus it is that the two-fold genesis, the two-fold Bergsonian history of intellect and matter rests entirely on a certain theory, on a certain critique of the *present nature* of the concept and of reason. If this critique is supposed to be *erroneous and ruinous,* then the genesis in question is nothing more than a gratuitous hypothesis. And we have just seen what we have to think of this critique.

One might, moreover, ask oneself what *is* a faculty of knowledge adapted to our practice and gradually made by evolution for the needs of the living thing. It is conceivable, if one is put to it, that an organ, a "thing" which subsists in a living being, should be thus determined. But to know is not to be a thing, to have this or that constitution; it is to assimilate the form of something else: and the intellect being a faculty of knowledge, can be understood only in a *relative* way, by relation to some *object* known. In saying that it is adapted to our practice and gradually made by evolution, we attribute to it a certain intrinsic constitution as to an organ, but at the same time we deprive it of its proper object, of the object without which it remains completely unintelligible. To know—what? If the intellect were like a hand, for example, which has a certain constitution in order to be able to effectuate a certain action, the Bergsonian thesis would afford a meaning; but the intellect does not manipulate things, it does not exert this or that action upon things. It knows them; that is to say, it must,—in order to *become* them,—be determined by them. And so, properly speaking, the Bergsonian thesis does not afford any meaning, because the only thing which can determine the intellect is being; the only thing which renders intelligence intelligible, the thing for which it is made, is truth. That being the case, the intellect has not been able to adapt itself to our practice, it can adapt itself only to being,—nor can it have been made by evolution for the needs of the living thing, it can only have been made by the author of being, and for truth.

One might also be surprised at the way in which Bergson understands human practice. It consists, for him, in manipulating solids.[1] In connection with this theory, Le Roy invokes the cave-man[2]; and in fact, a doctrine of this sort would seem made to fit those delightful text-book pictures in which one sees prehistoric men fashioning their instruments, or moving tree-trunks, or fighting wild oxen, in short, manipulating all sorts of more or less cumbersome solids. A strange conception of man and his operation, that is, of his ultimate perfection! *Fear God and keep His commandments: this is the whole of man,*[3] says the Preacher. This indeed is a point of view from which human practice appears under a very different light. It would be useless to seek in such a practice all that Bergson imputes to it: solids, geometry, kaleidoscope, the cinematograph and the rest; but one can readily understand that the knowledge of truth is its necessary condition.

As to the way in which Bergson presents the genesis of intellect and the genesis of matter, as to that two-fold progression and simultaneous fall by which things have gone in the direction of materiality, while we were headed toward intellectuality,[4] it seems to assume the following philosophical operations: substitute for the idea of corporal substance the idea of geometric extension; for the idea of geometric extension, the idea of multiplicity; for the idea of multiplicity, the image of a scattering. In like manner substitute for the idea of intellect the idea of reasoning; for the idea of reasoning the idea of a multiplicity of concepts; for the idea of this multiplicity, the image of a scattering. Put yourself next in a state of intellectual and moral concentration as intense as possible, and then pass progressively, by a skilful exercising of the imagination, to the state of mental dissolution of the above-mentioned imprudent runner and metaphysician so dear to Mr. Le Roy. You will thus have passed from concentrated Duration to scattered Duration; you will thus have lived over again, by means of a truly positive experiment, by a truly realistic philosophical procedure, the genesis of the intellect and the genesis of matter. . . .

Has Bergson's aim, the reconciliation of metaphysics with physics at the expense of the intellect, at least been achieved? The intellect, he tells us, which deforms the real everywhere else, gives us the truth in physics; there, as it were, it attains the absolute.[5] But why does the intellect thus succeed in the knowledge of matter? Because, Bergson says, matter, that relaxation, that falling-back of the vital impulse, is *ballasted with geometry;* so that no matter what may be the geometric forms it cuts out of matter, no matter what the

---

[1] Cf. *Creative Evolution*, pp. 137–139, 153–154.

[2] Cf. Édouard Le Roy, *Une philosophie nouvelle, Henri Bergson*, p. 17.

[3] *Eccl.*, XII, 13.

[4] Cf. *Creative Evolution*, pp. 199–202, 205–210.

[5] Considering at least in physics "only its general form, and not the detail of its realization." Cf. *Creative Evolution*, pp. 198, 206, 218, 230.

laws and mathematical relations it discerns in it, it will always succeed: it only completes the tendency toward homogeneity which constitutes the characteristic and the whole reality of matter. *"No one of the particular laws of the physical world taken separately has objective reality [. . .] And yet there is an approximately mathematical order immanent in matter [. . .] We can take it by any end and manipulate it in any way, it will always fall back into some one of our mathematical frames because it is ballasted with geometry."** It is obvious that Bergson considers, both in geometry and in mathematical physics, only the material element, extension, homogeneity, the possibility of being numbered; he leaves to one side the formal element, the geometric essences as well as the definite laws of physics. But one may doubt whether this conception of physics, where everything except the possibility of superimposing mathematics on nature is pure convention, is calculated to please the physicists; and in it the intellect has a very disconcerting way of attaining the absolute! For Bergsonism, the fragmented world of physics can be simply an ideal world, since all that is real in the material world, in Bergson's eyes, is universal *interaction.*† How then is it possible in conceiving that kind of a world, that fragmented world, for the intellect to attain truth, the absolute? I can see only one solution: this is to say that in fact, apart from this movement of descent and of relaxation which is real, objective, and which constitutes, in *Creative Evolution,* the genesis of matter, the material world has no objective reality at all and is only an ideal world. This time it is doubtful whether such a solution, in which are curiously mingled both realism and idealism, is calculated to please the metaphysicians.

IV

The Bergsonian theory of the intellect consists, in the last analysis, in declaring that the understanding deceives us in the formation of concepts, that reason deceives us in the analyses it makes of reality, that the intellect is not made for truth; that intellectual knowledge is a purely "practical" and "verbal" knowledge.[1]

Bergsonism *therefore snatches the truth from the intellect,* but only to try to give it to intuition as a present, as we shall see in the next chapter.

It is interesting to observe that the spiritualist disciples of Bergson often do not dare to formulate in all its strictness this critique of the intellect upon which all their philosophy rests.[2] It would perhaps be unfair, besides, to ask

* *Creative Evolution,* pp. 218, 220.
† *Ibid.,* pp. 11, 188.
[1] *Ibid.,* p. 307.
[2] For example, Lubac, in his book *La Valeur du Spiritualisme,* Paris, Grasset, 1912.

philosophers who despise reason and logic to follow their thought through to the very end. In any case, they sometimes hesitate to proclaim aloud the first principle of Bergsonism, namely the radical inaptitude of the intellect for the truth, and they strive to reconcile, at least in appearance, Bergsonian intuition with reason, pure becoming with common sense. As though there was a mean between the true and the false; as though intellectual knowledge could be "verbal," artificial, external to the real, and at the same time force itself upon us with evidence and claim to possess itself of what is, without being false and mendacious.

If the intellect breaks up, immobilizes, mechanizes reality, if it distorts things to meet the needs of practice and language, then it is deceitful by nature. It may be that reason errs in this case or that, although by essence it is suited to truth and made for it. It cannot be that the intellect as such, in its natural relation with the object, is by essence both true and false, both suited and unsuited to truth; and as its object is not this or that thing in particular but being itself, it cannot by nature be true in one domain (that of matter, for example) and false in another (that of life and duration): either it is made for telling what is, and it is purely and simply veridical; or it is not made for telling what is, and it is purely and simply false. There is no middle course.

But we have here, note well, another key to Bergsonism: Bergsonism refuses in fact, as much as that is possible for it to do, to choose between the *yes* and the *no,* or rather it seeks to keep simultaneously both the *yes* and the *no,* a *yes* all the more apparent as the *no* is more real, and thereby it puzzles many minds.

It is thus that there are, hidden in the very heart of Bergsonian intuition, rational operations without which the most Bergsonian philosopher could not even begin to philosophize. And it is thus, on the other hand, that there is in the heart of the most affirmative Bergsonian theses, a certain hidden negation which subtly destroys them from within. Most often, moreover, the philosophy of Bergson projects itself from the *yes* to the *no* and from the *no* to the *yes* by a shuttling movement so agile and so quick, that one might think, to look at things from a distance, that it had accomplished the masterpiece of constituting with both of them a new intelligible essence.

But there is no escaping the *yes* and the *no.* And Bergsonism tries to revoke—under the charge of fragmentation—the true divisions of being, operated by the intellect—only to create immediately, in the very heart of the real, schism and contradiction. It does not wish to recognize distinct *things* or *essences;* but it proceeds—which is much more serious—by "mis-oppositions" of *values.* And here is a final remark on the general spirit of Bergsonian philosophy. The general method of Bergsonism consists in dividing the real into two metaphysical portions, one naturally good, the other naturally bad. We recognize the method proper to *manicheism,* by which, as Saint Thomas says,[1] fire will be declared bad by nature, because, for example, it burned the house of some poor man.

Thus it is that Bergsonism opposes—as sharply, or almost as sharply as good and evil—duration and space, the intensive and the extensive, the spontaneous and the mechanical, change and being. It is above all in this way that it cuts our faculty of knowing in two, putting on one side intuition with truth, on the other, reasoning with error. Bergsonism rends the living unity of the intellect; it deprives it of its genuine nature, its immateriality; and of its genuine operation, the perception of being; and of its genuine light, that participation in the increate Light by which it enjoys an irreducible and vital activity; and finally of its primordial intuition, the intellectual intuition of the first principles of reason.

Bergsonism in the last analysis confuses thought with the material expression of thought, with language; and language itself, the word, which is what is most noble among material things, since it is matter putting on the immaterial and becoming one with it; this living word it confuses with the letter congealed in its materiality, or rather with I know not what automatic and passive repetition of practical signals and commonplaces: so that the intellect and logic are nothing more than a sort of blind mechanism "having as their essential function that of binding like to like."[2]

After having thus treated Intelligence as the Maenads treated Orpheus, it does not take much to despise it and abandon it to matter.

As for us, we know that intelligence is what, as they say, makes our specific difference, what makes us *men;* and that it is by the intellect that we possess our good, the *truth.* In it therefore we defend both our very nature, our humanity, and our beatitude, the joy of the truth.

That is what Christian philosophy proclaims. That is why there is no conciliation possible between Christian philosophy and any thought set up against the intellect.

[1] *Summa theol.,* I^a, q. 49, a. 3.
[2] *Creative Evolution,* p. 200.

Chapter Eight

INTUITION AND DURATION

The whole Bergsonian doctrine rests, in fact, as we have just seen, on a radical criticism of the intellectual faculty. Bergsonism must therefore be considered as an anti-intellectualist philosophy; it denies the intellect its privilege of being the faculty of the true.

But Bergson does not on that account abandon the ambition of attaining and possessing the truth, that ambition without which a philosopher is not a philosopher, a man is not a man. Far from it! Even Bergson is not a *pragmatist;* this intellect he seems to repudiate is too alive in him for him to claim to measure truth by its practical working. Who knows even if the anti-intellectualism of his doctrine does not interfere with some of his most intimate aspirations? And certainly, if he consented to consider what he calls *intellectuality,* that so-called intellectuality closely related to *materiality,* not as the intellect and reason, but as the blind exercise of reasoning WITHOUT INTELLIGENCE, on that condition his doctrine could doubtless be reconciled with Christian philosophy: because then he would have to abandon his theory of analysis, of the concept and of the genesis of intellect, and accept the only true and legitimate philosophical intuition, *intellectual perception.* But, in that case, would there be anything left to conciliate? Bergsonian metaphysics would have surrendered its basic and distinctive principles.

Aristotle said of Anaxagoras that he appeared in the midst of the other pre-Socratic philosophers like a fasting man in the midst of drunken and delirious revellers, because of those men who considered only the material cause, he alone had recognized the necessity of the νοῦς, of Intelligence. Bergson does not proclaim this primordial necessity, this necessary primacy of Intelligence, but by the very fact that he loves and desires truth and that he affirms the value and dignity of the purely speculative effort ordered to attain it, by the very fact that he desires to enter into possession of the absolute, to attach himself to transcendent realities, he pays homage in fact, in spite of his doctrine, to the light of the intellect, which is there, whatever one does, as soon as it is a question of truth and the absolute.

And thus, at the banquet of contemporary philosophy, in the midst of the Kantians and the neo-Kantians, of the Idealists, the Positivists, the Scientists, the Subjectivists, the Relativists, the Solipsists, the philosophers of Totem and Taboo, he appears really as a man fasting among revellers in their cups.

That is what explains the incontestable influence and renown of his philosophy. That is also what creates the inner conflict and anguish Bergsonian philosophy bears along with it. There we have a philosophy which commits us,—and that is its honour,—to the conquest of truth, of the absolute. But it immediately side-tracks us,—and that is its sin,—into anti-intellectualism, it turns us aside from the intellect, from our proper means of attaining the truth and the absolute. And thus, because it is strictly impossible to escape the principles one has first adopted, it leads us astray among phantoms—far from what we love,—and in the very name of what we love.

I.—INTUITION ACCORDING TO BERGSON

Bergsonian intuition is characterized essentially by its opposition to intellectual knowledge.

Intellectual knowledge is abstract, universal, and it uses reasoning or discourse. The intuitive knowledge required by Bergsonism will be experimental, singular,—excluding, at least in what constitutes it essentially,—reasoning and discourse. Intuition, Bergson tells us,[1] transcends intellect and reason, it is a sympathy of all our being with the real, by which we communicate fully and absolutely with it, although in a fleeting and, so to speak, vanishing manner. Maintained on the fringe of the unconscious at the cost of an effort contrary to our nature and sometimes painful, in which "the faculty of *seeing* twisted back upon itself [. . .] [becomes] one with the act of *willing*,"[2] condensing in a single marvellously simple perceptive act all that nebulosity of instinct and vegetative forces which envelops the human mind, it makes us vibrate with the reality in its innermost depths, it transports us at once to the heart of the real. And the metaphysics which rests upon it will be *integral experience.*[3]

Bergson disclaims any desire to introduce, with this admirable intuition, a novelty into the world. Although intuition goes against the grain of our essentially practical nature, all men, according to him, use it more or less, even and especially the great philosophers, but in so fleeting and so spontaneous a

[1] Cf. *Introduction à la Métaphysique* (*Revue de métaph. et de mor.*, January 1903), pp. 3, 22–25, 27, 29–36; *Creative Evolution*, pp. 177, 267, 268; *L'Intuition philosophique* (*Rev. de mét. et de mor.*, November 1911), pp. 809–827, published separately in 1928, Paris, Helleu et Sergent; and the (unpublished) lectures given by Bergson at the Collège de France.

[2] *Creative Evolution*, p. 237.

[3] *Introduction to Metaphysics*, in *Creative Mind*, p. 237.

manner that one ordinarily forgets, when one reflects upon the work once done, the share to be credited to intuition in the work *being done.* In Bergson's eyes, the knowledge a mother has of her child, and the living sympathy that unites her to it,—if she sleeps beside it, an imperceptible movement on the child's part awakens her, while the roar of a cannon would perhaps not waken her at all,—the knowledge a painter has of his model, or the knowledge a writer has of his hero, the great discoveries of science and metaphysics, the quasi-instinctive judgments of common sense, all these widely varied modes of knowledge, whose sole common trait is a certain irreducibility to rational processes and a certain spontaneity, have to do with intuition.

But intuition, no matter how frequently one has recourse to it, has so far been used only in a sporadic manner. What Bergsonian philosophy brings us is the regular, general and, to put it bluntly, systematic use of the intuitive method, thanks to which we have the hope of "dissolving again into the Whole," of "expanding the humanity in us and getting it to transcend itself."[2]

Let us notice, first of all, what is distinctive to Bergson's theory. It is not the statement that man possesses much knowledge not acquired by means of the syllogism and all of which is more or less spontaneous and lived: everyone admits that; it is that he groups all these variously acquired forms of knowledge by reference to one and the same power or cognitive function, *opposed to the intellect,* and that he attributes to that power and to it alone the virtue of apprehending the truth, thanks to a process of knowledge *sui generis,* thanks to an immediate contact, to an absolute coincidence with the real, that is, to intuition.

One might remark that none of the examples previously given correspond to an effort against nature, to a twisting back on itself of the faculty of seeing at one with the act of willing, to an actually experienced identification with the object, to an absolutely simple perception, in short, to all that Bergson describes *intuition* to be. Sympathy for others, moreover, will never transport us into their very consciousness.

One might also be astonished that Bergsonian intuition, a process *contrary,* as Bergson has so often said, to the *natural* inclination of our mind, should be presented to us precisely as the universal process of all *spontaneous* knowledge. But let us leave this and hurry on to find out what, in reality, Bergsonian intuition is worth.

And for that let us first examine what we should understand by intuition, not by Bergsonian intuition, but by intuition properly so-called, in general. A rather difficult task, for the word 'intuition' is one of those which have provoked in the philosophers, by the laws of a bitter destiny the most misunderstandings and obscurities.

2 *Creative Evolution,* pp. 191–192.

II.—INTUITION IN GENERAL

The word 'intuition' is, in its etymological sense, near neighbour to the word 'vision', for it goes back in the first place to visual perception, which will always remain the obvious type and the most convenient example of all intuition. The distinctive feature of intuition, taken in the very wide sense in which we understand it here, is that it is an *immediate* knowledge or perception, a *direct* knowledge or perception, in which the act of knowing terminates upon the thing known without any intermediary, without the interposition of a middle term,—in which it is *seen* in a word. Immediate, without intermediary, direct,—these words might give rise to a very serious confusion. We shall explain them shortly.

But first let us note a second meaning for the word 'intuition,' this time not philosophical or scholarly, but common. This second sense is that of *divination*; this is the way one usually speaks of "intuitions of the heart" and if we go back to the various examples of Bergsonian intuition we quoted a while ago, we shall see that they refer mainly to that sense. It is, then, no longer a question of the *immediacy*[1] of the act of cognition, but of the *spontaneity* with which the subject arrives in certain cases at that act of cognition. It is a question), of the relation of the very act of cognition to the object known. is a spurting forth of the right idea, an inclination of intelligence toward the true or the reinforcement of its virtue under some extrinsic influence; it is no longer a question (as in the purely philosophical sense of immediate perception), of the relation of the very act of cognition to the subject known.

It is the philosophical sense of the word 'intuition,' the sense of immediate or direct perception, which will interest us first.

III.—INTUITION IN THE SENSE OF DIRECT PERCEPTION

On the subject of intuition in the sense of direct perception we think it advisable to set forth, taking as our basis the Thomist doctrine, the following theses:

1) There is first a primary intuition, an intuition on which rests the whole of human knowledge, it is the intuition of the external world, sense perception.[2] In sensation, the object, by its action, produces in us a psychic likeness (*species*) of itself by means of which we perceive it directly, not in its essence but in its accidents, in its sensible qualities, and in the very action it exerts upon us. The living organ of sense therefore knows the concrete object im-

---

1 We shall see presently (pp. 150–151) in what sense this word is to be taken here. In the strict sense of the word it would designate a knowledge without *any* intermediary or mean, even subjective. It refers here to a knowledge without *objective* intermediary, that is to say which directly attains its object without the interposition of another term or object first known (as was the idea in the eyes of Descartes, and as it has remained for the moderns).

2 Cf. *Sum. theol.*, I^a, q. 78, a. 3.

mediately, in the materiality of its existence and of its individual and contingent action.

2) There is a second intuition, that of the active self, which intellectual consciousness does not know through the self's essence, but which it perceives in the self's operations, especially in the acts of intelligence which, by reflection upon itself, the intellect directly and immediately seizes.[1]

3) And finally there is a third kind of intuition, and that is the one of importance to us: intellectual perception.

Intuition or intellectual perception

The intellect is, in fact, of itself an *intuitive* faculty. When, fecundated by the intelligible form received in it, it produces in itself a living likeness of the thing known, which identifies it with the thing, not in the way the thing itself exists naturally, but in the immaterial way in which it, the intellect, exists, it *directly* perceives the intelligible object which it thus discovers in the real and which is but one with the real.

Here we must agree upon the words *immediate, without intermediary, direct,* which in general characterize intuitive knowledge. They do not at all imply that this knowledge should take place without any SUBJECTIVE intermediary, without the presence in the subject of a *means of presentation* of the object, whether a simple similitude merely *received* from it, as in sensation, or even (and here we take the words 'intuitive knowledge' in the broadest sense) an expressed similitude, an *idea*. In order that there may in fact be knowledge, the thing known, the object, must be in a certain manner in the subject, and it can be there only through a likeness of itself,[2] through a psychic, or as the An-

---

[1] Cf. *Sum. theol.,* I^a, q. 87, a. 1 and 3; *De Verit.,* q. 10, a. 8.

[2] Unless it is there *by itself,* and is at the same time *intelligible in act.* But this occurs only in the knowledge that God has of Himself; and, for creatures: 1) in the knowledge that the Angel has of himself; 2) in the beatific vision. If it were agreed to call *intuition stricto sensu* only that kind of knowledge in which the intellect is informed *"immediately"* by the essence or the substance of the thing known, *without the means of a subjective similitude of the thing,* we should then have to reserve the word 'intuition' in this very special sense to the three cases mentioned above. (Cf. *Sum. theol.,* I^a, q. 56, a. 1; q. 12, a. 2, ad 2um; *Contra Gent.,* II, cap. 98; III, cap. 51; *in Sent.,* liv. IV, dist. 49, q. 2, a. 1.) This we shall call the *absolutely restricted* meaning of the word 'intuition.'

There is a sense *less restricted but still strict* (the *proper sense* for the ancients) of the word 'intuition': this word then designates,—as in the case of sense perception in man and of the perception of things by angelic intellect,—a knowledge which, procured by means of a psychic similitude (*species impressa,* received from things in the case of the senses, infused by God in the case of the angels), attains the things however, as *physically present,* as given in actual existence and therefore also in its very singularity.

A third and *broader* sense of the word 'intuition,' refers to the introspective perception of the self. Here the intellect, informed immaterially by some psychic similitude (*species*) and determined thus to knowing directly some object other than the soul, perceives by a spontaneous reflection on its concrete and singular act the very existence of the soul that knows. This experimental knowledge indeed attains an object (the soul), *insofar as present itself and acting;* but as

cients used to say, an *intentional* likeness, a sort of living reflection of itself, produced in the subject: an idea or "mental word" if it is a question of intellectual knowledge, that is to say an expressed similitude in which the intellect, immaterially informed by the object, utters it to itself, presents it to itself in its own innermost activity. But this psychic likeness or similitude, this living reflection of the thing known is not the object in which the act of knowledge terminates: that is the essential point which we can never sufficiently stress! This likeness is *that through which* (or *in which*) knowledge take place, it is not that which is known. It is not the living reflection within us that we see, it is the thing itself reflected which we see in this reflection. And so the idea is not *that which* the intellect knows (the idea itself is known only by reflection), it is only *that by which* the intellect knows, that by which the intellect communicates with reality, that by which it grasps "intuitively," immediately, natures, objects of thought which are in things and which it brings forth from things by abstraction.[2]

Is all intellectual knowledge then such an "intuition"? No. Beside the intuitive or direct knowledge essential to intelligence as such, although of an inferior degree in us, there is another sort of knowledge, an indirect knowledge in which the object is known by the intermediary of another directly known OBJECT:[3] it is knowledge *by analogy,* that which takes place when we do not understand a thing in itself, by means of its idea, of its living reflection in us; but when we understand it by another thing which resembles it, and by means of the idea, of the living reflection of that other thing in us: thus it is that every created spirit knows God naturally through creatures, as in a mirror,[4] it is thus that we know pure spiritual natures.

---

it apprehends only the existence and the action, and not the nature of that object, and thus remains essentially obscure, the ancients refused to call it properly 'intuition.'

Finally, in the fourth place, the sense in which we use the word 'intuition' in order to apply it to the perception of things by the human intellect is a *very broad* sense (improper, like the preceding one, in the vocabulary of the ancients), for it is then a question of a knowledge which does not attain the object as present, as actually existing, but as enveloping in itself only a possible or an ideal existence. Since the abstract nature thus attained is, however, attained *directly* thanks to the idea (*species expressa*),—which is only a term *quo* or *in quo* ["formal sign"],—human intellectual perception indeed deserves the name of 'intuition' in the broader sense whose use modern gnoseology, with its fundamental misconception of the true rôle of the idea, makes obligatory, at least *ad hominem*, and in order to oppose errors which did not come upon the scene before Descartes and Kant. [Cf. *Réflexions sur l'Intelligence,* 2nd edition, Appendix II.]

[2] In "ipso [conceptu] immediate res cognita attingitur." John of Saint Thomas, *Curs. theol.,* t. IV (Vivès), q. XXVII, disp. XII, a. 5, p. 94.—"Scientia est assimilatio scientis *ad rem scitam* . . . secundum species universales." Saint Thomas, C. Gentes. II, 60.—Cf. *Ibid.,* II, 75, 77; *Sum. theol.,* I, 85, 2; *Comment. in de Anima,* lib. III, lect. 8, sub fine.

[3] Cf. *Sum. theol.,* Iª, q. 13, a. 5; q. 56, a. 3; q. 88, a. 1 and 2.

[4] It is the same, relatively speaking, even for the Angels (as to their natural mode of knowing God). For it is by their own nature intuitively known that the Angels know God. "The very nature of the Angel," by which the Angel knows God, "is a sort of mirror in which is reflected the divine likeness." *Sum. theol.,* Iª, q. 56, a. 3.

By opposition to this analogical knowledge, to this indirect intellection, we may call intuition, *intuition in general,* direct knowledge, the intellectual perception which takes place each time the intellect grasps an object which is *connatural* to it, as they say in scholasticism. Moreover knowledge by analogy or indirect intellection necessarily presupposes, as is quite evident, a primary direct intellection, that of the object through whose resemblance we conceive the object known by analogy.

Angelic perception and human perception

Thus it is that the operation proper to intelligence is an *intuitive* operation. If we now consider not intellection, the act of intelligence in itself, but the process by which the intellect produces it, we must distinguish two entirely different processes or *manners.*

In the one the intellect, in perceiving a thing (in an idea, as we have just said), attains that thing according even as it is present in its actual existence and its singularity; and not only does it grasp its essence through the root and in a way that is entirely manifest, but what is more it exhausts all its intelligibility, it sees in it immediately and all at once all the attributes, all the wealth of reality it comprises; this is the case of an *intuitive* understanding like that of the Angels.[1] Here we have *intellectual intuition in the strict sense of the word,*[2] which is found only in pure intelligences. Let us point out here this characteristic: that such a mode of knowledge excludes abstraction, the construction of propositions and reasoning, and constitutes a direct perception *entirely realized and all at once.*

On the contrary, in the other mode of knowledge, the intellect does not receive by infusion its ideas from God—but draws them from things by means of the senses and by abstraction; it therefore apprehends natures only according as their operations or their properties reveal them, and often by simple signs,—it is incapable of grasping at one fell swoop all the predicates which can be attributed to an essence; it is not enough, for example, for it to have the notion of *man* to know all that man is, it must proceed by way of reasoning; this is the case with a *discursive* understanding like our own, and this mode of knowledge which demands the construction of propositions and reasoning is accomplished, contrary to the first, with the help of *discourse.*

Discourse

Nevertheless if discourse as such, that is, the movement of reason going from proposition to proposition, is something else than intuition, it is essential to note the two following and very important points.

---

[1] Cf. *Sum. theol.,* I^a, qq. 54, 55 and especially 58.

[2] See note 2, p. 150. There, it is a case of *intuition in the proper sense* of the word in the vocabulary of the ancients (the second sense explained in that note).

In the first place discourse, far from *excluding* intuition in the sense of direct perception *achieved at once* (in a judgment), necessarily presupposes such an intuition, pre-requires in us a knowledge enjoying one of the characteristics of intellectual intuition in the strict sense of the word, thus forming as it were a common trait between our intellect and that of pure intelligences. As there is no movement without a starting point, there can be no discourse, no demonstration, without the existence, to serve as starting point for the discursive movement, of some truth evident in itself and therefore undemonstrable, the immediate perception of which we have right at once. This evident and undemonstrable truth is the principle of identity or non-contradiction, with all its accompanying principles. In the most common and most abstract concept, in the concept of *being,* which is the first spontaneously formed although the last scientifically elucidated, we see at once what can or cannot be attributed to being, in such a way that the primordial judgments, the first principles,—i.e.* all being is what it is, that which is cannot at the same time and in the same regard not be, everything which begins to be or whose existence is contingent has a cause, etc.,—spring up immediately in us, as soon as we think, under the action of the intellectual light which is in us; here we have perception without discourse, truly primary intuition, the principle of all truth, the very precious illumination without which our mind would remain irremediably deprived of its good; and this intuition of first principles which Pascal ascribed to the "heart," really belongs to the *intelligence.*

In the second place, as the point of arrival is no longer movement but the final result of movement, so knowledge acquired by means of discourse is no longer discourse, but the final result of discourse. And this final result of discourse is the act of the intellect through which, in a final judgment, we take possession of the object. Discourse is *only* for this act of intellectual apprehension, as moving is for attaining the goal and as seeking is for finding.[1]

In fact, it is a result of the weakness of the intellectual light in us that in none of our concepts—with the exception of the concept of being—do we see at first glance the attributes which do or do not suit the nature, the essence thus apprehended; and so, by the *formation of ideas,* by what is called the first operation of the mind, we have only an insufficient knowledge, a very incomplete perception.[2] By the sole fact that I have formed the concept *man,* for example, I indeed perceive (though dimly and obscurely) the *quiddity* of man, I perceive man as *something which is* (at least with a possible existence), *and which is of another type* from the rest of things, but I do not yet know

---

* On this subject, and for the scientific statement of first principles as well as for their relation to the principle of identity, see: Garrigou-Lagrange, *Le Sens commun, la Philosophie de l'être et les Formules dogmatiques,* 3rd edition, pp. 158–228.

[1] Cf. *Sum. theol.,* I^a, q. 79, a. 8.

[2] *Ibid.,* I^a, q. 16, a. 2 and q. 85, a. 3; *ad* 3; a. 5.

whether man is mortal, whether man is free, etc., nor what, scientifically defined, is the essence of man; I shall reach that complete knowledge only after a long discursive labour. To know things, our understanding must therefore not only construct assertions, construct ideas with ideas (the second operation of the mind), that is to say unite them by affirmation or divide them by negation, it must also *reason* (third operation of the mind), that is, go from a thing known to another which it knows next.

But reasoning is only a means, *it is a question of reaching a conclusion, a final judgment to which discourse well conducted will have brought the evidence of the first principles.* If, in this movement, we have not ceased to be faithful to the evidence, then, when our intellect pronounces within itself the conclusion, the final judgment, it will directly perceive the real in that subjective likeness of the object, in that living reflection it has produced in itself, and which the scholastics called the mental word.[1] This apprehension of the real by the intellect, at the final result of the discourse, is not a perception realized at once, like intuition in *the strict sense of the word;* it is a perception *realized after a progress.* But since it is an act of knowledge which terminates in the object itself, a perception accomplished thanks to constructions of concepts operated in the mind, but in which the intelligible real is attained (in these concepts) by the knowing subject without interposition of a previously known object, it is indeed the name of *intuition, in the very general sense of direct perception,* which suits it from this point of view. And so one can say that *any discourse or advance of reason begins by an intuition,*—originally by the intuition of first principles,—*and terminates in an intuition,* "discursus rationis semper incipit ab intellectu et terminatur ad intellectum."[2]

The Angel, because of the plenitude of intellectual light within him, knows at once what there is to know, infallibly and with perfect simplicity. As for us, on the contrary, we are forced to compose our knowledge from bits and pieces, with long detours, and skirting error at every moment, without our knowledge ever being completed. Thus the Angel and man each have a way of knowing proportionate to their nature. But we also understand by this why, as the pseudo-Dionysius put it, "when we reduce our varied notions to unity, human knowledge becomes in part angelical";[3] then does the man who, with a simple glance, grasps in a few principles a whole world of truth, seem to participate in the angelic nature and in "the marvelous fixity of the impulse which carries the Angels onward."[4] That is doubtless the most profound reason for the name we give the *Angelic Doctor.*

---

[1] The expression *mental word, verbum cordis,* refers not only to the *idea* but also to the *proposition,* upon which the judgment, one and indivisible as such, bears. *In quantum dicit verbum, anima cognoscit objectum.*

[2] *Sum. theol.,* II^a^–II^ae^, q. 8, a. 1, *ad* 2.

[3] *Divine Names,* VII, 2.

[4] *The Celestial Hierarchy,* VII, 4.

Bergsonian Intuition

Let us get back now to the Bergsonian doctrine of intuition; we can point out its essential vice: undertaking from a wrong angle to deal with the *immediate* character of intuitive knowledge, it supposes that all knowledge truly attaining the real must be a lived coincidence, *without subjective intermediary,* of the subject and the object, thus known, it is thought, in all the plenitude of its reality, thus exhausted to the very root; Bergsonism then opposes its intuition to the idea, to the concept, to abstract knowledge;—and to reason, to discursive knowledge.

It does not see that by suppressing in knowledge the idea, that is, the subjective likeness of the object, formed in the subject according to the subject's mode of being, it condemns itself to making of its intuitive knowledge an identification of the object and the subject according to the mode of being of the object; so that in order to have, in this sense the intuition of plant life or of matter, the philosopher in a certain way would himself have to become materially vegetable or mineral.

Bergson does not see either that in releasing his intuition from logical constraints and from the analytical progress of reasoning, he deprives it of any means by which the *evidence,* the primordial light of the first principles might be conveyed; nay more, he is led to deny the objective value of this initial intuition of the first principles, because this intuition is expressed in a construction of concepts and serves as the point of departure for discourse.

Quite on the contrary, a genuine intuition[1] comes at the starting-point and at the end of discourse, as that reasoning is only, so to speak, a transportation of intuitive light. Intellectual intuition, for our human understanding, far from being opposed to abstraction, can happen only through abstraction, the condition, as we shall see farther on, of the apprehension of the intelligible real by our mind. So that this apprehension of the real and this conforming to things which Bergson is looking for, we find in abstract knowledge: it is there that it occurs ever since God gave us, in our created intellectual light, a participation in His Light; and, as we see in the first principles, it is precisely at the summit of abstraction that we meet our primordial intellectual intuition.

Abstraction

This point, which is of capital importance, must be emphasized. Bergson is perfectly right in demanding that our knowledge, if it is true, if through it we actually conquer the real, be an assimilation of the subject and the object, and much more than a re-birth of the object through the subject, a birth of the subject in the object, and a vital identification with it. Yes, that is incontestable, and without it we never shall have *knowledge,* we shall flit restlessly about in

---

[1] In the broad sense of the word. Cf. above, note 2, p. 150.

a world of phantoms, we shall be forever walled-in prisoners. But by what unhappy misapprehension did he fail to see that the *idea* is the very means of that intuitive communication with the real, and not, as he, together with all the moderns imagines, I know not what screen interposed between the object and the intellect! By what unhappy misapprehension has he seen in the intellect only a mechanism for elaborating sensations and linking up words, and failed to see what it really is, the fountain of life by which the truth, the absolute, the real enter into our souls and expand them to the infinite, and by which the immensity of being co-operates in our perfecting.

The splendid ignorance which, for three centuries, has reigned in the modern philosophical tradition on the subject of the true nature and the origin of ideas would probably help to explain this misapprehension on the part of the most perspicacious of contemporary thinkers. Real *abstraction* is, in fact, very different from what modern psychologists call by that name, and the genuine idea has nothing in common with this pallid schema which, according to these psychologists, results from comparison and generalization, or from the reciprocal neutralization of several sensible images. It surges in us prior to any process of generalization, and in virtue of a specific operation, which is precisely the operation of abstraction.[1]

What the images which come from the senses present to us is indeed the being of sensible things, but not under its aspect of being; manifested only in its action upon us and in the shell, so to speak, of the *material* conditions peculiar to this or that individual in a certain place, at a certain time, in certain circumstances.—Let us try to isolate this sensible knowledge: our senses (external senses aided by memory and the "estimative") give us, for example, the image of *this lamp,* as of a certain ensemble acting upon our eyes by certain colours, a certain brilliance, according to a certain figure, certain dimensions, extremely variable moreover according to the changed position of ourselves or the object, and strictly determined by circumstances of time and place, by the *hic et nunc.* Were we to stop there, we should possess materially, organically, a knowledge impregnated with materiality: we should *see* this lamp (without being able to name it), we should not *think* it; what this lamp *is,* we should not know; and we should not know that there is an *I* perceiving it, for the sense does not turn back upon itself.—In order that we may know what the object is, in order that we may perceive its nature and its *being* as such, our knowledge of the object must absolutely be purely *immaterial.*

Then it will not be absorbed by the accidental and the momentary, it will assimilate us to the object, not according to the contingent particularities which come to the object from its material action on our organ, but according to what the object is; neither will it be limited to one category of objects rather

---

[1] *Sum. theol.,* I^a, q. 79, a. 2, 3, 4; q. 85, a. 1 and 2.

than to any other; it will be able to extend to all that is.—But how is this transformation to be obtained,—this immaterialization of knowledge,—how is knowledge to be made to pass from one order, from one essential degree, to another? Such a transformation would be positively impossible without the presence within us of a faculty or power that is wholly immaterial, namely, the intellect. Furthermore, since the images derived from the senses evidently cannot *by themselves* act upon such a faculty, we have to recognize the existence in our soul of an active faculty, a centre of intellectual light, called the *intellectus agens* (*formative intellect*) which, by means of the images that come from the senses acting as instrumental cause, will imprint upon the intelligence the likeness of the object, will convey to it the *form* of the latter in the Aristotelian sense of the word. But under what condition and in what way will the formative intellect attain this end? By actuating, by informing the intellect (*intellectus possibilis* as they say in the Schools, the *to-be-formed* intellect) only with the intelligible content which the sensible images potentially involved, a content not conditioned by the materiality proper to the object of the sense knowledge as such; in other terms, the formative intellect has to strip our knowledge of the material conditions implied in sensation and consequently, since it is in its very material individuation that the sensible thing is formally an object of sensation, it has to strip the object of intelligence of the *individuating* notes proper to the object of sensation as such; it has to draw, to bring forth from the singular (known materially by the senses) the universal which existed potentially in it, and which will exist separately, in act, only in the mind, where it is known immaterially. That is why this operation of the formative intellect is called abstraction.

By this we see that if intellectual knowledge, as it is in man, bears directly *only* on the universal, it is because it must bear on *what* things *are,* the necessity in which by nature we find ourselves of immaterializing sensible things in order to know them from the viewpoint of essence[1] thereby prevents our

[1] Let us note once and for all that the word "essence" in such a case signifies only *typical determination in being,* apprehended first in the commonest and most imperfect way.

As soon as I have the *idea* of what is called a lamp, I have before my mind's eye a certain *determined type of being* (which no sensation can give me). That does not mean that I thereby penetrate this type of being in its constitutive detail, that I know the secrets of the manufacture of lamps or the properties of the materials with which they are made, or the nature of combustion, etc.; this would be the case only after I had acquired a complete knowledge of lampmaking.

Abstraction presents to us "essences" in the most *imperfect and confused way,* simply as *something of a particular type.* That, however, is the primary condition for the work of reason, which will set out to acquire a distinct and *proper* knowledge of it. I must first have been introduced into the order of essence and have posited before my mind essence as an object *to be known,* so that I may next set to work to penetrate its intrinsic constitution and succeed in having this object before my mind as a thing *known,* which is the work of science. And very often (in the whole domain of the inductive sciences) our knowledge does but blindly attain essences, not in their distinctive traits, but in the signs which we see of them.

knowledge from going directly to the individual, singular nature and leaves it only the general or specific nature as its direct object.[2]

But in order that there may be knowledge, it is not enough that the intellect should have received, according to the process just described, the intelligible imprint of the object. Cognition is a vital operation and it takes place only when the intellect,—impregnated by the intelligible form received in it, that is to say, in the last analysis, by the object itself,—reacts, performs its own operation, *conceives* and gives birth within itself to a living likeness of the object, the idea, the concept, the *mental word,* which itself is not perceived except by reflection, but in which is directly perceived (in a manner at first exceedingly imperfect)[3] the nature or essence of the object, the object as type of being. It is thus that intellectual knowledge is the common act of the subject and the object joined in one and the same determination of being, which is the form of the object, and in one and the same vital operation. Thus it is that the concept, the concept thought, the concept as it is in the intelligence (not in the herbariums of the psychologists), is the living fruit of an eminently vital operation.

Intelligence lives, because what is proper to life is immanent action, action which dwells in the subject acting; and there is no action more immanent than that of the intellect engendering in itself a living fruit which dwells in it to enrich and perfect it.

The intellect lives because the intellectual light, the light of the formative intellect, is a participated likeness of the living divine Light. The intellect lives because under the action of that intellectual light and of objective reality, it produces, as long as truth requires it, new concepts, in the measure and likeness of things, which well up from the depths of its activity and which contain inexhaustible riches; for it is true as Bergson has expressed it, perhaps exaggerating a little,[1] that each of the great philosophers has spent his whole life in developing, in every possible direction, a single intuition, in reality the intuition in question has been an *intellectual* intuition, a living intellectual perception expressible in ideas or concepts.

[2] That is why the Angels,—who do not take their ideas from sensible experience, therefore in whom there is no *abstraction,* but who have received their ideas from God along with their nature,—know by their ideas the individual as well as the general. As for us, we start from a material knowledge which we must immaterialize, therefore, necessarily disindividualize; so that we know immaterially only the general; and we know the singular (directly) only materially. The Angels, on the contrary, do not start from a material knowledge. Their knowledge is immaterial from the beginning; so that they know immaterially the singular as well as the universal. Cf. *Summa theol.,* Iª, q. 55, a. 2; q. 57, a. 1 and 2.

Let us add that, as our intellect turns back upon (singular) images from whence ideas are taken, we have of the singular not only a *direct* knowledge through the *sense,* but also an *indirect intellectual* knowledge (by "reflection on the images"). Cf. below, note 3, p. 160.

[3] See note 1, p. 157.

[1] *L'Intuition Philosophique,* a lecture given at the Philosophical Congress in Bologne (*Rev. de Mét. et de Mor.,* November, 1911); published separately in 1928 (Paris, Helleu and Sergent).

Bergsonian philosophy and the intellect

Why then does Bergsonian philosophy so wrongfully oppose life and intelligence, direct perception and abstraction? Let us point out some of the causes which may have led it into this error.

First of all,—and this seems an indirect result of our original fall—it is relatively rare that we really accomplish an act of pure intelligence,—I do not mean that we think without at the same time calling up images,—a thing Saint Thomas declares to be impossible,*—I mean that in this natural co-operation of intelligence and imagination we rarely allow intelligence the sovereign domination which is its due. That explains why on the one hand so many philosophers, and especially the later scholastics, should be content to repeat mechanically ready-made formulae without ever referring to the reality they signify, thereby offering a pretext to Bergsonian philosophy for declaring the intellect by nature unsuited to truth. And why, on the other hand, many philosophers, not *thinking,* not being able or not wanting to *live* in their intelligence those truths taught by the eternal metaphysics, declare that these are only words and formulae;—that is one of the most important reasons why the new philosophy,—and here I am speaking much less of Bergson than of those Catholic philosophers who seek to follow him,—is led so abundantly to malign the scholastics with whom it is so little acquainted.

Let us then imagine a person accustomed either to the kind of intellectual somnolence of which Kant has spoken, or to the uncertain philosophy taught by our academic masters. If he should happen to read the works of Bergson how could he fail to come under the spell of that unknown world which opens out before him, that marvellous duration which grows larger as it advances, the bursting rockets, the palpitating real on the fringe of the unconscious, the continual shimmer of sensations and images? How could he help feeling awaken within him that springtime of fresh emotions, extolled with so much lyricism by Le Roy in his book on Bergson?[1]

He will think he has awakened to thought; in reality, *it is his imagination* which will have awakened. And that is a great deal, for imagination is better than nothingness, and is so close a neighbour to intelligence, that it might perhaps, on the rebound, manage to awaken this too. But if we stop there, we also risk abandoning ourselves to a sort of philosophical impressionism, and straying into a search, as Saint Augustine says,[2] not for the substance, but for the odour, as it were, of ideas.

* Cf. *Sum. theol.,* I[a], q. 84, a. 7 and 8.

[1] *Une philosophie nouvelle, Henri Bergson,* pp. 5–7, 112.

[2] "Quia non secum ferebat nisi amantem memoriam, et quasi olfacta desiderantem, quae comedere nondum posset . . ." The Church, in its liturgy, has adopted this text from the *Confessions* (festival of Saint Augustine, 3rd response of the first Nocturne, in the Dominican breviary).

Now, if it is true that the new philosophy gives the image precedence over thought, it is equally true, as has already been pointed out, that it ascribes to thought what really belongs to imagination substituted for intelligence. What happens, for example, when the mechanicists, who in fact proceed more by imagination than by intelligence, suppose that in the place of sensible qualities there exist only vibratory movements? For a certain image, for the image of the world that we see, hear, touch, they substitute another image in which there are only atoms in movement. Bergsonian philosophy admits that the intellect proceeds thus and that it *substitutes* for the universe perceived by our senses, a whole world cut out of cardboard, composed of entities, of laws, of genera and species, as a child builds himself a miniature fort or sheep-fold. This only goes to show that this philosophy *thinks* philosophical propositions less than it *imagines* them, and thinks that we imagine them also; of all intellectual notions it makes a sort of rudimentary and confused imagery which replaces for us, as it thinks, reality. We can therefore understand how it is that it accuses abstraction of *impoverishing* reality, of robbing it of colour, of congealing it, of falsifying it, etc. We can even understand the kind of holy anger which grips William James when he happens to speak of ideas, and the indignation with which he pursues Socrates and the Universals.[1]

This philosopher, precisely, speaks of all the sub-universes (there are at least seven of them) which correspond, for man, to various superposed systems of representations, from the universe of common knowledge to that of the various supernatural worlds affirmed by religions and by the authors of literary fiction.[2] Let him express himself as he will, but at least let him do the Author of the world the courtesy of distinguishing His universe from the universe of the dime-novel; and let him understand that our knowledge does not *substitute* one imaginative representation for another, but attains and brings out varying aspects of the one universe God has made: it is this same and unique universe that we know by our senses and by our intellect. Abstract knowledge considers separately certain things, it does not consider them as being separate; it does not substitute for the image of man as he is perceived by our senses, the image of a man in general who would be neither tall nor short, neither fair nor dark, etc. It considers human nature separately in an abstract idea, but knowing that this nature exists in reality only in these or those individuals;[3] so that all our knowledge has reference to that

---

[1] Cf. William James, *Principles of Psychology*, Fr. trans., *Précis de Psychologie*, p. 317.

[2] *Prin. of Psychology*, II, pp. 292–293.

[3] Thus it is that intellect, by reflection on the images from which it takes its ideas, knows the singular, by a concept, proper but *indirect and reflex*, which returns from the universal upon the felt singular (which the universal concept connoted *in obliquo*, as the term from which it was taken, and which it left behind). Cf. *Summa theol.*, I[a], q. 86, a. 1; Comm. in *de Anima*, lib. III, lect. 8; John of Saint Thomas, *Phil. nat.*, III P., q. 10, a. 4.

unique world, marvellously rich and varied, which we know first by our senses and in which, by our intellect, we perceive separately—but not as severed in existence from the individuals which alone are real—those general or specific essences which are singularized in individuals and exist separately only in our minds.

What is at the bottom of the reproaches addressed by the new philosophy to abstract knowledge is impatience with the laws and limitations peculiar to our nature. This philosophy will not resign itself to perceiving the real only by a variety of manifold faculties, to the inability to drain reality to the dregs, to the absence of an experimental knowledge of the essence of things. In this ambition of making nature transcend itself, an ambition which is usually accompanied by an incomprehension of or refusal to accept the supernatural order, must be seen, transported here into an anti-intellectualist thesis, the proper sin of absolute intellectualism.

It is true that we have not by our intellect direct knowledge of the singular, —but we have our senses for knowing the singular! And it is equally barbarous to wish to sacrifice the senses to the intellect, or the intellect to the senses, for these two orders of faculties are made to cooperate in the same perfection of human nature. As to perceiving by one and the same faculty the singular and the general alike, the abstract and the concrete, that is reserved for Angels, for pure Intelligences. Now Bergsonian philosophy does not respect this order, it wants to *precipitate* matters, it cannot resign itself to a complexity in our manner of knowing which our very nature requires. It claims to give man the means of perceiving both the general and the singular at the same time, by one and the same act, by one and the same effort contrary to nature, by philosophical *intuition*. . . .

Let us point out, concerning knowledge of the singular, an ambiguity we constantly meet in Bergsonian philosophy:—The singular, it is said, is inexpressible.—Yes, of course; for we have no direct idea of individual things, *as such*.

Nevertheless, we have a direct idea of the general or specific nature which we draw precisely from singular things, so that individual things, that is all things, are essentially expressible as having a certain nature, although material individual things are inexpressible as individual. But they do not think of those two words: *as individual*, and they proclaim that things are *absolutely* inexpressible, that the real is ineffable.

The truth is quite the contrary. All that is, is expressible and namable, of course not *for us, men* (especially as regards either purely spiritual things, or material things taken in their singularity): but expressible and namable *in itself*. And even for us these things are expressible and namable in a certain way, the first by analogy and the second in the generality they potentially contain. The reproaches Bergson makes to intellectual knowledge amount to saying that this knowledge is not the thing itself or the sensible or experimental knowledge of the thing; that the idea of illness is neither the illness nor the experience of the illness, and who ever said it was? This idea is nonetheless fit to procure a true knowledge. All that is can be *uttered* (imperfectly, no doubt, like everything we do) by human intelligence, either directly or by analogy. And there is only one truly and absolutely ineffable reality (that is, no creature can express it *as it is*), in other words the divine essence: not that it is ineffable in itself, far from it! for it utters itself to itself in the eternal generation of the Word; or that we can in any way express and name it, for if its infinity overflows our concepts and our names, these nevertheless give us a view of it which is true even though analogical. If contemplative souls invite silence, it is not because they put pure and simple silence above the spoken word. It is because in silence unbroken by any human word, they hear in their innermost selves the living Word which bestows being upon all that is.

Let us note finally that intellectual knowledge, by the very fact that it does not claim to exhaust the object in its entirety, but gives us only what matters most about it, or extracts, if I may say so, only its marrow,—that is, the general or specific being; by the very fact that it is not experimental and that it turns aside from sensible individuating notes; finally by the very fact that it begins with a very modest germ, namely the intuition of the most simple of entities, of being in general, and the intellectual perception, at first quite incomplete, of the *quiddities* of sensible things; for all these reasons intellectual knowledge corresponds to the most profound laws of our nature: to the necessity of detaching ourselves from the sensible, to the necessity for humble and patient effort, to the necessity for a certain sobriety in knowing. *Sapere,* says Saint Paul, *sed sapere ad sobrietatem.* On the contrary, Bergsonian intuition wants to take possession of the real in its entirety, by a sudden and fleeting impulse; it wants to experience the absolute.

It demurs at the kind of sacrifice that the intact and supreme immateriality of intellectual knowledge demands of our sensibility even as it sets us free.

IV.—INTUITION IN THE SENSE OF KNOWLEDGE OF INCLINATION,
OF SPONTANEOUS OR INSTINCTIVE KNOWLEDGE

It remains for us to examine a second sense of the word intuition, not scholarly and philosophical this time, but popular; to have an intuition in that sense means to divine, to know without reasoning, to form a just idea or correct judgment without any discursive preparation. We must pause a bit over this divination-intuition. It would be absurd to deny its existence, even though the more or less romantic literature devoted to the new philosophy ordinarily makes excessive use of it. All that we maintain is that in order to *divine*, to know or judge without discourse, we do not have recourse to a special cognitive power, distinct from the intellect and upon which by right the apprehension of the truth would devolve; and that when it is not a question of a purely sensitive instinct, everything boils down to the spontaneous exercise of the *intelligence* under the influence of certain causes, above all in its vital imbrication with the imagination. The intellect, in a similar case, produces its act without having been led to do so by its normal mode of advancing, by reasoning or by discourse. It is the spontaneous welling up of this act which gives it its "divinatory" aspect; but as a result it finds itself deprived of demonstrative certitude.—One cannot too much insist upon this fundamental spontaneity of intelligence and on the importance of similar "intuitions" which, more or less confused, always precede and accompany intellectual elaboration, which cause the solution to be foreseen before it has been verified and demonstrated, and which are at the origin of the great conquests of thought. But these acts are far from being foreign or contrary to the intelligence,—they are intellectual acts; it is more than ever a question of intelligence.

If innumerable causes can intervene in this spontaneous play of the intellectual faculty, we must not in any case forget the principal cause, namely *the force and activity of the intellect itself, as well as the disposition proper to it.* The more or less great power of intellectual light (which, according to Saint Thomas,[1] discloses a difference between souls as to their individual substance), and the possession in the state of habit of certain more or less extensive forms of knowledge will certainly make the intellect more or less capable of perceiving in a principle, with a simple glance, a conclusion hitherto hidden; and the purer and more untrammeled the soul is, the more its intuitions have their origin in intelligence itself, the less they will depend on the capricious associations of the imagination.

But over and above intelligence it is the activity of the whole soul which, by the infinitely varied influences of its diverse powers on the exercise of the intellectual faculty, takes part in the process of knowledge, and especially of that knowledge which divines before demonstrating. For "intellectualism" has never claimed,—as ill-informed adversaries often accuse it of doing,—to enclose each of our faculties in an ivory tower, and reduce all our ways of knowing to the syllogism. To affirm that the organs of movement are the muscles is not to deny that our whole organism is interested in each of our movements, and that the state of the heart or the lungs, for example, can influence our walking. Thus it is that we affirm that the intellect is the faculty of truth: but absurd as it would be to make truth the common object of

[1] *Sum. theol.*, I[a], q. 85, a. 7.

all our faculties monstrously confused, it would be just as absurd to deny that the soul as a whole is interested in the possession of truth, and that faculties different from the intellect can, in a sometimes preponderant way, have an influence on the mode according to which the intellect acquires truth. Does not Saint Thomas, to prove the unity of our soul, insist upon the interdependence of all our powers, which means that what happens in one has its repercussions through our whole being, and even that the too-intense operation of a power hinders the other from acting?[1] That is what scholastic philosophy calls the *coherence* of the faculties.[2]

Sensibility and intellect

In the question of the inferior faculties, of sensibility, it is well enough known that for traditional philosophy the intuition of the senses, sensible experience, is the very basis and primary origin of all human knowledge; and that memory and imagination have so important although subordinate a rôle in knowledge, that the intellect never understands, Saint Thomas tells us,[3] without turning toward images, and that one of the reasons which establish a difference of intellectual value between men, is the greater or less perfection of the sensitive faculties which depend on the complexion of the body.—The present dispositions of sensible memory and imagination, presenting the intellect with more or less happy combinations of images, will naturally influence intellectual research, and all the more so as the knowledge is more concrete and the mind more imaginative. Do not certain scientists tell us that the idea of their discoveries has come to them after the most unlikely or even the most trifling play of an imagination wandering at random?

The cogitative and intellect

But it must be noted here that the scholastics admitted the existence of a special *sensitive* faculty, properly divinatory, since its object is to seize, on the occasion of a sensible perception, concrete notions—inaccessible in themselves to the external senses,—which lie dormant in the animal, and which reveal in its psychic organization the mysterious correspondences of the plan of creation. If, for example, the lamb runs away as soon as it sees a wolf, it is not, Saint Thomas says, that the form and colour of the wolf have offended its eye; it is because it perceived in the wolf its "natural enemy."[4] It is this *estimative* faculty with its purely sensible perception of the advantageous, the good, the harmful, etc., in short, of the concrete relations to the well-be-

---

[1] *De Verit.*, q. 26, a. 10; *Sum. theol.*, I^a, q. 76, a. 3; I^a II^{ae}, q. 37, a. 1.
[2] Hugon, *Curs. Phil. Thomist.* (Lethielleux), III, 231.
[3] *Sum. theol.*, I^a, q. 84, a. 7; q. 85, a. 7.
[4] *Ibid.*, I^a, q. 78, a. 4.

ing of the living thing, which accounts for the instinct and the individual experience of animals. This kind of particular reason or animal reason evidently has nothing in common with the intellect since it does not grasp the universal and in no way penetrates to essence, but is purely sensitive and, as such, limited to the particular, to the *hic et nunc,* and embedded in matter. In man it acquires, from the fact of its proximity to intelligence, a flexibility and variety unknown in the animal; it is then called *cogitative,*[2] because the concrete and sensible notions it furnishes are no longer derived solely from the natural instinct but also, in addition, from a certain combination or active collation, *co-agitatio,* but it always remains as blind to the essence of things as touch or taste.

To this sensitive faculty must be related many antipathies and instinctive sympathies and "presentiments." On it depends the sense knowledge as it were divinatory, that uncultured men, shepherds, carters, poachers, machine tenders, sometimes have of the animals with which they live or of the machine with which they are familiar. To it in short, as much as to the influence of maternal love, must be attributed the concrete knowledge a mother has of her child and the elective sympathy which unites her to it.

But most often the *cogitative* works with the other sensible powers in the service of the intellect. In this case we see why it can create in us, aside from our organic faculties, a certain sympathy or *connaturality* with beings that are themselves corporal or with material objects, in virtue of which the intellect will be spontaneously inclined toward this or that judgment. That explains the fact that the use of laboratories or the practice of scientific methods gives scientists a sort of sentiment, or instinct, or flair, whichever you wish to call it, that nothing can replace.

In the same way, in his work the artist is directed by a kind of sensible sympathy which unites him to both the living reality he wishes to express and the means of expression he employs; thus he makes his model confess, as Carrière I think it was, said; and the poet knows his heroes the better for the fact that it is always some aspect of himself that he expresses in them. One might say that art attempts precisely to make us divine sensibly in its very singularity that individual nature that our senses give us in its accidents and its material operations but not in itself, and which our intellect, as we said a while back, does not know directly as individual; that is why, even from the point of view of the perfection of our *knowledge,* we have so great a need of art and artists.

Will and intellect

Yet it is not only on the side of the sensitive faculties that the intellect can be aided or influenced in its operation. Christian philosophy also shows us,

---

2 Saint Thomas, *ibid.; de Anima,* a. 13; cf. *Opusc.* (unauthentic) *de potentiis animae,* chap. 4.

but this time preferably with regard to the higher truths, that the affective faculties, the heart or the will, exert in several ways an influence on intelligence.

First, and this is a quite general psychological law, it is the will which turns the intellect to the consideration of one thing rather than another. Moreover, the influence of the will or of love aids the sensitive faculties the intellect uses, memory, imagination, the cogitative, to make their activity converge toward one same point, and the exercise of the intellect is facilitated to that extent.

But especially is intelligence itself fortified in its operation by love. For all operative power has a natural inclination which the scholastics call *nisus* or *conatus* or *inclinatio*,[1] toward its act and its good: for example, the intellect has a natural appetite for being, for truth. But the stronger this appetite is, the more perfect is the operation of the power; and how could the ardent will to truth fail to reinforce the appetite the intelligence has for truth, how could the love for the primary Truth fail to make the intellect adhere with greater force and greater impulse to the mysteries of faith as well as to the truths which our reason can attain, and make the intellectual operation freer from and less hampered by obstacles?

From another angle, as soon as there is love the imprint of what is loved is in some way in the will of the one who loves, not as image or likeness, but as impetus or impulsion. "The thing loved," says Saint Thomas,[2] "exists in the will like a weight which inclines the one who loves and in some way pushes him with an inner thrust toward what is loved, [. . .] and as the term of the movement exists already in the impulse which creates between it and the moving body a proportion and conformity." And thereby, if love is habitual that which is loved will be constantly in him who loves, in the manner of an impetus or an impulsion which will ceaselessly urge him on. Then, at the least relaxation, on the slightest propitious occasion, the soul will be invaded by the thought of what is loved; and where reason could not have recognized it, love will do so. Thus it is that the disciples at Emmaus did not recognize their Master from the explanation of Scripture, but recognized Him in the breaking of the bread; and that Saint Mary Magdalene recognized Him when He said: Mary; and that Saint John, while he was fishing with Peter and the others, hearing Him speak from the water's edge, suddenly cried: *Dominus est*. In all these cases, in which moreover it is a question of *recognizing* and not of knowing, truth surges up in intelligence under the stimulus of love, and thus it can be said that the mind is taught by the heart.[3]

---

[1] Cf. Hugon, *Curs. Philos. thomist.*, III, p. 230.

[2] *C. Gent.*, lib. IV, cap. 19. Cf. *Sum. theol.*, I^a, q. 27, a. 4.

[3] It was in this sense that Ernest Hello wrote: "He who loves greatness and who loves the forsaken, when he passes close to the forsaken, will recognize greatness if greatness is there."

Moreover, from the sole fact that the will is directed by love to the things that the intellect knows, the risks of error are, to a certain extent, diminished; for it often happens that the practical consequence of a truth turns the soul from that truth if the will is perverse, or that, the coldness of the heart making a truth unbearable to the will, the intellect together with the whole soul is carried far from that truth.

Quite on the contrary, when love is there, it pulls the intellect along together with the whole soul toward truth—*amor meus pondus meum*—at least if it is a question of truths which are, as Saint Thomas says, *secundum pietatem,* according to divine goodness; and thus it causes many secrets to be divined because it tends by instinct toward what renders most glory to God.

Finally, briefly characterizing the relation of the life of the soul in general with the intellect, Saint Thomas[1] says that the presence within us of a certain *habitus* or permanent disposition, of the *habitus* of a virtue for instance, inclines the intellect spontaneously and without reasoning to judge correctly the things which relate to that *habitus.* We then have, with the things we know, a certain *connaturality.* It is in this sense that *he who does not love, does not know God,* and that Christ says in Saint John: "If any man will do the will of my Father he shall know of the doctrine, whether it be of God. . . ."[2]

Thus it is that will and love give to knowledge an ultimate and incomparable perfection, by transforming science into wisdom, otherwise expressed, doctrinal wisdom into wisdom lived. Thus it is that according to Aristotle, *the virtuous man is the measure and rule of human acts,* and that in the testimony of pseudo-Dionysius *Hierotheus was instructed in divine things, less for having learned them than for having lived or suffered them non solum discens, sed et patiens divina.*[3]

Thus it is that the seventh gift of the Holy Spirit, the gift of Wisdom, makes us judge in an experimental way of divine things and conveys their savour to us,—*sapida sapientia,*—thereby crowning the *habitus* of charity which introduces the soul into divine familiarity, gives it a genuine congeniality, a connaturality, *compassio sive connaturalitas,*[4] with the things of God, and unites it to God according to the word of Saint Paul: *qui adhaeret Deo, unus spiritus est.*

That is how lived knowledge,—knowledge by sympathy or connaturality,— was neglected by the scholastic doctors, who made it wisdom *par excel-*

---

[1] *Sum. theol.,* I^a, q. 1, a. 6, *ad* 3. Cf. John of Saint Thomas, *in* I^am II^ae, q. 58, disp. 18, a. 2, 3, 4; Aristotle, *Ethic.,* lib. X, cap. v, 1176 a 17–18; cf. lib. III, cap. iv.

[2] John, cap. vii, 17.

[3] *Div. Names,* cap. ii, 9.

[4] *Sum. theol.,* II^a II^ae, q. 45, a. 2.

lence, and discovered some twenty years ago by the philosophers of intuition and the philosophers of action!

All these remarks help us to understand why and in what sense the truth must be lived, meaning especially truth which interests the soul and God, in order the better to know it, that is to say once more, in order that the intellect may function under the best conditions of exercise, or that it may be borne as though by instinct toward truth. *Qui facit veritatem venit ad lucem.*—But one very clear conclusion arises out of the analysis we have just sketched: it is, first, that in no case can we establish the presence in us of a faculty of knowledge superior to the intellect: all these "intuitions," these divinations, all these judgments by inclination, far from having anything in common with angelic intuition (which they resemble in a wholly negative way, by the absence of the discursive process), are deprived, whatever the certitude with which they impose themselves upon us, of the light of *evidence* properly so-called. That is true even and especially of that contemplative union of which we spoke last,[1] which is, however, wholly supernatural, which brings us as close as possible to the vision of God, and in which the intellect is raised above its ordinary processes, but which takes place only in the divine shadow, under the dazzling cloud of which the Saints speak.

In the second place, we see that, wherever it is not a question of animal-like and unconscious knowledge given by the senses and the *ratio particularis,* wherever it is a question of a knowledge in any way attaining the truth about the being of things, there is knowledge only if there is intelligence; since if anything other than intelligence plays a rôle in knowledge, it is by exercising an influence on intelligence. Nay more, it is intelligence and reason—resting on the first principles of the natural order and on sense experience or on the principles of faith, or on the very experience of infused wisdom—which alone have power to *judge* the various forms of knowledge by inclination of which we have spoken; for instead of a divination or a knowledge lived, one can have only an illusion, and if it is true that authentic mystical experience and even certain charismatic graces bring with them an infallible certainty, it is equally true that the Devil sometimes disguises himself as an Angel of light. And what instrument, what faculty will mankind and the Church itself use to decide definitively if not reason, illuminated,—when it is a question of a supernatural object,—by the light of the living faith.

---

[1] When they deal with the gifts of the Holy Ghost theologians explain that the gift of *intelligence* includes a certain *evidence* of divine things, but it is a question of an *evidence* either *negative* (making these things distinguishable from all sensible contamination and all error) or *extrinsic* (showing their credibility), it is not a question of a *positive and intrinsic evidence* which will be given only in the beatific vision. Cf. John of Saint Thomas, *Curs. theol.,* t. VI (Vivès), in I–II, q. 70, disp. 18, a. 3, numbers 27–44.

Bergsonian intuition

Let us return now to the Bergsonian doctrine; this doctrine plays with the two meanings, philosophical and popular, of the word 'intuition,' thus piling up the confusions and ambiguities. But if it fails to recognize real intellectual intuition, on the other hand it denatures intuition in the sense of divinatory knowledge or knowledge lived, since it claims to separate it from intelligence and make it the operation of a power other than the intellect, a special faculty or rather a confusion of all the faculties.

All the influences of which we have just spoken, influences so diverse and complex and so delicate, too, which derive from the coherence of our faculties, and which presuppose the cooperation and harmony of all the forces of the soul, are thought to constitute one single and sole operation *sui generis* because they have been joined under one and the same name, intuition. In reality, Bergsonian intuition can appear to us only as a forcing and wholly artificial concentration of *some* of our faculties.—What is more, the intellect being excluded, at least in principle, there remains nothing in the foreground but the sensitive faculties. Hence the preponderance, in the intuitions on which the philosophy of Bergson feeds, of the imagination and the cogitative, of metaphor and emotion. It does not claim to explain all things by water, air and fire, like the early Greek evolutionists: they dealt with the sensible, but at least they *thought* it. The philosopher now sets himself to *feel* reality.

And this dilation of the sense is to attain the truth, the absolute, make us coincide with the essence of things! No matter how much sensibility puffs itself up, exerts itself, it will never succeed. The philosopher therefore is compelled, in fact, to re-introduce—without admitting it, and with more or less friction in the process—intelligence, intellectual perception. He begins by forcing sensibility, and then in spite of himself he adds to this disorganized sensibility intellectual operations as disguised, as transposed as possible, and out of all this he makes a single whole, a *simple* operation: that is what is called[1] "re-absorbing intellect into instinct or re-integrating instinct into intellect." In short, it is a question of *thinking* with the *senses* and of thus obtaining a supra-intellectual knowledge. The painful efforts that such an intuition demands are easily understood. It is, in fact, outside of nature.

Bergsonian intuition and truth

When we are told that truth is a matter of intuition not of reason, and that we must transcend intelligence and find something better to attain the true, we instinctively understand that it is a question of finding a *perfecting* of the intellect, something which completes and improves our reason; and as we know our reason to be very weak and as we aspire to something other

---

[1] Éd. Le Roy, *Une Philosophie nouvelle,* p. 107.

than seeing in a glass darkly realities from on high, we do not perceive, before more serious reflection, any impossibility in this thesis; we thus run the risk of being seduced by it. But if it were, on the contrary, a question of a radical opposition to intellectual knowledge, we should less readily give it credence. For if all knowledge capable of being expressed by the intellect is thereby incapable of revealing to us what is, as we can always (however imperfectly and indirectly) express intelligibly what we know,[1] all our knowledge becomes false, there is no more truth for us.

That is why eclectic Bergsonians refuse to sacrifice the intellect to intuition and claim to have an equal veneration for both of them. Bergson himself, after having attempted a wholly nihilistic criticism of the intellect and reason, tries to reconcile intellect and intuition: it is especially in *Creative Evolution*[2] that the doctrine receives this useful amendment. Did not Bergson elsewhere declare that if the results of an intuition are contradicted by reason this intuition is only a "hollow dream,"—however scandalous it might be to have a lived coincidence with the absolute controlled by a faculty made to manipulate solids?

Let us remember, however, that the intuition he is talking about is not expressible in conceptual terms. It can be suggested only by sense metaphors or very imperfectly communicated by supple concepts that are flexible, mobile, almost fluid, very "different from those we usually handle," and which apply to "only one single thing."[3] What becomes then, of the truth of the assertions of common intelligence, of philosophy, of moral law, assertions such as: "the whole is greater than the sum of its parts," or "do not return evil for evil," which are certainly not sense metaphors or fluid judgments?

Furthermore, from the moment that the intellect in its very nature *becomes* and evolves, any conceptual proposition which, according to popular opinion, would immutably express a truth, must in reality change, evolve, *become*, with the intellect itself and the progress of humanity. "Axioms and categories, [. . .] all become, all evolve," Le Roy tells us.[4] In other words the

---

[1] See above, pp. 161–162.

[2] *Creative Evolution*, pp. 195–208 (science and metaphysics); and especially p. 238 (dialectics and intuition).

[3] *Introduction à la Métaphysique*, pp. 9, 15, 27.

[4] Éd. Le Roy, *Sur quelques objections adressées à la Nouvelle Philosophie*, (*Revue de Métaphysique et de Morale*, 1901, page 305): "Who does not know that evidence evolves? That is an undeniable fact." *Ibid.*, page 428: "Axioms and categories, forms of understanding and sensibility, all that becomes, all that evolves. The human mind is pliable and can change its most intimate desires provided it takes, I do not say the required *time*, but the required *duration*. That is the thesis I maintain." In this case it is doubtless against Kantism in particular that Le Roy sustains this thesis, but the fact remains that he does uphold it and that, for him, axioms evolve. Cf. again *Comment se pose le problème de Dieu, ibid.*, 1907, pages 492–493: "The thought to be taken under consideration is thought as creative activity, the same which manifests itself in invention—which is the work of genius—and in biological evolution,—in short, *thought action*. Pure intelligence, or the faculty of critical reflection, of conceptual analysis, is only a form of it,

truth of the enunciation evolves, truth changes. Then either notional, philosophical or dogmatic formulas will themselves change, and in order to think in accordance with the real it will be necessary first to affirm an assertion and then to deny it. Or else these formulas themselves will not change, but the truth that they state will have changed, and in order to think in conformity with the real it will be necessary not to think what one says. I regret having to express myself here with a certain bluntness, but what is at issue is too momentous: the Bergsonian theory of intuition reduces intelligence to nothing, irremediably dispossesses man's thought of the truth.

It is true that Bergson does not deny himself the privilege of using conceptual propositions, of uttering judgments on the real and of writing books on philosophy. But it is not always necessary for a philosophy to *perform* what it *signifies:* otherwise idealism, for example, would never have been able to bestow its profundities upon us. Thanks to a subtle art, and by a sort of philosophical *tour de force*, Bergson manages to keep an apparent equilibrium between the contradictory tendencies of his system. But his philosophy itself goes inevitably wherever his principles take it. It is sometimes said that Bergson regrets the anti-intellectualist reputation of his system, and it seems that he hesitated to call "intelligence" the faculty he sets up against his intuition. But it is not a mere question of words. The conciliation of Bergsonism with a sane philosophy of intelligence is possible only on condition that we abandon Bergsonian intuition, the critique of concept and reason, and consequently *duration*.

---

a function like clear consciousness in relation to the subliminal. It is a determination or particular adaptation of it, the part organized in view of practical life, the part consolidated in discourse. Consequently we can conceive without any vicious circle a genesis of intellect, while for thought taken in its broader sense such a genesis is absurdity itself." But, by the very fact that it overflows intelligence, this thought-action cannot find a fixed term in any conceptual enunciation. These enunciations, to the extent that they are conceptual, are fraught with relativity and contingency: "Contradiction, causality, primacy of act, what more? Just so many obscure mysteries as soon as one endeavours to attain their ultimate roots. Assuredly these principles carry with them a certain necessity, contain basically an absolute exigency. And yet they are explicit only in their applications, in contact with definite hypotheses, and then they are contaminated with contingency. How are we to discriminate between their profound soul and their transitory bodies? [. . .] Were we to seek a formula universal in application, we should see the principle dissolve in an indeterminable vagueness. We *feel* indeed that there still subsists in the last analysis some necessity or other, a residual exigency which dominates all particular cases and is manifest in each one. But of apprehending this exigency in its pure state and of saying what precise necessity is involved, we are incapable." (*Ibid.*, July 1907, pages 474–475.) These are the inestimable confessions of a philosophy which, in order to know, turns to the very thing which in our psychic life is subjacent to intelligence and overflows it: *if we seek a formula universal in application, the principle dissolves in an indeterminable vagueness.* That is to say that, insofar as they are necessary and universal, the conceptual formulas which express the principles of reason are, for us, empty of all determinately knowable content; and that, insofar as they bring us a content determinately knowable and which the mind can deal with, they are contingent and transitory and subject to evolution. *The truth I am speaking is true for all time but I do not know what I am speaking, or the truth that I speak is true today but will be false tomorrow:* the evolutionist theory of intelligence and the speculations depending upon it will never get out of that dilemma.

V.—BERGSONIAN DURATION

The study of Bergsonian Duration cannot bring us new conclusions, but can only confirm those to which we have been led in examining Bergsonian Intuition. There is, in fact, proportionality between the object known and the faculty knowing, and what *being* is to *intelligence*, *duration* according to Bergson is to *intuition* according to Bergson. The Duration of his metaphysics is nothing but non-being asserted in existence.

Time and change

Duration, for Bergson, is reality itself. And for him duration is simple time, what he calls concrete and genuine time.[1] Bergson has perfectly well seen that time is not a *thing;* and in fact it is only a continuous passing of impermanent existence constituting a very particular sort of (flowing) quantity. But with that he declares that time is the *stuff* of things:[2] the stuff of things, that is a way of saying the substance of things. Here we have then a substance which is not a thing, a substance which is not a substance. Here we have a being which is nothing.

The notion of Time is one of the most difficult and most complex notions we meet in philosophy. Without going into the technical discussion of the problem,[3] let us say simply that time is not the duration,—that is to say, the perseverance in being, of a *thing* which endures and still less the thing itself which endures.

Time *measures* the duration of mutable things, and it is itself the duration of what endures only by unceasingly losing existence and receiving it again, that is, of continuous change: numerable and measurable duration, like continuous change itself, by reason of spatial continuity which is the very first principle of the continuity of change. It is in this regard that time is a certain quantity.

As soon as there is movement or change, there is before and after, just as when there is space there is length, width and depth. But to say that a change is continuous, is to say that if we distinguish parts in it, no one of those parts, no one of those portions of change exists separately in the change—except in a potential manner,—before we have distinguished the parts in question. Furthermore, one of these parts has already disappeared when the other is about to be there, for change is something successive, and this is so for any

---

[1] Cf. *Essai sur les données immédiates de la conscience, Time and Free Will*, pp. 99–132.

[2] *Creative Evolution*, pp. 4–11; cf. pp. 337–342.

[3] On this subject, see Saint Thomas, *Sum. theol.*, Iᵃ, q. 10; q. 53, a. 3; *Comment. in Physic. Arist.*, lessons 15–23; *opusc.* (*unauthentic*) *de Instantibus;* John of Saint Thomas, *Philos. natur.*, I, P., q. 18; Pègues, *Commentaire à la Somme, Traité des Anges*, pp. 266–324. See also above, preface footnote p. 24, n. 3, and below, chap. X. [In the second edition of *Théonas* (chap. VI), I tried to complete the theory of time sketched here.]

portion of change, no matter how small we make it; so that we can continue this division of change as much as we like, we shall never have finished, we shall never reach a portion, a part which is not itself change, a part which remains. And this is not surprising since continuous change is not made up of parts distinct in act, for if it were it would be discontinuous. Continuous change is indeed made up of parts, but of parts which are distinct only potentially.

It is the same thing for continuous and successive quantity which is linked to continuous change according to the before and after, and which is its duration (numbered or numbering). This continuous quantity which flows unceasingly, is time. No portion, no part, absolutely nothing of this quantity remains, and the present instant, the *nunc fluens,* which is not a *part* of time, but the *limit,* or *terminus,* the indivisible point which unites past time which has been and is no longer, to future time, which still is not, continually dies and is born again. And so time is indeed a flux, a pure flowing, as Bergson says. But it is not a flowing without anything which flows, there is something which flows and which serves as *subject* for time, it is the movement of the thing which changes.—Now in order to number that flowing quantity using any conventional unity we like, and in order to retain it in thus numbering it, a memory, a mind is necessary: in this sense Aristotle says that without the soul there would be no time.[1] We see that time, or, according to the classical definition, the number of movement according to before and after, is not only a mode (quantity of duration) of an accident (I mean of movement); but also that it is completely itself only because the human mind is there. That is what the philosophy of intuition has chosen to be the essence and stuff of things.

What must be retained here of the Bergsonian doctrine is, in the first place, that time in its reality, like movement in its reality, is something other than what mathematics call time and movement, which is only the translation of time and movement into the register of abstract quantity. Exactly like move-

---

1 " Ἀδύνατον εἶναι χρόνον ψυχῆς μὴ οὔσης," Aristotle, *Phys.* IV, 14, 233, a. 26. An assertion whose implication is explained and limited by Saint Thomas in his commentary on the *Physics* (*lect.* 23): "Esse rerum numeratarum non dependet ab intellectu, nisi sit aliquis intellectus qui sit causa rerum, sicut est intellectus divinus; non autem dependent ab intellectu animae, unde nec numerus rerum ab intellectu animae dependet, sed solum ipsa numeratio, quae est actus animae, ab intellectu animae dependet . . . Sed motus non habet esse fixum in rebus . . . Sic igitur et tempus non habet esse extra animam nisi secundum suum indivisibile. Ipsa tamen totalitas temporis accipitur per ordinationem animae numerantis prius et posterius in motu . . .; et ideo signanter dicit Philosophus quod tempus non exsistente anima est utcumque ens, id est imperfecte; sicut et si dicatur quod motus contingit esse sine anima imperfecte . . . Patet enim ex praedictis quod [tempus] non habet *esse perfectum* extra animam sicut nec motus." In his commentary on the Sentences Saint Thomas had already written: "Tempus habet *fundamentum* in motu, scilicet prius et posterius motus; sed quantum ad id quod est *formale* in tempore, scilicet numeratio, completur per operationam intellectus numerantis." (*in Sent.,* I, *dist.* 19, q. 10, a. 4.)

ment, time, by the real it contains, is something absolute even though the unity chosen to number it is conventional and relative.

In the second place Bergson's accusations against mechanicism and atomism, for which "everything is given," and which deny all real production of novelty in the world, are as accurate as they are penetrating, and he is right in stating that modern philosophy is generally powerless to account for change, —because modern philosophy has an aversion for the doctrine of potentiality and act, which is the only possible foundation for the philosophical theory of movement and becoming.

While Parmenides declared that movement, becoming, and the production of novelty is impossible because new being can come neither from being, which is already all that is, nor from non-being which is not at all, and while Heraclitus for the same reasons declared that being does not exist and that there is only movement,—Aristotle, founding metaphysics, has recognized that being, affirmed with evidence by the intellect, and change attested with evidence by the senses, are equally real and do not contradict one another in the least, because being in act comes neither from non-being, nor from another being in act, but from being *in potency*: that is to say that before change, the new being, the term of the change, was in no way given in act and nevertheless was not pure nothingness; but that before change, this new being, the term of the change, was in the mutable thing in the capacity of *real possibility*, which will be transformed into actual reality under the influence of a cause itself in act: thus it is, for example, that a man sleeping is *in potency* (in real possibility) with regard to the acts of speaking, walking, etc., or that the acorn is *in potency* with regard to the oak it will produce.

By the distinction of being in act and being in potency, the intellect reaches an authentic perception of change in function of being. *Since nature,* Aristotle said,[1] *is the principle of movement and change, [...] to ignore change would be to ignore nature also.*

Now the intellect does not ignore change, it succeeds, not without effort it is true (for truth is not easy), it succeeds in acquiring an accurate scientific *idea* of change, as of the continuum, as of life, as of all those realities to which Bergson refuses it access.

The fact is that Bergson, too, rejects the doctrine of potency and act. For him, the intellect, which he confuses with a visual imagination eager to philosophize, conceives change, the continuous change with which we are presently concerned, only by supposing it to be composed of distinct parts in act and of immobile states, and by having recourse to a psychic cinematograph in order next to give itself the illusion of movement. And then, in order to re-establish the continuity of the change it has thus destroyed, the intellect supposes a fictitious unity subjacent to those artificially distinguished states,

[1] *Phys.,* III, 1, 200 b 12–15.

an imaginary thread that joins them, and which it calls substance, the subject of change. This interpretation of the processes of the intellect is entirely gratuitous.* It leads Bergson to posit *pure Change* as sole reality. *Pure Change,* that is the real name of Bergsonian Duration. Born of a penetrating introspective observation (unfortunately transposed into an unthinkable metaphysic) of the flux of our inner life, this Duration can afford the psychologist valuable aid in renewing the manner of his approach to and apprehension of the concrete. It is not from this point of view that we are considering it here; it is its metaphysical signification that we must examine, it is according to its metaphysical pretensions themselves, to its absolute value, that we must name it.

Pure change

Heraclitus, the great ancestor of the new philosophy, said that all is movement. What is the consequence of this principle of Heraclitus? The Greek Sophists brought it to light long since: if all is movement, if it is not true that movement, or the passing to new determinations, necessarily supposes the permanence of the being which thus passes, that is to say of substance, or of subject, immutable as such; and if it is not true that "even for mutable things there are relations which do not change,"[1] then, any expressed proposition will be false of itself, since the flux of the real will have flowed by before one can have made a judgment about it; there will be no more truth.

But Bergson pushes the demonstration even further. He declares in fact that *if change is not everything, it is nothing,*[2] that it is not only *real,* but *constitutive of all reality,*[3] that it is *the very substance of things.*[4] One cannot over-emphasize texts laden with so much significance, and which give us the key to *Creative Evolution.* "*There are changes,*" Bergson writes, "*but there are underneath the change no things which change: change has no need of a support. There are movements, but there is no inert or invariable object which moves: movement does not imply a mobile.*"[5]

The utilitarian preoccupations of the sense of sight have no doubt accustomed us to cutting movement up into successive states, in such a way that "movement is as it were superadded to the mobile like an accident."[5] "But we already have less difficulty in perceiving movements and change as independent realities if we appeal to the sense of hearing. Let us listen to a melody, allowing ourselves to be lulled by it: have we not the clear perception

---

* *Creative Evolution,* pp. 298–329.
[1] *Sum. theol.,* I^a, q. 84, a. 1, *ad* 3.
[2] "The Perception of Change," in *Creative Mind,* Bergson, p. 171.
[3] *Ibid.,* p. 177.
[4] *Ibid.,* p. 184.
[5] *Ibid.,* p. 173. See p. 317, n. 1.

of a movement which is not attached to a mobile, of a *change without any-thing changing?* This change is enough, it is the thing itself."*

If we do not dwell on these spatial images, *pure change remains, sufficient unto itself, in no way divided, in no way attached to a "thing" which changes.*†

"Let us come back, then, to sight. In further concentrating our attention upon it we perceive that even here movement does not demand a vehicle nor change a substance . . ."[1] "But nowhere is the *substantiality* of change so visible, so palpable as in the domain of the inner life . . ."[2] "Thus, whether it is a question of the internal or the external, of ourselves or of things, reality is mobility itself. That is what I was expressing when I said that there is change, but that there are not things which change."[3]

"Before the spectacle of this universal mobility there may be some who will be seized with dizziness. They are accustomed to terra firma . . . They think that if everything passes, nothing exists; and that if reality is mobility, it has already ceased to exist at the moment one thinks it,—it eludes thought. . . . Let them be reassured! Change, if they consent to look directly at it without an interposed veil, will very quickly appear to them to be the *most substantial and durable thing possible.*"[4]

Bergsonian metaphysics is indeed therefore the metaphysics of pure change. Bergsonian duration is nothing else than time,—"*real duration* is what we have always called *time,* but time perceived as indivisible,"[5]—time so continuous that, even though successive, no distinct "before" and "after" can be designated in it,[6] time indivisible in which the past endures (for "we are inclined to think of our past as inexistent, and the philosophers encourage this natural tendency in us. For them and for us the present alone exists by itself . . . ," but "that is a mistake!" no doubt useful, "necessary to action," but "fatal to speculation").[7] "The preservation of the past in the present is nothing else than the indivisibility of change."[8] "It is enough to be convinced once and for all that reality is change, that change is indivisible, and that in an indivisible change the past is one with the present."[9] These four lines give us the complete metaphysical picture of Bergsonian duration.

"Let us imbibe this truth and we shall see a good many philosophical

---

* *Ibid.,* p. 174. The italics are mine.
† *Ibid.,* p. 174. The italics are mine.
[1] *Ibid.*
[2] *Ibid.,* p. 175.
[3] *Ibid.,* p. 177.
[4] *Ibid.,* p. 177. The italics are mine.
[5] *Ibid.,* p. 176.
[6] *Ibid.*
[7] *Ibid.,* p. 177.
[8] *Ibid.,* p. 183. I have tried to show (above, pp. 132–133) what must be thought of this *indivisibility* of change. We see here what an important part this notion plays in Bergsonian metaphysics, and to what conclusions it leads.
[9] *Ibid.,* p. 183.

enigmas melt away and evaporate. Certain great problems such as that of substance, of change, and of their relation to one another will no longer arise. All the difficulties raised around these points—difficulties which have caused substance to recede little by little to the regions of the unknowable—came from the fact that we shut our eyes to the indivisibility of change. If change, which is evidently constitutive of all our experience, is the fleeting thing most philosophers have spoken of, if we see in it only a multiplicity of states replacing other states, we are obliged to re-establish the continuity between these states by an artificial bond; but this immobile substratum of mobility, being incapable of possessing any of the attributes we know—since all are changes—recedes as we try to approach it: it is as elusive as the phantom of change it was called upon to fix. Let us, on the contrary, endeavour to perceive change as it is in its natural indivisibility: we see that it is *the very substance of things*."* And thus "... difficulties raised by the ancients around the question of movement and by the moderns around the question of substance disappear, the former because movement and change are substantial, the latter because substance is movement and change."†

These long quotations were necessary. They throw a vivid light on the characteristic processes of the Bergsonian method, which, wishing to install philosophical intuition in movement itself (in the passage from potency to act), can only appeal to the sense of hearing, then to the sense of sight, then to introspection, to establish the knowledge of change, and can philosophize only by allowing itself to be lulled by a melody or by listening to the "uninterrupted humming of life's depths,"[1] in short, remains entirely immersed in the senses and in images, in the phenomenon; thinking it is exorcising substance, it succeeds only in stopping the idea of substance (which the most anti-intellectualist intellect cannot, after all, do without) with sensation itself or the feeling of change, with change purely felt, which is consequently substantified. But especially do these texts give us one of the primary secrets of post-Cartesian metaphysics, in so far as it is no more than an extrapolation of the sciences of phenomena. We see taking shape in them the bond which unites the thesis of the substantiality of change to that of creative time. This last expression must be understood in all rigour; it is a question of a strictly creative time, movement is the absolute, and that absolute grows by itself, it creates and creates itself as it advances; "following the new conception to the end," we succeed *"in seeing in time a progressive growth of the absolute."*[2]

All this amounts to saying that change is being, and that becoming *is* by itself, enjoys *aseity* as well as creative virtue. It is enough to have A given in

* *Ibid.*, pp. 183–4. The italics are mine.
† *Ibid.*, p. 184.
[1] *Ibid.*, p. 176.
[2] *Creative Evolution*, p. 244. The italics are mine.

reality in order to have *more than A,* or *other than A.* The contingent and becoming, change and diversity are posited from themselves. Posit time and things arise from themselves. If, moreover, change is *indivisible,* if, consequently, one cannot distinguish in it parts which succeed one another, something which precedes and something which follows; if the past, the past as such, far from ceasing to be, remains and "preserves itself by itself, automatically,"[3] it is because with the absolute phenomenalism of Bergsonian philosophy one refuses to the very end to concede the reality of substance (whatever implicit use one may make of the notion) for in that case the slightest change is a change of the whole of being and all we have are continual *creations* following one another. There is no more change, that is, no more passing from one manner of being to another, or from one being to another,—unless we dare to affirm the unthinkable and declare that the past as such (and not only the *thing* which existed in the past, since we do not admit such *things*), continues to exist and becomes an integral part of the present, or in other words, that *what is no longer, is.* The radical suppression of being; the philosophy of the nothing which changes.

It is dangerous to prefer imagination to intelligence, and perception dilated into philosophical intuition to what the Ancients called the *natural light.* "Let us take care," says Plato,[1] "not to become misologues, as some become misanthropists. For to hate reason is the greatest of all misfortunes . . . Those who have often trusted reasonings which have betrayed them as they would trust false friends finally come to think after many disillusionings, that they have become very wise and that they alone have succeeded in discovering that neither in things nor in reasonings is there anything true or stable, but that all is in a continual ebb and flow like the Euripus channel, and that nothing ever remains for a single instant in the same state. Would it not therefore be a regrettable evil if, instead of blaming oneself, one finally became thus embittered against reason, and spent the rest of one's life hating and calumniating it, thus depriving oneself of truth and knowledge?"

Thus depriving oneself also, we must add, of the divine Truth and the revealed Word. Insofar as the vital connections between philosophical ideas and religious faith are concerned, the conclusion to these studies on the criticism of intellect, on Bergsonian intuition and duration, unexceptionably imposes itself. I do not speak here for those who believe that all that glitters is gold, that all that is modern is new, that all that is movement is life, and who at the same time and without any apparent great danger entertain the most contrary thoughts. But taking ideas in their full objective logic and assuming minds

[3] *The Perception of Change, Creative Mind,* p. 180.
[1] *Phaedo,* chap. XXXIX (89D-90D.).

truly coherent with themselves, it must be stated that with regard to the theological incidences of Bergsonism, Bergsonian metaphysics would lead one gradually to regard dogmas as the momentary and indefinitely improvable expression of a certain religious sentiment in evolution. If there are no eternal truths[1] and if axioms evolve,[2] why would not also dogmas evolve?

Lord, the religious soul would say, I believe all that Thou teachest, I accept all Thy words, I resist nothing . . . But *I do not understand Thee*; I know not what Thou intendest; give me the intuition of the Holy Trinity or of the mystery of Redemption. Otherwise I am no doubt willing to believe, but I shall only adopt certain practical attitudes, I shall have a soul empty of all reality; for, to me, Thy Word is only words, words which have allowed the real to escape as a net allows water to run out through its meshes . . .

In destroying Intelligence and Reason and natural Truth, one destroys the foundations of Faith. That is why a philosophy which blasphemes intelligence will never be Catholic.—Reality, for Bergsonian philosophy, is neither *yes* nor *no*, we must seek beyond the *yes* and the *no*.—*I am the Way, the Truth and the Life*, says Christ, in Whom, says Saint Paul, there is not the *yes* and the *no*, but in Whom all is *yes*. *I am the Principle, I am the Resurrection and the Life, I am the true Vine and the Bread from Heaven* . . .—*As for you let all your discourse be yea, yea; nay, nay. All the rest is of the devil.*

[1] Éd. Le Roy: "Are there any eternal and necessary truths? We may doubt it. It seems in fact that all particular truth, all distinctly formulable truth is relative, contingent." (*Comment se pose le problème de Dieu, Rev. de mét. et de mor.*, March 1907, p. 167.)

[2] Éd. Le Roy, *Revue de mét. et de mor.*, 1901, p. 428. See above, p. 170, n. 4.

Chapter Nine

GOD

I.—THE EXISTENCE OF GOD

Those who call themselves *intellectuals* ordinarily affect a fine disdain for what are called the proofs of the existence of God, first, because in most cases they are ignorant of them; next, because in reality these proofs are not made for those whom Pascal called the 'demi-habiles,' the half-clever ones. They are too *simple* for such people.

As natural perceptions of common sense they presuppose an integrity, a balance and a spontaneity of the faculties of knowledge one more frequently meets in the illiterate than among philosophers; and they presuppose above all that one has not the prejudicial scorn with regard to common sense that characterizes the doctors of modern science.

As scientific demonstrations they presuppose the power of discerning in the things of this world, by the abstractive force of the intellect, the most general and consequently the simplest realities and of resting firmly on these fundamental realities to raise oneself up to the universal cause. This simplicity of gaze and straightforwardness of reason are generally rare in minds loaded with human wisdom. But who could flatter himself that he has kept them intact,—except by the effect of faith, which can maintain everything and cure everything,—in a time in which philosophical intelligence, debased and degraded by the chafing of innumerable errors, slowly poisoned by attentive educators, made cowardly and pusillanimous by the incessant itching to be modern and to conform to the age, cannot take one step forward without asking itself in terror whether the external world really does exist, whether reality is knowable, whether the principle of causality is not a synthetic judgment *a priori,* and reason a mechanism with blind shackles (and then what is the good of philosophising? and have these propositions themselves any meaning?) and whether our ideas, our consciousness and the intellectual evidence are not the residue of biological or sociological accidents.

All these questions are taken to be the mark of philosophical genius, when in reality, as Aristotle has already pointed out, they are merely the sign of a weakness of the intellect: ἀρρωστία τις διανοίας.[1]

The saintly doctors of olden times, who in the fullness and humanity, if I may say it, of their pacific wisdom, remained by heart and intellect the friends of the people whom they taught, and whose difficult and profound science was a tranquil flowering of that fair knowledge *ex natura* common to all men, would have pitied the intellectuals of our time, who set their pride and sometimes their piety—if they are religious—to depriving human intelligence of its most glorious fruits, and of the very end for which it is made, namely the knowledge of God. Faith can of course in such a case make good the deficiency of reason. But since grace completes and consequently presupposes nature, integral vitality of faith cannot exist where reason lacks health.

The Thomistic proofs[2]

The existence of God is not for mankind a truth evident in itself, that is to say it is not enough, as Descartes believed, to have the idea of God to know that God exists: the ontological argument proves, in fact, only one thing: that Being *a se* exists necessarily, *if it exists;* it does not prove *that it exists.* It is not with one single ambitious leap, with an idea of our minds as starting-point, that God wishes us to go to Him; it is by passing through His creatures and by making use of the things He has made. But so easy is that way, so natural and spontaneous that passage, that man cannot exert his reason without heaven and earth showing him his Creator, to the point that the knowledge of the existence of God is for him a *dowery from nature,* it happens in him without instruction, as the first fruit of the activity of his living intelligence; and if he really rejects so natural an instinctive certitude it is because in that case his will is deflected or because he has been blinded by his teachers.[3]

Is it a question of putting this spontaneous knowledge into demonstrative form, and of establishing it by well-assured metaphysical or scientific proofs? It is obvious, Saint Thomas tells us in his first argument which, although admirably simple, is often wrongly understood, it is obvious that there are things in the world which change or are in movement. Our senses infallibly attest this for what is other than ourselves, and our consciousness for ourselves. *Now, all that is moved or that changes, is moved or changed by something other than itself.*

Therein lies one of the first principles of reason, an absolutely universal

---

[1] Aristotle, *Phys.*, VIII, iii, 253 a 33–34.

[2] Cf. *Sum. theol.*, I[a], q. 2, a. 3 to q. 3, a. 4; q. 45, a. 5; q. 61, a. 1; q. 65; q. 79, a. 4; q. 103, 104, 105.—I[a] II[ae], q. 9, a. 4. See also the work by Garrigou-Lagrange, *Dieu, son existence et sa nature,* Beauchesne.

[3] Cf. below, Part III, *The Two Bergsonisms,* chap. III.

and necessary principle, which derives directly from the intellectual intuition of being. In the intuition of being we have the immediate and infallible perception of the principle of identity: "all being is what it is," or in a negative form: "a being cannot, at the same time and in the same regard, be and not be." But in the intuition of being we also see, infallibly, that all that is has what it needs in order to be, that by which it is, in short all that is has its *raison d'être*.* Furthermore, all being which *begins* to be has not in itself the reason for its existence, or as one might say, does not exist by itself, for if it did it would always be. That which begins to be therefore necessarily has the reason for its existence in something else, that is, in a cause other than itself.[1]

In short, to say that a thing changes or moves, that it becomes this or that it arrives here, is to say that it was not *this,* or that it was not *here* first, it is to say that it begins to be this or here; consequently it must have a cause of its changing, of its beginning to be in a new way, that is to say, that which moves or changes must have a mover other than itself. This principle cannot be denied without, in that very act, denying the principle of identity, and the primordial intuition of being, without which we can neither think nor speak.[2]

---

* The principle of reason, or the principle of universal intelligibility, being evident in itself cannot be deduced from the principle of identity by direct demonstration; but it is connected with it by *reductio ad absurdum*. To deny this principle, that is, to suppose that *a being is which has no raison d'être, which has not that by which it is,* is in fact to deny the principle of non-contradiction. For *that by which a being is* signifies *that without which this being is not. Without that,* therefore, the being in question *is not.* And thus the being which is, without having any *raison d'être,* is and is not, both at the same time, which destroys the principle of non-contradiction.— Unless we say that *that by which a being is* does not signify *that without which it is not.* In which case the being in question *is* indeed *without that.* But then *that by which it is* is identical to *that without which it is; the same thing is both *that by which* and *that without which,*— which likewise destroys the principle of non-contradiction.

[1] Whether we give it this formula, or the more profound formula: "All being which can *not be* has a cause," the principle of causality, being evident in itself, cannot be deduced from the principle of identity by direct demonstration; but it is connected with it by *reductio ad absurdum*. To deny the principle of causality would, in fact, be either to deny the principle of sufficient reason by saying that being which begins to be (or contingent being) has no reason for its existence, or to deny the principle of identity by saying that that which begins to be (or which is contingent), that is, which is not of itself, has in itself the reason for its existence, that is to say, *is* by itself.

[2] On the subject of local movement the formula which, after Galileo and Descartes, is given to the principle of inertia,—namely that bodies left to themselves continue indefinitely in their state of rest or *of movement,* and that thus, supposing all resistance abolished, movement once imparted continues and is transmitted without diminution,—this formula is, for the scientist (cf. H. Poincaré, *Science et hypothèse,* pp. 112–119), one of those well-founded symbols (*ens rationis cum fundamento in re*) which it is legitimate to construct for the easier establishment of the mathematical knowledge of nature. The philosopher is not obliged to regard it as the ontological expression of the behaviour of the real. Local movement in fact is not a *state* but a *passing,* and like all change, it requires at each instant an actual cause (whose real nature it is the business of the *philosophia naturalis* to seek out, and to determine whether or not it is, at least at the limit, compatible with indefinite continuation of movement). However that may be, and even if movement should be considered as a *state,* it is the Aristotelio-Thomist theory of local movement that would suffer, not the axiom: *quidquid movetur ab alio movetur.* It

And now that which moves here below, is first moved; the millstone which grinds the grain, is itself moved by the wheel of the mill. But is it possible that in the series of movers which thus move one another, there is not a first? If there is no first one which sets all the others going, there will never be movement or change. And yet movement, change exist in fact. Therefore there exists a first mover. First? that is to say one which is not itself moved, which is moved by no kind of movement, which consequently acts by itself, that is, which is its action, for if it were other than its action, it would have to proceed into action under the influence of some cause other than itself, and it would no longer be the first. And as there is no potentiality in its action, so there is no potentiality in its being, for that which *acts* by itself, necessarily *is* by itself, and if it were by another, it would no longer be the first mover. This first mover, this first cause without cause and without any mixture of potentiality, this *pure act* absolutely immobile, not with the immobility of inertia,— far from it,—but with the immobility of pure and supreme activity, which has nothing to acquire and which can become nothing because it has in itself all that can be had and because it is by itself all that one can be, it is this that we call God. Note carefully that in this proof it is not a question of a series of causes following one another in duration nor of a first mover far back at the beginning of time and giving an initial fillip to the universe. That there should be in time an infinite and innumerable multitude of causes succeeding one another is, in fact, not at all impossible, as long as the actual *presence* of the action of all these causes is not required in order that the last of them may

---

would always be necessary to assign some other cause than the mobile, making it pass into this or that state of movement (to say nothing of the causes which constantly maintain it in being). Let us add that the principle of inertia in the form: inanimate bodies are incapable by themselves of modifying their *state,* is an undeniable principle deriving from the truth that living beings *alone* are capable of acting upon themselves.

As to living beings, it is certainly true that they *move themselves,* that is to say, that their action is immanent, that their action terminates with themselves. But they cannot escape the universal principle: *Quidquid movetur ab alio movetur,* for: 1) there is a cause other than themselves which makes them move themselves; 2) it is not in the same connection that they are moved and are movers. For this whole discussion see the afore-mentioned work by Garrigou-Lagrange, *Dieu, son existence et sa nature,* Paris, 5th. ed., pp. 241–266, and appendix II.

"*Omne quod movetur ab alio movetur.* There also," writes Le Roy, "one might find a *petitio principii. Ab alio?* That, in short, is the whole question. The force of the argument depends upon the spatial image employed: a row of billiard balls starts moving only through an initial shock, through an original fillip." (*Rev. de mét. et de mor.,* March 1907, p. 135.) Did Aristotle and Saint Thomas really have in mind only that row of balls? Why not preferably admit that they were playing billiards rather than philosophizing? The whole modernist criticism of the proofs of the existence of God is reduced to the infinitely crude confusion between spatial imagery and thought. Like all philosophies which cannot rise to the intuition of intelligible being, this doctrine which believes that perennial metaphysics abandons itself to the "idols of practical imagination" (*ibid.,* p. 150), and that "we make for ourselves separate ideas in the image of independent bodies" (*ibid.,* July 1899, p. 392), can see in metaphysical principles nothing but dialectical formulae or purely verbal statements. After hearing certain philosophers so often repeat that the principles of reason are only empty forms, one is inclined to agree that *for them* that is certainly so and that they are really incapable of discerning in them anything but words.

act;[1] thus it is that the causal action of the father, grandfather, great-grand-father, etc., need not be present in order that the son may beget in his turn; or that, if a smith striking the anvil changes hammers at each stroke, the causal action of each hammer is not required to be present for the following hammer to act in its turn. And so there is no impossibility in supposing that the smith uses an infinite number of hammers one after the other.[2] But it *is* a question in this proof of a series of causes holding one another in the very act of causing and of a first mover placed at the summit of the hierarchy of beings, infinitely above everything, and giving all things continually, at every instant, being and activity. For it is absolutely impossible that there should exist a series of causes actuating one another at this given moment without there being a first cause of that series, because in that case the actions of all these causes would be without cause, which is absurd. So that even though (contrary to what we know by revelation), creation had taken place from all eternity, from all eternity change in creatures would have manifested the existence of the first immutable cause of all change.

That is how the proof called the proof of the first mover, by starting from movement and becoming, leads us to God, and shows us in Him, both the One Who is by Himself—the pure Act—and the One Who acts by Himself, the first Activity without which nothing is made.

Saint Thomas's second proof,—starting from the fact that there are new *beings* in the world, beings which are caused by a cause other than themselves, and which require in consequence a first cause, itself uncaused, always acting, which produces and preserves all that is,—shows us God as first efficient cause. Starting from the fact that there are in the world beings who cease to exist, therefore who can *not be,* that is to say who are contingent, the third proof shows us God as first necessary: for if there are *only contingent beings,* it is impossible for them to have existed always; to exist without beginning belongs *per se* only to that which is by itself, and could belong to a series of contingent beings only if these had always been receiving existence from a Being Who exists by Himself, that is to say, from a necessary Being;[3] if then

---

[1] And as long as one supposes a being *necessary and eternal in itself* setting in movement, *ab aeterno,* that infinite series of second causes. For an infinite series, in time, of contingent beings (that is, beings who do not exist by themselves) is *absolutely impossible* without a Being Who exists by Himself and Who gives it being from all eternity. Supposing, in fact, that this Being does not exist and that consequently there is only the series of contingent beings, either there will be a first (contingent) cause at the beginning of this series, and in that case it *will no longer be infinite,* or else there will be no first cause at the beginning of this series,—that is to say that taken together the contingent beings who compose it will be without any *raison d'être,* and then the series *will not be.* Supposing then that there are only contingent beings, they could form only a finite series in time. It is precisely upon this that Saint Thomas bases his third proof.

[2] Cf. *Sum. theol.,* I[a], q. 46, a. 2; *C. Gentil.,* II, 38.—Aristotle, *Metaph.,* I, XII, c. 6 (lesson 5 of Saint Thomas).

[3] See note 1; *supposing* that only a contingent series exists, it would perforce be *finite in time.*

there are only contingent beings, these have begun, and before that beginning there was nothing at all: now, "let there at one moment be nothing, and eternally there will be nothing." There must therefore be some being which is necessary, that is, which cannot not exist, and if that being is not necessary by itself, it derives its necessity from another, and since here again we cannot go on ad infinitum, we must conclude the existence of a Being Who is to Himself the reason of His being and of His duration, a Being absolutely necessary, by Whom the being and duration of all the rest is explained.

Starting from the fact that there is in things a diversity of being and perfection, and various degrees of perfection, that is to say various degrees of being, from whence it follows that there is a being which occupies the highest degree, who has the most being, the fourth proof shows us God as the first Being, the cause of all being and all perfection; for that which has the most being cannot receive being from something else, but necessarily possesses being by itself, by virtue of that which constitutes it; it is Being itself, *ipsum esse subsistens,* Being without any admixture of non-being, without limit to its perfection, absolutely simple and pure, *mare pacifico,* as Saint Catherine of Sienna said, the tranquil Ocean of Being.

Finally, starting from the order of the world, that is, from a multiplicity of beings with opposing inclinations which nevertheless co-operate toward a single end—that of their mutual preservation and the good of the whole, the fifth proof shows us God as the first Intelligence, therefore as uncaused Being, since if this Being were caused there would be presupposed before It an intelligence which would cause It for an end, and It would no longer be the first Intelligence directing all things toward their final end, which is Himself.

So, therefore, in any case and in any way, it is because things are, and because they are in such a way that their being is not sufficient of itself, it is by their being that things make us know the existence of God; and it is thanks to the intellectual intuition of being, it is by means of the principle of identity and the principles which are linked to this supreme principle, it is by that sole means, primordially implied in the natural play of intelligence, that our reason raises itself to God. So that we can neither think nor speak, and by that very fact affirm, at least implicitly, the principle of identity, without demonstrating implicitly the existence of God; so that the fool who says in his heart: "there is no God," declares in reality that to be and not to be are identical, that all is absurd and that his thought is only a non-sense. So also that he who denies the principle of identity and who calls the primordial intuition of being untrue, in reality denies, do what he will, the existence of God.

The existence of God and Bergsonian anti-intellectualism

Bergsonian philosophy, as we have seen, replacing intelligence by "intuition," and being by "duration," by becoming or pure change, suppresses in things that by which they resemble God and that by which they show God to us, it suppresses in us, in spite of the philosopher's wishes, our sole natural means of knowing God.

The philosophy of duration or of universal mobilism declares that change or becoming posits itself through itself. It thereby denies the principle of identity since it admits that it is enough to posit A to have non-A,[1] and its true formula is that what evolves creates itself, otherwise stated, that the contingent is cause of itself[2] and has no need of cause.[3]

Did not Bergson take care to justify this thesis by a criticism of the idea of nothingness[4] which amounts to claiming that since the idea of absolute non-being is, as he asserts, a pseudo-idea, it is illusory to seek a cause for the contingent, or rather that the distinction between the necessary and the contingent is itself illusory?—To which we may reply that the idea of nothingness is not at all a pseudo-idea; and that moreover in the idea of contingence and of the consequent fundamental indigence of that being which is not by itself, the idea of absolute non-being is not implied, but only the idea of the non-being of that given thing, the contingent being by definition that which might not be.

In a letter addressed to Father de Tonquédec, Bergson, commenting on his own text, says that his argument tends to prove only one thing, namely "that

---

[1] *Existing consists in changing,* says Bergson. (*Creative Evolution,* p. 8.)

[2] The very expression "cause of itself" (*in essendo*) is inadmissible for, in order to be "cause of oneself" one must first be. GOD, necessary Being, *is by Himself* and *is without cause.* He is not "cause of Himself."

[3] Such indeed is the formula of *creative evolution* expressed in thinkable terms, in "conceptual" terms. The philosophy of duration does not itself declare that the contingent is cause of itself, precisely because this formula would manifest too clearly its internal contradictions; rather it refuses, as tainted with intellectualism, the distinction between contingent and necessary. This distinction however is one of the first divisions of being; intellect cannot escape it. So the philosophy of duration is inevitably disposed to deny both the absolute necessity of the creating One and the real contingency of the created multiple. In order to impose on God and on things the (unthinkable) condition of pure change, it tends to make God contingent like things, while at the same time it tends to make things necessary like God. This slipping toward the negation of the real contingency of particular beings is clearly marked in certain passages of Le Roy's. "To tell the truth," he writes, for example, "each object is only a point of view, a centre of perspective on universal continuity, an aspect rather than a section, a useful abstraction rather than a true reality, in short, a moment of total necessity. It appears contingent to the extent that one either isolates it, or separates it, or tears it out of the tissue or correlations of which it is a knot, or pulls it from that duration of which it is a wave, that is to say, in short, to the extent that it is not. Its contingency signifies therefore in the last analysis only the unreality of the fragmentation." (*Comment se pose le problème de Dieu, Rev. de Métaph. et de Morale,* March 1907, p. 139.) As though it were necessary to pass through the contingency of the universe in order to be sure of the contingency of a certain event resulting from a simple meeting of causes, so that itself it is properly "without cause" ordered by itself to produce it (cf. *Sum. theol.,* I, 115, 6), or from a cause ordered by itself to a certain event or a certain being, but which can suffer hindrance. The new philosophy is in this case nearer than it thinks to Spinoza.

[4] *Creative Evolution,* pp. 275–299. On the application of this Bergsonian theory in the modernist criticism of proofs of the existence of God, see Le Roy, *Rev. de mét. et de mor.,* July 1907, p. 481.

something has always existed; on the nature of that something it provides, it is true, no positive conclusion."* *Something has always existed,*—who would think of denying so manifest a truth? To establish it, there was no need for a very subtle analysis, for it is a primary evidence that being cannot come from nothingness.

In reality the Bergsonian argument goes much further.† It first attacks an imaginary enemy, a pseudo-problem which would consist in asking: why, by what cause does being, *being by itself* as well as contingent being, exist? An absurd problem for to be caused, to have a why and wherefore, is not essential to being as such, to what purely and simply is, and only belongs necessarily to contingent being, to what is by participation; being by itself, that which is by essence, has no why, has no cause; it is, and it is for itself its own *raison d'être*. But once embarked on this pseudo-problem, and resolved to show that it should not be propounded, but without pointing out in what its absurdity consists and without distinguishing being by itself and contingent being, Bergson's argument, whatever his intentions may have been, can only end in one conclusion, namely that *contingent being* as well as being by itself has no need of cause, or in other words that the contingent exists by itself. If "it in no way says that what has always existed is the world itself,"[1] it says that what has always existed is not necessarily *ens a se*, pure act, and is itself only a *becoming* in which, however concentrated one makes it, it is impossible to perceive any essential and absolute distinction from the universe of the contingent.

There is more, says Bergson,[2] in movement than in the immobile. From whence it follows that movement has no need of cause, and the mobile no need of mover. Moreover, according to Bergsonism the distinction between the mobile and the mover, between effect and cause, is only a result of the conceptual fragmentation and an artificial division of the moving continuum in terms of space; and the principle of causality, for Bergson, is the very principle of mechanistic error.[3] "Why not simply identify being with becoming,"[4] asks Le Roy. "Things *being* movement, there is no longer any need to ask oneself how they *receive* it."[5]

These philosophers, who move among images, do not see that simply identifying being with becoming is simply to declare that potential and inde-

---

* *Études*, February 20, 1912, p. 516.
† See *supra*, First Section, chap. III.
[1] *Études*, number quoted above, p. 516. See *supra*, p. 92, n. 1.
[2] *Creative Evolution*, p. 316.
[3] See *supra*, p. 128, n. 2, and *infra*, p. 259, n. 3. For reasons at first glance different from Bergson's, in reality very close to them, a theorist of the sciences such as Meyerson will likewise admit that the natural functioning of explicative thought tends automatically to mechanicism. These philosophers conceive rational thought only according to the eleatic pattern.
[4] *Comment se pose le problème de Dieu* (*Rev. de Mét. et de Morale*, March 1907, p. 150).
[5] *Ibid.*, p. 135.

terminate being in the act of being determined and actuated, is being itself and all being, or in other words that it determines and actualizes itself by itself, or that it gives itself what it has not, and finally that what is not, is. They do not see that the distinction between the mobile and the mover, between effect and cause, does not in any way result from the fragmentation of the sensible continuum into spatial images in juxtaposition to one another, but ineluctably results as we have just seen, from the exigencies of the primordial intuition of being.[1]

They do not see that what is more than movement, what accounts for movement, is what is opposed to movement *for the intellect*, is being, act, the actual and active possession of the real, it is not what is opposed to movement *for the senses,* namely the state of rest of inertia, potentiality, the simple aptitude for being, where there is certainly less than in movement in which there is less than in actual being.

As a result it appears obvious that for such a philosophy there is no possibility of showing by reason, with the help of creatures, the existence of God, either by starting from movement, since for such a philosophy what is moved is not moved by another, or by starting from new beings, since for it the new is produced from itself, or by starting from contingent beings since, for it, becoming and the contingent need no *raison d'être*, or by starting from degrees of perfection since, for it, potentiality and movement take precedence over being and act, or by starting from the order of the world since, for this philosophy, the order of things exists by itself, without there being any need of an end pursued by an intelligence. Such is indeed the scope of the critique of the idea of disorder set forth in *Creative Evolution*.[2] In this critique Bergson, forgetting that the principle of finality: "every agent acts for an end," is a necessary and universal principle of reason which is connected immediately with the principle of *raison d'être,* for without an end, without a specifying *raison d'être* an agent would not be determined to one action any more than to another and consequently would never act; forgetting also that every order, that is to say every convergence of multiple and diverse things toward one

---

[1] "Why not simply identify being with becoming? There would be no numerical series, no scale of distinct terms each realizing statically a degree of perfection; rather would there be mobile continuities, dynamic progress, spectrums of colours dissipated in a perpetual spurting; and perfection would present itself as a sense of genesis, not as a final point or a primary source." Éd. Le Roy, *Rev. de Mét. et de Mor.,* 1907, p. 150. And again: "Why should not perfection be quite simply the infinity of progress when envisaged globally and when its convergence is symbolized by a limit? Why, in a word, would not the perfect be an ascension, a growth, rather than an immobile plenitude?" (*Ibid.,* July 1907, p. 482). *Why? Simply* because the philosopher who would identify being with becoming could not think what he says, because he would be philosophizing without ever having had the intellectual perception of being, and would therefore be spreading himself in a pure verbal flood, in an illusory flow of images.

[2] *Creative Evolution,* pp. 218–236.—On the use of this Bergsonian theory in the modernist criticism of the proofs of the existence of God, see Le Roy, *Rev. de Mét. et de Mor.,* July 1907, pp. 467–477.

and the same end, demands an intelligence which knows that end and sub-
mits the multiplicity of means to the unity of that end, Bergson tries to show
that what he calls *the vital order* has no need of a wherefore and spontaneously
results from the evolutive impulse (very much as the order of an army if I
may suggest an example, would create itself alone, without chief and without
discipline, by the simple impulse toward victory). While what he calls *geometric or automatic order* results spontaneously from the interruption of the
vital order, and consequently does not demand a wherefore either (somewhat
as rout and panic would result spontaneously from the interruption of the impulse toward victory of an army ordered along Bergsonian principles . . .)

The universe our hands touch and our eyes of flesh see is better made than
the universe of the philosophers; and it knows neither rout nor panic because it marches under one single chief, which is Intelligence itself. No matter what we do we shall never find in the multiple as such the reason for
unity. One may question whether in certain particular cases one is dealing
with a real order or with an imaginary order (again due to intelligence, I
mean to the intelligence of the observer). But each time that one has to deal
with a real order, it is certain he will find himself facing some trace of the
mind. Any calculation of probabilities presupposes in the beginning determined conditions which have to do either with natural finality or with voluntary finality. One can moreover imagine he is calculating the chances that
words thrown at random will compose the Aeneid, and can say that the
chances of that happening are infinitely small: yet in reality, in making (or
imagining) such a calculation one *takes it for granted* that the event in question is *possible,* and that is what is false. In the real, the chances in question
are strictly nil, it is metaphysically impossible for a real order to derive from
chance. It is also impossible for it to derive from an impulse without intelligence such as the one accepted in *Creative Evolution.* If a certain automatic
order can spring from the mere corruption of the vital order, it is because
absolute disorder is impossible, the dispersed materials always keeping at
least their nature and the ordinations it comprises; and the vital order itself, implying essentially self-regulation and the investment of the parts by
the whole, implies to a supreme degree that finality to which all *nature* already bears witness, and which is in the substance of things the imprint of
the Intelligence by which everything has been made.

The existence of God and Bergsonian intuition

If reason dispossessed of truth cannot do so, can Bergsonian intuition at
least, make us know the existence of God?

"Just as," says Bergson, "a consciousness of colour, which would harmonize
inwardly with orange [. . .] would feel itself caught between red and yellow,
would perhaps even have, beneath the latter colour, a presentiment of a

whole spectrum in which is naturally prolonged the continuity which goes from red to yellow, so the intuition of our duration [. . .] puts us in contact with a whole continuity of durations which we should try to follow either downwardly or upwardly: in both cases we can dilate ourselves indefinitely by a more and more vigorous effort, in both cases we transcend ourselves. In the first case we advance toward a duration more and more scattered [. . .] At the limit would be the pure homogeneous [. . .], materiality. Advancing in the other direction, we go toward a duration which stretches, tightens and becomes more and more intensified: at the limit would be eternity."[1] That is the means by which Bergsonian philosophy gives us the hope of knowing the existence of God and claims to "put at last" "at the base of things" "a Principle of creation"[2] which is a "centre of shooting-out."[3] Bergsonian duration, the time-stuff of things, the contingent and the new which is posited by itself being the sole reality,—by the intuition of this duration shall we raise ourselves to God: a perilous ascent indeed if this duration is only a myth. . . .

Bergson's metaphorical argument takes on an air of plausibility from its distant analogy with the proof by degrees of perfection: that is a kind of mirage, due to the fact that the intelligence, going instinctively to the intelligible and seeking everywhere its good,—even in the "consciousness of colour,"[4]—involuntarily corrects the Bergsonian metaphor and sees in it, in spite of anything, the very thing that the Bergsonian thesis excludes. But, in reality, the proof by degrees of perfection rests wholly on the intuition of being and the principle of identity, which Bergsonian metaphysics jeopardizes: it stresses the radical poverty of the contingent which, according to that metaphysics, is self-sufficient and self-asserting, and it leads us to God by a rational and analogical knowledge, not by any kind of experimental knowledge.

In the Bergsonian doctrine, on the other hand, if we are to place a "principle of creation" "at the base" of duration, of the vital impulse, is it in virt of the laws of causality, of sufficient reason, of identity? Assuredly not, fo we should then fall back into conceptual fragmentation and the sin of reasoning. Is it because our senses have always shown us that water-fountains or clusters of fireworks, have a centre of spurting, and that in the spectrum orange comes after yellow and green? There is not much chance, I dare say, of deriving any metaphysical truth from that. Only one resource remains and that is to say that by the intuition of a created duration, of our duration for example, we manage, by dilating ourselves sufficiently, to enter into contact with the divine essence, with the duration which is the "concretion of all du-

---

[1] *Introduction à la Métaphysique* (*Rev. de Métaph. et de Morale*, January 1903, pp. 24–25). (Cf. *Creative Mind*, p. 221.)

[2] *Creative Evolution*, p. 275.

[3] *Ibid.*, p. 248.

[4] Cf. Farges, *La Philosophie de M. Bergson*, pp. 23–25.

ration."* In this connection Bergson speaks of a going to the limit. But in a metaphysics which claims to be an *integral experience,* that operation cannot in any way relate to a conclusion established by reason passing from one concept to another concept. It can signify only one thing: that by dint of dilating or transcending ourselves, and of intensifying the intuition of our duration, we should succeed, if only in a flash of evanescent intuition, in perceiving God intuitively: an obviously untenable thesis! As though there were not an infinite distance between the divine nature and our own, as though the intuitive knowledge of God were accessible to metaphysical effort and not the most supernatural gift of His mercy, that which constitutes, according to Saint Thomas, our very beatitude.†

Shall it now be said that Bergsonian intuition, however vigorous its efforts may be, intends to remain always infinitely distant from divine reality, and that it only indicates a direction? Then what means have we of passing, by following this direction, from the finite to the infinite, and of affirming the existence of God as a necessary truth? Neither intuition (by hypothesis), nor reason (since it has been done away with). The existence of God will always remain irremediably hypothetical.

The Existence of God and reason

As for Christian philosophy, it affirms with the Catholic Church that *"reasoning* can with certainty demonstrate the existence of God."[1] For, since the creation of the world, as Saint Paul says, *invisibilia Dei per ea quae facta sunt, intellecta conspiciuntur.*[2]

I do not maintain, be it observed, that the heart, the will, the experience of life do not, in certain cases, play a preponderant rôle when a soul, after having by accident lost the primordial certitudes which are our natural portion, gradually finds belief again, even purely natural belief, in God. And this not only in the sense that the will, in becoming upright, suppresses the obstacles it raised against the normal exercise of reason; but also in the sense that the profound sentiment of our indigence, and the need for order, and the desire for good, and the progress of the will and "the effort of the whole

* *Rev. de Mét. et de Mor.,* January 1903, p. 25. (Cf. *Creative Mind,* p. 221.)

† Saint Thomas, *Sum. theol.,* Iª, q. 12, a. 4.—We know that the theologians admit that Moses and Saint Paul were raised in a transitory way to the vision of divine essence; but there it is a question of the highest graces of prophecy and infused contemplation. We also know that an experimental knowledge of God, as it were, takes place through the gift of wisdom. But this knowledge, which is essentially supernatural (since it supposes charity), far from being intuitive here below, is produced in the darkness of faith.

1 A proposition imposed by the Congregation of the Index under the signature of the Abbé Bautain in 1840, and of Bonnetty in 1855. (Denzinger-Bannwart, 1622, 1650–1652.)

2 *Rom.,* I, 20.

soul" "living and acting"[3] can, even when we are still dulled by the habit of error and not in condition to *demonstrate,* cause us to divine, give us the practical conviction that He in Whom is all good, all order, all plenitude, exists necessarily.

What I do maintain is that it is unworthy of human nature to limit to this conviction, especially practical and objectively insufficient as it is, our natural knowledge of the existence of God. Even in the practical and objectively insufficient conviction of which we have just spoken, there is persuasive force only because the intelligence (which one would not dare to believe if it spoke in its own name, for one is still not cured of the habit of error), comes into play unawares, under cover of feeling and moral aspirations, and starts at least somehow returning to the instinctive proofs of common sense,—which are but philosophical demonstrations in the implicit state, and which are all based on the intellectual intuition of being.

Thus, for example, if the desire for good, or the intelligible commandment of the moral law, can lead us to God, it is because in reality "one single aspiration of the soul toward the better and the perfect is a more than geometrical demonstration of the existence of God";[1] it is (according to Saint Thomas's fourth argument, the argument by degrees of perfection) because our will, seeking in all contingent good the absolute good for which it has a desire rooted in nature,—this absolute Good, by reason of which all the other goods are goods must necessarily exist; and it is also because the universal and necessary imperative of duty having its final justification only in the absolute good, this absolute Good must exist necessarily.

So, finally, when a man accustomed to thinking at the surface of his mind one day manages to perceive that he lives, that he is, that he really and truly possesses being, and by the same token feels all the worth yet all the indigence of that being, he understands by instinct that the source of being, that *being by itself* exists necessarily; and he is then ready to understand the word that God addressed to Saint Catherine of Sienna: "I am Who Am, thou art who is not."

It may be that in many people the life of reason is so feeble that rational perceptions most efficacious in themselves and most certain have need of a sort of reinforcement by motives of sentiment and practice less removed from the life of the senses and acting precisely in the way of *sensitizers.* But it is nevertheless the life of the reason, however hidden it may sometimes be, which here again plays the essential rôle. The fact still and in any case remains that man knows the existence of God naturally only because he leans upon the intellectual intuition of being. To suppress being is to posit atheism.

---

[3] As Laberthonnière says, in his *Essais de Philosophie religieuse,* in other respects so open to criticism (2nd. edition, Paris, 1903, p. 78, note).

[1] Hemsterhuys, quoted by Garrigou-Lagrange, *op. cit.,* p. 306. Cf. Saint Thomas, *Sum. theol.,* I^a II^{ae}, q. 2, a. 7 and 8; q. 3, a. 1 and 8; q. 91, a. 1 and 2; q. 93, a. 1 and 2; q. 94, a. 2.

II.—THE NATURE AND PERFECTIONS OF GOD

In spite of the weaknesses of Bergsonian metaphysics, Bergson was led to affirm less and less conditionally and doubtfully the existence of God.*

This God of Bergsonism,—we must now ask ourselves what His nature is, what His attributes are and whether He is the true God.

The Doctrine of Saint Thomas

We cannot, by our natural forces alone, know the divine nature in what constitutes it by right, for in order to do that we should have to *see* God Himself; but we can know the divine nature in an inadequate way, by means of creatures, which are likenesses of it. The five great ways, the five great Thomist proofs by which reason demonstrates the existence of God, lead us to God as first Mover, first Cause, first Necessary, first Being, first Intelligence. First, that is, Who has nothing before Him, nothing above Him, nothing which moves Him, nothing which causes Him, nothing which accounts for Him. God must therefore be in Himself the reason for His action, the reason for His being, the reason for His thought. God is by Himself.

This attribute of *aseity,* of existence by oneself, of absolute Independence in being itself, is the profoundest thing human reason can say on the subject of divine essence; it is the attribute from which all God's other perfections are deduced: unity, truth, goodness, infinity, immensity, immutability, eternity, incomprehensibility, intelligence, life, liberty, providence, justice and mercy, omnipotence, absolute beatitude.[1] In every contingent thing, in each one of us for example, our nature, our humanity, *what* we are, is something else than *existing,* or *esse,* than the positive and beneficent act *par excellence* by which we are "situated outside of nothingness"; that is what is expressed when we say that in every contingent thing essence and existence are distinct. And it is clear that the existence of things is distinct from their nature, since they can cease to be! In God, in Being by itself, essence and existence are one and the same reality: because He can neither give Himself existence, which would be absurd, nor receive it from another. God has not being, He is being; He is subsisting being itself, without any admixture of potentiality, without limit, incomprehensibly rich in all perfection, He Who is and Who cannot not be. That is the fundamental truth of Christian philosophy.[2]

From this derives, or rather in this very fact consists the absolute *simplicity* of God. In God there is no composition, all that is in God is God; God is His Existence, He is His Divinity, He is His Intelligence, He is His Goodness,

* Cf. for example the letters, previously quoted, to de Tonquédec, *Études,* February 20th, 1912. —And also *La Perception du Changement,* p. 37.

[1] Cf. Saint Thomas, *Sum. theol.,* Iª, q. 3 to 26.

[2] Cf. del Prado, *De Veritate fundamentali philosophiae Christianae,* Fribourg, Switzerland, 1899–1906.

He is His Duration, He is His Life and His Joy, and all the perfections we discern in Him separately because of the infirmity of our thought, are actually but one with one another and with Him. Hence His *unity,* because divine nature being identical with God's being, cannot be communicated to any other than God Himself. Hence also His *immutability,* because He is pure Being, pure Act, without any admixture of potentiality, and because the unlimited plenitude of Being excludes in Him all becoming.—From that derives, in that consists the infinite transcendence of the divine nature and its absolute distinction, real and essential, from the world, from everything in which essence is distinct from existence, from everything that implies, in any possible way, multiplicity, composition, change or possibility of change.

If therefore the world exists, it is because it has been *created,* that is, made *out of nothing,* of no pre-existing matter. Reason without Revelation cannot decide whether creation began in time,[1] but in any case it affirms that if the world had always endured, then creation would have always endured also. For all that is, and that is not God, can only be created, that is, *caused in its whole being;* God alone, being the universal and all-powerful Cause, has the power to create; and He creates with the most absolute freedom, not at all to receive, solely to give, because He Himself suffices, fully and infinitely, for the perfection of His goodness; and if the effect of the creative act, as we know by Revelation, began in or rather with time, the creative act itself which is one with the divine essence, the free choice by which God wills and loves His creatures, is eternal like God; and if things continue to have being, and if things act and are causes in their turn, and if we think, and if we love, and if we freely will, it is because God positively preserves the being of things, by the same action which created them, and because He acts in everything that acts, being present by His action in the innermost heart of each thing Himself operating in the innermost heart of each thing, Himself moving, as primary mover, each thing, each thought, each love, each will, since it is He Who *causes* all that is *to be.*

Finally, what enables us to speak of God, to name Him, to know Him, is the fact that being and the notions connected with being, the one, that is to say being as undivided, the true, that is, being as facing intelligence, the good, that is, being as facing will, etc., are notions which overflow any genus or any category of things and which, consequently, imply in their essence no limitation. These notions, which for that reason are called transcendental, are found in all that is; as a result, they do not belong exclusively to any species of beings; they are ascribed to the one and the other *by analogy;* a man is good in his manner as a fruit is good in its manner or a word is good in

[1] *Sum. theol.,* I^a, q. 46, a. 2. On the creation and conservation of things, see I^a, q. 45 and q. 104 and 105.

its manner, and being must indeed be an essentially *analogous* notion, since things which differ really from one another, and since all of them nevertheless are, all of them truly and properly have being. Hence we can attribute to God, truly and properly, all the realities or perfections of the transcendental order, such as being or those defined in relation to being, even though we first got our idea of them from the consideration of creatures.

While the realities essentially enclosed in a genus and implying in their definition an imperfection, a limitation, can be said of God only in a metaphorical way, as when we say that God is a lion, a fire, a torrent, a rock, a spring of living water, because all the beauty and perfection these things have exist eminently in God, but in Him have a *formality* unknown to us,—the realities of the transcendental order, being, unity, truth, beauty, intelligence, will, etc., are said of God by right, by very reason of the essentially *analogous* value of such concepts. These perfections exist in God *formally*-eminently.*

But the *mode* in which these realities exist in God, this mode which is infinite, this mode which is that of subsisting Being itself, how, in what way, to what point God is, God is true, God is good, no idea will ever suffice to show,—by very reason of the analogous character of all natural knowledge of God. All that we know from this point of view is that the divine reality everywhere overflows our concepts, that all that we know in a separate way is but one in the absolute simplicity of the divine essence, that our knowledge of God here below is irreducibly inadequate, and that what is truest and most worthy of God is to say, with the pseudo-Dionysius in his "negative theology," with Saint Thomas and with the whole Church, that God is nothing of what is, is not as things are, is not good as things are good, is above all being and all thought.

It is thus that we know God by analogy, in a glass darkly. It is thus that Christian wisdom, going from one extreme to the other with strength and gentleness, shows us that God infinitely exceeds our knowledge by His essence and at the same time, that we can know Him inadequately, but with an absolute truth, by His creatures; know Him with more certitude than we know our brother, our friend, our own heart;[1] as it shows us at the same time the ineffable transcendence of the divine nature and the sovereign immanence of divine operation; as it shows us both the very redoubtable holiness and the superabundant mercy of Him Who is.[2]

But in any case it is ever the idea of being which is our light. By it, even though it also is infinitely overflowed by the divine reality, by the *deity,* which

---

* On this question see *Sum. theol.,* I^a, q. 12 and q. 13; John of Saint Thomas, *Cursus philos.,* t. I, Log. II P., q. 13 and 14; Garrigou-Lagrange, *La valeur transcendantale et analogique des notions premières* (*Revue thomiste,* 1912–1913).

[1] Cf. Garrigou-Lagrange, *Dieu, son existence et sa nature,* pp. 378–379; *le Sens commun, la Philosophie de l'être et les formules dogmatiques.* 3rd. edition, 1922, pp. 307–312, 317–318.

[2] Cf. *Sum. theol.,* I^a, q. 21, a. 4.

is super-being just as it is super-goodness and super-beauty,—it is by the idea of being that we give God the name which suits Him *par excellence,* and that we see His absolute distinction from the world; by it, because of its analogous value, we can found our knowledge of God without giving either agnosticism or pantheism the slightest hold.

The Bergsonian theory

Bergsonian philosophy, on the contrary, by the very fact that it tries to do without being, is logically incapable of establishing an *absolute and total, real and essential* distinction between God and things.

The doctrine of analogy, it is quite evident, can have no place in an anti-intellectualist philosophy. It follows either that God is unknowable,—whence agnosticism,—or else that God is directly attained in Himself by the same knowledge which allows us to attain creatures,—whence monism. Let us recall furthermore the manner in which Bergson tries to show us the existence of God. The intuition of our own duration puts us in contact with a whole continuity of durations that we can follow, transcending ourselves, and going toward a duration which stretches, tightens, and becomes more and more intensified. "At the limit would be eternity." At the limit, by dint of transcending ourselves, we should touch God, were it only in the fading of a fleeting ecstasy! There, then, by intensifying the intuition of our duration, by progressively emphasizing our intuition of created natures, do we succeed in perceiving by *intuition* God Himself and, to use the terms by which Bergson describes his intuition, in coinciding with Him, in reliving Him; there in any case we have the process by which we know things, enabling us to attain God directly in things . . .

Bergson moreover, in the lines following the text I have just quoted, has this to say about the God he has caught sight of: "A living *and consequently still moving* Eternity [. . .]," he says, *"which would be the concretion of all duration as materiality is its dispersion."*[1] If God is the concretion of all duration, is it probably because all duration is the dispersion of God? If He is the concretion of all duration as materiality is its dispersion, is it probably because living eternity and materiality are two opposite extremes within an identical genus which is duration?

In claiming that becoming or movement is more than being, and that the principle of identity must yield before "the flowing of duration," the new philosophy renders impossible any real and essential distinction between God and the world. On one hand it attributes to things what appertains only to God: aseity, since it claims that movement is sufficient unto itself, that the

---

[1] *Rev. de Mét. et de Mor.,* January 1903, p. 25. Cf. *Creative Mind,* p. 221. The italics are mine.

contingent is self-positing, that becoming is its own reason; simplicity, since in its eyes, things are their action and their duration; incomprehensibility, ineffability, since our concepts are radically incapable of expressing the real; and finally creative power, since duration or action increases as it advances, and creates in proportion to its progress,[1] since "we experience creation within us" "as soon as we act freely," since *evolution* is *creative*. Did Bergson not see that in order to act it is first necessary to be and that to create it is necessary to be *a se?*

On the other hand, Bergsonian philosophy attributes to its God what pertains to things; it makes him contingent like them, indigent like them, changing, moving, becoming like them. God "has nothing of the already-made,"[2] says Bergson; and elsewhere: He is a "still moving" duration. And certainly, in the Increate there is nothing of the *made*. But let us take the philosopher's words in the very sense in which he constantly uses them. If God has nothing of the already-made, is it then, that He is *in the making?* With nothing *perfect* in Him? Pure Need instead of Pure Act?

"Our life," wrote Le Roy, "is incessant creation. And it is the same for the world [. . .] If we declare God immanent, it is because we consider *of Him what has become in us or in the world;* but for the world and for us there still remains an infinity to become, an infinity which will be creation properly so-called, not simply development; and from this point of view God appears transcendent."[3] It is in vain that, refusing to accept the idea of being as means of attaining the *Ego sum qui sum,* one tries to restore the truth of divine things in terms of becoming. To call creation what is becoming, to know God as immanent in turning back upon what has *become*, as transcendent in turning toward what is *to become* of the creature, without manifesting ontologically the difference of essences, is to take all real meaning away from divine transcendence. "That amounts to saying," Le Roy further wrote, "that God is known to us by His very life in us, in the work of our own deification. In this sense one can say again that, for us, God is not, but becomes. His becoming is our very progress. . . ."[4] For us, God is not? Before this moral

---

[1] *Creative Evolution*, p. 249.

[2] *Ibid.*, Chevalier (*op. cit.*, p. 237[2]), while defending this formula, forgets that for Bergson, as it happens, there is no *freedom* except in the *being-made*.

It seems that Bergson is struck by the thought that if God is immutable Being, *apud quem non est transmutatio nec vicissitudinis obumbratio*, He is no longer the living God. It is quite evident that when one says He is immutable it is *by analogy*, to express the perfection of an activity which lacks nothing and which, as a result, cannot change, but not at all to compare His nature with the nature of things we see immobile here below and in which are the least being and activity. Moreover, even in creatures, the higher one goes in the scale of beings the more movement becomes immanent. In the highest forms of life, in thought for example, it remains entire in the one who acts. In which sense it can be said, by analogy also, naturally—that God moves. Cf. *Summa theol.*, I[a], q. 18, a. 3, *ad* 1.

[3] *Rev. de Mét. et de Mor.*, July 1907, p. 512. (The italics are mine.)

[4] "Comment se pose le problème de Dieu" (*Rev. de Mét. et de Mor.*, July 1907, p. 509).

"becoming" of Him in us (or rather of us in Him) we do not *know* that He *is?* Then it is only in thinking Him unknowable that one will be able not to think that He is Himself pure becoming. How is absurdity at the summit of things to be avoided, when one has begun by putting absurdity at the root of everything, by suppressing being and the principle of identity, and by positing becoming as the fundamental reality? Aristotle says,[3] "It is impossible for anyone ever to think that the same thing exists and does not exist. Heraclitus is of another opinion, according to some, but it is not necessary for one to think everything that he says [. . .] The cause of this opinion, is that [the old evolutionist Ionians], while they sought the truth about beings, admitted only the sensible as being [. . .], and as they saw that all sensible nature is in a perpetual movement, and that about pure change as such nothing true can be said, some people like Cratylus have thought that we should no longer say anything. He contented himself with wagging his finger." Would to heaven that all the enemies of reason would imitate the discretion of Cratylus!

Between Bergson's God and the world there is in reality only a difference of degree or intensity, or of tension or contraction in duration; that will never make an authentic difference of nature or of essence. "Let us imagine," writes Bergson,[1] "a recipient full of steam at high pressure, and here and there in its sides a crack through which the steam is escaping in a jet. The steam thrown into the air is nearly all condensed into little drops which fall, and this condensation and this fall represent simply the loss of something, an interruption, a deficit. But a small part of the jet of steam subsists, uncondensed, for some seconds; it is making an effort to raise the drops which are falling; it succeeds at most in retarding their fall. So, from an immense reservoir of life, jets must be gushing out unceasingly, each one of which, in falling, is a world. . . ." With this difference, that the "crack, the jet of steam, the raising of the drops, are determined necessarily, whereas the creation of a world is a free act, and life within the material world participates in this freedom. Let us rather think then of an action like that of raising the arm; then let us suppose that the arm, left to itself, falls back, and yet that there subsists in it, striving to raise it up again, something of the will that animated it. In this image of a *creative action which unmakes itself* we already have a more exact representation of matter. We shall then see in vital activity what subsists of the direct movement in the inverted movement, *a reality which is making itself through a reality which is being unmade.*" God appears then as a "centre from which worlds shoot out as it were like rockets in a fireworks display,—provided however that I do not present this centre as

[3] *Métaph.,* lib. IV, c. 3 and 5 (1005 b 23-26; 1010 a 1-3, 7-9, 12-13).
[1] *Creative Evolution,* pp. 247–248. The words are in italics in the original text.

a *thing,* but as a continuity of shooting out."* If these words have a meaning they signify that the world is, or that worlds are, an *emanation* from God. This emanation is creative, creating and created, as much as you like, since the word 'creation,' in a philosophy which rejects the idea of being, no longer has any meaning, and can be said of anything and everything; but it is still an emanation in the sense of production of what is identical in nature. The Bergsonians imagine that all that is necessary to silence criticism and avoid pantheism is to call *creation* what everybody else calls becoming or movement (and *free* what everyone else calls *spontaneous*). But it is a creation without a *thing which creates,* as Bergson says, and without *things created;* it is a creative action, a pure change which is common to God and the world; hence the world can only be an impulse or a spurting which is distinguished from the divine fountain-head only while continuing it.

There is no denying that Bergson *does not intend* to be pantheistic and monistic: "I speak of God," he wrote to Father de Tonquédec, "as of the *fountain-head* from whence come one after the other, through an effect of His liberty, the 'currents' or 'impulses' each one of which will form a world: He therefore remains distinct from them";[1] and again: "From all this we get a clear idea of a creative and free God, generator of both matter and life, *whose effort of creation continues* on the side of life, through the evolution of species and the constitution of human personalities. From all this, consequently, we get the refutation of pantheism and monism in general."[2] —Alas no! From all this we see that Bergson is not a pantheist in the way Spinoza was nor a monist in the way Haeckel was; but here again the doctrine is stronger than the philosopher. To avoid pantheism, it is not enough to say that God is distinct from the world as the centre of spurting is distinct from the rockets which shoot out, or as the fountain-head is distinct from the springs into which it divides, or as the sap is distinct from the tree, or as any created cause is distinct from its effect. The world is absolutely distinct from God *by essence;* there is nothing, absolutely nothing in common, except by analogy, between the being of God and the being of the world. And because in Bergsonian philosophy there cannot be between God and the world an absolute distinction of nature or essence, but only a difference of degree or intensity,—because pure becoming is the ultimate reality, the same ultimate reality for God as for the world, and because the becoming of the world which is making itself, that is of the *creative gesture,* is necessarily in continuity with the becoming of the God who is making Himself, the Author of the creative gesture,—because the vital impulse, the reality which is making itself through the reality which is being unmade is only the continuation of

* *Ibid.,* p. 249.
[1] *Études,* February 20, 1912; Ire Lettre (May 12, 1908), p. 517.
[2] *Ibid.,* IIe Lettre (June 12, 1911), p. 515. (The italics are mine.) See *supra,* p. 92, n. 1.

what Bergson calls, with characteristic incorrectness of terms, the *effort* of creation,—because matter itself is only "inverted psychic," and because thus what gives the impulse, and what shoots out, and what falls back is but one and the same essential reality, pure becoming at various degrees of concentration, now ascending, now descending, here at the maximum of intensity, there at the maximum of dispersion and dissipation, it must be said that Bergsonian metaphysics in spite of itself, falls a prey to pantheism: an original pantheism certainly, and quite opposite to Spinoza's, a pantheism of creation, through self-production or self-increase of the absolute in "real duration," in substantial and creative time.—In refusing to admit the principle of substance, in constructing a doctrine of metaphysical reality on an absolute phenomenism Bergson, in spite of his desire to mark the originality or even the irreducibility of the diversities of the real, prohibited himself from admitting any *essential* distinction between beings: however "heterogeneous" we may picture things as being, they can as a result (under pain of being substances!) only form one single and sole continuity of nature,—the continuity of duration, of pure change. They are one, not in Spinozist *substance,* but in *pure becoming.* Bergson thereby condemned himself in advance to a monism which was also original,—a monism by a gushing of ever new modes of self-sufficient change, —but a monism still deserving of the reproaches Aristotle once formulated: "To admit that all things are one in what constitutes their being, is to maintain the Heraclitean opinion. [...] Then good and evil will be the same thing, man and horse will no longer be substantially distinct. But in this case we are no longer philosophizing on the unity of things, but on their nothingness."[1]

Perhaps it would be advisable to emphasize this point still further, for a per-

---

[1] *Phys.,* 1, I, c. ii, 185 b 19–25.—Cf. Garrigou-Lagrange, *Le Sens commun, la Philosophie de l'être et les Formules dogmatiques,* 3rd. edition, pp. 244–246. "Bergson [...] goes so far as to say that modern philosophy's last word, insofar as it is in opposition to ancient philosophy, consists in stating that the *fundamental reality is becoming.* Now that amounts to saying, as Hegel recognized, that *the intimate nature of things is a realized contradiction.* To deny the principle of identity as the fundamental law of the real, is evidently to affirm that contradiction is at the very heart of the real, since the principle of non-contradiction is only the negative formula of the principle of identity. *To suppress pure Act which is to being as A is to A, to suppress divine transcendence, is to root everything in absurdity.* Bergson's anti-intellectualism is nothing more than a Hegelianism turned upside-down. These two extreme systems were bound to join one another in a common evolutionistic monism; if they did not exist they would have had to be invented for they constitute the most remarkable proofs by *reductio ad absurdum* of the existence of the transcendent God, absolutely One and immutable . . .

. . . Only three positions are possible in general metaphysics and theodicy: 1) *Admit the primacy of being over becoming and deny potentiality;* then willy-nilly we must get back to Parmenides [...], absorb the world in God [...] and *deny the world* in denying all multiplicity and all becoming. 2) *Admit the primacy of being, and also admit potentiality;* then, with Aristotle, we *must affirm divine transcendence,* implied in the concept of pure Act; 3) *Deny the primacy of being and affirm that of becoming,* with Heraclitus, which is [...] to deny the objective value of the principle of identity and place absurdity at the very heart of the real [...] absorb God in the world [...] and finally *deny God.*

The alternative amounts to this other: God or radical absurdity."

fect metaphysical purification of the idea of primary Cause is rarer than one would think, and even though we have a horror of pantheism, it often happens that we still harbour in our thought notions whose wholly pantheistic affinity has not been eliminated. The partisans of Bergsonian philosophy are not alone in this. In order properly to understand the essential difference between God and the world, it is not enough to recognize a God distinct from the world as one man is distinct from another, or a mind from a body, or one thing here below from any other thing here below, no matter how different they may be. *No word of ours* is applicable to God in the same way that it is to the things of which we have experience. Between Him and creatures it is being itself in its depths and its totality, the metaphysical structure of being that differs; in Him an infinity of being infinitely different, infinitely separated from all that, outside Him, we call being, from all being which appears and can appear before our eyes and before our reason. That is why *what* God *is,* is known to us in reflections and in riddles, we do not know it in itself: *nos non scimus de Deo quid est.** In this being of the deity, essentially different from the entire being of the world, is hidden and rooted the universe of the supernatural order (supernatural *quoad substantiam*), which is the divine life itself participated in. Scarcely does that life come down into the world, when the scandal of the cross and the hatred of the world immediately *illustrate,* in a tangible way, the *real and essential distinction between God and the world . . .*

Far from being infinitely transcendent to the world, the God of Bergsonian metaphysics cannot be conceived without the world (either this world or other worlds) : its life consists in being a *centre of gushing.*

To designate this God, or what of Him is continued in the vital impulse, Bergsonian philosophy uses the words of consciousness or rather of super-consciousness, of effort, of will tremendously stretched and tightened, of "need of creation."[1] But this God is a still changing and moving God. He has not the intelligence, the *august and holy intelligence* that Plato claimed for Him,[2] and consequently He has not providence, He creates without having any plan,[3] leaving the vital impulse with the responsibility of inventing, hit or miss, if I may say so, the solution required by the various stages of evolution; and far from His knowledge being the cause of things, no primary knowledge can regulate in advance the invention of the new by concrete time. Bergson, we are careful not to forget, wishes with all his heart to have life and freedom recog-

---

* Saint Thomas, *Sum. theol.*, Iᵃ, q. 2, a. 1.

[1] *Creative Evolution*, p. 261.

[2] *Soph.*, 248 E. "Τί δὲ πρὸς Διός; ὡς ἀληθῶς κίνησιν καὶ ζωὴν καὶ ψυχὴν καὶ φρόνησιν ἦ ῥᾳδίως πεισθησόμεθα τῷ παντελῶς ὄντι μὴ παρεῖναι, μηδὲ ζῆν αὐτὸ μηδὲ φρονεῖν ‚ἀλλὰ σεμνὸν καὶ ἅγιον νοῦν οὐκ ἔχον, ἀκίνητον ἑστὸς εἶναι ;"

[3] Cf. *Creative Evolution*, p. 103. "So also evolution [. . .] is not the realization of a plan," etc.

nized in the Principle of things; but he himself does not succeed in doing so. For there is freedom only where there is intelligence, and what Bergson calls free choice, free act, is only pure and simple spontaneity. There is life only where there is immanent activity, and in life Bergson sees only invention and mobility. As to eternity, it is indeed a duration, but essentially different from time, from succession, since it is *the whole* SIMULTANEOUS *and perfect possession of life without end.* One destroys it if one confuses it with time, however compressed the latter may be.

Bergson calls the immutable and peaceful eternity of God an eternity of death; he does not see that divine immutability has nothing in common with inertia, with the immobility of material things, of what here below has the least being and activity, the least perfection. This wholly relative immobility —for in reality, nothing is more mutable, nothing is more the slave of time and becoming than inanimate things—consists in the fact that those things are capable only of "transitive" activity and are *in potency* in a multitude of respects. He does not see that the divine immutability consists, on the contrary, in the supreme perfection and infinite plenitude of being and activity. Containing in His being no potentiality, God absolutely excludes from Himself all becoming and all change, but that is because He "is by essence His own activity, and He has no need to pass over into action in order to act." He is all being, all act, all activity, pure Act.

Life, in short, does not essentially involve change and becoming,—far from it! Becoming, change, is only a consequence of the imperfection of all created life, and especially of all material life. What constitutes life is immanent activity, the activity whose beginning is in the acting subject, and whose term is still in the acting subject.[1] And the higher one goes in the scale of the living, the more this immanence of the vital activity increases. So that what is most living in the world is intelligence, which by its own activity perfects itself from what it knows. "Life is in God," Aristotle had already said, "for the action of intelligence is a life and God is the actuality of intelligence; this actuality taken in itself is His perfect and eternal life."[2]—Created intelligence needs to be objectively moved by an external truth, for it is not subsisting Being. And so its life is not perfect. God, on the contrary, is His being, His intelligence and His action. Pure activity, infinite fire burning without matter, inaccessible spirit, His action is His very being. "It is Truth itself in the state of thought always actual, always living, Good itself in the state of eternal love."[3] Not only therefore is He living, but He is the Life, sovereignly perfect and eternal

---

[1] Cf. *Sum. theol.*, Iª, q. 18, a. 1 and 3.

[2] *Mét.*, XII, c. 7. «Καὶ ζωὴ δε γ' ὑπάρχει· ἡ γὰρ νοῦ ἐνέργεια ζωή. ἐκεῖνος δὲ ἡ ἐνέργεια· ἐνέργεια δὲ ἡ καθ' αὑτὴν ἐκείνου ζωὴ ἀρίστη καὶ ἀΐδιος. φαμὲν δὴ τὸν θεὸν εἶναι ζῷον ἀΐδιον ἄριστον. ὥστε ζωὴ καὶ αἰὼν συνεχὴς καὶ ἀΐδιος ὑπάρχει τῷ θεῷ· τοῦτο γὰρ ὁ θεός.» A, 7, 1072 b 26–30.

[3] Garrigou-Lagrange, *op. cit.*, pp. 498–499.

life.—There is thus,[1] indeed, as Plato said,[2] "motion" in God, if one means by motion (in an altogether improper sense) all that which is activity and fertility; but there is in Him absolute immutability. This is what reason affirms, even before Revelation tells us that all that has been made, is life in God, and, in disclosing the names of the Persons of the Trinity, makes us dimly aware of what activity, what fertility, what beatitude exist in divine Life.

[1] *Sum. theol.*, I^a, q. 18, a. 3, *ad* 1.
[2] *Phaedrus,* chap. XXIV, 245 D: ‹οὕτω δὴ κινήσεως μὲν ἀρχὴ τὸ αὐτὸ αὑτὸ κινοῦν. τοῦτο δὲ οὔτ' ἀπόλλυσθαι οὔτε γίγνεσθαι δυνατόν . . . ›

Chapter Ten

MAN

I.—SOUL AND BODY IN THE BERGSONIAN THEORY

After Descartes had made of the soul and the body two complete substances, two things existing each in itself and for itself, and defined, the first by thought, the second by extension,—human nature became absolutely incomprehensible to philosophers. How can two substances, each existing for itself, combine to form one and the same being, one and the same nature? How could the thinking substance act upon the extended substance, except "from without," in moving it, which creates between them a purely accidental union? And especially how could the extended substance act upon the thinking substance? With Descartes, or after Descartes, philosophers came to ascribe to the body alone, to the "extended substance," all the physiological phenomena, and to the soul alone, to "thought," all the psychological phenomena, sensations, emotions, etc., as well as intellectual and voluntary operations,—thereby making it easy for the materialists, but at the same time opening the gate to idealism and subjectivism, perception being no longer anything more than a modification of the soul or of "thought," and giving us knowledge only of states of our consciousness. They also came to divide the activity of the soul, of the soul alone, into sensibility (alleged special faculty of pleasure and pain), intelligence (including external perception!) and will (including instinct and the sensitive tendencies).[1] As to man, he was, as the imprudent Le Roy (I am speaking of Regius) confessed, to his master's indignation, only an *accidental* whole; and philosophy, if it did not wish to explain everything by materialistic monism, which explains nothing at all, had to admit a *preestablished harmony* between the operations of the thinking substance and those of the extended substance, a brilliantly lazy solution.

It is this solution, born of a wholly *a priori* metaphysics, which passed, as a scientific postulate and under the name of *psycho-physiological parallelism,* into the minds of most of those psychologists who set themselves up as being adversaries and despisers of metaphysical apriorism. The progress of science,

---

[1] An absurd classification which separates what is most intimately united (will, love, joy, for example) and which joins those things which are farthest removed from one another (intellectual act and sense perception, for example, or even carnal pleasure and love of truth).

especially of neurology and mental pathology, and the theory of cerebral localizations, had confirmed what common sense had always found, namely, the strict dependence, the intimate union of physiological and psychological functions. These psychologists did not, as the scholastics did, conclude in the first place that the sensitive powers are organic and consequently localized powers, powers of the soul and body taken together, and, in the second place, that the intellect and the will, even though purely spiritual and therefore without corporeal organs, receive the effects of corporeal and cerebral disturbances because of the sensitive and organic powers which are the condition and means of their exercise. But, as it had been resolved to banish from science any vestige of metaphysics and especially the idea of power or faculty and that of substance, it was conceded that corporeal events or *phenomena* (above all, the modifications of the cerebral cortex), on the one hand, and the events or *phenomena* of consciousness on the other, each formed a self-sufficient series, in such a way that these two series corresponded term for term, element for element, and could be considered as the translation of the same text into two different languages,—but without there being any communication or interaction between them. Thus, to any mental phenomenon there was a corresponding cerebral phenomenon; and whoever followed, with the help of some marvellous microscope, all the vibrations of the cerebral cells could have read in them the events which were unrolling in the other series, the psychological series. Such was the doctrine of *parallelism*.

The more prudent ones accepted it as a hypothesis, without asking themselves why there were these two series, or why they corresponded to one another. The bolder ones, no longer seeing the need for two isolated series where one would serve the purpose so well, considered consciousness to be an "epiphenomenon" or a phosphorescence of matter, and concluded logically that if Virgil and Dante had not known what they were writing and had possessed neither intelligence nor consciousness, the *Aeneid* and *The Divine Comedy* would nevertheless have been just what they are, because the modifications of the nerve cells and the muscular mechanisms would necessarily be sufficient, according to the hypothesis, to explain all the movements effectuated by the hand of these *writers*.

This hypothesis of parallelism is today practically abandoned, and the fine works of Hans Driesch in Germany seem to have dealt it a mortal blow.[1] But when Bergson was publishing his earliest works it was in full swing, reigning and even tyrannizing, and he freed the knowledge of the soul from a long slavery by taking a stand against this hypothesis with a firmness and tenacity worthy of admiration. All the negative and critical part of Bergson's work,—

1 Cf. Hans Driesch, *Die "Seele" als elementarer Naturfaktor*, Leipzig, Engelmann; *Philosophie des Organischen*, 2 vol., Engelmann (French Translation: *Science et Philosophie de l'Organisme*, Rivière edition).

in which he reduces to absurdity the materialist theses and the claims of pseudo-science, as well as associationism and English idealism,—exerted for many minds a genuinely liberating virtue and destroyed many arrogant errors in a way we may hope was definitive.

The Bergsonian method

Bergson not only attacked parallelism in a purely dialectical fashion, and by trying to show that whatever language is used, idealist or realist, parallelism implies contradiction,[1] he also endeavoured to refute it on the basis of experience, and this, it would seem, is the essential object of his book *Matter and Memory*, where his aim has been to make as precise as possible, by the objective study of facts alone, the nature of the psycho-physical relation.

Let it at once be observed, with regard to the method employed, that scholastics cannot too highly approve of Bergson for wishing to establish his philosophy of human nature on facts, either immediate perceptions of consciousness or observational data, although Bergsonism, elsewhere, denies *facts* any real objectivity and makes them out to be merely an invention of the scientist or an artificial cutting up. Metaphysics, like any science of the real, is nothing if it is not based upon observation and experience.

But Bergson goes much farther. For him, metaphysics should not only be based on observation: observation, in fact, is to replace metaphysics; the metaphysics or the "integral experience" of Bergsonian philosophy will be nothing else than an observation considerably intensified and sufficiently dilated by intuition. We shall therefore get along without any strictly metaphysical notion; we shall treat metaphysics with the kind of disdain that clever people like;[2] in short, we shall, as far as possible, do without philosophical reason and its principles. A remarkable survival of positivist prejudices in so free a thinker as Bergson.

That is why he declares, while dealing with the union of the soul and the body, that "it cannot here be a question of constructing a theory of matter" or of mind,[3] for "one can distinguish two things from one another, and determine their relations up to a point, without knowing the nature of either."[4]

---

[1] *Le Paralogisme psycho-physiologique* (*Rev. de Métaph. et de Mor.*, November 1904, pp. 895–908). [Reprinted in *L'Énergie spirituelle* under the title: *Le cerveau et la pensée, une illusion philosophique.*] This, it seems, is how one might translate with slight modifications Bergson's argumentation into scholastic language: supposing that cognoscitive psychological phenomena are a "lining," as it were, of physical phenomena; in view of their representative character they must be the "lining" (*in esse intentionali*) of all the phenomena of the known universe. But the parallelist hypothesis makes it the "lining" of a tiny part of these phenomena, namely cerebral phenomena. It therefore implies this absurdity: that the "lining" of a part is at the same time the "lining" of the whole.

[2] Cf. *Foi et Vie*, December 16, 1912, p. 717; January 1, 1913, p. 15. [*L'Énergie spirituelle*, pp. 40, 61–62.]

[3] *Matter and Memory*, pp. 246, 320.

[4] *L'Ame et le Corps* (*Foi et Vie*, December 16, 1912, p. 714). [*L'Énergie spirituelle*, p. 31.]

A very praiseworthy bit of prudence for a starting point, but very strange as a conclusion: it appears difficult in fact to explain how the body and soul are united and how they act upon one another before knowing what they are. Instead of starting from *operation,*—which alone is directly accessible to observation, though as a simple factual datum,—in order to reach scientific knowledge of being or of nature, and from there scientific knowledge of *operation* itself or of *action,* for every being acts according as it is,—Bergson limits himself to studying operation or activity or phenomenon as though they were self-sufficient and without passing through being or nature. From the methodological point of view, that is the root of his theory of duration, which is action without being.

Consequently Bergson's intention in the point under discussion is only to "formulate" as well as possible "the relation of mental activity to cerebral activity";[3] in order to do that he will "place himself at the confluence of mind and matter, desirous chiefly of seeing the one flow into the other" and of "retaining, of the spontaneity of intelligence only its junction point with a corporeal mechanism."[4]

It is obvious that the modesty of the Bergsonian method is more apparent than real. Ostensibly in order to avoid metaphysical pride one claims to take up a position at the junction of mind and matter and to perceive, by means of observation or intuition, their mutual relationship. Not only does this method presume infinitely too much for our knowledge, it also vitiates the problem in advance because it leads one to envisage the union of the soul and the body not with respect to the whole living body, but solely with respect to the brain, and even solely with respect to those cerebral centres attributed to memory.

Matter and memory

I cannot possibly undertake here to give a summary of that very complex ensemble of theories and hypotheses which constitutes *Matter and Memory.* I shall simply emphasize the following points as far as it is possible to single them out from the rest. The relation of cerebral to mental activity, of corporeal to psychological phenomena does not appear to Bergson—and in this he is quite right—at all like that relation of one series to another, to another equivalent whole, or of a text to its translation, evoked by parallelism. But for Bergson, the cerebral phenomenon is in a relation *sui generis* to the mental phenomenon, in what might be called the relation of the part to the whole, or be compared to the relation of a frame to the various pictures one might put into it. The frame, from the fact that it has a certain form and certain dimensions, eliminates a great many pictures. But several different ones can never-

---

[3] *L'Ame et le Corps* (*Foi et Vie,* January 1, 1913, p. 7). [*L'Énergie spirituelle,* p. 44.]
[4] *Matter and Memory,* p. 321.

theless fit into that frame, and it would be useless to seek in the frame the determination or the equivalent of the content of the picture. In the same way cerebral activity delineates at every instant the frame into which the mental activity can fit, but in no way determines the content of that activity.

In the functioning of the sensitive or organic powers, it is of course true for scholastic philosophy that the physical phenomenon observable in the brain is in no way the equivalent of the psychic phenomenon, for the very good reason that the genuine operation of the organ, like that of the power, *is the psychic phenomenon,* not the physical, which is only a condition of or an accompaniment to it. But Bergson, as we have just seen, gives an entirely different interpretation of this fact since he makes the physical phenomenon as such the operation proper to the organ, constituting the frame in which the psychical, hence entirely inorganic or immaterial in itself, phenomenon will take place.

This relation of frame to picture no doubt suits the relation of the present *sensation* and the action begun to the interpretive *images* furnished by the memory, that is, to the relation between two equally psychic and equally organic phenomena. Bergson applies it to the relation of the cerebral centres to the memory, and he thinks he has thus put his finger on the junction point between mind and matter, between Soul and Body; he thinks he "thus sees mind and matter *flow* into one another," and that he is present at their union.

In order that his doctrine may be understood, the following points which I consider essential should be emphasized. In the first place, as he sees it, the brain serves only to "transmit and divide movement."[1] The part the brain plays consists solely in preparing gestures, attitudes, movements, in setting up an indefinite number of motor mechanisms. It is a machine for transforming movement, nothing more.

In the second place, while the scholastics recognize the existence of two distinct memories, the memory of the sensible concrete, the "internal sense" whose organ is in the brain, and the intellectual memory which is one with intelligence, for Bergson there is only one memory,[2] which has no organ and is nothing but the soul or the spirit, (for according to him, the spirit becomes what it is only through memory), and which at the same time, far from being the intellect, actualizes and manifests itself only by sense images.[3] It is

[1] *Ibid.,* p. 20.

[2] See note 3, and *infra,* p. 212, n. 5.

[3] He also clearly distinguishes, besides *memory* properly so-called, *a motor memory,* but this *motor memory* is nothing else than the assemblage of cerebro-spinal apparatus, mechanisms set up in the brain and the medulla, which assure a suitable reply to the various possible interpellations. It is, therefore, not memory at all, it is merely corporal habit, "it acts our past experience, but does not evoke the image of it; it has nothing in common either with intellectual memory or with memory in the "inner sense". (Cf. *Matter and Memory,* pp. 88–104; 195.)

the *memory of the sensible concrete* considered as spiritual. Instead, therefore, of the recollections being placed in the cerebral centres as in a box,—Bergson imputes this materialist theory to all his adversaries,—they exist only in the mind as *pure recollections*.

And finally, in the third place,—and here is the fundamental dogma of Bergsonian philosophy,—the past as such preserves itself; this past which preserves itelf and increases as it proceeds is our recollection itself, or our soul, and the *pure recollections* are the elements of this past which still remain, which are present, even though they have passed.

External perception

If sense perception makes us really communicate with the world, it is because, in what Bergson calls *pure perception* subject and object are not yet separate;[1] from which it follows that the mind of each of us, in this pure perception, is not yet distinct from that kind of universal subconsciousness which is matter, which in turn is only a relapse of the vital impulse, a lowering of the psychic,—merely "psychic energy inverted."[2]

It seems impossible to give any other interpretation of the Bergsonian theory which defines material things as "present images,"[3] virtual representations which neutralize one another in universal interaction, so that it is definitely in things and nowhere else that the image of things is *formed and perceived*,[4] so that "our perception is outside our bodies"[5] and there are no centres or organs *of sensation* anywhere in us.

If we now have, not a virtual representation of the whole universe (as is the case[6] for any unconscious material point whatever), but a real and conscious representation of certain objects, Bergson says it is because we are, in the universe, "centres of indetermination." According to the needs and necessities of our practice, we therefore automatically isolate and retain certain virtual representations in preference to others. By the very fact that they are separated from the rest, moreover, these representations become real and conscious; and thus are retained only those which correspond to possible actions by our self upon things, which solicit our activity, "put our bodies into relation with points of space which directly invite them to make a choice";[7]—that is, with those points of space acting physically on our nervous system which, being

---

[1] Cf. Éd. Le Roy, *Une philosophie nouvelle*, p. 179.—"Pure perception, which is the lowest degree of the mind,—mind without memory,—is really part of matter as we understand it," writes Bergson (*Matter and Memory*, p. 297). This is an important revelation of what the new philosophy means by *mind*.

[2] *Creative Evolution*, p. 202.

[3] *Matter and Memory*, p. 27.

[4] *Ibid.*, p. 37.

[5] *Ibid.*, p. 59.

[6] *Ibid.*, p. 30.

[7] *Ibid.*, p. 40.

made solely to gather up movement and give it back in the form of "voluntary" actions, is the very instrument of choice, the instrument of indeterminate will.

Thus it is that the body serves not to feel, but to select sensations readymade, if I may put it that way, already virtually given in the ocean of slumbering consciousness in which we and all things bathe. By that fact it plays a necessary but occasional and extrinsic rôle in sense knowledge; it has no essential intrinsic part in the *act* of sense knowledge.

Pure perception thus defined is, in short, if I may so express it, nothing but pure present (or rather something chosen, something separated, in the universal pure present); this present, this sort of constantly-repeated instantaneous, is itself only matter. Finally, "the material universe" itself is only "a kind of consciousness, a consciousness in which everything compensates and neutralizes everything else, a consciousness of which all the potential parts, balancing each other by a reaction which is always equal to the action, reciprocally hinder each other from standing out."*—Thus perception is an *instantaneous and vanishing intuition* of matter, (an intuition in the Bergsonian sense, that is, a knowledge of the object which is but one with the object).

It must now be added that our perception is something more than "pure perception," something more than a series of instantaneous and vanishing visions. But that is because our *memory,* in contracting the millions of instantaneous vibrations (which are also qualitative, but with a slackened, diluted quality) of intuitive *pure perception,* and especially in projecting into it the images of recollection, makes it conscious perception properly so-called. So that "the basis of real and so-to-speak instantaneous intuition upon which our perception of the external world is developed, is a small matter compared with all that memory adds to it."[1]

Memory and general ideas

"When we pass from pure perception to memory, we definitely abandon matter for [spirit]."[2] It is by our memory that we are distinct from things; and the life of our memory is the very life of our spirit.

Following a diagram given by Bergson himself,[3] let us imagine an upturned cone with its apex resting on a horizontal plane. This cone will represent memory as a whole or the human person; the base will represent the *past* which is preserved, the plane of pure recollection; the apex will represent the body which, like the material world of which it forms a part, is only an in-

* *Ibid.,* p. 313.
[1] *Ibid.,* p. 70.
[2] *Ibid.,* p. 313.
[3] *Ibid.,* pp. 196, 210–211.

stantaneous *present* ceaselessly repeated, and continually progressing (as though the cone lengthened constantly); the plane will represent the material world, intuitively known by pure perception, in which action takes place.

The life of the spirit (or of memory) consists in the "movement" by which it goes from the base of the cone, from the plane of pure past or pure recollection, which Bergson also calls the dream plane, to the "plane of action," to the "plane in which our body has condensed its past into motor habits,"[4] through a whole series of "planes of consciousness" which the mind finds or rather "unceasingly creates anew."

It is "this double movement of memory between its two extreme limits (which) also sketches out [. . .] the first general ideas,—motor habits ascending to seek similar images coming down towards motor habits, to free themselves, for example, in the automatic utterance of the word which makes them one."[5]

The motor habit, therefore, is all that constitutes the unity and universality of the general idea.

At first this habit is related to a movement or an attitude of our body. Then the identity of our motor reactions to faintly different actions brings it about that the generality—that is to say, the resemblance between different individuals—is "automatically acted" before being thought. So that the general idea is, in the beginning, only "our consciousness of a likeness of attitude in a diversity of situations"; it is "habit itself, mounting from the sphere of movement to that of thought."[1]

The motor habit is related in the next place not to a corporeal attitude but to an uttered word. Once in possession of the idea of genus we do in fact voluntarily construct an unlimited number of general ideas by setting up motor mechanisms, artificial in this case, each of which will constitute an identical motor habit corresponding to an unlimited number of individual images; "the assemblage of these mechanisms is articulate speech."[2]

In any case, then, the general idea receives its unity, its fixity, its generality from a motor habit. It constantly oscillates between the apex and the base of the cone. At the apex "it would take the clear-cut form of a corporeal attitude or an uttered word"; mounting toward the base "it would wear the aspect no less defined of the thousand individual images into which its fragile unity would break up."[3] It is "always ready either to crystallize into uttered words,

[4] *Ibid.*, p. 322. Cf. the remarkable article by Bergson on *l'Effort intellectuel* (*Revue philosophique*, January, 1902); according to him intellectual effort takes place on the point of crossing between the "schéma dynamique" (the recollection trying to actualize itself) and the image. [This article was reprinted in *l'Énergie spirituelle*, chap. VI.]

[5] *Ibid.*, p. 324.

[1] *Ibid.*, p. 209.

[2] *Ibid.*, p. 209.

[3] *Ibid.*, p. 210.

or to evaporate into recollections."* A word at one extremity, individual recollections at the other,—in reality, its *essence* is *to move unceasingly back and forth between the sphere of action and that of pure memory.*†

Recognition

The recognition of perceived objects, the essential function of memory, takes place, according to Bergson, in two absolutely different ways. Sometimes "by entirely passive recognition, acted rather than thought, the body responds to a perception that recurs by a movement or attitude that has become automatic." In this case "everything is explained by the motor apparatus which habit has set up in the body":[1] either the motor tendencies suffice to give us the feeling of familiarity and recognition;[2] or the memory takes advantage of the opportunity to slip into the perception of the present moment images which can be prolonged in the movements already outlined by the body.[3]—Sometimes, on the other hand, "recognition is produced actively by memory-images which go out to meet the present perception." In such cases, far from it being a question of "a mechanical awakening of memories dormant in the brain," recognition "implies, on the contrary, a more or less high degree of tension in consciousness which goes out to fetch pure recollections in pure memory, in order to materialize them progressively by contact with the present perception."[4] This pure recollection[5] is nothing but the past itself, the past which is preserved, which is virtually there, in a state of "nebulosity,"[6] but which can only be realized in becoming present, that is, in first becoming a memory-image and finally motor action. The operation of active recognition "does not consist at all in a regression from the present to the past, but on the contrary in a progress from the past to the present. It is in the past that we place ourselves straight away. We start from a *virtual state*"—that is, from pure recollection,—"which we lead onwards step by step through a series of

* *Ibid.*, p. 211.
† *Ibid.*, p. 210.
[1] *Ibid.*, p. 316.
[2] *Ibid.*, p. 113.
[3] *Ibid.*, pp. 113–114.
[4] *Ibid.*, p. 317.
[5] This pure recollection has nothing in common, let this essential point be noted, with the intellectual memory, the "organless" memory of the scholastics, which is indistinguishable from intelligence. Bergson occasionally calls his pure recollection *idea;* but for him there is no difference in nature between the idea and the image. Pure recollection differs from image only because it is of the *past,* while image is of the *present;* it is the original (virtual) state which develops and actualizes itself in an image. "Pure recollection, though independent in theory, manifests itself as a rule only in the coloured and living image which reveals it." (*Matter and Memory*, p. 170.) As we remarked above, the pure memory of the Bergsonian theory is only the *memory of the sensible concrete,* assumed to be at the same time non-organic and susceptible to various degrees of tension and materiality.
[6] *Ibid.*, p. 154.

different *planes of consciousness,* up to the goal where it is materialized in an actual perception; that is to say, up to the point where it becomes a present, active state";* in which it continues, for example, in the nascent movements "which help us to dwell upon the outlines of the object."†

Memory and the brain

To these two modes of recognition correspond two kinds of pathological disorders. Sometimes "our body can no longer automatically adopt under the influence of the external stimulus the precise attitude by means of which a selection could be made among our recollections; sometimes the recollections can no longer find in the body a point of application, a means of prolonging themselves in action."[1] "In the first case, the lesion affects the mechanisms which continue in an automatically executed movement, the stimulation received";[2] it will hinder "the body from taking, in regard to the object, the attitude that may call back its memory-image."[3] In the second case, the lesion "will sever the bonds between remembrance and the present reality"; "suppressing the last phase of the realization of a memory,—the phase of action,— they [will] thereby hinder the memory from becoming actual";[4] that is to say, "it [will] involve those particular cortical centres which *prepare* voluntary movements,"[5] and which constitute as it were the internal keyboard ("mental ear" or mental retina symmetrical to the external keyboard of the eye or ear) upon which recollections—*virtual objects* so to speak—act to set in motion from within the so-called sensory centres and thereby to prolong themselves and be realized in movements.[6] "But in either case, it is actual movements which are hindered or future movements which are no longer prepared; there has been no destruction of memories."[7] And more, the memory itself has remained intact, only the purely motor mechanisms have been hindered. The memory (memory of the lived concrete, which "actualizes itself in images"

* *Ibid.,* p. 319.
† *Ibid.,* p. 118.
[1] *Ibid.,* p. 132.
[2] *Ibid.*
[3] *Ibid.,* p. 120.
[4] *Ibid.*
[5] *Ibid.,* p. 132.
[6] *Ibid.,* pp. 166–167. Let me quote the following paragraph, which very clearly summarizes this part of the theory: "In other terms, the centres in which the elementary sensations seem to originate may be actuated, in some sort, from two different sides, from in front and from behind. From the front they receive impressions sent in by the sense-organs and consequently by a *real object;* from behind they are subject, through successive intermediaries, to the influence of a *virtual object.* The centres of images, if these exist, can only be the organs that are exactly symmetrical with the organs of the senses in reference to the sensory centres. They are no more the depositories of pure memories, that is, of virtual objects, than the organs of the senses are depositories of real objects." (*Matter and Memory,* pp. 166–167.)
[7] *Ibid.,* p. 132. Cf. pp. 315–317.

and which belongs in the sensory order—and that is the only one Bergson mentions), the memory has no organ.

The brain is, therefore, not the organ of memory. "The state of the brain continues the remembrance; it gives it a hold on the present by the materiality which it confers upon it: but pure recollection is a spiritual manifestation."[1] The brain, for Bergson, is only "the organ of attention to life"; it does not serve to preserve the past, but first to mask it, then to allow what is practically useful to show through; since all recollections, the past as a whole, are virtually present, that only is actualized which sets in motion the cerebral mechanisms that enable "the [spirit] to respond to the action of things by motor reactions, effectuated or simply nascent, whose accuracy assures the perfect insertion of [the spirit] into reality."[2] The brain, "the point of insertion of [the spirit] into matter," explains forgetfulness, that is, the actual non-utilization of a recollection, it does not explain memory, which has no need of explanation, since it is the spirit itself.

The self

We are a memory, an individual duration, that is, a pure change which is *indivisible,* which is therefore entirely preserved from our birth. That is our ego, or our soul, or our consciousness, or our memory, four quasi-synonyms. We are constantly transporting ourselves, as we have seen above, from the deeper self to the superficial self, from the plane of the dream to the plane of action. Between these two extreme planes is an infinite number of intermediary planes.

There is thus an infinity of degrees between spirituality and materiality. The soul, the consciousness or our integral duration, expands beyond the body or the brain in all directions, in extension by perception, in a sense, but especially in time by memory. Turned entirely toward action it constantly brings pressure on the body in order to put more of itself into the present action; the body, on the contrary, eliminates from this past with its tendency to actualize itself, all that does not square with the present action. The body, while purely material and having only a motor function (the transformation of external vibrations into muscular reactions, and the actualizing of pure recollection into movement), thus constitutes the sharp *point* by which the soul acts in the world.

The "disorders of personality" will, then, be explained by the too great weight of the mass of recollections seeking to actualize themselves in relation to the accidentally-weakened mechanisms they utilise; in such cases these recollections, in order to remedy the inability of the present to carry the past,

---

[1] *Ibid.,* pp. 320–321.
[2] *L'Ame et le Corps (Foi et Vie,* January 1, 1913, p. 10). [*L'Énergie spirituelle,* p. 52.] Cf. *Matter and Memory,* pp. 225–227.

will, for example, split up into two or more distinct "selves," as a result of a scission in the "sensori-motor connections," in the cerebral mechanisms by which they are inserted into present reality.[1]

The whole relation of soul to body, of spirit to matter, is therefore in the final analysis that of an indivisible duration which is entirely preserved, to a duration which is no more or almost no more than an instantaneous present constantly beginning again; an infinite number of transitions permit continuous passage from one to the other, and the first acts and actualizes itself by the second. Thus[2] Bergsonian philosophy proposes *to distinguish and unite the soul and the body, not in terms of space,* as Bergson claims the Cartesians did, *but in terms of time.*

Such, in brief outline, does this doctrine appear to be—a doctrine in which vast and audacious hypotheses slip through a heap of obscure scientific facts scrupulously and minutely studied, and in which a sort of grand metaphysical dream mingles with many a subtle and profound psychological observation. Shall we, like Le Roy, claim it to be the *positive* observation of the junction point, the "living contact" of matter with mind?

It would be absurd, of course, to try to distinguish the soul and body in terms of space. Why? Because space follows upon the accident of quantity, and because it is a question of the *substance* of man. To see the distinction as well as the union of the soul and the body, only one point of view is possible and that is the point of view of being. As for Bergson, he distinguishes them neither in terms of being nor in terms of space, but in terms of time; of time, that is to say, in terms of the least substantial reality, of the most accidental condition (however infrangible, however despotic) imposed upon us by matter. Hence all that is of the essence of man is obscured, fugitive like time itself. The soul is no more than one certain manner of enduring, the body another.

But before emphasizing this aspect of the Bergsonian doctrine, we must briefly examine, from the psychological point of view, the different theories set forth in *Matter and Memory*. We shall see that they often contain a large part of truth, but that they are unfortunately vitiated by the metaphysical principles of Bergsonian philosophy.

On the theory of external perception

Bergson must be given thanks for having tried to re-establish, against most modern psychologists, the intuitive character of sensation. But he makes us pay dearly for this truth, which is, in his system, bound up with the strangest kind of monism.

[1] Cf. *Matter and Memory*, pp. 229–230; and in *Études* (November 20, 1911) the article in which Grivet sums up one of Bergson's lectures on personality (1910–1911).

[2] *Matter and Memory*, pp. 294–296.

For scholastic philosophy bodies, by their active qualities, act upon the sense organ and by means of their physical action on the organ[1] imprint upon the sense (a power of the soul linked to matter but for the purpose of acting in a way superior to matter), psychic (immaterial, "intentional") likenesses of themselves which determine the sense and set it in act; and the sense, then entering into vital and immanent operation, *becomes immaterially* the object, (which means to perceive it) at the same time that it produces an image of it in the internal sense.[2] Thus sensation is an *intuition* of the object and is *extensive*;[3] but the sensitive operation (though it does not happen exclusively in the cerebral centres, as is claimed by the current theory Bergson rightly criticizes) takes place however in the peripheral sense organ (taken in its entirety).[4]

According to Bergson, on the contrary, as we have already seen, sensations are "a part of things rather than of us," "our perception is outside of our body," "the images of things are formed and perceived in things," the function of the so-called sensory organs being only to receive and transmit movement. In order to try to save the objectivity of sensible knowledge Bergsonian philosophy therefore posits that "the material universe is itself a kind of consciousness," that there is nothing real or positive in matter except "psychic energy inverted," and in short, that by our body, our "point," we are one in nature with the whole world, from which our body is distinct only by the indetermination of its action, not by its substance.

This theory, like the theory of intuition in general, results, it seems from the erroneous principle that we have already tried to elucidate,[5] a principle latent in the whole Bergsonian philosophy, and according to which knowledge is *intuitive* only if it occurs without any subjective intermediary, only if it is an absorption of the subject in the object, an assimilation or even an identity of the object and subject *secundum modum cogniti*.

This theory does not, however, *solve* the problem of external perception, it *suppresses* it, since it assumes that sensations already pre-exist, virtually, in

---

[1] In this (transitive) action, in which the medium plays an *instrumental* rôle, the *agent* (the object) communicates to the *patient* (to the animate organ) the very form (the sensible quality) by which it acts, in virtue of the principle that action and passion are one and the same movement. But it is *secundum esse immateriale* that this action and this form are received by the senses. Cf. Aristotle, *Phys.*, III, chap. 4, 202b 5–22; *de Anima*, II, chap. 11 and 12 (lessons XXII, XXIII and XXIV of Saint Thomas; see also lesson V of Saint Thomas on this same book II).

[2] Cf. *Sum. theol.*, Iᵃ, q. 78, a. 3; a. 4, *ad* 2.

[3] In the sense that not only is its object from the outset known as extensive, but also that the mode of knowing is itself essentially bound up with the extensivity of the object, as with the materiality of the organ in which the sense operation takes place.

[4] This "peripheric" organ can extend more or less by its roots, into the interior of the organism, for example, take root in this or that particular cerebral territory; it is not for philosophy to determine its anatomical limits.

[5] See above, *supra*, p. 169.

things: moreover, it cannot make clear how a "virtual" representation becomes "real" and "conscious" from the fact that it is separated from other "virtual representations" which "neutralize" it in the "sort of consciousness" which the material universe is; nor how we can *feel* without having any *properly sensitive organ*: for we can think without any organ because thought is immaterial,—but sensation is not immaterial.

The Bergsonian theory considers perception in its concrete form "as a synthesis of pure memory and pure perception, that is, *of spirit and matter*."* From which we are forced to conclude that *the spirit* according to Bergsonian philosophy is the portion of animals as well as of man, since animals deprived of reason enjoy, like us, sense perception. In reality, and more simply, perception must be regarded as a synthesis of sensation properly so-called and of interpretive complements furnished by the "internal senses" according to this or that dominant direction of psychic activity. But the Bergsonian theory destroys sensation properly so-called, the sensible intuition of the object, by reducing it to nothing more than an instantaneous and vanishing "pure perception" which is a part of things rather than of us; it thus robs it of its primordial character,—that of being an intuitive *knowledge* (by no means instantaneous or vanishing); it does not see that sensation, being essentially an intuitive knowledge of the object, a knowledge impregnated with materiality, can be only the operation of an animate organ, or of a faculty of the "human compound."

Because of this, Bergson, in spite of his desire for objectivity, is led to exaggerate the importance of the subject in external perception, to replace the *principal* rôle the nucleus of real sensation plays in it by the "not very much" that "pure perception" represents, and to outline, while he is still on the subject of perception,[1] the theory of knowledge-as-an-artificial-breaking-up. In the same way bodies vanish; these he no doubt presents to us as existing objectively, but they melt immediately into the "universal interaction." And finally, matter vanishes and the physical *qualities* which, first posited as real, soon resolve into a duration tending toward pure repetition, into diluted qualities tending toward pure homogeneity, into a "succession of infinitely rapid, 'almost instantaneous' moments."

On the theory of the general idea

The Bergsonian theory tries to explain the general idea by a to-and-fro movement of the memory. We were right in seeing in this theory radical *nominalism* and *sensualism*;[2] for according to it the universal is neither in things nor even in the mind, it is nothing more than a motor habit.

---

* *Matter and Memory*, p. 325. The italics are mine.
[1] Cf. Éd. Le Roy, *Une philosophie nouvelle*, pp. 22–32.
[2] See *supra*, pp. 140–141.

The explanation offered by Bergson would at most account for the manner in which animal experience, while being sensitive and singular, prepares and, as it were, mimics in advance intellectual knowledge of objects. But how could it account for the general idea which is *thought* as such? How could the uniting of several different images with one and the same bodily attitude, one and the same motor mechanism, replace *abstraction,* and magically transform these images into an idea?

As to the procedure by which we are supposed to construct—with recollections and movements—an unlimited number of "general ideas" by making an indefinite multitude of individual images correspond to one motor mechanism (in this case artificially set up)—namely, to the utterance of a word—it is strictly impossible in the Bergsonian theory itself. These images in fact cannot receive their unity from the mechanism to which they are connected since this mechanism is artificial, and their connection with it conventional, and since in order to connect to some uttered word certain images rather than all others, it would be necessary, on the contrary, first to have perceived or established between them the unity in question (which in reality can only take place through veritable *ideas* and thanks to abstraction). The Bergsonian theory should logically limit itself to explaining the general idea by an identity of attitude or natural reaction of our body toward things,—an explanation which, as we have just seen, is absolutely vain and manifestly belied by the simple fact that we have an indefinite multitude of general ideas, whereas our corporal attitudes toward things are limited to a small number of types.

Bergson considers he is refuting nominalism by saying that general ideas are neither the words into which they crystallize, nor the recollections into which they evaporate, but the *movement* which goes from one to the other.[1] As though an image ceases to be an image because it moves! Bergson is not a nominalist after the manner of the English psychologists, but his theory of the to-and-fro is none the less a radical nominalism since according to him all that is *thought* in the universal is "the representation, at least virtual, of a number of remembered images,"[2] and since for him there is nothing more in the general idea than a word or an attitude, recollection and movement.

He did not see that the idea, by the very fact that it is abstract, that is, free of *any* individuating note, that it is universal, that is, applicable *as such,* without any retouching or modification, to an infinite number of individuals, and above all by the fact that it seeks in the object what the object *is,* is necessarily

---

[1] Cf. *Matter and Memory,* p. 324. "It will always be easy for a certain philosophy . . . to make it (the general idea) crystallize into words or evaporate into memories, whereas it really consists in the transit of the mind as it passes from one term to the other."

[2] *Matter and Memory,* p. 201.

of another nature or another order than the image,[3] is wholly spiritual while the image is impregnated with materiality. Here again the philosopher, it seems, has been misled by his imagination. He has confused with the idea that multitude of varied, moving images, ceaselessly oscillating between the vague and the precise, which always *accompany* the *idea*.

On the theory of recognition

Whether or not it is necessary to distinguish in an absolute manner, with Bergson, two different kinds of recognition,[1] and whatever psychological

[3] It is generally known that studies in experimental psychology have confirmed this essential thesis in every particular. See especially the works of Binet (*L'Intelligence*, Schleicher, 1903. "All the logic of thought escapes imagery," he writes, p. 309); of Woodworth (*Imageless Thought, Journal of Phil., Psych., and Scientific Meth.*, 1906, 701–708); and those of Marbe, of Messer and of Bühler as described or adopted by Bovet (*Étude expérim. du jugem. et de la pensée, Archiv. de Psych.*, t. VIII, p. 37: "The existence of thought distinct from image is recognized").

[1] In my opinion Bergson there touched upon, but *in obliquo* and without revealing its essential principles, a fundamental distinction: the distinction between the entitative and dynamic enriching of our being (of the *subject*), by the whole series of our experiences, and the preservation of the past itself as *object* by a function of knowledge.

In the first case *we are not dealing with memory*, and if then we speak of the preservation of the past, it is in an improper sense; it can only be a question of the preservation of the past *as not passed*, I mean of the permanence of the modifications the past has left behind it, in us. In the second case it is properly a question of *memory, a function of knowledge*, and of the preservation of the past *as passed* (but according to the intentional existence which things known to the soul have in it; see *infra*, p. 220, n. 1). To the first case would be related what in a general way the moderns call motor mechanisms, habits, acquired tendencies, "engrammes," etc., what the ancients called dispositions and *habitus:* modifications of the subject and its dynamism; the first kind of recognition admitted by Bergson, acted recognition, would belong to it (but let us add that it is not only in our flesh that the past is thus preserved; there are also habits of the mind). To the second case would be related what the ancients called *species*, what the moderns in less adequate language call images and representations (including Bergsonian *pure memory* as well as the images in which it actualizes itself). Under this second case would come the second type of recognition admitted by Bergson (but ascribable to a properly sensitive cerebral function, and not only to the corticle preparation of movements to come and of motor attitudes); —let us add (see *infra*, p. 220, n. 1) that if memory, to the very extent that it is a function of knowledge, includes immateriality (it is this immateriality that the works of Bergson have remarkably thrown into light), that does not make it (I am speaking of sensitive memory) a *spiritual faculty*, that is, intrinsically independent of any organ in its being and in its operation proper.

It seems that from another point of view, there would be reason to distinguish two sorts of recognition, the one bearing on the object *as object* in perception, the other bearing on the memory (or the object) *as part of our past*. Could we not connect the first to imagination properly so-called, the second to memory properly so-called? It is known that for scholastic philosophy imagination and memory are two distinct faculties, constituting within the soul two worlds in reserve, so to speak, the one corresponding simply to the world of sensation and external data, the other being the world proper of the experience of the subject, in which the contribution of the external senses is preserved with all the interpretative values with which the *estimative* clothes it. Recollections, in the latter case, would thus be organized and preserved by reason of their very connection with the *lived*, the *experienced*, so that they would bear within them from the outset the coloration, the mark of the past (of the already-lived),—a thesis which seems to be confirmed by modern psychology. Cf. Peillaube, *Les Images*, pp. 336–338 (see *infra*, p. 234, n. 2).

thesis one adopts on the subject of recognition, in any case nothing in the known facts obliges us—and nothing authorizes us—to suppose that the past automatically remains in its own reality, and that memory (the memory by which the world of sense perceptions and affections exists within us, for that is the one we are discussing here), is the spirit.[2]

No more than he distinguishes in things perceived the being of nature according to which they exist in themselves and the intentional being according to which they exist in the soul, does Bergson distinguish in the past the true reality of the experiences that the soul has lived and that have left in the soul permanent modifications but which have ceased to be,—let us say the *being of nature* of the past,—and the purely representative or immaterial existence according to which the past subsists in the apprehension of the soul, —let us say the *intentional being* of this same past. The lack of so indispensable a distinction gives his theory of memory a thoroughly equivocal aspect and finally vitiates his whole doctrine. Let us make this distinction and we shall see how the terms of the problem should be stated.

That our past states are preserved in us we certainly do not deny, and who has ever denied it? That they are preserved other than by a material inscription on a recording disc we do not deny either. But it is not in their concrete existence and their *being of nature, in esse naturali,* that these states are preserved,—being past they no longer are;—neither is it in the modifications they may have left behind them in our being, particularly in the cerebral centres, modifications which in any case could be nothing more than pre-requisite conditions; it is in the *intentional* or immaterial existence demanded by any function of knowing, it is *in esse immateriali*[1] that our past remains in us by means

---

One can conceive the "recording" of images and memories not as a material inscription comparable to that of a phonogram, but as an (intentional, psychic) informing of the faculty, imagination or memory, according to certain organized synthetic groupings.

An object of perception would be recognized when it would thus be repeated in one of these synthetic groupings, like a word heard and at the same time mentally repeated in a word-group. An object, an event, a memory would be recognized as *passed,* when that word-group, at least vaguely indicated, is the weft itself of time, of the succession of the lived, preserved and partially uttered by the memory. [Cf. H. Delacroix, in Dumas, *Traité de Psych.,* t. II, p. 80.] The activity of the memory and the imagination can furthermore be either coherent and systematized, or more or less disintegrated.

2 "Pure memory is a spiritual manifestation. With memory we are in very truth in the domain of the spirit." (*Matter and Memory,* p. 320.) Let us repeat that it is a question here of the memory of the sensible concrete. Bergson has perhaps been the victim of the impropriety of modern philosophical language, which often confuses *knowledge* (mere sense knowledge) with spirit. But one thing is certain and that is that this confusion essentially affects his doctrine, since for him the body never participates intrinsically in the functions of knowledge, even sense knowledge; the brain is exclusively a "pantomime organ." (*L'Énergie spirituelle,* p. 50.)

1 "Hujusmodi autem viventia . . . habent duplex esse. Unum quidem materiale, in quo conveniunt cum aliis rebus materialibus. Aliud autem immateriale, in quo communicant cum substantiis superioribus aliqualiter. Est autem differentia inter utrumque esse: quia secundum esse materiale, quod est per materium contractum, unaquaeque res est hoc solum quod est, sicut hic

of a form which doubtless modifies, thanks to the organ, the faculty of the soul, but only in order to be present in it immaterially as vicariously standing for things that were and that were known, and as a principle of reference or of tendency, in the order of knowing, to those very things which no longer are. There lies the real mystery of memory,[2] a function of knowledge and a privilege of the living things which have awareness (the plant does not remember), and which, capable of being not only themselves but others, can also be not only what they are but what they no longer are. That "pure recollection" is the past itself not yet made actual and broken up into "particular images," let us grant,—[3] but the past in the *intentional* state, not in the proper existence according to which it was "posited outside the nought"; the past as an object retained in the soul by means of a pure "sign," not as actual reality lived in the nature of things.[4] Because he does not make this distinction Bergson refuses

lapis non est aliud quam hic lapis; secundum vero esse immateriale, quod est amplum, et quodammodo infinitum, inquantum non est per materiam terminatum, res non solum est id quod est, sed etiam est quodammodo alia . . . Hujusmodi autem immateriale esse habet duos gradus in istis inferioribus. Nam quoddam est penitus immateriale, sicut esse intelligibile . . . Esse autem sensibile est medium inter utrumque. Nam in sensu *res habet esse sine materia,* non tamen absque conditionibus materialibus individuantibus, neque absque organo corporali." Saint Thomas, *in de Anima,* lib. II, lect. V.

Thus *immateriality,*—the immaterial presence of things in the subject,—is essential to all knowledge, but it does not therefore mean that the senses and memory are *spiritual,* that is to say, independent of a definite organ in their being and in their activity. For the sense can exist and exert itself only in and by an organ, but it nevertheless already transcends matter in that its operation proper, accomplished by and in the organ, is in itself an assimilation immaterial to the object. What we are saying of the sense and sensation must also be said of memory, the "internal sense," and of the preservation of the *species.* What Bergson, in my opinion, has thrown much light upon, and what seems to me so much to the good, is the fact that this preservation, takes place itself *secundum esse immateriale,*— that is, if it intrinsically supposes organic and material conditions (at least the partial preservation of the organ and perhaps of certain dispositions in it, just as recording and evocation suppose its activation). Bergson thus got back to the sensitive *soul;* he thought he had discovered the *mind.* From this immaterial informing of memory (insofar as it is a faculty of knowledge) by recollection, his error was to conclude in favour of the *spirituality* of the sensitive memory, therefore identifying memory and mind.

[2] I am speaking of memory properly so-called, not of motor habits, or adaptations, or of "engrammes" affecting the dynamism of a faculty. See *infra,* p. 219, n. 1.

[3] It would then be a question of integral preservation, in a sort of symphonic score composed as it went along by the vital activity of the faculty, of the *species* furnished to the memory by the external and internal senses. This virtual symphony would become actual only by making consciousness hear short fragments emerging from the whole ("images" in the Bergsonian vocabulary) themselves united by association or condensation to other fragments according to various combinations. Without forgetting that in man, memory, because of its closeness to the spiritual faculties, has for evocation as well as for forgetting, a complexity and a freedom of play that are unique.

[4] "In its entirety, probably, it (the past) follows us at every instant; all that we have felt, thought and willed from our earliest infancy is there, leaning over the present which is about to join it, pressing against the portals of consciousness that would fain leave it outside." (Bergson, *Creative Evolution,* p. 5.) Nothing could be truer. But here we must recognize two orders of things perfectly distinct in themselves, even though closely interwoven: the one which be-

to distinguish the past from the memory of the past, and to admit that memory is a power or special faculty of our soul; in so doing he dovetails his psychology into the most venturesome of metaphysics. Instead of being content to show,—and this would have meant a considerable gain for psychology, —that the preservation of recollections supposes, like any function of knowledge, even the lowest, a certain immateriality and that while remaining intrinsically bound to organic conditions and consequently while remaining essentially distinct from properly spiritual functions, it is what comes closest to the spirit in the life of the senses, he has purely and simply identified memory and spirit.

Things should be interpreted in another way. If we grant that the past— the recollection of the past—is preserved whole, the "inner sense" of memory is perfectly sufficient for that integral preservation which is a living and continual organization of images. If we grant that in "active recognition" we go *from the past to the present,* it is because memory goes progressively from a potential state in which the recollection of all the past is there, but in potency, to an actual state in which some element of this past, taken from the flood it raises with it, will be told again to the consciousness: in that however there can be no question of a completely spiritual *pure recollection* gradually becoming material, but only of a cognitive (organic) faculty which passes from potency into act, (either, as in the animal, in strict dependence on the external world and sensation, or, in virtue of a power possessed by man, by reason of an active incitement originating from within and which, as Bergson notes in pages unmatched for pure psychological description, makes the past, preserved in virtual or dynamic form, pass through a series of different planes of consciousness in order to bring it into contact with the present and its particular determinations).

In this operation recollection is actualized *as recollection.* It would, on the contrary, be impossible that "pure recollection" should become an image, simply by setting a motor keyboard in motion and, in short, should pass to act *in the form of movement.* Not only would that be passing from one order to another, but it also seems clear that it is movement (any movement other than a simple reflex) which first supposes the image or recollection as realized, far from the image or recollection requiring movement in order to be realized, be that movement merely nascent or simply prepared. Driesch has established convincingly that the action of animals receives its "individuality" only from a representation which commands it.[1] The stimuli received by the hypotheti-

---

longs to the accumulation of dispositions and tendencies *entitatively* modifying all our faculties, the other belonging to the accumulation and preservation of the events of our past *by mode of knowledge.* In the former the past leaves in us, though it passes on itself, subsisting modifications; in the latter it subsists itself, but in the apprehensivity of the soul.

[1] Cf. H. Driesch, *Phil. des Organischen,* vol. II, pp. 49 and ff.

cal "mental ear" or cortical retina cannot, any more than those stimuli reaching the organ of external sense, be individualized otherwise than by a cognoscitive act transcending them. So in the diseases affecting recognition, it is inadmissible that the organic lesion which hinders the actualization of a recollection should relate to an organ whose function is solely motor.[2] What is injured in such cases is a *sensitive* organ, it is the organ of an "internal sense," memory or imagination. We do not deny the importance of motor attitudes and nascent movements in the mental life or that motor tendency is woven into the very tissue of images and recollections; we do deny that the body's share in the sensitive life can be reduced to pure motivity.—As for "acted recognition," either it is purely *acted* and motor, in which case it is only an attitude or an impulsion, or else it is truly *recognition,* and in this case the attitude or movement released by habit only provokes or facilitates the formation of a synthesis of images which alone properly constitutes recognition. Here again, consequently, it must be concluded that in the diseases which affect recognition the cerebral lesion must directly affect the memory (of the sensible concrete) or the imagination.[1]

[2] As has been rightly pointed out (Quercy, *Annales médico-psychologiques,* October 1925, p. 15 of the separate printing), the Bergsonian position is, from a certain point of view, very close to the Cartesian position: as Descartes saw in the body only a machine, Bergson sees in the brain only an organ of transformation for movement (it is certainly that, but the question is to know whether it is only that). One might even wonder whether there is not some analogy between the way in which Bergson's pure memory sets in motion the "mental ear" of the temporal lobe and from there the sensorial centre, and the way in which Descartes' soul set the pineal gland in motion.

That the *parallelist* hypothesis which has passed from Spinoza's metaphysics over into the domain of experimental psychology must be replaced by the notion of the *solidarity* between the body and the soul; and that in such disorders as sensory aphasia, for example, it is not particular images which are lost but the function of *actualizing memories* which is impaired, Bergsonians and Thomists agree. The question at issue between them is to know whether this function of actualization is only a motor function or whether it is a properly sensitive function; whether all psychic is spiritual, everything cerebral purely motor and the body nothing but a collection of motor contrivances used by the soul in order to act; or whether the body is partaking both of the vegetative life and the sensitive life, because wholly informed by the soul; whether what is cerebral is not only motor but also sensitive; whether the psychic is organic in the whole order of sensitive life, and properly spiritual only in the order of intellectual and voluntary life.

[1] "To recognize a common object is mainly to know how to use it . . . But to know how to use a thing is to sketch out the movements which adapt themselves to it, it is to take a certain attitude." (*Matter and Memory,* p. 111.)—No doubt, but ordinarily this motor adaptation is not purely mechanical and reflex, it assumes first an organization, a synthesis of images. Furthermore, the moment that recognition is properly recognition, that is to say perceived, conscious, this organization of images is indispensable; it is this organization, or more precisely the integration, at least begun or vaguely indicated, of present sensation with a synthesis, with a melody of (virtual) images organized beforehand, which makes recognition.

If there are cases in which recognition is injured (psychic blindness, for example) in spite of the preservation of visual images, it is because the integration of the actual sensation with a synthetic whole—essential to the act of recognition—is an entirely different thing from the preservation of an image.

It is the same for the reverse case (a case studied by Charcot and reported by Bergson, *op. cit.,* p. 109). If there is sometimes a (relative) persistence of the power of recognition in spite of the

On the theory of memory and the brain

A simple motor disturbance, the impossibility of a present or future movement, is therefore absolutely insufficient to explain the deficiency of a recollection or an image. It appears that the Bergsonian theory fails in accounting for the very facts that it invokes first of all, the diseases affecting recognition.

It is indeed true that "in the different types of aphasia and in the diseases of visual or auditory recognition, we do not find that certain definite recollections are as it were torn from their seat, but that it is the whole faculty of remembering that is more or less diminished *in its vitality*."[2]

---

total eclipse of visual images, it is because the integration in question can still take place by utilizing images other than visual ones.

[For that matter (cf. Quercy, *Encéphale*, XX, February 1925), the experimental material itself is here insufficiently elucidated and does not allow really decisive conclusions, both in the case observed by Charcot and in the opposite category (the cases of Wilbrand, Lissauer and Mueller: the case of Wilbrand is said not to have involved in reality any loss of recognition, and in the two others the presence of visual images evoked spontaneously or in response to auditive perceptions is not proved).]

In three interesting notes (*Congrès des médecins aliénistes et neurologistes,* Brussels, August 1–7, 1924, *Encéphale,* February, 1926, *Annales médico-psychologiques,* October 1925), Quercy had shown that the Bergsonian theory of memory might on certain points lend itself to experimental verifications, in particular on the point of knowing whether the so-called sensory corticle centres (the cuneus, to take Quercy's example) are actuated "from in front" by the real object acting first on the retina and at the same time "from behind" by the pure recollection or the virtual object actuating first on the so-called imaginative corticle centres (the 'curved fold,' for example, taken as "mental retina"). He points out that in the Bergsonian theory recollection being actualized in images only by means of the excitation of the same centre which is brought into play by sensation, the destruction of the cuneus for example ought to make the actualization of visual images impossible. It seems however that in the corticle hemianopsias, in the middle of a "blind field," there can be visual hallucinations; and in cases of complete corticle cecity by the destruction of the two calcarinian regions,—images, hallucinations and visual dreams.

Likewise, insofar as sensorial aphasia is concerned, disorders of motivity and of orientation and verbal cecity do not vary in a parallel way, and it also seems that alexia can persist when the power of copying has recovered. On these various points neurology would seem to refute the Bergsonian theory. I quote these remarks as a reminder, being perfectly aware that by themselves alone scientific data will always have a great deal of trouble in proving or ruining a philosophical doctrine (even when it claims to cling as close to experience as do the Bergsonian doctrines), all the more so since other facts and other scientific constructions can always arise and modify the interpretation put upon the earlier ones (as here for example, the distinction admitted by Ramsay Hunt and by Mourgue between "paleo-kinetic system" and "neo-kinetic system"). The fact remains that from the neurological point of view it is by no means established that agnosia is purely motor in origin; and that however important the rôle of nascent movements and motor attitudes may be in mental life, however useful it may be for neurology to turn its research at the present time in that direction, the disorders of motivity alone are in themselves insufficient to explain the disorders of the sensitive functions.

Insofar as recognition is concerned, in any case, it is generally admitted today that "the motor theory is not enough." (H. Delacroix, in Dumas, *Traité de Psych.,* t. II, p. 75.)]

[2] *Matter and Memory,* p. 316.

It is well known that, following G. Bernheim of Nancy (cf. the article by Fernand Bernheim in the *Semaine médicale* of November 7, 1906), Pierre Marie, in some important articles (cf.

Semaine médicale, May 23, October 17, November 28, 1906; *Revue de philosophie,* March 1907) has decisively undermined the classical theory of aphasia. (Cf. also Peillaube, *Les Images,* pp. 179–189; Dagnan-Bouveret, *Journ. de Psych. norm. et pathol.,* 1907, pp. 558–560; 1911, 9–34; *Rev. de Mét. et de Mor.,* 1908, p. 468; Moutier, *L'aphasie de broca,* Paris, 1908.) According to these works a complete revision of all research on cerebral localizations is necessary. The disorders noted in aphasia are due not to the loss of certain determined images, but to a general weakness in the use of all images, and one would have to infer the nonexistence of special centres for language images. [As has been noted by L. Boule, who rightly criticizes the exaggeration in the ideas of those who oppose the localizing theory,—not without clinging, himself, too narrowly in my opinion to the classical conception of localizations (*Les localisations cérébrales et la philosophie spiritualiste,* Revue des questions scientifiques, t. XXIII, 1913, pp. 192–228, 352–388), —Pierre Marie is hostile to the idea of cerebral localizations in the classical sense (that is, in a mechanistic and atomistic sense, as it were, making each cerebral region into a chess-board with separate centres for each category of images), but he by no means denies localizations as assigning globally to a certain comprehensive psychic function a certain encephalic region; he even pushes the localizing doctrine to an untenable excess, since he makes Wernicke's zone into a centre of *"intellectual* elaboration." See also L. Barat's very just objections to this localizing theory of Pierre Marie's, in the *Traité de Psychologie* by Dumas, t. I, p. 748.]

"The problem of cerebral localizations," writes de la Vaissière (*Éléments de psychologie expérimentale,* 1912, p. 115), "has received no definite solution, if one wishes to affirm more than a general correspondence between the cerebral state and the regime of representations. Two points, however, seem to be established: 1) 'It is not the cerebral centre which creates the function, but the function which organizes the centre . . .' (VAN BIERVLIET, *Mémoire,* Paris, Doin, 1902, p. 44); 2) The existence of the vicariating function has been demonstrated: if in the normal man a definite portion of the cortex serves for vision, for example, after the removal of that visual sphere other neighbouring cortical parts fill the same functions. (VAN BIERVLIET, *loc. cit.,* p. 43)."

[On this question of localizations special mention should be made of von Monakow's important work, *die Lokalisation im Grosshirn.* Concerning sensorial aphasia in particular, von Monakow writes: "What is first of all destroyed in sensorial aphasia are, in my opinion, the relatively elementary physiological processes serving to awaken the comprehension of words and facilitating the comprehension of the verbal sound. Here it is a question of nerve mechanisms seated in the region of the aphasia,—essentially of channels of association. It is not the 'mnemonic images of sound' which have disappeared, but only the possibility of making them appear or of rousing them from the very first cortical ways of entry of central acoustic radiations." (p. 857).

Observations made during the war have shown that "those having brain wounds with loss of substance may present, outside of attenuated and transitory disorders of abulia and amnesia, no psychic disorder." (Porot and Hesnard, *Psychiatrie de Guerre,* 1919, p. 92. The authors are here quoting Brodier, *La Trépanation,* 1916, and Raffegeau, *Soc. méd-psych.,* November 27, 1916.) Mignard writes, for his part: "The observer is first struck, when considering most of those wounded in the brain, by the relative integrity of their psychic functions [. . .] I have never noticed the disappearance, the weakening, or the particular disorder of this or that mental function (attention, will, judgment, sentiment) in connection with the special lesion of a certain region of the brain. Superior psychism is by no means analysed by the various deficiencies of cerebral matter which the cranial region attacked allows us to suppose. It does not even seem possible to assign it, on the whole, a definite organ such as the frontal lobes, for example [. . .] It is only in its inferior, subconscious, involuntary, emotional manifestations that psychism seems sometimes to be influenced by the seat of the lesion. And even then it happens in an intermittent manner and only in connection with the sensory-motor functions, language and habits. As for the rest, the psychic syndrome which is revealed in the various lesions of the brain presents, on the contrary, a very remarkable unity. With the exception of cases in which one can admit the evolution of a diffuse meningo-encephalitis one notices most frequently a state of inactivity, of torpor, of more or less pronounced laziness in which the psychic functions, without being suppressed or even seriously harmed, are slowed down, impeded in the exercise of their activity." It is a sort of sluggishness of all the faculties which Mignard calls "atopic syndrome," that is to say, implying no precise localization of the lesion. (*Annales médico-psychologiques,* 1918, pp.

On the other hand the progress of amnesia follows an order absolutely incompatible with the topographical advance of the lesion,[3] and in fact, it is absurd to assume a definite cerebral centre for *each image* when each image participates at once in a multitude of other images which in the hypothesis, however, ought to have their seat at different points in the brain.[4]

241–243. Mignard's observations are based on 258 cranial wounds observed at the neurological centre of Montpellier.)

I do not consider that these facts constitute anatomical and histological evidence (the lesion of a cortical region does not necessarily mean total and perfect destruction) that is strong enough to invalidate the argument for localization, not, to be sure, of each recollection, but at least of memory as a whole and of the other sensitive faculties within various parts of the brain. But what is certain is that they succeed in reducing to nought, in the field of experimental psychology, the parallelist theory and the materialist conception of localizations. From another angle they demonstrate the Bergsonian theory of memory-mind and of the brain as an organ of pure motivity, a pure "pantomime organ," no more than they demonstrate the Aristotelio-Thomistic theory as we have explained it here. Even though one would have to say with Flourens (what I consider false and what Bergson himself does not at all admit, because for him there is a cerebral topography with distinctly defined functions, although purely motor, cf. *Matter and Memory*, pp. 164–167, *L'Énergie spirituelle*, pp. 137, 143), that each part of the brain is capable of substituting for all of them (cf. Troude, *Cerveau et Pensée*, Revue scientifique, June 26, 1920), the fact would still remain that this organ is intrinsically necessary for the existence in act and the exercise of the sensitive faculties, and takes an intrinsic part (although one which concerns only the entitative conditions prerequisite to cognoscitive immaterial actuation) in the operation proper of the sensitive memory and the imagination, as the retina and striata area take an intrinsic part in the proper act of vision. In reality, what has been fully confirmed by observations on cranial wounds and by war psychiatry, is that the superior psychic functions (intellectual and voluntary in the strict sense) are not localized. As to the inferior psychic functions (relating to the sensitive and sensory-motor life) their localization remains certain but it must be understood in quite a different sense than the one in which Broca and Charcot understood it.

If research in cyto-architectonics has given a still more precise and still more certain value to the fact of the histological differentiations of the cortex, the scientific interpretation of these differentiations with regard to the mental functions gets farther and farther away from the parallelist and materialist theories; and the views enunciated by Brodmann, for example, from the experimental point of view (cf. Tournay, in the *Traité de Psychologie* by Dumas, t. 1, p. 196) might easily be integrated to the philosophical views proposed here.

Similarly, the new tendencies of neuro-biology and neuro-pathology, the remarkable works of Sherrington, von Monakow, Radl, von Uexhüll, Toulouse and Mignard, etc.,—from which attempts have been made to draw confirmation for the Bergsonian thesis (cf. Mourgue, "Le point de vue neuro-biologique dans l'oeuvre de M. Bergson et les données actuelles de la science," *Rev. de Métaph, et de Morale*, January–March, 1920),—all certainly seem to converge (when they do not reflect the prejudices of any particular school, and approach realistically the dynamic of the nervous system) toward a radical negation of psychological atomism and of parallelism. But far from being open to an interpretation in line with Bergson's ideas only, these tendencies and these works (if we pass from the purely experimental register, from the language of conditionalism to that of causality), can receive in the Aristotelio-Thomistic theory an interpretation quite as easy, more direct from certain points of view and in any case much freer from arbitrary metaphysical hypotheses. The same must be said for the research in animal psychology of the eminent Dutch biologist, Buytendijk.

[3] Peillaube, *Les Images*, pp. 158–160.

[4] Ebbinghaus, *Précis de Psychologie*, Alcan, 1910, pp. 108–109. This argument does not prove that the functioning of the faculty may not *organize* the cerebral "centre," in such a way that a definite topographical portion (for example, the temporal lobe) would be assigned to the evocation of a *certain global category* of images (for example, the evocation of auditive images).

It also seems clear that in many cases of amnesia there is not so much loss or destruction of recollections as inability to reproduce the recollections preserved.[1]

We have a right to conclude from these facts that parallelism and epiphenomenalism—untenable in other respects—are refuted by science on grounds of their own choosing, on the grounds of cerebral localizations.

But from that, to conclude as Bergson does, that the brain has a purely motor rôle, that cerebral lesions leave the memory of the sensible concrete intact, that this memory is inorganic and is identical with the spirit, is a whole world of difference. Memory of the sensible concrete, and the imagination, preserving images inseparably riveted in their representative function to conditions of materiality, images which have their origin in the external senses themselves organic, are necessarily organic faculties. All of which in no way implies that images and recollections are inscribed in the nerve substance as though on a phonographic disc, or deposited in the brain as though put into a box, but only that the faculty is subjected or localized in a definite organ, and that the operation of the faculty is at the same time the operation of that organ. The faculty can actualize only by the play of the organ the recollections which immaterially inform it, and which subsist in it in a state of habit. It could therefore be a question only of a global relation between the physical organ and the psychic faculty, or of a "general correspondence between the state of the brain and the tissue of representations";[2] and it would be absurd to seek in the details of a purely physical functioning of the organ the reason or the equivalent of its functioning properly so-called, which is of the psychological order.[3]

As to the theory of memory-spirit, and of an entirely spiritual "pure recollection" which is progressively materialized, and which acts, after the manner of a "virtual object," on cerebral centres comparable, for example, to a "mental ear,"[4] not only does it, like the Bergsonian theory of perception, bestow *spirit* on animals, since they have memory as well as sensation,[5] but it also makes of the body a simple instrument *possessed* and actuated by a mind, a more

---

With the remarkable theory of chronogenic localization, of von Monakow, science seems to open the way for the general idea of an organization of the centre by the function.

[1] Cf. De la Vaissière, *Elém. de Psych. expér.*, 1912, pp. 125–126; William James, *Princ. of Psychology*, I, 682; L. Barat, in Dumas, *Traité de Psychologie*, t. I, p. 526. In quite different cases, in dementia and mental confusion, there is likewise, according to Toulouse and Mignard (*Annales médico-psychologiques*, 1914) not so much loss of psychic functions as lack of power to use them correctly, or loss of *auto-conduction*.

[2] See *supra*, p. 224, n. 2.

[3] See *supra*, pp. 207–208.

[4] *Matter and Memory*, p. 166.

[5] This seems true of *all* animals. For example, the existence of memory in fish, batrachians, the tortoise, crustaceans, insects, molluscs, etc. has been experimentally demonstrated. (Cf. Piéron, *L'Évolution de la Mémoire*. Flammarion, 1910; F. Buytendijk, *Psychologie des Animaux*, chap. VII.)

"spiritist" than spiritualist conception, and one which ruins the unity of the human being.

Finally let us not forget that in addition to the memory which retains and reproduces images, there is in man, and in man alone, another memory of whose existence Bergson tells us nothing: it is the intellectual memory, which is one with intelligence.[3] The understanding, in fact, which Aristotle calls *the place of intelligible forms,*[4] keeps and retains within itself—in the state of *habitus*—the abstract knowledge that perfects it, acquired *science,* and in such a manner that it cannot lose it, being itself "of a much more stable and immutable nature than corporal matter";[5] that is why intellectual memory subsists in the separate soul.[6] This memory cannot "materialize itself progressively," and it has no organ. Yet in order to exercise itself (under the conditions of this present life), it requires the assistance of the sensible memory, as the intellect requires the assistance of the imagination. If Bergson had recognized its existence, he would by that very fact have had to recognize both the existence of true intelligence and its authentic spirituality.

On the theory of self

The results of the metaphysical principles which direct, like occult forces, the whole psychological discussion of *Matter and Memory* will now stand out more and more clearly.

The Bergsonian theory which constantly moves around the notions of *potency* and *act,* without managing to formulate and use them in a rational way, might at a certain point of view appear to be an inversion of Aristotle's doctrine. As it is attached to movement, not to being, to sense data, not to intelligible reality, to action which passes, not to the act as the perfection and principle of being, instead of seeing *in the soul the act of the living body,* rather does it see *in the body the actualization of the soul.* "For the spirit, to live is essentially to concentrate on the act to accomplish,"—[1] and it is through the body that act takes place. Therefore, by a strange yet inevitable contradiction, the spirit in its very life and proper activity appears as depending upon

[3] On this particular memory rests, in reality, the so-called *rational* way of learning as opposed to what was called the "mechanical" method of learning. (Cf. Myers, *Textbook,* pp. 179–180.)

[4] *De Anima,* lib. III, c. IV, 429 a 27–28.

[5] Saint Thomas, *Sum. theol.,* I[a], q. 79, a. 6.—Intellectual memory moreover does not know under their guise of *things past* the *objects* it remembers, since intelligence does not perceive things directly except in their universal nature, apart from the concrete conditions of time and place. It does however bear upon the past, insofar as intelligence knows that *its act* has existed in the past (*Ibid.,* q. 79, a. 6, *ad* 2).

[6] *Ibid.,* q. 89, a. 5 and 6.

[1] "(To live, for the mind) is therefore to insert itself into things by a mechanism which will extract from consciousness all that is utilizable for action, even if it obscures the greater part of the rest." *L'Ame et le Corps (Foi et Vie,* January 1, 1913, p. 14). [*L'Énergie spirituelle,* p. 60.]

the body which is, after all, only a dissipation or distension of the psychic; the spirit appears as 'finalized' by the body which serves it.

Is not the "plane" on which the spirit is most spirit also the "plane of the dream"? And is not the plane on which the spirit is the least spirit and materializes into movement, also the plane on which the spirit acts and "inserts itself into reality"? So that the "deeper self" is the self of the dream or the "lower self" concentrating in order to produce an outward action? One can perfectly well admit within us the existence of different "planes of consciousness," of different states or degrees of actualization of the prodigiously complex and moving inner world of our potencies. But by what astounding misapprehension can one confuse this actualization with the act brought about by means of the "sensori-motor mechanisms," and reduce it to the tension of the organic faculties upon the present moment? Even for this purely practical tension or attention, a coordination of the forces of the soul is necessary which, in man, has its root in the activity of the will. And it is especially by the exercise of the wholly spiritual faculties of the intellect and the will that we truly actualize ourselves; that is why the most immanent act, contemplation, is *par excellence* the act of man.

But Bergson has in view only the purely transitive act of *homo faber*. He does not see that the body, being made for the soul, is made for the operation of the soul—that is, for the spiritual possession of being—because the human soul, being the least perfect of intellectual natures and having to draw its ideas, by abstraction, from sensible experience, must, *in order to know*, be united to a body.[1] In his eyes, on the contrary, it is the soul that is made, not

---

1 True, because the human soul is spiritual, intelligence emanates from its substantial basis intelligibly informed by it (not, however, that this radical auto-intellection can actualize itself here below). So that if the soul were not joined to a body which made one single substance, one sole primary subject of action with it, it would enjoy that intuitive knowledge of its own essence which the union with the body and the law of activity which this union implies, make impossible now. (Cf. John of Saint Thomas, *Curs. phil.*, III, P. *de Anima*, q. IX, a. 1, Vivès, t. III, pp. 434-436; *Curs. theol.*, *de Angelis*, disp. XXI, a. 2, par. 13; Gardeil, *La structure d l'âme et l'expérience mystique*, t. I, book II, question IV.) But so feeble is the intellectual light of the human soul and so inferior its condition, that such a knowledge would remain insufficient to enable it properly to know all that it should know, especially concerning God: a mirror which reflects God yet which cannot distinctly read in itself the reflection it bears. The human soul therefore could not find, like the angelic spirit, in the knowledge of itself by itself, the original and principal perfection (in the natural order) of its life of knowledge. It is by the multiplicity of ideas that it draws from things, by turning first toward external realities, that it must tend toward this perfection before it turns back upon itself in knowing itself by its acts, and before it experiences within itself,—this time supernaturally, through the connatural knowledge proper to the gifts of the Holy Ghost,—the One Whom it knows naturally only by visible things.

One can thus understand, in my opinion, why the human soul which, as spirit, knows itself by its essence in the state of separation, nevertheless finds in the good of its operation proper which is knowledge (and ensuing love), the final reason for its union with the body which, in virtue of its nature and its proper degree in the scale of beings, it is its function to inform substantially. "*Si animae humanae sic essent institutae a Deo, ut intelligerent per modum qui competit substantiis separatis, non haberent cognitionem perfectam, sed confusam in communi.*" *Sum. theol.*, I, 89, 1.

for the body doubtless, but *for the act* accomplished by means of the body.

Consequently he can form only a wholly physical idea, or rather image, of the soul; he can conceive it only as a sort of mass which is propelled by an *élan* or an impulsive force and which contracts upon its "point." That image is not a simple occasional metaphor. It is an integral part of the philosopher's thought; it is impossible to do without it for an instant in the Bergsonian theory, more particularly in the theory of the disorders of the personality, a theory which tends, furthermore, to have us take the disorders which can affect only the faculties,—and directly, only the sensitive faculties,—for diseases, scissions, which would affect the *person* itself.[2]

The confusion which Bergsonian philosophy constantly makes between the self or the person and the memory would be completely inexplicable were we to forget that for this philosophy memory is the past itself and finally duration surging forward, and that the self is thus an *uninterrupted change*.[3] A very superficial doctrine from the psychological point of view, for though our sensations and impressions are ceaselessly changing, nevertheless in reality we have within us more of the definitive than of the transitory; there are in us certitudes and choices which do not change; and the more man is raised above matter, the more stable are his thought and his will.

This is a doctrine which is, strictly speaking, inconceivable from the metaphysical point of view because it confuses our operations with our substance, that which is of us with that which is ourselves, change with the thing that changes.

In reality, it destroys the human person. For Bergsonian philosophy the self is not,—it becomes. It is not a being, it is a continuous change.[1] Now, if I say that "I CHANGE," I think that I am acquiring a certain being—an accidental being—which I did not have, and by that very fact I think that before the change I had another being,—a substantial being, or one constitutive of my self,—(otherwise I should not have changed, I should have been created all of a piece), and I also think that this substantial being is still there after the change (otherwise I should not have changed, I should have been transformed into another, therefore I should not be able to remember the first *I* which would no longer be myself); and thus I think that I am, that I am a person or a substance, and that this substance remains the same while being the subject of the change. But to say that "I CHANGE," that "I am a pure change, without a thing which changes," is to say that there is no substance subject of this change, therefore no *I* which changes, and that I am not a person for the

[2] Cf. Jules Grivet, *La théorie de la personne d'après H. Bergson, Études,* November 20, 1911. (Articles on Bergson, by the same author, in *Études* of July 20, 1910, October 5 and November 20, 1909.)

[3] "The Perception of Change," in *Creative Mind,* p. 172.

[1] *Ibid.;* cf. *Creative Evolution,* pp. 1-8.

very good reason that *I* am not, that *I* do not succeed in being, and that there is only pure becoming. It is therefore impossible, in the Bergsonian thesis, to say or to think *I*. A result of our language habits? It is not indeed a question of language, but of thought. I defy anyone to *think* this absolute phenomenalism. It is absolutely unintelligible.

Bergson tries to replace the permanence of substance by the permanence of what he calls indivisible change, by the automatic preservation of the past in its reality proper.

That in living beings capable of knowledge, and most eminently in man, the past is preserved,—in other words, that these living beings are *capable of experience* in such a way that their power to act is modified and enriched by their very activity is, as we said above, a fact that no one denies.* But, as we also said, it is not in its existence proper, in its natural being, that the past is thus preserved: it is in the *intentional* being which happens to things when they are detached from themselves and no longer exist except in the soul in order to specify the knowing activity of the latter. The Bergsonian theory of the preservation of the past could have made a precious contribution to psychology if the philosopher had distinguished between natural being and intentional being and had noted that in his thought only the latter was concerned. But this distinction which supposes a strictly realist metaphysics is entirely foreign to Bergson's doctrine. It was therefore to the preservation of the past in *nature* that, in spite of himself, he was inevitably to be led, and the thesis of *The Perception of Change* which we quoted above[1] must serve as a key to the interpretation of *Matter and Memory* and of *Creative Evolution*.

It may happen that, profiting once more from the instinctive rectifications of common sense in the reader, the Bergsonian theory will for him at first find its expression more or less confusedly in an affirmation of an integral preservation of the past *in the 'apprehensivity' of the soul* (*in apprehensione mentis*). The reader is at once struck by the great psychological significance of this affirmation; but if he is more attentive to the metaphysical significance of the doctrine he must surely realize that for the latter it is a question of the preservation of the past *in its reality proper* as well as in the apprehensivity of the soul. This was inevitable from the moment the philosopher failed to get clear of the idealist postulates and to make up his mind first on the problem of the relations of knowing and being. "We are inclined to think of our past as inexistent. . . . This is a profound mistake!"[2] "It is enough to be convinced

---

* See *supra*, pp. 220–221.—Let us once more remark that I am speaking here of *experience* properly so-called, implying memory and the preservation of the past itself. All the facts of adaptation, of perfectioning through use, of anaphylaxis, etc., in short, of entitative enriching through duration that one already meets in the realm of the vegetable life do not concern the preservation of the past itself, but only habitual modifications left in a subject which endures by events which pass.

[1] See *supra*, pp. 175–178.
[2] "The Perception of Change," pp. 177–178 of *Creative Mind*.

once and for all that reality is change, that change is indivisible, and that in an indivisible change the past is one with the present."* "The preservation of the past in the present is nothing else than the indivisibility of change."† "Of course, if we shut our eyes to the indivisibility of change, to the fact that our most distant past adheres to our present and constitutes with it one single and identical uninterrupted change, it seems that the past is normally what is abolished and that there is something extraordinary about the preservation of the past: we think ourselves obliged to conjure up an apparatus whose function would be to record the parts of the past capable of reappearing in our consciousness. But if we take into consideration the continuity of the inner life and consequently its indivisibility we no longer have to explain the preservation of the past, but rather its apparent abolition."¹ What could be clearer? Of that immaterial being according to which the past subsists in the soul by reason of the exigencies proper to the functions of knowing, there appears not the slightest suspicion here; all that is mentioned—to deny it—is the natural being of a material apparatus as recorder of the past and—to affirm it—the natural being of indivisible change in which the past adheres to the present. That is why the problem proper of memory is simply suppressed. "Memory therefore has no need of explanation. Or rather, there is no special faculty whose rôle is to retain quantities of past in order to pour it into the present. The past preserves itself automatically."²

It would be particularly instructive to consider at this point the symmetrical errors of the philosophy of clear ideas and the philosophy of pure change. To tell the truth, the extreme positions of Descartes and Bergson can be ascribed to the same confusion between *what endures* IN *time* or through time, and *time itself*.³ They both confuse the novelty of the *instant*, which did

* *Ibid.*, p. 183.
† *Ibid.*, p. 183.
¹ *Ibid.*, pp. 180–181.
² *Ibid.*, p. 180.—"I shall accept, however, if you insist," writes Bergson elsewhere (*L'Énergie spirituelle*, p. 59), "but taking it in a purely metaphorical sense, the idea of a container in which recollections are lodged, and I shall then say quite simply that they are in the mind." Let us take care that it is not here a question of an intentional informing of the "mind" (or of the faculty of the soul) by the past, but of the automatic preservation of the states themselves lived by the mind, and which are abolished only in appearance. That is why the idea of a *containing*, even in the mind, can be taken only in a "purely metaphorical sense."—Cf. again *Creative Evolution*, p. 4: "Duration is the continuous progress of the past which gnaws into the future and which swells as it advances. And as the past grows without ceasing, so also there is no limit to its preservation. Memory, as we have tried to prove, is not a faculty of putting away recollections in a drawer, or of inscribing them in a register. There is no register, no drawer; there is not even, properly speaking, a faculty, for a faculty works intermittently, when it will or when it can, whilst the piling up of the past upon the past goes on without relaxation. In reality, the past is preserved by itself, automatically."
³ Aristotle had, however, taken care to put the philosophers on their guard against that confusion. Cf. *Phys.*, lib. IV, c. 12, 220 b 32–222 a 9: *lect.* XX of Saint Thomas.

not exist a moment ago and which already no longer exists, or of the *moment of change,* which comes into existence with each new instant, and the novelty (a so-called novelty) of the very being of substance,—let us say in short that they confuse the *flux of time* and the *duration of substances.*

Descartes conceived time as being a ready-made medium (analogous to geometrical space) awaiting events; its parts, which he takes to be indivisibles —for him time was *composed of* independent *instants*[4]—will successively be *filled* by things. According to him then, if I do not yet exist in some future instant now empty but which my existence will fill, that means,—not that before this instant ideally indicated and not yet given in being there already existed the *I* that will exist at the instant in question,—but rather that before this instant the *I* which will fill it did not yet exist; it will spurt into being with the instant itself, it will therefore be *created* anew. So that time is composed of instants of creation, discontinuous but infinitely close together, and substances are continually re-created by God at each of these instants; they endure atomically. Instead of meaning: *the present instant* alone exists in act *in time,* it meant: the *instantaneous* alone exists *in things.* Thus it is that Descartes, confusing the instants of time (regarded by him as the parts of time) with the duration of things in time, *substantified* time and at the same time pulverized the duration of created substances, which was a radical sacrificing of the continuity of time and of memory, and led to all the inextricable difficulties which caused so much rejoicing in the second half of the seventeenth century.

At the opposite extreme Bergson, looking upon substance as constituted by pure change itself without a thing which changes, or by the flux of real time, thinks that if our present is only the point by which our past, constantly increasing, inserts itself into the universe,—it is not that we are a substance which exists and endures in time, which continues there in being, and whose immanent activity emerges enough above matter to be also—*intentionally* or

---

[4] In his thesis on *Le rôle de l'Idée de l'instant dans la philosophie de Descartes* (Alcan 1920), Jean Wahl quite rightly remarks that "the two ideas of independence of instants and dependence of the creature, of discontinuous time and continuous creation are indissolubly bound up in the thought of Descartes. It seems that his work has consisted here in profoundly uniting to the idea of continued creation as it presented itself in scholasticism, the idea of discontinuous time, as it took shape in the mechanics and the physics of the Renaissance" (p. 24).—For Descartes "duration is the fact that the thing which endures ceases to be at each moment." (p. 24).— It is unnecessary to point out that *continued creation* (that is to say, *perpetually renewed* creation) in the sense of the Cartesians differs *toto caelo* from the *preservation* of things or *continued creation* in the Thomists' sense. The latter regard the preservation of things as the non-cessation,—as regards the effect produced, or things themselves,—of creative action, in itself above time and movement, eternal. Cf. *Sum. theol.,* I, q. 104, a. 1, *ad* 4. I may add that for Saint Thomas the instant is not a part of time (the parts of time are always times, and always divisible however small they may be supposed), but the indivisible term by which time continues with time; the present instant is thus the indivisible term, the present without duration by which time past continues with future time and by reason of which time exists in act.

in the order of knowing—what it no longer is *really* or in the order of its existence proper, in short, enough to *retain time;* no! it is that our past itself preserves itself and continues in being; it is called 'past' only through the effect of an incidence of our practical interests on our manner of conceiving; in reality it is a present which does not abolish itself, which prolongs itself unceasingly in the indivisibility of change; so that in real time or indivisible change nothing, in reality, ceases to exist. Instead of saying: *being* endures *in things,* Bergsonism says: *the present* endures *in time.* Confusing the duration of things in time with the flux of time itself, and if I may say so, thus *chronifying* substance, the Bergsonian doctrine solidifies time, which is a radical sacrifice of the *successiveness* essential to it, and which leads to insoluble contradictions.

Let us recall here the argument often invoked by Bergson; I give it just as he formulated it in a philosophical causerie: "In pronouncing the word 'causerie,' " he said, "when I articulate the last syllable, the first two are already a part of the past, and this last syllable 'rie' itself has not been instantaneously pronounced.[1] However I perceive this word, all at once, in one identical *present,* and what is more the other words which precede it are still there, in my consciousness, "otherwise I should have lost the thread of my discourse."

Does that mean, as everyone agrees, that without a special faculty called memory it would not be possible for us to speak, or to understand speech? And does that also mean that in time *felt,* in subjective or apparent time (we refer here not to things which are in time, but to the weft of time itself), there is a *felt present,* which is not instantaneous like the indivisible *nunc fluens* of real time, but which occupies a variable duration?[2]

Not at all. The distinction of the present and the past, says Bergson, is purely practical and wholly relative. This felt *present,* which lasts some hundredths or tenths of a second, extends in reality to all the time a real change endures: to convince oneself of this, it is enough to conceive a sensation suf-

---

[1] Cf. *L'Ame et le Corps* (*Foi et Vie,* January 1, 1913, pp. 13–14). [*L'Énergie spirituelle,* pp. 59–60.] See also *The Perception of Change,* in *Creative Mind,* pp. 180–181.

[2] This duration would vary between $1/100$ or $75/100$ of a second and 5 or 12 seconds as extreme limits (even though the psycho-physicists have here measured the times that sensation can appreciate, rather than the times that the sensation of the present can endure).—See concerning this question Peillaube, *Les Images,* pp. 321–338.—*This sensible present* is perceived by the senses. The *sensible past* is perceived by the estimative: *ratio praeteriti, quam attendit memoria, inter hujusmodi intentiones (aestimativae) computatur.* (*Sum. theol.,* I[a], q. 78, a. 4.) That is why, as I have already said (p. 219, n. 1), recollections preserved by the memory already bear within them the mark or colouring of the *past.*—Time, as Albert the Great says (*de Mem.,* tract. I, c. II) is thus *felt* in the present when the event is (sensibly) present (that is, in short, as long as a simple act of sensation lasts), it is *felt* in the past when the event passes (cf. Wm. James, *Psychology, Précis de psychologie,* p. 374), one has a *presentiment* of it in the future when the event approaches: *hoc est obscure percipere tempus.*—Let us point out a remarkable similarity between these observations by the great scholastics and the views set forth by Henri Delacroix on recognition (insofar as it bears upon the past) and on memory as "the consciousness of time" (in the *Traité de Psychologie* by Dumas, t. II, p. 80).

ficiently dilated, which would comprise, like a compass between its points, not just a few fractions of a second, but a whole human life, for example: thus time is *only a present which endures*,[1] all our past events remain, not in their images which a special faculty preserves, but in themselves, and "our past is there intact, subconscious." In short, that which is no longer, still is.

Bergson, in this singularly fallacious argumentation, confuses in one identical contradictory concept true *time*, which the intelligence alone can know in its reality,[2] and the *present* of felt time, of time as sensation makes it known (indeed in a confused and rudimentary manner,—time being after all only a "common sensible," not a "proper sensible"). He forgets that the felt present, whereas it occupies objectively a certain time, and therefore *objectively* implies a certain *succession*, comprises, on the contrary, no succession (therefore no change) *for sensation*, and is felt as simultaneous, as *instantaneous*. He forgets that the felt present is thus only a sensible and imperfect substitute for the present instant properly so-called, which does not endure but is always flying by,—for that indivisible instant whose flux constitutes time and which intellect conceives by *purifying* the sensible notion of time, by its awareness of the fact that the sensible present, which in reality endures for a certain *time*, is instantaneous and *present* as a whole only in appearance, because it is absolutely impossible and contradictory that a thing in which there is succession should be at the same time instantaneous. So that if there is, in fact, an *indivisible duration* and a *present which endures*, an "instant which remains,"[3] that duration excludes all movement, all change, all

---

1 "The distinction we make between our present and past is therefore, if not arbitrary, at least relative to the extent of the field which our attention to life can embrace." ("The Perception of Change," in *Creative Mind*, p. 179.) "In a word, our present falls back into the past when we cease to attribute to it an immediate interest." . . . "Consequently, nothing prevents us from carrying back as far as possible the line of separation between our present and our past. An attention to life, sufficiently powerful and sufficiently separated from all practical interest, would thus include in an undivided present the entire past history of the conscious person,—[. . .] What we have is a present which endures." (*Ibid.*, pp. 179–180.)

The past has not ceased to exist, says Bergson further, but has *simply ceased to be useful* (*Matter and Memory*, p. 193).—So therefore, if I heard the music of Bach yesterday and that of Schönberg today, must I say that I am still hearing Bach as I listen to Schönberg, but that I am not paying any attention to it? If I went for a walk yesterday in Lyons, and if today I am in Paris, must I say that my walk in Lyons has not ceased to exist but has ceased to be useful? If yesterday I was happy and today I am sad, must I say that my happiness has not ceased to exist but that it has ceased to be useful? What a consolation for people to think that what they took for the recollection of past happiness is this very happiness itself, which is "automatically preserved"! And what delight for the philosopher to think that the same being is both ignorant and learned, a child and an old man, etc.

Let us add that there is no need, if after all one denies that wonderful past which is preserved, to suppose that the universe "perishes and is reborn, through a veritable miracle, at every moment of duration" (*Ibid.*, p. 193). All we have to do is to recognize that *substance* continues to be and remains beneath change.

2 See *supra*, pp. 172–173.

3 Boëthius, *de Trin.*, chap. 4.

succession. This is the case with eternity which, being simultaneously all and entire, excludes from its essence any kind of time.[4] How can Bergson help but see that it is absurd on the contrary to combine in a single concept this felt *present* (felt as instantaneous and simultaneous) and the *succession* which measures it objectively, and then to say that time is both continuous succession and permanent present, therefore that time is a simultaneous succession, that *time subsists?*

In so doing Bergsonism falls, in reality, into the error with which it never ceases to reproach others. In admitting a duration which flows, that is, which is a successive continuum, and which nevertheless remains, which is therefore a simultaneous continuum, it confuses the successive continuum with the simultaneous continuum, *time* with *space*. Its duration, that precious reality discovered by intuition,—an unfortunate hybrid of these two concepts! Thus does intelligence take its revenge.

Intelligence alone, in fact,—and not the senses, as Bergsonian philosophy keeps falsely repeating,—really perceives the successive continuum; it alone clearly knows that time never subsists, but ceaselessly *becomes.*

Thus we see that Bergsonian duration is properly unthinkable, the idea of a simultaneous succession being as contradictory as the idea of a square circle. The soul in Bergsonian philosophy, the cone, the point, the plane and all the rest is swallowed up by a metaphysical myth which resists any intelligible formulation.

To try to understand, in spite of everything, the relation that Bergsonism establishes between the soul and the body, between "time which is preserved" and the "present which is repeated," one might venture to say that for Bergson the soul would be to the body very much what eternity is to time; eternity co-exists, in fact, with every moment of time,—it is an indivisible endless present. But, as a matter of fact, eternity excludes any kind of change or possibility of change, any kind of past or of future. Furthermore, there is no transition possible between eternity and time, and eternity and time can never combine to form one single nature. Whereas Bergsonian duration is nothing else than change which remains and the past which preserves itself; and whereas between this duration and the "instantaneous" there is an infinity of degrees; and they must both constitute human nature. . . .

[4] Eternity measures the duration of the *absolutely immutable* Being. Time measures the duration of what is *mutable as to substance;* the *aevum* measures the duration of what is *immutable as to substance,* but which in other respects admits of *accidental changes* producing for the subject a certain succession of before and after,—the *aevum* is the duration proper of angelic stability (*Sum. theol.,* I[a], q. 10). From the fact that a certain succession of volitions and thoughts is found in Angels, a certain time, measuring that succession, will be joined to the *aevum.* This time of the Angels is *composed* of instants *which endure* (contrary to the instants of our time, which do not endure and which are not *parts* of our time). But in fact each of these instants, as long as it endures, excludes all change and all succession; and they follow one another discontinuously. (*Sum. theol.,* I[a], q. 53, a. 3; cf. Opusc. [unauthentic] *De Instantibus;* Pègues, *op. cit., Traité des Anges,* pp. 291 ff.)

The spirituality of the soul

The Bergsonian theory admits for the soul an infinity of degrees and transitions between spirituality and materiality.[1] It admits moreover that the spirit *actualizes itself* only in *materializing itself*. What Bergson calls spirituality therefore has nothing in common with true spirituality, which consists, on the contrary, in an intrinsic independence with regard to matter, as to being and as to operation, and which begins at a perfectly determined stage in the scale of beings.

And after all, where is this immaterial operation of the soul in the Bergsonian theory? The more the soul acts, the more it uses the brain, since the body is the point by which our action inserts itself into the real. As to the idea, it is of the same order as the image, and the intellect is a most material activity within us. Would it be the intuition? But that violent operation assumes the coming into play of all our potencies and the re-absorption of intellect in instinct which, I imagine, is not pure spirituality.

We must not allow ourselves to be over-awed by words. There is no place for *the spirit* properly so-called in an anti-intellectualist philosophy.

Dualism and monism

The Bergsonian theory, moreover, does not escape the drawbacks of dualism, for in it soul and body form an accidental whole, not an essential whole; in it man cannot be regarded as a being composed of a body and a spiritual soul, but only as a soul making use of a body in order to act, and it is the soul by itself alone which would constitute the first subject of action, the human *person* in the metaphysical sense of the word, if the *person* could subsist in it.

On the other hand, the Bergsonian theory has all the drawbacks of monism, for it admits between soul and body only a difference of degree or intensity, not a difference in nature; since, according to Bergson, we go by continuous transitions from spirit to matter, since matter is only "inverted psychic," since the sole reality is becoming, pure change, concrete duration, now ascending, now descending, now concentrated, now diluted, since in short opposites are identical with one another and all is in everything.

Opposites are thus made identical: instead of showing how the soul and the body, while fundamentally distinct, constitute one single and same being, and how opposites harmonize, Bergsonian metaphysics, in fact, seeks progressively to *attenuate* one of the opposites and then the other, to the point that, by

---

[1] See *supra*, pp. 210–214, etc. It would be too bad not to read, on this subject, the following text which is a good example of the ordinary language of the new philosophy: "Between inert *matter* and the *mind* most capable of reflection there are all possible *intensities* of *memory* or, what comes to the same thing, all the *degrees of freedom*." (*Matter and Memory*, p. 296.) (The italics are mine.)

scarcely perceptible transitions, one passes on to some notion which is not properly suited to either, but in which each of them disappears. There they are then, placed in continuity and in fact identified; they no longer appear to be anything but different degrees of the same thing (which is not thing, but rather action). This is the way that Bergson identifies body and soul in a certain *extensivity*, intermediate between the inextended and the extended,[1] in a certain *tension*, intermediate between quality and quantity,[2] in a certain spontaneity and a certain contingency intermediate between freedom and necessity.[3]

It was all in vain then that Bergson sought, at the cost of an extraordinary philosophical effort, to find (through intellectualized plastic imagination and through intuition chosen in preference to the intellect and its rational equipment, and by having recourse to time, not being) the true distinction between soul and body, and their real unity, and the living personality of man, all those truths for which he had the desire and, as it were, the divination. This attempt on the part of a marvellously gifted mind, a mind in which *endless patience* and a capacity for hard work were not wanting, could not help but come to grief, because its *principles* were not fashioned to the measure of what is.

Bergson claims to rely on experience and to limit himself to the immediate. And he imagines, with regard to very obscure psychological facts, studied, moreover, with great care—but which (with a similar expenditure of talent but with other metaphysical principles) could have produced equally fruitful interpretations—a whole world of gratuitous hypotheses which infinitely transcend the facts observed, which often contradict other facts, and which above all claim to renew philosophy to its foundations. To find the exact place of a grain of sand he turns the solar systems topsy-turvy. And as all this is grasped with the keenest *imagination,* is therefore seen, felt, hence immediate, hence absolutely certain, we have no right to discuss it and we manifest, in seeking to understand, the most refractory obtuseness. Because he wanted to do without the intellect and reason, he constantly confuses the accidental and the essential, whose distinction is a matter for intelligence, not sensibility. That is how he translated the commonplace fact that we are constantly changing into the original theory that we *are* change; the commonplace fact that we are constantly modifying ourselves, and that we are constantly enriching ourselves with our past, into that original theory that we create ourselves ontologically, and that our past is preserved in its natural being; the commonplace fact that every spirit presupposes the fac-

---

[1] *Matter and Memory*, pp. 325, 326 and 327.
[2] *Ibid.*, pp. 238, 328.
[3] *Ibid.*, pp. 330, 331, 332.

ulty of recollection, into the original theory that memory is spirit. Because he wanted to do without the intellect and reason, he blurs the meaning of words, and establishes between spirit, memory, consciousness, soul, person, action, freedom, duration, will, creative effort, a sort of generalized osmotic 'compenetration': all these notions become more or less synonymous and are used interchangeably according to the needs of the *philosophical feeling* to be suggested. Ostensibly in order to make metaphysics an *integral experience,* from which the idea of being is excluded, he extenuates, he reduces to nothing the spiritualist theses he proposes to restore.

II.—SOUL AND BODY IN THOMIST PHILOSOPHY

As to Thomist philosophy, it is not the philosophy of time, but the philosophy of being. And it is in terms of being, the formal object of the intelligence, that it knows the distinction and the unity of the soul and the body.

Substance

The idea of *substance* is the primary and absolutely necessary determination of the idea of being. Substance is that whose function it is to be, in the primordial sense of this word, it is that whose function it is to have existence in itself. If there is no substance, if there is nothing which has being in itself, of a certainty there is no being, that is perfectly evident. The sole question is to attribute to the words 'being,' 'existence' and to those related to them, a real meaning, or in other words, to think that thought is not vain, and that the philosopher has the right to speak philosophy in his innermost intelligence, and to express it outwardly in some other way than by wagging his finger.

Substance being the object of intellectual perception, being grasped as such by the intellect,—by the intellect alone—on the occasion of a perception of the senses or of consciousness, it is easy to understand why the sensualists who hold to be true only what comes under sense observation, regard substance as a philosophical fiction; it is understandable too that Bergsonian philosophy, which philosophizes with the senses and the imagination, should consider substance as a spatial image arbitrarily isolated and solidified, as an empty framework, an inert medium, a cord on which to thread phenomena, a "piece of matter" situated beneath phenomena,—in short, to use William James's felicitous expression, a sort of theoretical stop-gap,—and should exert itself with extraordinary fervour to banish the idea of substance from human thought.[1] In reality, this idea has nothing whatever to do with space and the sense continuum, it is related solely to being. Substance is to such an extent being, the formal object of the intelligence, in its primary and pri-

---

[1] Cf. Wm. James, *A Pluralistic Universe,* p. 210; Laberthonnière, *Annales de Phil. chrét.,* November, 1910, p. 178. Bergson sees in the philosophical idea of the person only the idea of "a formless *ego*" (*Creative Evolution,* p. 3).

mordially indispensable acceptation, that when they claimed to expel substance from philosophy, the phenomenalists simply expelled accident from
it. In the phenomenalist doctrine, there is nothing but substances which they
call *sensations, images, states of consciousness,* etc., there is nothing but
thousands of tiny imaginary substances among which they have parcelled
out our ego.

As to those who have been led astray by pure becoming and change without
any thing which changes, in spite of themselves they think "substance" when
Bergson speaks to them of "duration," "profound self," "streams of consciousness," etc. But it is at the cost of a flagrant misconception, for Bergsonian
philosophy radically excludes the idea of substance; it is a far cry from this
idea to what Bergson calls the "uninterrupted humming [and continuous
rumbling] of life's depths,"[1] replacing as always, and calling it immediate
data, *reality* the object of intelligence by what *appears* to the senses or to introspection.

If the opponents of the idea of substance ordinarily have a very poor understanding of that idea, they have even much less understanding of the idea
of accident, so that substance is indebted to accident for its many enemies.

When we think of a being we think first of all of a thing which is, of a
nature or essence which has existence in itself, that is, of a substance. But observation shows us that there are many realities—colour, sound, movement,
states of consciousness, etc.,—which do not correspond to that idea, which are
not subsisting things; they modify, complete, finish another thing in which
they have being. Thus it is that Peter and Paul can be musicians or philosophers; whether they are or not, they will be neither more nor less human
beings; the habitual science of philosophy or of music is a reality which is not
sufficient in itself for existence, but which is added to the reality, already fully
constituted in the order of substance, of this or that human being.

Intelligence then, elaborates a new concept, "made to measure," as Bergson
says,—the concept of a nature or essence whose function is not to exist in itself but in something else, of an added reality incapable of possessing being
on its own account but by which the subject flowers and reaches completion
in every way, and forming with the subject a single whole all the more one
because it is united to it by its very being, by the act of existing it receives in
it. This something which is not properly *a being,* but rather *of a being,* is accident. If one correctly understood the concept of accident, one would avoid
the error which consists in treating states of consciousness as things ready
made, as pseudo-substances juxtaposed to one another or set inside one
another, and one would also spare oneself the trouble of accusing Aristotelian
intellectualism of the same error.

---

[1] "The Perception of Change," in *Creative Mind,* p. 176.

As to the idea of substance, once the idea of accident is made precise, it becomes precise in turn. Since the substance of a thing is that which, in each thing, receives first and foremost existence,—if it changed as such the thing in question would cease to be; as long as the thing is or exists, its substance *as such,* considered separately by the mind, cannot therefore change. It changes, but by and in its accidents.

Moreover, a thing being, and being what it is, as a whole as well as in each of its parts, substance as such, that which constitutes the thing in being, must necessarily have in the whole and in each of the parts its whole nature; a drop of water is neither more nor less water than the ocean; it is this which forms the basis of the scholastic adage: *remota quantitate, substantia remanet indivisibilis.* The (corporal) substance is extended in space, and it is divisible, but by and in the primary accident of bodies (quantity).

It follows that substance *as such* is a pure intelligible, it is nothing in itself of what makes things visible and sensible, mutable and divisible. But through it the thing has primary being, and through it all the accidents are maintained in being. Far from being an empty medium, a frame for phenomena, it is the primary ontological root of all and sundry in its permanent actuality, in its essential unity, in its irreducible reality, in its specific and individual originality, so far from being empty and inert that it is the source of all the faculties, of all the operations, of all the activity and the causality of the subject.

This division into substance and accident is a consequence of the very condition of the created being. Created things cannot fill their whole being right away, and they comprise various degrees in being itself. They cannot have immediately and totally completed all the perfection they possess simply because they have their nature; hence their metaphysical composition, hence the fact that they have potency and act, substance and accident: distinctions which suppose another still more profound distinction and which derive in a word from the fact that in God alone essence and existence are one: His nature or divinity is the same thing as His act of being, whereas in the creature *this* and *exist* are necessarily distinct, since it is not Being by itself.

Corporal substance

Let us consider a corporal substance, a drop of water for example. (That the word 'water' designates a specific nature, a *species naturalis,* we take for granted. If in actual fact and in the particular case this is not so, water, or the "solution" called by that name, will have been only a substitute for such a nature; and that there are such natures in the world of bodies one can demonstrate as being a primary datum of our intellectual knowledge of this world. As for knowing in addition whether, considered in its physical state, this drop of water is or is not a simple aggregate without any substantial unity of a multitude of individual molecules, that has no importance here.) We can divide it so that instead of one drop we shall have ten or twenty, which will still be water, which will have the same nature and which will differ only numerically. And this division can be pushed by the imagination to the point of separating the molecules from each other. That there are thus several *individuals* of the same specific nature, necessarily supposes that *what causes them to be* of such a specific nature is found in like manner in each of them; but if in order to constitute them there was nothing more than this same determining principle of being, they could not be several. There is in them therefore another first principle of being which does not cause them to be of a certain nature, which does not in any way determine them, but which is solely determinable, and which brings it about that the determining principle of being can be multiplied into a plurality of individuals.

Similarly, a molecule of water can be broken up into hydrogen and oxygen, which are substances of a specific nature other than water, (assuming, as we have granted, that water has an essence or nature proper and is not a simple whole by accident). Before the breaking up the hydrogen and oxygen did not therefore exist in the water with their proper nature, the first principle of being which causes them to be hydrogen and oxygen, which determines them to this or that essence, was not there; they could exist in water only by reason of another first principle of being, by no means determining, solely determinable (and by reason of their joint and harmonized qualities).[1]

And finally, one corporal substance can be transformed into another, as happens when an aliment is assimilated by a living being. In this transformation of one substance into another, the principle which determined it to be this or that essence therefore disappears, and the subject of the change can be only a principle of being which is not at all determinant, but solely determinable.

The first of these two principles of being, the one which causes (something) to be, the one which determines this or that specific essence, which radically determines all the being and hence all the activity of the subject, the Aristotelians call *substantial form;* the other principle of being, the one which receives determination, and which permits numerical multiplicity, elementary composition and substantial transformations of corporal things, they call *prime matter,* pure potency in the order of substantiality. These words, (alas, only too easy to visualize, which run the risk of betraying the doctrine they translate), are borrowed from what takes place in the order of accidental being, as when a sculptor determines a certain *matter* to this or that accidental

---

[1] Elements exist *virtually* in the compound, in the sense that, at least in the same line, each superior form contains within it the perfection and virtue of the inferior forms, and that the divergent qualitative dispositions of the elements, more or less tempered to one another, in consequence remain joined to one another in the compound in a more or less stable or unstable way. Cf. *Sum. theol.,* I^a, q. 76, a. 3, *ad* 4; a. 4, *ad* 4; *de Anima,* a. 9, *ad* 10; *Comm. in de Gener. et Corruptione,* lib. II; the opuscule (of doubtful authenticity) *de nat. materiae,* c. 8; the opuscule *de mixtione elementorum.*

form; but they refer to the constitutive principles of being itself, of the substance of corporal things. Whereas the wholly spiritual substances, such as Angels, are pure forms subsisting in themselves, all corporal substances are composed of *prime matter* and *substantial form,* and that in their very essence. It is by the composition of these two principles that corporal things *are what they are.* Matter which receives an accidental form has such and such a nature before being this or that statue. But *prime matter,* which receives substantial form, that is to say which receives the first principle which causes a thing to be such and such a nature, evidently cannot have by itself any form, or any determination, or any nature. From which it follows that prime matter can never, in any case, exist alone; it exists only in the compound of matter and form; it is not a being, it is only a principle of being, a principle of pure passivity, of pure potency, of pure indetermination, a simple potentiality for being. Let us note further that in corporal substances not endowed with intelligence, neither can substantial form exist without matter; so that these substances are, they have being, through the uniting or the composition of two principles of being, of two halves of being so to speak, absolutely incapable of being or existing separately. The accident *quantity,* let us also note, has to do with corporal substances by reason of matter; the accident *quality,* by reason of form.

Living corporal substance

If we pass now to animate beings, we note that they differ from inanimate bodies in that they are able *to move themselves,* in that their activity, instead of being turned solely outward, terminates in themselves and thus concurs in their own perfectioning. Life, which is not something superadded to the being of living beings, but which is that being itself,—according to the scholastic formula, *for the living to live is to be,*—life therefore constitutes a superior degree of being. And we call by a special name, by the name of *soul,* the substantial form of living bodies. But in all material living beings other than man, this soul is completely submerged in matter, similar in this respect to the substantial form of non-living bodies; it cannot be, it cannot act in any way without the matter it informs; it is therefore incapable of subsisting after the death of the plant or animal; it is not a being, it is only a principle of being.

Furthermore, the mere consideration of animate beings is enough to demonstrate with evidence the existence in them of an ontological factor which corresponds to the notion of substantial form, and this by reason of the functions of nutrition (it would otherwise be impossible for the substance of the living being to remain one and identical, in spite of the perpetual renewal of its material elements), and by reason of the functions of growth, of reproduction and in the case of animals, of sensation, none of which (and fresh proof of this has been provided by Driesch's remarkable experiments)[1] can be explained by any *mechanism* of physico-chemical agents whatsoever.

Man

And finally we come to man. Man is a substance, a corporal substance, a living substance, an intellectual substance. This substance is one, it is the same being, it is the same self which thinks, and feels and lives. Therefore this substance, like any corporal substance, is a compound of prime matter and substantial form; like any living corporal substance it is composed of a body and a soul, a principle of being and of life, and here, in man, a principle of intelligence also since substantial form is the radically determining principle of all the activity as of all the being of the subject.[2]—But this soul, contrary to the souls of other living beings, is not only a substantial principle; it is a substance, a being; it is *subsistant.*[3]

Why? Because the soul is the principle of the intellect (and of will). Now the operation of the intellect implies in itself absolutely nothing corporal, is, in what properly constitutes it, entirely free and independent of matter, because, if its proportionate ("connatural") object is the nature of things known by the senses, it is nevertheless on sensible objects *of whatever kind* that it thus bears; while any operation in which matter intrinsically intervenes is limited by that very fact to a certain category of material objects, as happens for the operations of the senses, which can perceive only what is suited by its action to the physical constitution of the organ; and by the same token the operation of the intellect does not stop at sensible objects, it goes beyond them and knows by analogy spiritual natures; it extends to the world of possibles; its field is infinitely wide. This operation is moreover strictly immaterial in itself, because it bears, as on its specificating object, on being, on the essence of things, by means of an abstract and universal idea free, as we saw with regard to abstraction, from the conditions that matter imposes on sense perception; finally because the intelligence, by reflection, comes back entirely upon itself, so that it can contain itself and its principle (the existing self) in its activity; and this any material agent is essentially incapable of doing. One could likewise show that the will, which follows upon intelligence, and which determines itself with a dominating indifference of which no material agent is capable, has an operation in itself independent of matter. But the first principle of proper and independent operations necessarily has a nature independent also and subsistant in itself; this is all the clearer since every being acts according as it is. Therefore the human soul, the primary

---

1 Cf. Hans Driesch, *Die Lokalisation morphogenetischer Vorgänge* (Leipzig, Engelmann); *Die organischen Regulationen; Philosophie des Organischen*, Bk. I, pp. 119–148 and Bk. II, pp. 67–76.

2 Cf. *Sum. theol.*, I^a, q. 76, a. 1.

3 *Sum. theol.*, I^a, q. 75, a. 2.

principle of intellectual operation as of voluntary operation, is really a substance, a being, a subsisting being. It has no need of matter in order to be; it is
a *spiritual* substance.

Moreover, the sole consideration of man suffices to demonstrate the existence of the soul as substantial form; for man is endowed with intelligence,
and the principle of intelligence, as we have just seen, is independent of matter in its being and in its (intellectual and voluntary) operation; it is spiritual.
But when we say that someone thinks, performs an act of intelligence, it is not
in an accidental way, according as he is tall or short, a soldier or a musician;
it is evidently according as he is man, according to his essence, that we ascribe
to him this act. Is it then by virtue of that which totally constitutes himself,
as though he were only intelligence, that this man thinks, as Plato and Descartes believed? Assuredly not, for it is the same man who thinks and who
feels, and there is no sensation without a body. Therefore the body also forms
a part of man. Hence the principle of the intellect is not all of man: it is a
part of man, but an essential part, a part of his substance. And because man
is not an aggregate or an accidental whole, but a single whole by nature, *one*
being, a substance that is *one,* and because a compound substance, if it is not
an aggregate, if it is *one,* can only be composed of a purely potential principle
not already having in itself any determined nature, any act—that is what we
call prime matter—and of another principle which is the *act* by which this
substance is constituted in its nature, and by reason of which it possesses existence—that is what we call substantial form—it must be said with Saint
Thomas that the intellect, or more precisely the soul, the primary principle
of intellectual operation, is the form of the human body.[1]

Such is the admirable feat of authentic realism: basing itself on the *unity*
of man, an intelligent corporal substance, it distinguishes in him *two* principles, each incomplete, whose union makes up the human being. It is impossible more profoundly to distinguish the soul and the body, since this soul
has a proper activity and life, independent (at least if one considers them in
their intrinsic structure) of the body itself which it informs. It is impossible
more closely to unite them, since they constitute one single essence and exist
in one and the same existence (which is that of the soul communicated to the
body). The body *is* not, it cannot be without the soul. It is not a machine
once made which then receives life, and which the soul directs from the middle of the brain, like Descartes's fountain-maker, "who must be at the observation points where all the pipes of his machinery converge."[2] For it, to
be is to live; from the sole fact that it is, it is living and organic, because what
causes it to be is the union of prime matter, pure ontological potency, with
the soul which informs it and which, being in the body as substantial form,

1 *Sum. theol.,* I^a, q. 76, a. 1. Cf. Cajetan's commentary (no. 31).
2 *De Homine,* II, 16.

is entirely in all the body and in each of its parts. As to the soul, it is spiritual and subsistant, it is a substance, it can be without the body, but without the body it is an *incomplete* substance because it has in its nature not only to be able to exercise the spiritual operations of the intellect and the will, but also to inform the body substantially: so that according to its natural mode of operating, the very exercise of its spiritual operations depends (*extrinsically*) on the body and the sensitive faculties. Thus the soul alone is not man, the human person.* Although it derives from the soul both its subsistence and the characteristic properties of personality (that is intelligence and the control of its acts), the human person is the complete substance, composed of spiritual soul and of body; to the point that the soul, when separate,—deprived moreover of the exercise of the sensitive faculties, which *are* not without the body, —cannot as an incomplete substance (incomplete *in ratione speciei*) be called a person, the very metaphysical notion of person requiring the integrity of nature. Thus it is that philosophy prepares the way for the revealed dogma of the resurrection of the body.

Here we are then, far from the ingenuous scorn of the body and the sensitive faculties professed by the spiritualists of the school of Descartes or of Plato. But at the same time all the being, the life, the actuality that man has he derives from his soul, and that soul is an immaterial substance:—a doctrine which is truly the friend of truth and of peace, truly human, which honours all that God has made.

From this doctrine it follows that the soul of each man is immediately created by God, so that its infusion into the germ makes the germ properly human; for being immaterial, it cannot be made of anything pre-existent, neither can it emanate from the soul of the parents, the soul like any subsisting form being simple and indivisible; it is therefore made *ex nihilo,* that is to say, created.

It follows also that the human soul is incorruptible or immortal. No doubt God can, by His absolute power, annihilate it. But by His ordered power He cannot, for "being the Author of nature, He could not withdraw from things what is proper to their natures."[1] Now, of itself, the soul, from the moment it is, can no longer cease to be. It cannot, in fact, become corrupt by occasion, from the fact that the body becomes corrupt, for it is subsistant, nor can it become corrupt of itself, because it is simple, and because, being a form or an act, it possesses being by reason of itself. "Every being," Saint Thomas goes on to say,[2] "tends naturally to exist in conformity with the requirements of its nature; and in natures endowed with knowledge this desire is pro-

---

* *Sum. theol.,* I^a, q. 75, a. 4.
1 *Sum. contra Gentiles,* lib. II, c. 55.
2 *Sum. theol.,* I^a, q. 75, a. 6.

portionate to their knowledge. Now the sense knows being only as determined to a certain place and to a certain moment, riveted to the present. Intelligence, on the contrary, seizes being absolutely and according as it dominates all the diversities of time. Whence it comes that every intelligent being desires, with a desire essential to nature, to be always. And because a desire essential to nature cannot be frustrated, it follows that every intellectual substance is incorruptible."

As to the operations of the human soul, they are not of the order of substance because there is absolutely God alone, Being *a se,* Whose operation is substance. They are therefore of the accidental order, and consequently they proceed, as from their proximate principles, from powers or faculties which are accidents distinct from the substance of the soul.[1] That is why one cannot say, with Descartes, that the soul is thought, or with Bergson, that the soul is memory. It has memory; it has thought.—Among these powers, some have action only on the body to which the soul is joined,—they are the vegetative and motor powers; by the others the soul knows other bodies in their action on its body and their significance for it—they are the sensory powers, the internal and external senses. And the soul proceeds toward what it knows in this way—that is the sense appetite. All these powers are faculties, not of the soul alone, but of the compound, soul and body: it is not the soul alone which sees, it is the animate organ which sees.

And finally, through other powers the soul attains a truly universal object, not only the bodies capable of acting on its own, but, in a universal fashion, all being: that is the intellect. And it is attracted toward what it knows in that way; that is the intellective appetite or the will. These latter powers are those of the soul alone, inorganic, wholly spiritual powers.

With his marvellous diversity of powers man is the most complex thing in the world. It is so because he is the highest and most perfect of material beings—the substantial forms which by their union with matter constitute corporal substances being the more excellent the less they are immersed in matter and the more they go beyond it by their operation, and thus ranging themselves in an ascending hierarchy: the forms of simple bodies or elements, of composites, of organic compounds, of plants, which live a wholly material life, of animals, which have knowledge but a knowledge limited to the particular and to matter, and finally of man, who has intelligence.

Through the intellect, whose being and operation are immaterial and which perceives the eternal truths, man emerges above matter and time—*intellectus supra tempus*—and already takes his place, as it were, in eternity. And while the beings below him have as their end nothing but particular

---

[1] *Sum. theol.,* I[a], q. 77, a. 1. Cf. *de Anima,* a. 1.

goods, he has as his end the absolute good, and he loves it and is capable of attaining beatitude. But man is also at the lowest degree among beings endowed with spiritual activity; he is the least perfect and the most mortified of spiritual natures. "That is why the human soul has need of multiple and diverse operations. The Angels for their part have less diversity of powers. And God has no other action, or other power, than His essence itself."*

Thus it is, by that *admirable connection of things,* that according to Saint Thomas's expression, the human soul is "a sort of horizon, and as it were the confines of the corporal and the incorporal world."† Thus it is that in man the virtues and activities of bodies and of spirits combine and rejoin, and that, assembling in himself, so to speak, the material universe of which he is the summit, and reflecting in his soul the eternal light, man is by nature designated to offer freely to God, in the name of all beings, sacrifice and thanksgiving.

III.—MAN IN CREATIVE EVOLUTION

Let us now call to mind Bergsonian metaphysics and *Creative Evolution.* In it man appears not as the "outcome of the whole of evolution, for evolution has been accomplished on several divergent lines,"[1] but as a success of evolution, a wholly fortuitous success except for the impulsion of the vital impulse toward "freedom" and "consciousness." *"It is,"* writes Bergson,[2] *"as if a vague and formless being whom we may call as we will, man or super-man, had sought to realize himself and had succeeded only by abandoning a part of himself on the way.* These losses are represented by the rest of the animal world and even by the vegetable world, at least in what these have that is positive and above the accidents of evolution." Nevertheless it has been necessary to abandon along the way valuable possessions, in particular intuition and consequently truth, which we can no longer find except by an effort contrary to nature, by re-absorbing, according to Bergson, intellect in instinct. This man or this superman who was not and who was seeking to become, would therefore be complete only by recovering what he left in animals and plants, and it is for this work of re-fusion into the whole that the philosophy which "introduces us into the spiritual life"[3] will henceforth occupy itself in "thrusting the intellect out of doors."[4]

As for man such as he is, such as the hazy and indistinct superman who sought to realize himself has successfully turned him out, he is alone, alone in being intelligent, in a world which seems to be deprived of the governance

---

* *Sum. theol.,* I[a], q. 77, a. 2.
† *Sum. contra Gentiles,* lib. II, chap. 68.
[1] *Creative Evolution,* p. 266.
[2] *Ibid.,* p. 266.
[3] *Ibid.,* p. 268.
[4] *Ibid.,* p. 193.

of any superior Intelligence, and where the life of each one is only an effort to make himself, to become, to push forward, to create himself. It is a sort of metaphysical social climbing, a transcendental race for success.

Man is made to act, *homo faber;* he is "harnessed, like an ox to the plough, to a heavy task"[1] which consists in inserting his action into reality, in *working* in the world. Did we then receive our soul in order to act on things? Nowhere do we see anything to indicate that Bergsonian philosophy assigns to us any other end. So that if we indulged in a little speculative activity it would only be through violence and, as it were, by cheating and by an inversion of our thinking nature. It is true that if we contemplate men, one may imagine that they feel more at ease, as a rule, busying themselves in servile occupations. Let us, however, guard against confusing a state of fact, due to all the accidents and misfortunes of the existential condition of man, with what is proper to his very essence. Such a confusion is parallel to the one which causes a disorder of intelligence to be taken for intelligence itself. Certainly man is made for his action, action being the ultimate perfection of all being. But the action suitable for man by essence is only secondarily transitive action, his principal action does not consist in manipulating solids. It is immanent action which above all is suitable for him, action *par excellence,* which is the act of knowing and of loving and which supernaturally finds its fulfillment in contemplation and in divine charity. And so no philosopher can tell us what in reality is the ultimate end of our existence. It is God Who has taught us that, He Who made us in order that we might at last see Him as He sees us.

For Bergson, intellect is common, although in widely differing degrees, to man and to vertebrates:[2] what makes the difference between man and animals is the superior organization of the human brain, "which enables him to

---

[1] *Ibid.,* p. 191.

[2] *Ibid.,* pp. 132–150.—These pages contain a good many views it would be well to examine closely: "The cardinal error," writes Bergson (p. 135), "which, from Aristotle onwards, has vitiated most of the philosophies of nature, is to see in vegetative and rational life, three successive degrees of the development of one and the same tendency, whereas they are three divergent directions of an activity that has split up as it grew." As a matter of fact Aristotle did not regard *vegetative* life, *sensitive* life and *intellective* life as "three successive degrees of the development of one and the same tendency," but rather as three specifically distinct degrees of one perfection (life) which is distributed in ontologically hierarchized types, in such a way that the plant has the first degree of life only, the non-rational animal the first and second, man all three at once. As for the picture Bergson sketches for us of the universe of life and the complementary divergencies of the vegetable kingdom, of that of the arthropods and that of the vertebrates, in my opinion it would constitute a remarkably true and fruitful account of natural philosophy, did the evolutionist ideology (I use the word "evolutionist" in the metaphysical, not the biological sense) not come along to spoil it, and especially if the formulas in which he expresses himself were not vitiated by a fundamental confusion between the wholly spiritual intelligence come from on high and the *ratio particularis* of the animal, which emerges from matter as the highest function of the senses. It is not by the search for *intelligence,* itself characterized as "the faculty of making and using inorganic instruments," and by the progress toward *instinct,* characterized as "the faculty of using and even of constructing organic instru-

set up an unlimited number of motor mechanisms,"[3] and thanks to which man avoids automatism. But that, in spite of what the philosopher may say, is an accidental difference, not a difference of nature. Let us not forget that Bergson, in giving vertebrates intelligence and even, as we have seen,[1] "spirit" to all animals, deprives human nature of its specific difference. To say that evolution has passed from animals to man by a sudden leap and not by a gentle gradation is still admitting the reality of the passing. And where there is

---

ments" that we must distinguish the world of vertebrates from the world of insects. It is indeed rather by the progress toward *cognoscitive experience* and toward *individuality of behaviour* (preparation for intelligence and freedom, which appear only in man), and therefore toward a memory and an estimative (faculty) (*ratio particularis*) with greater variability in play,—and on the other hand by the progress toward the *organization of tendencies* and *specific perfection of behaviour*, and therefore toward a memory and an estimative as fixed as possible.

A passage such as the following (the italics are mine) shows clearly to what a point the most philosophical evolutionism remains obsessed by the profoundly anti-philosophical preoccupation to ruin essences and essential distinctions. *"It is because intelligence and instinct, having originally been interpenetrating, retain something of their common origin.* Neither is ever found in a pure state. *We said that in the plant the consciousness and mobility of the animal, which lie dormant, can be awakened;* and that the animal lives under the constant menace of being drawn aside to the vegetative life. *The two tendencies—that of the plant and that of the animal—were so thoroughly interpenetrating to begin with,* that there has never been a complete severance between them; they haunt each other continually; *everywhere we find them mingled; it is the proportion that differs.* There is no intelligence in which some traces of instinct are not to be discovered, *more especially no instinct that is not surrounded with a fringe of intelligence."* (P. 136.)—That in organisms a superior degree of life is always more or less penetrated,—and menaced,—by the lower degree upon which it rests (and from which it remains always essentially distinct in itself), is perfectly true. But the converse is entirely unacceptable, and directly contradicted by experience. On the essential ("typological") difference between plant *irritability* and animal *sensibility* see Hans André's study ("La Typologie des Plantes") in the second *Cahier de philosophie de la nature* (Paris, Vrin, 1929). This very remarkable work shows of what profit for the scholar himself the Aristotelian training can be; it also shows what advantages (if not in metaphysics, at least in natural philosophy) and in spite of all its lacunae, the *phenomenologistic* conception, especially as a method, presents over any evolutionist conception.

"Now let us open a collection of anecdotes," Bergson again says (p. 137), "on the intelligence of animals; we shall see that besides many acts explicable by imitation or by the automatic association of images, there are some that we do not hesitate to call intelligent: foremost among them are those that bear witness to some idea of *manufacture*, whether the animal succeeds in fashioning a crude instrument or uses for its advantage an object made by man. [. . .] Invention becomes complete when it is materialized in a manufactured instrument. Toward that achievement the intelligence of animals tends as toward an ideal." (Let us here note that a hive gives evidence of a power to *manufacture* instruments,—in this case an architectural instrument,— that is quite superior to any that Monkeys or Elephants can offer from this point of view. Should Hymenoptera then be declared much more *intelligent* than the superior Vertebrates?) "While nature has frankly evolved in the direction of instinct in the arthropods, we observe in almost all the vertebrates," continues Bergson (p. 142), "the striving after rather than the expansion of intelligence. It is still instinct which forms the basis of their psychic activity; but *intelligence is there*, and would fain supersede it. Intelligence does not yet succeed in inventing instruments; but at least it tries to, by performing as many variations as possible on the instinct which it would like to dispense with. *It gains complete self-possession only in man* . . ." (My italics.) All these pages show clearly how for Bergson intelligence is common, although in widely varying degrees, to man and the vertebrates.

[3] *Creative Evolution*, p. 264.

[1] See *supra*, pp. 216–217 and 227–228.

a difference of nature, such a passing over, if it is conditioned by the simple progress of secondary causes, is impossible.

In the system of creative evolution, human souls are not immediately created by God. It is life as a whole, the flood or stream of universal consciousness, which "flowing through human generations, subdivides into individuals" in virtue of "the matter it bears along with it."* "Thus souls that nevertheless in a certain sense pre-existed, are continually being created. They are nothing else than the little rills into which the great river of life divides as it flows through the body of humanity,"—that great river of life which begins in the primitive "monera."

Lastly Bergson admits "the possibility and even the probability of survival of the human soul for an x quantity of time."† But in what does this merely hypothetical survival consist when we cannot even tell whether it is unlimited? All it is is the continuation beyond the body of the "tremendous push" of the vital impulse and of humanity which "bestriding animality," itself resting upon plant life, "gallops beside and before and behind each one of us in an overwhelming charge able to beat down every resistance and clear the most formidable obstacles, perhaps even death."‡ In this hypothetical immortality which is merely the perpetuation of an impulse or a gallop, how are we to understand that souls, no longer having matter to keep them divided, do not, like rivulets, flow back into the great wide stream of universal life?[1]

Bergson has made the sincerest possible effort to reach within the limits of his system the great spiritual truths restored and rejuvenated. He considers that the philosophy of intelligence and being is perfectly right in distinguishing between soul and body, in believing in the reality of the person, in attributing to man a privileged place in nature, in affirming the "survival" of the soul.[2] But (like Descartes in an earlier age) he thinks it has failed to establish these verities. So, discarding the value of the intellect, he has attempted to attain them more surely with metaphysical imagination and intuition. It is to be feared that the philosophy of pure change, while filling us with a desire for these supreme certitudes, will leave us nothing but words—and a regret.

---

* *Creative Evolution*, p. 269.

† *L'Ame et le corps* (*Foi et Vie*, January 1, 1913, p. 14): reprinted in *l'Énergie spirituelle*, p. 62. For Bergson, this survival is "so probable that the burden of proof rests with the one who denies it, rather than with the one who affirms it." (*Ibid.*) It still, however, belongs to the order of likelihood and probability.

‡ *Creative Evolution*, p. 271.

1 The Thomist doctrine is known to consider human souls as individuated not by their factual union with matter, but in virtue of their transcendental relation to matter (*materia signata quantitate*). Each one, having to inform an individual body, is created individual substance and naturally keeps its individuality in the state of separation.

2 *Creative Evolution*, pp. 268–269.

Chapter Eleven

FREEDOM

I.—THE PROBLEM OF FREEDOM

It remains for us to investigate what makes our acts properly human acts, by reason of which we ourselves are good or bad, for it is by his operation, by his action proper, that each one attains or misses his fulfillment in being,—it remains for us to examine the freedom, the free will of man.

The argument most worthy of attention that one can bring against the existence of human freedom, is the argument of psychological determinism as formulated by Leibnitz, for example. This argument, which, like the arguments of Parmenides against movement, stirs human reason in its depths, consists in saying that if free will really exists then the will determines itself without motives, therefore without reason or intelligibility; the free act would therefore be an act without any *raison d'être;* freedom would be the power of acting without reason, without motive, or in spite of motives, and consequently freedom is strictly impossible, because the principle of universal intelligibility—which cannot be denied, as we recalled in a preceding chapter,[1] without thereby denying the principle of identity,—the principle of universal intelligibility demands that everything that is have its *raison d'être*: one could thus, seemingly, affirm freedom only on condition that one denied being, the formal object of intelligence, and hence suppressed all truth.

From another point of view the existence of free will is the most certain *fact* there is. As evidenced by the judgments of practical reason in each one of us and the principles of social life and the universal consent of mankind, freedom is an immediate datum of consciousness; it is perceived by an intuition as infallible as the intuition of the active self by the consciousness, or of the external world by the senses, or of being by intelligence; not that we immediately apprehend, through consciousness, the essence of the will or its power; but because we immediately apprehend in its action,—by reason of the immanence of spiritual things to themselves,—the dominating indetermination of our will, because we perceive as an existing fact in the operation of the will that it is we who give to the determining motive its determining

[1] See *supra*, p. 182.

value, and to the sufficient reason of our act its complete sufficiency or its efficacity; which means that our will is not determined by any of the particular goods presented to it; whence it follows that we could, in the same circumstances, have acted differently or not at all.

It seems therefore that anti-intellectualism has things all its own way. Since it questions the primary affirmation of the intellect, since it refuses to concede any value to the idea of being and posits the inner reality as unintelligible, it will have no scruples about destroying the principle of universal intelligibility along with all the others; and having brought the *raison d'être* to naught it will not accuse itself of parricide as Plato did when he "struck at" being and grappled with Parmenides. In circumstances like these there will no longer be any obstacle to the affirmation of freedom (unless perhaps freedom, being *something* positive, has also disappeared in the annihilation of everything).

II.—THE BERGSONIAN SOLUTION

Bergson hopes to defend freedom in this way, thereby joining, as has been said, the philosophers of the *libertist* school who, like Secrétan and Lequier,[1] not to mention those as far back as Descartes and Ockham, give will primacy over intelligence, and the free act primacy over being.

It is absurd, Bergson explains at length,[2] to say with the determinists that of the great diversity of the motives which tempt us, it is the strongest motive which necessarily prevails. But why? Because the question itself is meaningless. Because in comparison with the deeper and truly personal life of the consciousness there is neither diversity of motives pulling the mind in opposite directions nor one motive stronger than the others which finally prevails, since the idea of positing in the psychic life a distinct multiplicity, and in the states of consciousness intensive magnitudes, is nothing more than an illusory conceptualization due to the obsession of spatiality, by which we transform the psychological continuum into numerable and measurable things "spread out in space." The idea of the greater or less intensity of a psychic state is the result of a "compromise between pure quality, which is the state of consciousness, and pure quantity, which is necessarily space."[3] The idea of number, or of "distinct multiplicity,"[4] is the result of another compromise between the distinction of material objects in space and the dynamic interpenetration of facts of consciousness. The more the psychological life deepens, the more the real appears in it as solely constituted by duration which grows as it advances,

---

[1] Cf. Secrétan, *La Philosophie de la Liberté;* Lequier, *La Recherche d'une première vérité.* See on this point Garrigou-Lagrange, *Intellectualisme et Liberté chez saint Thomas,* in *Revue des Sciences philosophiques et théologiques,* 1907, pp. 649–673; and 1908, pp. 5–32 (repeated in the book *Dieu, son existence et sa nature,* pp. 595–654).

[2] *Time and Free Will,* pp. 1–139; 155–174; 222–231.

[3] *Ibid.,* pp. 223, 224.

[4] *Ibid.,* p. 226.

in which everything is qualitative heterogeneity, fusion and interpenetration.

To which one might reply that if there is fusion there must certainly be multiple states which fuse. Bergson here seems regularly to confuse *exteriority* in space and *distinction*,[3] (as though metaphysical entities were not, as such, perfectly distinct from one another without on that account being planted in space). How then could he avoid positing in the life of the soul a *multiplicity* and a *heterogeneity* without *distinction*, which seems indeed to be a contradiction in terms? For that matter, to affirm that there is pure heterogeneity and that there is not any more or less in psychology, would be to affirm willy-nilly that love, for example, in *increasing* (to use language common to everyone), becomes something radically heterogeneous to what it was, that is to say, becomes non-love: for in fact, if there is anything really common, *gleichartig,* in spite of all possible diversities, or even discordances in orchestration, to a sentiment in the nascent state and a great effective outburst which we call by the same name, it is because one same *quality* can pass through various states of intension and remission.

In reality the ideas of distinct multiplicity and of intensive magnitude are accompanied, like any idea, by an imaginative and consequently spatial representation which Bergson has, as usual, fused with the idea. But these ideas by themselves and in their object proper do not necessarily imply space. If number properly so-called (quantitative number) implies spatiality, since it arises from the division of the continuum (without however at all demanding on that account the "compromise" imagined by Bergson, for the mensurability of the divided parts by one of them, or in other words the unity of the number as a whole, results from the very homogeneity of the spatial continuum), there is, on the other hand, a *transcendental multitude* (and also a *transcendental number*) entirely different from *quantitative number,* in that they do not presuppose in things a certain accident (quantity, spatiality) added to their nature, but on the contrary add to the thing about which they are said, no other notional complement than indivision concerning each,[1] so that these things, having nothing in them which be-

---

[3] "But the determinist, even when he refrains from regarding the more serious emotions or deep-seated psychic states as forces, nevertheless distinguishes them from one another and is *thus* led to a *mechanical* conception of the self." (*Ibid.,* p. 170.) "What is duration within us? A qualitative *multiplicity,* with no likeness to number, [. . .] a pure heterogeneity within which there are no *distinct* qualities. In a word, the moments of inner duration are not *external* to one another." (*Ibid.,* p. 226.) If these elements melt into one another is it not because they were distinct from one another? All these passages presuppose the confusion of *distinction* (or of logical "exteriority") with *spatial exteriority.*

[1] Cf. *Sum. theol.,* I^a, q. 30, a. 3, the body of the article, and *ad* 2: "Multitudo, quae ponit aliquid in rebus creatis, est species quantitatis, quae non transumitur in divinam praedicationem, sed tantum multitudo transcendens, quae non addit supra ea, de quibus dicitur, nisi indivisionem circa singula." Likewise, the multitude found in the operation of the Angels and in the time which measures these operations is the *multitude belonging to the transcendentals.* (Cf. the apocryphal opuscule *De Instantibus;* Pégues, *Traité des Anges,* p. 298.)

comes larger because of their plurality, cannot be added up.* And there is an *intensive quantity* (*quantitas virtutis*) which differs completely from quantity properly so-called, from *dimensive quantity* (*quantitas molis*), for it also belongs to the transcendental order, and refers to the being itself, of the things concerned without adding to them any accident (as is quantity properly so-called or spatiality),[1] so that this *intensive quantity* cannot be mathematically measured, at least in itself. Thus it is that the more or less profound rooting of charity in the soul, or the more or less great beauty of a work of art, has nothing to do with space. To note, as Bergson rightly does, that the intensity of a quality is itself "felt," is itself qualitative, itself a "shade," a "coloration"[2] of that quality, does not therefore in the least signify that it is incompatible with the *more* and the *less* which all intensity comprises in actual fact, for there it is precisely a question of a *more* and a *less of quality*, not of *spatiality*. And likewise to note that the multiplicity of states of consciousness is not a "multiplicity of juxtaposition," but,—and the more profoundly one goes into the inner life,—a "multiplicity of fusion or of mutual penetration,"[3] does not mean that all distinct (or numerical) multiplicity,[4] that all diversity *of nature* and all formal distinction between faculties, habits or operations, should be excluded from psychological life. This multi-

* Thus it is, to take approximate examples, that in a hundred Frenchmen there is not (except insofar as one possesses certain traits of national character that another does not, or possesses to a lesser degree) more of the *quality of Frenchness* than in a single one; or again, that in themselves (except for the mind that receives them and which may be more sensitive to some than to others) ten good reasons have no more *demonstrative value* than a single one. Cf. *Sum. theol.*, I^a, q. 30, a. 1, *ad* 4: ". . . in rebus quidem creatis unum est pars duorum, et duo trium, ut unus homo duorum, et duo trium: sed non est sic in Deo, quis tantus est Pater, quanto tota Trinitas."

1 A notion is transcendental when it is defined *in relation to being*. Now in order to define *the more and the less* one may say that one being is *more* than another when in order to become that other it would have to *cease to be* in some manner. The idea of degrees of being or perfection is thus a transcendental notion, defined solely by means of the notions of *being* and *non-being*, and in itself independent of any idea of dimensive quantity and space.

The more and the less, augmentation and diminution, can be said of forms or qualities: 1) according to the very perfection of the form or the nature considered, *secundum ipsam perfectionem formae vel naturae;* 2) according to the more or less perfect actuation of the subject by the quality, according to the more or less profound "rooting" of a virtue like charity, for example, in the soul; 3) according as the quality extends to a more or less great number of objects (like science to a more or less great number of truths), or again,—but this only for material qualities,—according as the subjects in which they are found increase or diminish in number; and finally, 4) according to the *effects* of the form or the quality, in particular according to the power to act of the being under consideration (*intensive quantity* thereby falls *indirectly* below measure).—On all these points see *Sum. theol.*, I^a, q. 42, a. 1 (*ad* 1) and a. 4; q. 48, a. 4; I^a II^ae, q. 52, a. 2; II^a II^ae, q. 24, a. 5; *I Sent.*, dist. 17, q. 2, a. 1 and 2.

2 Cf. *Time and Free Will*, pp. 186–187.

3 *Ibid.*, pp. 161–162.

4 "Numerical" in the sense of transcendental number. All distinct (and finite) multiplicity is a *numerical* multiplicity in the sense of *transcendental number*, but *not* in the sense of *quantitative number*, which implies spatiality.

plicity of powers, habits and operations, which are *accidents,* not *things,* does not prevent the unity of the soul itself which is a *substance,* or the unity and the continuity of the "stream of consciousness," precisely because that is a substance which endures through time, and whose diverse powers, mutually articulated according to an order superior to spatiality, act upon one another in a vital immanence much more perfect than that of material organisms.

The reply to the determinists here, which Bergson does not afford, is that motives (in the strict sense of the word) can in no way be compared to more or less great forces acting upon us because they are not inclinations and mobiles, but ideas or judgments of the intelligence.

It is absurd, Bergson goes on to explain,* to say with the determinists that our will cannot choose between several equally possible courses. But why? Because the question itself is meaningless. Because there are not several equally possible courses to choose from. Again it is this wretched space which suggests such a thought by causing us to imagine these courses to be taken as so many "ready-made" roads branching off from the same point; while for our duration which grows as it advances, and whose progress is invention, there was in reality only one single course, the one taken,—that is, invented or created,—without our being able to find any sense in the question of knowing whether another course could or could not have been taken.

It is indeed true that the two courses to take are not pre-existent like two roads already well trodden (already *actual*), between which to choose. But what is in question, and what it is perfectly reasonable to ask oneself is whether, in the moment I am about to choose and at the very instant in which I take a certain course, and all the prerequisite antecedents for the act being given, I decide in favour of that course only by *choosing* it properly speaking, by exercising a power of mine to will it or not to will it; or in other words, it is a question of knowing whether before my choice is made, and at the instant it is made,[1] I am or am not necessitated *ad unum,* necessitated to one course rather than to another, to act rather than not to act, whereas the two courses are there before me not as things "ready-made" or in act, but as *possibles* represented by the *intelligence* and of which only the bringing in of my will, will make one actual. But that Bergson does not make clear to us. He attributes to the partisans as well as to the adversaries of free will a "clumsy symbolism,"[2] in virtue of which they imagine "deliberation under the form of an oscillation in space,"[3] and the progress of our inner movement as a road which bifurcates at a given moment. Has so crude

* *Time and Free Will,* pp. 175–183.
[1] See *infra,* p. 273, n. 1 (composed sense and divided sense).
[2] *Time and Free Will,* pp. 181–182.
[3] *Ibid.,* pp. 179 and 182.

an imagery in fact ever haunted the mind of a metaphysician? Bergson clearly sees that the courses between which we choose are not paths traced in space or forces which draw us in this or that direction; he does not see that they are *objects* of judgment and that they have a hold over our deliberate will only by means of our intellect, which knows them in advance as possibles. He shows clearly how the determinists materialize and spatialize the life of the spirit; but no more than they does he take into account the primary condition of the life of the spirit, I mean to say of the *noésis,* of the immaterial ("intentional") and supra-subjective manner in which the spirit, through intellection, is itself and the others, and presents to itself its objects.

It is absurd, continues Bergson,[1] to say with the determinists that the act of the will, supposing that one knows all the circumstances ahead of time, must necessarily, in virtue of the principle of causality, be able to be foreseen. Because the question itself is meaningless. Because one can foresee any psychological event whatever only at the very moment it occurs.

This is an argument which can signify two things: in the first place, that there is never, in the psychological life, a repetition of the same causes;—which is true (if it is a question of absolute identity, and in all details), not only of the psychological life, but even of the physical life, and which is false (if it is a question of a basic identity limited to the essential), not only for the physical world, but even for the psychological life as well, seeing that true causality does not reside in phenomena, but in the powers or faculties. Strictly speaking, never does an *event* re-occur exactly the same, either in nature or *a fortiori* in the mind. But the *causes* of events, which are active powers, do not have to re-occur or repeat; they endure, with the substance or nature whose radical causality they express, they traverse time, even in the material world and all the more rightfully in the mind. However that may be, moreover, even if the Bergsonian argument were valid purely and simply in the first sense, it would only prove that the required condition, "supposing that one knows all the circumstances in advance," is unrealizable in fact,[2]—

---

[1] *Ibid.,* pp. 183–198.

[2] "Hence it is a question devoid of meaning to ask: Could or could not the act be foreseen, given the sum total of its antecedents?" (*Time and Free Will,* p. 189.) [Because "dynamically" assimilating these antecedents is not foreseeing the act, but becoming the one who accomplishes it, "passing through the same series of states, and thus getting back to the very moment at which the act is performed"; and assimilating them "statically," is presupposing the act itself as already performed, "by the mere fact of annexing to the qualitative description of the previous states the quantitative appreciation of their importance."] Whereupon one may ask whether a pure spirit could not know by divine revelation (but not becoming the agent himself except intentionally, in order to be intent in advance on the latter's various states) the whole series of antecedents which succeed one another up to the very instant (with the exception of that instant itself) in which the act of choice is accomplished; so that the question of knowing whether this pure spirit would or would not know in advance with certitude what would be the act of choice, in other words, the question of knowing whether of itself the act is or is not infallibly foreseeable in its antecedents, is by no means a question devoid of sense.

in no way does it answer the question as to what would actually take place if this condition could be realized.

But the Bergsonian argument has a further very different meaning: it also signifies that in the progress of pure becoming, of Bergsonian *duration*, there is a continual creation of acts or events which are *absolutely new*, therefore *essentially* unforeseeable, because the effect is not virtually contained in its cause and is not determined by it, but wells up of itself without requiring a proportionate *raison d'être;* because the contingent is posited of itself, because the principle of causality (and as much should be said of the principle of universal intelligibility, which Bergson does not mention), engenders "so profound an illusion," so "tenacious a prejudice," that it surely rests on an "equivocation."*

It is absurd to say with the determinists, Bergson concludes,† that the act of the will is necessarily determined to be this or that by its *raison d'être*. Because the question itself is absurd. And the philosopher, treating the concept of cause as a pure conflict of images, shows it to be a compromise between the mechanical image of a pre-formed future *already-made, already wholly in act* in the bosom of the present (as he sees it, like a theorem in a definition), and the merely introspective image of a future pre-formed in the bosom of the present as *simply possible* (as he sees it, like action in effort). In the first case it would be absolute determinism, but to the extent that the reality of nature would disappear to give place to the pure mathematical, or better still to pure and simple "relation of identity"; in the second case, it would be the exclusion of all determinism, but also the disappearance, in the whole field of the real, of all necessary determination. As a matter of fact, between a conception for which the effect is already in the cause, just as it is and ready-made, with its actuality proper, and a conception for which the effect "is no longer given in the cause," except "in the state of pure possibility,"[1] causality properly so-called disappears. For true causality implies the pre-formation of the effect in the nature or in the intelligence of the cause,—not as a simple possible, and not as existing already for itself,—but as more or less proximately determined to being, and as ultimately determined to being at the very moment of causation: at that moment the effect is itself posited in existence (for causation in ultimate act and effectuation are simultaneous). If Bergson did not see that the notion of universal intelligibility and of causal determination is by no means linked to mechanicism, if he holds the principle of causality to be a compromise between "two contradictory conceptions of duration,"[2] it is because instead of conceiving causality metaphysically, in terms of intelligible

---

* *Time and Free Will*, pp. 199–221.
† *Ibid.*, p. 202.
[1] *Ibid.*, p. 212.
[2] *Ibid.*, p. 215.

being, and as actuation of what passes to the act by what already is in act, he envisaged it only in terms of time, in terms of future and of present, in short, from the point of view of the succession of phenomena. Consequently, he cannot discover in it anything but either a mathematical diagram linking like to like, or a consciousness of the auto-creative power of concrete time. In the second case causality itself cuts becoming loose from the bonds of *raison d'être;* in the first, it is from causality itself that becoming is freed; the principle of causality, insofar as it binds the future to the present, must "never take the form of a necessary principle."[3] All of which amounts to affirming the primacy of contingency, and to saying that the real is contingent in its very essence, and that the contingent is self-sufficient.

Thus it is that Bergson refutes and confounds determinism. Not because the truth would be contrary to the determinist *solution,* but because the very *question* determinism answers is, according to him, meaningless, ascribable to the obsession of the idea of space, and because the principles of reason which, like all reasoning, determinist reasoning invokes are, in short, practically valid but speculatively illusory approximations.

But what becomes of freedom in all this? If the partisans of determinism are wrong in answering *no* to a meaningless question, it seems that the partisans of free will are equally wrong in answering *yes* to the same question. Does the will act according to a sufficient reason by which it is necessitated to produce this act rather than some other?—Yes and no, answers Bergsonian philosophy; furthermore I do not understand the question.

Freedom exists, Bergson says. But it is impossible to define the free act, that is, to distinguish it from other acts by "saying of this act, when it is once done, that it might have been left undone"; impossible to define it by saying "that it could not be foreseen," supposing as known "all the conditions in ad-

---

3 "Thus understood, the relation of causality is a necessary relation in the sense that it will indefinitely approach the relation of identity, as a curve approaches its asymptote . . . But the principle of causality, insofar as it is supposed to bind the future to the present, could never take the form of a necessary principle; for the successive moments of real time are not bound up with one another, and no effort of logic will succeed in proving that what has been will be or will continue to be, that the same antecedents will always give rise to identical consequents." (*Ibid.,* pp. 207–208.) Cf. *Creative Evolution,* pp. 213–215, where Bergson clearly shows to what extent, for the new philosophy, the principle of causality is *imagined* instead of being *thought.* The intelligence, as a matter of fact, sees in this principle a demand of the intuition of being; but for the senses and the imagination, it can only consist in the expectation of seeing "automatically completed" a certain isolated system in the grand total.

Let me further quote the following text which clearly shows to what an extent the idea of causal determination or of motivation is, for Bergson, linked to that of mechanism: "If we question ourselves carefully we shall see that we sometimes weigh motives and deliberate over them, when our mind is already made up. An inner voice, hardly perceivable, whispers: 'Why this deliberation? You know the result and you are quite certain of what you are going to do.' But no matter! it seems that we make a point of *safe-guarding the principle of mechanism and of conforming to the laws of the association of ideas.*" (*Time and Free Will,* pp. 157–158. The italics are mine.)

vance"; impossible to define it by saying that the will, in producing it, "is not necessarily determined" by the cause or reason which makes it act.[1]

What then is freedom, for Bergson?

"We can now," he announces, fifteen pages before the end of his thesis on the *Données immédiates de la Conscience,* "formulate our conception of freedom."

"Freedom is the relation of the concrete self to the act which it performs. This relation is indefinable, just because we *are* free. [. . .] Any positive definition of freedom," he adds in a formula which is an insult to intelligence, "will ensure the victory of determinism."[2]

When he comes to deal (in *Matter and Memory*) with the relation of thought to the brain Bergson will consider an object—the memory of the sensible concrete—inferior to the domain of the *spirit* properly so-called and he will transfer it into this domain, confusing, as we have seen, the veritable spirituality of those powers which are intrinsically independent of any organ with that kind of immateriality which memory, like every cognitive function even when organic, implies in virtue of *becoming another.* In the *Essai sur les Données immédiate de la Conscience* an inverse shift had occurred—the origin of all Bergsonian confusions between the psychic and the spiritual. Here, insofar as he was dealing with freedom, it was in the domain of the spirit itself that the philosopher found himself placed from the beginning. Instead of consenting to perform the work proper to philosophy and seeking to *define* the free act, in respecting the wishes of the intelligence and hence bringing out the relation of freedom to the principle of universal intelligibility and preserving them both at once, he preferred not to define the free act, to sacrifice the principle of causality and the principle of universal intelligibility, and to demand of psychological intuition and a sort of spiritual super-empiricism an affirmation of the radical contingency of all creative becoming. But it is the same thing with the definition as with the philosophy itself: one cannot give them up except by continuing to practise them. Because he refused to define freedom Bergson, in spite of himself, defines it *in actu exercito* and without ever saying so, by a common and much too wide notion which shifts that wholly spiritual essence to the domain of the psychic and of the vital taken in general. Properly speaking, and even though Bergson himself does not use that designation, Bergsonian freedom is nothing other than spontaneity,[3] *libertas a coactione,* and this is in varying degrees the prerogative of all living beings; (nay more; we find a ves-

---

[1] *Time and Free Will,* pp. 219–221.

[2] *Ibid.,* p. 219. And again: "All determinism will thus be refuted by experience, but every attempt to define freedom will open the way to determinism." (P. 230.)

[3] "Freedom is not hereby, [. . .] reduced," writes Bergson (*Matter and Memory,* p. 243), "to sensible spontaneity. At most this would be the case in the animal, of which the psychical life

tige of it in any *nature,* even non-living, each time a being acts without undergoing violence, by following the radical principle of oriented activity which precisely constitutes its *physis*).[1]

At the same time freedom takes along with it into this inferior domain to which it descends something peculiar to freedom itself, namely, the radical contingency of the effect (of the act of choice) with relation to its cause (to the will) considered in its nature,—so that for Bergson an absolute metaphysical contingentism will affect the whole domain of spontaneity itself and, as we have seen, of all that has to do with concrete time.

"Free decision emanates from the whole soul, ξὺν ὁλῇ τῇ ψυχῇ," writes Bergson,[2] . . . "There are not (in reality) two tendencies, or even two directions, but a self which lives and develops by means of its very hesitations, until the free act drops from it like an over-ripe fruit[3] . . . In a word, if it is agreed to call every act free which springs from the self and from the self alone, the act which bears the mark of our personality is truly free, for our self alone will lay claim to its paternity."[4] And that is no doubt true, but it is

---

is mainly affective. [*Thus freedom is already in the animal!*] But in man, the thinking being, the free act may be termed a synthesis of feelings and ideas, and the evolution which leads to it a reasonable evolution." This assertion by no means answers the objection. I do not claim that Bergsonian philosophy reduces freedom to *sensible* spontaneity alone, I claim that it confuses freedom with spontaneity understood in all its fulness. I willingly grant that freedom, for Bergson, is not only the spontaneity of the life of the senses; I think that for him, if we wish to express ourselves in well-defined terms, freedom is confused with the spontaneity of the whole soul, intelligence and will as well as sensibility,—with the spontaneity of this "reasonable evolution" which leads to a "synthesis of sentiments and ideas."

[1] Spontaneity is absolute only in God, Who does not depend on any cause. Bodies of non-living nature present the most imperfect resemblance to that divine spontaneity, for since they are turned exclusively toward the external world, in the exercising of their real activity they are in complete dependence with regard to what is outside of them. Life, with its activity turned inward, offers a spontaneity which is much more profound, but still imperfect: for vegetative activity enters into play only as it is dependent upon external energies and all the conditioning of the physical world; the sense acts as dependent only upon the object present, the intelligence itself exercises the purest spontaneity here below only as dependent upon intelligibles other than itself. Let us add that if the living moves itself it is because one of its parts activates the other, or because in act in a certain respect it determines itself under another in such a way that the principle of causality applies just as well in this order of immanent action as in that of transitive action proper to inanimate matter, and because nowhere is there place for a creative becoming in the Bergsonian sense. As to freedom, it is indeed at the superior degree of spontaneity proper to the intellective life that we find it; but it is something different from this spontaneity; something entirely new begins with it, while the interiority and spontaneity of spiritual functions do themselves no more than mark a higher degree of a perfection common to the vital and the psychic in general.

[2] *Time and Free Will,* pp. 167–168.

[3] *Ibid.,* p. 175.

[4] *Ibid.,* pp. 172–173. Cf. p. 165: "And the outward manifestation of this inner state will be just what is called a free act, since the self alone will have been the author of it and since it will express the wole of the self." Page 169: "Moreover we will grant to determinism that we often resign our freedom in more serious circumstances, and that by sluggishness or indolence, we allow this same local process to run its course when our whole personality ought, so to speak, to vibrate."

not enough as long as we are not given the *why* of that perfect personalization of the free act. To say that the difference between a free act and an act which is not free consists in this that the first is the expression of "our whole personality," while the second is produced by one of those partial mechanisms which are, so to speak, at the surface of our ego,[5] is perhaps to reach in a confused sort of way, enveloped in a very general and vaguely determined effect, the true nature of freedom, but it is not to bring out or expressly signify this nature; as long as we confine ourselves to such formulas, as long as we do not show *in what way and in what capacity,* by virtue of what active and dominating indetermination of will with regard to the motivating object itself, the free act expresses our personality, we do not get beyond the difference between the *automatic* and the *spontaneous.* Even though one were to regard the latter as a stumbling-block for the principle of causality, one would not on that account have touched freedom; one would only have added one confusion to another.

It happens then that on the one hand the field of frequency of free acts is limited to excess, as though freedom occurred only in those all-too-rare moments when we have the feeling of expressing ourselves completely, of involving our whole life in an action. "Many live this kind of life and die without having known true freedom."[1] And freedom doubtless admits of degrees, as Bergson quite rightly indicates against[2] a certain spiritualism (of Descartes), but he himself seems to forget that the slightest moral act,—to the extent that it remains moral, and even though it would not affect our profoundest sentiments and inclinations, and even though it would fall a prey to a great deal of automatism and consist, for example, in yielding to the automatism of a habitual weakness,—still comprises a measure of genuine freedom.

On the other hand, the very nature of this freedom is circumscribed so ambiguously that on the one hand it seems almost reserved for the spiritual man capable of saying: *anima mea in manibus meis semper,* but on the other hand the ψυχικὸς ἄνθρωπος, wholly possessed by a great passion or a great vice is at the same time allowed to claim for himself in the moment of his most complete abandonment that plenitude of autonomy by which without being defined free will seems to have been characterized. For after all if it is true that "passion, even sudden passion, would no longer bear the stamp of fatality if the whole history of the person were reflected in it, as in Alceste's indignation, and the most authoritative education would not curtail any of our freedom if it only imparted to us ideas and feelings capable of impreg-

[5] *Ibid.*, pp. 165–170.
[1] *Ibid.*, p. 166.
[2] *Ibid.*, p. 166.

nating the whole soul";[3] if it is true that as soon as a sentiment has "attained sufficient depth" it represents the "whole soul," so that to say that the soul determines itself under its influence is to "recognize that it is self-determined";[4] in short, if it is true that "we are free when our acts spring from our whole personality, when they express it, when they have that indefinable resemblance to it which one sometimes finds between the artist and his work,"[5] how will it not be sufficient for a soul to allow itself to be wholly impregnated by a dominating sentiment, to surrender to it all its history and its whole personality in order to know *true freedom*?

This interweaving of freedom in the sense of *free will* with freedom in the sense of *autonomy* (*ubi Spiritus, ibi libertas*) is, moreover, not without having contributed still further to obscure the Bergsonian notion of freedom. But we see thereby all the more clearly to what an extent the notion of free will is for Bergsonian philosophy, in fact, identified with the notion of spontaneity,— of spontaneity whose spiritual autonomy is the highest form, but which in its less elevated degrees begins in regions that are very inferior to the life of the spirit. The consequence is that the specificity of free will has, to tell the truth, vanished.

No doubt for Bergson man is free by eminent right in opposition to animals, but it is only because of the superiority of his brain, which can set up an indefinite number of motor mechanisms. Man, if we wish to express ourselves in exact terms, is therefore characterized by a spontaneity which remains open and always available, and the animal by a spontaneity which is "the prisoner of mechanisms it has itself set up." This freedom-spontaneity is therefore already in the animal, although a prisoner and limited; it is in the impulse of universal life which is freedom as it is consciousness; it is in all efficacious activity.

At bottom, Bergsonian freedom is still and always, or rather (since *Time and Free Will* has chronological priority in Bergson's work), it was already duration, that extraordinary master-key which solves all problems (because the problem is wrong in positing itself and because contraries when sufficiently thinned down finally become identical). It is still and always, it was already this marvellous Proteus of Bergsonian philosophy, here *freedom* as spontaneous action, there *soul* and *ego* and *memory* as duration which preserves itself, elsewhere *vital impulse, stream of universal consciousness, creative effort,* etc. To freedom taken as simple spontaneity, as we have already noted, a new character is thus added, more profoundly Bergsonian,—it is the affirmation that the contingent creates itself and that potency passes of itself to the act, since duration is pure change, change which

[3] *Ibid.*, p. 167.
[4] *Ibid.*, p. 165.
[5] *Ibid.*, p. 172.

is self-sufficient; we perceive then the authentic resonance, grasp all the metaphysical scope of psychological analysis to whose spell it would be easy to yield. The free act, they tell us, is the one which, prepared well beneath arguments juxtaposed at the surface of ourselves, emanates from the explosion, from the "revolt," from the "irresistible thrust" of the "self from below coming up to the surface," from a "gradual heating and a sudden boiling over of feelings and ideas, not unperceived, but rather unnoticed";[1] in short, the truly free act is the one on which, by reflection, "we find that we have decided without any reason and perhaps even against every reason," and which thereby attests that power of "choosing without a motive" of which one is wrong to "look for examples in the ordinary and even indifferent circumstances of life."[2] Thus a psycho-motive spontaneity which thrusts itself

[1] *Ibid.*, p. 169.—Intelligence, in Bergson's eyes, plays so small a part in freedom that its practical judgments might, according to him, be compared to pretexts invented after the event by subjects who have yielded to a post-hypnotic suggestion. (*Ibid.*, pp. 156–158.)

[2] *Ibid.*, p. 169.—The passage, moreover, is of the highest quality, and remarkable on more than one count. Let me quote it at length: "When our most trustworthy friends agree in advising us to take some important step, the sentiments which they utter with so much insistence lodge on the surface of our ego and there get solidified in the same way as the ideas of which we spoke just now. Little by little they will form a thick crust which will cover up our own sentiments; we shall believe that we are acting freely, and it is only by looking back to the past, later on, that we shall see how much we were mistaken. But then, at the very minute when the act is going to be performed, *something* may revolt against it. It is the deep-seated self rushing up to the surface. It is the outer crust bursting, suddenly giving way to an irresistible thrust. Hence in the depths of the self, below this most reasonable pondering over most reasonable pieces of advice, something else was going on—a gradual heating and a sudden boiling over of feelings and ideas, not unperceived, but rather unnoticed. If we turn back to them and carefully scrutinize our memory, we shall see that we had ourselves shaped these ideas, ourselves lived these feelings, but that, through some strange reluctance to exercise our will, we had thrust them back into the darkest depths of our soul whenever they came up to the surface. And this is why we seek in vain to explain our sudden change of mind by the visible circumstances which preceded it. We wish to know the reason why we have made up our mind, and we find that we have decided without any reason, and perhaps even against every reason. But, in certain cases, that is the best of reasons. For the action which has been performed does not then express some superficial idea, almost external to ourselves, distinct and easy to account for: it agrees with the whole of our most intimate feelings, thoughts and aspirations, with that particular conception of life which is the equivalent of all our past experience, in a word, with our personal idea of happiness and of honour. Hence it has been a mistake to look for examples in the ordinary and even indifferent circumstances of life in order to prove that man is capable of choosing without a motive. It might easily be shown that these insignificant actions are bound up with some determining reason. It is at the great and solemn crisis, decisive of our reputation with others, and yet more with ourselves, that we choose in defiance of what is conventionally called a motive, and this absence of any tangible reason is the more striking the deeper our freedom goes."

This remarkable analysis suffers from an irremediable ambiguity. It could have been the enunciation of the purest truths had Bergson been careful to show that the motives of which he speaks are only the pseudo-motives of associationist determinism; that the outer crust beneath which the real choice occurs is that of the opinions of others lodged on the surface of our soul without our having assimilated them by a vital act of intelligence, in short, that it relates, if you will, to the social self, but not to the intellectual or rational self. And finally and above all that the most intimate depths, the truly spiritual depths of our being are not those regions

into existence, invents and engages itself wholly without submitting to the law of universal intelligibility, a pure creative unforeseeability, an absolute contingency swollen with impulsions and accumulated energies, in short an *advancing force,* that is what is left of human freedom.

Although Bergsonian philosophy has abandoned being and the intellect, in so doing it has not saved freedom, for its spontaneity cannot in any way be true freedom, *libertas a necessitate,* such as the testimony of consciousness affirms it. No matter how much we accumulate the most exquisite dubitations of psychological analysis, never shall we prevent consciousness from affirming that we are not necessitated to one act rather than to another, and that we are free, in a given circumstance, to act or to not act; one can never force consciousness to admit that in bringing this testimony it is making a meaningless affirmation and expressing a "bastard" and unintelligible idea. This affirmation is, on the contrary, eminently intelligible, because it is formulated in terms of the primary ideas of being, of cause and of action.

Bergson has dealt with the problem of freedom from the point of view of the associationists and phenomenalists. His criticism is undoubtedly directed against the imaginings of these philosophers who conceived motives as flying machines coming to light upon us and weighing down on our will. But he forgets, along with them, that psychological causality, the true radiance of the substance of the soul, is in the faculties or powers of the soul, not in phenomena and that it is by reason of the powers (not of phenomena) of the will and intellect (not "motives" and states of consciousness) that the problem should be posited and dealt with. He remains a prisoner of sensualism and nominalism, he does not establish any distinction in nature between the idea and the image. He therefore cannot bring to light what is the very root of freedom, namely, the perception of the universal by intelligence. For him, there is nothing but the particular in us: hence if one will not regard the soul as a system of given and therefore determined forces, attractions, impulses, one must look upon it as a confused self in the process of making itself, but also determined in the last analysis, unless we posit chance at the base of everything. In which case we temper determinism by unintelligibility, but without keeping anything of freedom but the word itself.

III.—THE THOMIST DOCTRINE OF FREEDOM

Here we have it then; the most thorough-going, most intelligent anti-intellectualism,—Bergsonian anti-intellectualism,—compromises and destroys

---

where sentiments and ideas seethe, but rather those very chasms of the will enrooted in the intelligence in the most secret recesses of substance, the chasms of those infrangible desirings (*appétitions*) and those immaterial acts of judgment which the better express our whole personality according as they are bathed in more intellectual light and conveyed with a firmer lucidity. Such are the true *motives* and they do not necessitate the will, because their efficacity comes from it.

man's freedom just as much as the intellectualism of Parmenides, Spinoza, Leibnitz and Hegel. Let us realize that intelligence alone can correct intelligence and that if we wish to cure the soul of the false intellectualism of Spinoza and Hegel, which measures being upon thought and to which the dogmatism of our pseudo-savants bears but a faint and crude resemblance, there is only one means, only one remedy: authentic intellectualism,—submissive to the real,—which measures thought upon being. Intelligence, moreover, is the better able to establish the existence of freedom since it is intelligence which is its foundation in reality. The root of freedom, says Saint Thomas, is constituted in the intellect or reason. *Totius libertatis radix est in ratione constituta.*[1]

We cannot review in a few pages the Thomist doctrine of freedom, in which are joined both metaphysical profundity and a wealth of concrete analysis which modern philosophy might well envy, and which would enable it singularly to illuminate its finest discoveries. Let us attempt however to indicate its essential points.[2]

Freedom

Every appetite is a power which directs us toward the good that we know: that we previously know, either by the senses, or by the intellect, for in itself appetite is a blind faculty. So that the desire for a thing that is absolutely unknown is absolutely impossible, *ignoti nulla cupido,* and nothing is willed if it is not first known: *nihil volitum nisi praecognitum.* So that the will is subordinate to the intellect, practice to theory, action to truth and the will cannot produce its operation proper without a judgment of the intelligence which is the reason for this operation.

For the will is an appetite, it is characterized by desire, its primordial act is love; it is not that imaginary and puritanical faculty which wills without desiring, claimed by Kant and Thomas Reid. Thus we understand why the final end, the ultimate act of the will, does not consist in producing outwardly, but in resting in the possession of the desired good; we also understand why before the *reflection* of the intellect, there are in the will, upon the simple intellectual apprehension of a good, undeliberate movements for which we are not responsible.

What distinguishes will from sense appetite as it is found isolated in the animal deprived of reason, is that the sense appetite has its root in sense knowledge: by the sense appetite the animal proceeds (spontaneously and necessarily, according to the system of its actual dispositions) toward the

[1] *De Veritate,* q. 24, a. 2.
[2] I am especially indebted, in this account, to the study by Garrigou-Lagrange, *Intellectualisme et Liberté chez Saint Thomas,* already mentioned above. Cf. also *Sum. theol.,* I^a, q. 82, a. 1 and 2; q. 83, a. 1; I^a II^{ae}, q. 10, a. 2; *de Malo,* q. 6.

particular and concrete goods its *senses* make known to it, but without investing them with the intelligible value or objective note of *good,* for the sense does not know good as such any more than being or unity as such; whereas by the will we proceed toward things that are good to the extent that we know them by the *intellect,* that is, insofar as they participate in the intelligible value or formal aspect of *good* in general; for the intellect does know good as such, since good is being itself as desirable.[1]

And it is because the intellect knows good under its very value of good, and in terms of being,—a knowledge essentially distinct from sense knowledge,—it is for this reason that, in any nature which has intelligence must exist a faculty of desire or of love essentially distinct from sense appetite and which tends toward the good according to its universal ampleness and according as it transcendentally imbibes every good thing; toward the good intelligibly apprehended, not toward certain particular good things known only by the sense: and this is the rational appetite or the will, which has its root in intelligence.

Thus the will is founded in nature and is itself a certain nature. It must therefore, like each nature, have a necessary determination, it must have an operation which, as it is produced by mode of nature, is necessarily determined; there must be something which it wills *in very virtue of what it is,* something which it wills necessarily.[2] Moreover, if there is something the will wills contingently, that perforce supposes that there is something else it wills first necessarily, for what is contingent, what is not by itself, always supposes before it that which is by itself, that which is necessary. And thus as there is no movement without something immovable, so freedom presupposes necessity; there is no free act without some necessary act.

But what then does the will thus necessarily will? It is what it wills by nature, and its nature is to be the appetite which follows upon intelligence; it is therefore the good in its typical form or value as intelligence makes it stand out from the shadows of sensible goods, let us say *pure good.* From whence it follows, in the first place, that the will can never will evil as evil; it can will only what the intellect rightly or wrongly regards as a good; for it wills good by the very fact that it exercises itself; to will good, is the very urge and expression of its being. In the second place, it follows that it cannot, from the instant it exercises itself, not will an ultimate aim, a primary good, for which

---

1 The good is qualified to move desire, either for the perfection it includes and which makes it desirable in itself,—the good properly so-called, good as an END in itself, that the School calls the *bonum honestum*—or for another good it will procure for us—the *useful good,* which is only a MEANS,—or for the pleasure we take in it or the joy we get out of it,—*the delectable good,* which is only an effect or a repercussion of the possession of a good: REST in the good possessed. (Cf. Saint Thomas, *Sum. theol.,* Iª, q. 5, a. 6.)

2 Cf. *Sum. theol.,* Iª, q. 82, a. 1; Iª IIªe, q. 10, a. 1.

all others are willed, that is to say good in all its fulness, universal good, absolute good, unmixed good, beatitude; so that we are not free not to will the good which saturates all desire (where it resides is another question), and we cannot voluntarily wiggle our finger without manifesting that we are made for beatitude, and that we necessarily will it. The adequate object of the will, what it cannot, from the moment it wills, not will, what determines it necessarily, is therefore absolute and universal good.*

That is the capacity of the human will. But what is the result of all this? If what necessarily determines the will is absolute and universal good, it follows evidently that all that is not absolute and universal good cannot determine the will necessarily. "Any particular or partial good remains inadequate to that infinite capacity for loving."† Any particular or partial good, any good which the hand can grasp is fundamentally incapable of moving the will of man necessarily, of determining it by itself to will it. With regard to any object which is not pure good, the rational appetite, the will, is *undetermined,* "*indifferent.*"

Now it is intelligence or reason which is the root of this fundamental indetermination of the will with regard to the particular; because the universal capacity of the will is proportionate to the universal capacity of the intellect, and because in any particular good which it knows, the intellect sees that this good is not universal good. We can therefore say with Saint Thomas: It is necessary that man be free by the very fact of his rational nature,[1] and again: The root of freedom *as subject* is the will, but *as cause* is reason.[2]

Finally, if there is indetermination (indetermination that is active and dominating) in the will, it is because there is indetermination (indetermination to be dominated) in being itself, it is because all that is is not Being, and because all goods are not *the* Good; it is because no one created thing is pure Act, in its infinite Perfection (for where is pure good in reality, if not in subsisting Good itself? That is why every will, even the most perverse, desires God without knowing it; atheism, if it could be lived to the very root of will, would disorganize, would metaphysically kill the will; it is not by accident, it is by a strictly necessary effect, inscribed in the nature of things, that every genuine experience of atheism, if it is consciously and rigorously conducted, in the end provokes psychic dissolution). If there is indetermination in the will, it is because in every desirable thing, save God, there is a mixture of potentiality; and because intelligence sees this indetermination, this funda-

---

* In these lines I did not distinguish (as I should have done) between *felicity* or *happiness in general,* to which the human will tends necessarily by virtue of a natural desire, and *absolute happiness or beatitude,* to which it tends necessarily by virtue of a trans-natural desire.

† Garrigou-Lagrange, *Intellectualisme et Liberté chez Saint Thomas,* p. 15 in the separate printing.

[1] *Sum. theol.,* Iª, q. 83, a. 1.

[2] *Sum. theol.,* Iª IIªᵉ, q. 17, a. 1 *ad* 2.

mental imperfection, this mixture in all things. To deny freedom, as to deny movement, is to say that all is act, that there is no potency in things, it is to say that every being is God.

Election or the free act

The will, because of the intellect, is indeterminate or indifferent with regard to all particular goods. In order the better to understand this, let us remember that the reason for the operations of the will lies in intelligence. But in what form? In the form of the proper and complete operation of the intellect, namely of a judgment. But not of just any judgment: of a judgment bearing upon a particular and concrete act to be accomplished *hic et nunc,* of a *practico-practical* judgment, as the scholastics say. This judgment alone, once it is brought to bear, determines the will, and without this judgment there is no voluntary act possible; that is an essential thesis which modern psychology,[1] as we may say in passing, discovers anew and in its own way. And the whole psychological problem of free will consists of the relation between practical judgment and the will.

It is expedient here to distinguish with the scholastics three kinds of judgment: in the first place *purely speculative* judgment, the one which in no way concerns action, for example: the whole is greater than its parts, man is a rational animal; in the second place *speculative-practical* judgment, the one which concerns action, but by enunciating a universal truth, leaving out of account concrete circumstances and the singular reality of the act to be accomplished, for example: one should do good; one should not kill; one should love one's neighbour. Finally *practico-practical* judgment, the one which prescribes a determined action, in strictly individual and concrete circumstances, for example: I must, in fact, now give a certain piece of advice to such and such a friend.

Now the *speculative-practical* judgment, the universal judgment, is incapable by itself of determining the will necessarily. Why? Because it bears upon a universal truth, on an action in general to be done in general, for example: man should help his neighbour, from which it follows that being a man it is my duty to advise my friend, *in virtue of a universal law applicable to human action in general.*[2] But the act that I have to do is a concrete and par-

---

1 Cf. William James, *Principles of Psychology,* Bk. II, pp. 569 ff.; Dürr, *Die Lehre von der Aufmerksamkeit,* Leipzig, 1907; and the works of Ach and of Michotte and Prüm (Cf. De la Vaissière, *op. cit.,* 1912, pp. 289–294), whatever objections we might have to these works in other connections along with Ch. Blondel (Dumas, *Traité de Psych.,* t. II, pp. 354–369).

2 The intelligence without the will can judge that a certain definite act, taken in its general aspect as a human act, should be accomplished in virtue of the *universal* law. It shows obligation in general (*speculative-practical* judgment). The intelligence (presupposing the will in its dispositions, for example, in the moral virtues), can in addition judge that a certain particular act, in certain particular circumstances, should be posited *hic et nunc* by the subject. It then shows obligation in particular: *video meliora.* This judgment, although particular, remains

ticular act; it is not a human act in general, nor an act of my own simply determined as human; it is essentially an act of *mine, determined as my own.* The will requires of the intellect, in order to be determined to such an action, *a decree which bears in particular on that action as my own,* as a concrete and singular act relating to my end and to my personal and singular will of my end. This means that it absolutely requires of the intellect a *practico-practical* judgment.

In another respect *practico-practical* judgment, the immediate determining principle of the will, is, for intelligence left to itself, absolutely indifferent. This capital truth cannot be too greatly emphasized for it derives from the very essence of the intellect, which, left only to itself, is simply speculative. Intelligence is, by nature, fundamentally indetermined to formulating, after reflection, the judgment: "it is absolutely advisable for me, *hic et nunc,* to do this act, to seek this particular good." Why? Because this judgment does not bear upon the relation of my act to being or truth, in which case one would have a *speculative-practical* judgment, such as: "it is good, or it is my duty, to advise my friend,"—it bears on the relation of my act, considered *hic et nunc,* to what I need, I who produce it. Now what I need is Good, absolute good. And the act in question is only a particular good, which therefore lacks some good and which thereby appears as a non-good; it is a good in one aspect, a non-good in another. I therefore do not need it necessarily; I need it in one respect but not in another; in one respect it is advisable for me to accomplish this act but in another it is not; that is all that intelligence alone, the pure faculty of knowledge, can tell me.

It is impossible for me ever, by making use of intelligence alone, to decide that: "I must, *hic et nunc,* accomplish this act, absolutely; this good in fact will be for me as though it were *the* Good"; and that because of the *infinite* disproportion between the absolute Good and this particular good.[1]

---

speculative-practical as long as the singularity of the act is determined in terms of that *universal truth,* which shows in absolute good the goal of human acting. It is still insufficient to determine action. It is only when the intelligence (presupposing the will in its act of election) determines the singularity of the act to be posited in terms of the *singular will itself* that the subject has of his own absolute good, and which in that case plays the part of major premise, that one has to do with a definite *practico-practical* judgment, with a judgment that is completely individuated, proper to the act in question insofar as it is mine—and this judgment may be in contradiction with the first: *deteriora sequor.* Thus, in the case of moral fault then, the sinner judges speculatively that he should do good; that is precisely what constitutes advertence in sin. But "at the very moment that he sins he judges practically that it is appropriate to sin: *hoc simpliciter est bonum mihi hic et nunc.*" (Garrigou-Lagrange, *op. cit.,* p. 22.)

[1] To be a geometrician is good; but it is not being either a soldier or a poet, and thereby it is a non-good. To obey God is good, but it is not to possess beatitude, and to that extent it is a non-good. And much as the intelligence is capable of making by itself this *speculative-practical* judgment: "to be a geometrician is preferable in order to attain the goal I have set myself" or "one must always obey God," and consequently: "it suits me, *in abstracto,* to be a geometrician," or "it is my duty to obey God," if left to itself it is just as incapable, constitutionally, from the fact of

But from another standpoint action, the act which I accomplish, being doubtless not a creation as Bergson says but really a production of novelty in the world, can be prescribed only by an absolute judgment; for in acting I *cause* something *to be* which was not and I thereby exclude from being all other possibles. The *practico-practical* judgment, this incommunicable judgment exclusively mine, in which I commit myself completely and by which I say to myself, "I must, *hic et nunc,* accomplish this act," cannot therefore be expressed except in the absolute: *fiat!*

And thus the basic indetermination of intelligence in its *practico-practical* judgment is the very cause and root of the basic indetermination of the will with regard to its operation, when the latter is to bear upon a particular good. The intellect by itself, in such a case, would always remain indifferent, it could not get rid of its indetermination. But will the will remain indifferent? Is it never to will when its sole function is to will? The operation by which it triumphs over indetermination, by which it determines *itself,* is the very act of *free will.*

For the will can thus determine itself only through the intellect, without which its operation would be without any *raison d'être,* that is to say, would never take place. It is therefore the will which makes the intellect pass from *speculative-practical* judgment unfitted to determine it, or from indeterminate *practico-practical* judgment, to a determinate *practico-practical* judgment, the only one fit to determine the will. And thus we see that the operation of free will is common to the intellect and to the will, which here are, so to speak, integral parts of one another.

But this operation is really *free.* Since the intellect alone, as we have just seen, is not capable of determining itself to an unconditional *practico-practical* judgment, since left to itself it cannot absolutely affirm: "I must, in fact, act rather than not act," it is the will which will intervene in order that this judgment may be made; the will it is which specifies and determines the *practico-practical* judgment.— But how without a vicious circle can the will thus determine the judgment which determines itself? Here is the very knot of the problem of free will. The answer is in Aristotle's axiom: *causae ad invicem sunt causae,* causes of a different kind cause one another. At the end of deliberation, in that instantaneous[1] operation which constitutes the act of free will, the will and the intellect determine one another, but in different respects. Since the intellect separately taken presents the judgment: "I must act" both as having and not having to be made, the act of free will or election

its speculative nature, of making absolutely and *in concreto* this *practico-practical* judgment: "it suits me *hic et nunc,* purely and simply, to be a geometrician," or "I must, *hic et nunc,* purely and simply, obey God."

[1] *Sum. theol.,* I^a II^{ae}, q. 113, a. 7, ad 4.

consists of the following instantaneous process: on the one hand the will as *efficient cause* and by virtue of its inclination toward one or other of the alternatives, applies the intellect to judge, for example: "I must act," rather than: "I must not act"; on the other hand, and that at the same time, this very judgment, acting as *formal extrinsic cause,* and being made, by virtue of the exercise of the will, capable of biting into existence, fixes and determines in its nature, specifies the action and inclination of the will: here is the choice, the instantaneous election which metaphysical analysis seizes on the wing, in its two-fold and undisjointed relation of causality.

The will is thus the cause of the very attraction it undergoes,[1] of the efficacity of the form which actuates it. A free cause, because the efficient cause in the order of action has absolute priority (in the nature) over other causes,[2] the formal causality of judgment coming into play, in actual existence, only if the efficient causality of the will is first exercised; and because without the movement of the will proceeding toward a certain specification to be received, thus making of a certain particular good the very means, signified *hic et nunc,* of the perfect good it naturally wills, there is nothing in the world, neither external circumstances, nor internal dispositions, which can determine the intellect to judge that a certain partial good is the good I must have, the good which fits my will for absolute good,[3] and to make by itself alone an unconditional *practico-practical* judgment; nothing in the world therefore which can necessitate the will,—since this is the only kind of judgment (save for the vision of God) which can necessitate it. It is indeed therefore by a free act, without being necessitated by anything, that the will leaves its state of indetermination.[4] But it is not by an act without reason. For the will exerts its efficient causality only by being to the same extent formally determined by intellect. When it bends the intellect to a certain *practico-prac-*

---

[1] Garrigou-Lagrange, *op. cit.,* p. 43.

[2] Salmant., t. IV, p. 680, par. 270.

[3] In making the *practico-practical* judgment under the motion of the will the intellect does not judge, in relation to being, that a certain partial good is absolute good; it judges, *in relation to the will,* that a certain partial good is *hic et nunc* the means of absolute good, is good purely and simply in relation to the will thus disposed. Thus "the truth of the practico-practical judgment, in opposition to the truth of the speculative or speculative-practical judgment, takes itself *non per conformitatem ad rem, sed per conformitatem ad appetitum rectum.*" (Garrigou-Lagrange, *op. cit.,* p. 24.) Cf. *Sum. theol.,* Iᵃ IIᵃᵉ, q. 58, a. 5.

[4] It triumphs, 1) over the indetermination of the object (both good and not good, because it is not the Good itself), 2) over the passive indetermination which affects it itself (and which is a sign of imperfection: it is not always in act like the will of God). It triumphs over this double indetermination by exerting its *active and dominating indetermination or indifference,* which is the very essence of freedom. It is because they have not distinguished between passive indifference and active or dominating indifference in our will that many authors have so completely misunderstood the Thomist doctrine of free will. Cf. John of Saint Thomas, *De Anima,* q. xii, a. 2; Prado, *De Gratia et Libero arbitrio,* t. I, pp. 159 and ff.; t. II, pp. 167 and ff.

tical judgment rather than to another, it does not act without motive or reason, its motive or reason is precisely the partial good, represented by the intellect, which it thus chooses. But it is a motive or reason *which does not necessitate it*.[5] Because this good, not being its adequate determining motive, namely perfect good, is incapable of moving it necessarily. So that the will is free with regard to it, it can will it or not. That is the very definition of freedom: "the power of choosing between the means while the ordination to the end remains fixed," or again, as the moderns put it, the proper act of "a power, which, once all the conditions prerequisite[1] for acting are posited, can act or not act." To be free is to be master of one's acts and consequently master of one's judgment, *liberi arbitrii:* for if the will had not mastery over the judgment by which it is moved, it would not have full mastery over its actions.[2]

We see therefore that the will is free even though it always follows the in-

---

[5] Cf. *Sum. theol.*, Iᵃ IIᵃᵉ, q. 10, a. 2, *ad* 1. "Sufficiens motivum alicujus potentiae non est nisi objectum, quod totaliter habet rationem motivi [per respectum ad voluntatem hoc est bonum perfectum]; si autem in aliquo deficiat non ex necessitate movebit."

[1] It is understood that if it is a question of prerequisite conditions of a priority *in time* it can act or not act *etiam in sensu composito;* if it is a question of prerequisite conditions of a priority not in time, but only *in nature* (such as the final practical judgment and the motion of the first Cause, which are *simultaneous* with the act of choice), it can act or not act *in sensu diviso tantum.*
Let me explain these locutions. At the instant I choose to stand up, I retain (but deciding not to actualize it) the *power* of choosing to remain seated. The judgment which determines my choice does not suppress the power that I have of willing or not willing, since it is precisely in exercising this power that I bring this judgment to bear. It is clear that one does not lose a power from the fact that one exercises it; it is then, on the contrary, that it is most manifest. Given the final practical judgment, *if one considers the relation between my will and the object of choice taken in itself,*—for example, to make or not to make a certain promise,—this relation always remains what it is essentially: a relation of dominating indifference, with the power *ad utrumlibet.* That is what the Thomists are expressing when they say that *in sensu diviso* the will, *stante judicio practico,* retains (and more than ever) its dominating indifference.
At the instant that the final practical judgment is made, the will cannot choose otherwise *in sensu composito* (the ACT of choosing otherwise is incompossible with the positing of the final practical judgment; in other words, if our mind joins in a conditional statement the positing of the practical judgment and the act of choice, saying for example; "if the final practical judgment is: I must promise,—the will will choose to promise," there is necessity in THE CONSEQUENCE, that is, the proposition: "the will will choose to promise" necessarily follows, in the mind, from the condition posited); but *in sensu diviso,* the power the will has to choose otherwise, for example not to promise, even though it is not actualized, remains intact, and it is that very thing which constitutes its freedom. The POWER of choosing otherwise is not incompossible with the positing of the final practical judgment; in other words, even though the positing of the final practical judgment and the act of choice are united in the real, the mode of egression of the act of choice, considered in itself, remains necessarily what it is by nature, namely, free: there is no necessity in THE CONSEQUENT (in the choice itself), that is to say that in reality the manner in which the act of choice comes out of the will does not change in nature. By the very nature of things, the act of choice cannot issue from the will unless it is *able* not to issue from it.

[2] Cf. John of Saint Thomas, *de Anima*, q. xii, a. 2. "Indifferentia libertatis consistit in potestate dominativa voluntatis non solum super actum suum ad quem movet, sed etiam super judicium a quo movetur: et hoc est necessarium ut voluntas habeat plenum dominium suarum actionum." Saint Thomas, *de Veritate*, q. 24, a. 2; *ibid.*, a. 1: "Homo non solum est causa sui ipsius movendo, sed judicando, et ideo est liberi arbitrii; ac si diceretur liberi judicii de agendo vel non agendo."

tellect: *voluntas in omnibus suis actibus sequitur ductum intellectus*. We see also that it is free, even though necessarily determined[3] by the final *practico-practical* judgment, because it is through its freedom that this judgment is, and is what it is.

From this point of view it is right to say with Bergson, but in a deeper sense, that "our motives are what we make them." And again: that our "reasons have determined us only at the moment that they became determining, that is to say, at the moment the act was virtually accomplished."[4] Because in reality, as Garrigou-Lagrange so excellently puts it, in the act of free will the will "goes to meet an attraction which is incapable of coming all the way to it"; because "the free act is a gratuitous answer, from the infinite depths of the will, to the unavailing solicitation of a finite good."[5]

The intellect and freedom

Thus it is that the "intellectualism" of Saint Thomas, as it recognizes that the created being is a mixture of potency and act, that all being is not Being, and that all good is not Good, recognizes by that very fact that all *raison d'être* is not necessitating, but that when it is a question of determining the infinite by the finite, the infinite capacity of the will by a finite good, every motive, every reason, sufficient in its order, finds itself fundamentally insufficient and incapable of necessitating such a faculty to act: it is by itself that it will act, freely, being able not to act, keeping mastery over its act in such a way that this act (and it alone) is *absolutely* unforeseeable. If God knows free acts in advance, it is not that He sees them pre-determined *in their cause,* in created will, it is that He sees them present *themselves* in His eternity, and because from all eternity He wills or permits them.

Thus it is that Thomist philosophy establishes the freedom of man in the very terms of intellect and being. It shows us in human will a bottomless pit which subsisting Good, which God alone can fill; and in human freedom a participated similitude of divine freedom, thanks to which, without being able to *create* anything properly speaking (*ex nihilo*), we, however, as we please, cause that to be which was not and also form ourselves; thanks to which we are persons and, like gods, intervene in the order of the world by acts of endless scope; so much so that the mystery of our *acting* is as marvellous and as terrifying for whoever can be conscious of it, as the very mystery of our *being.*

Thomist philosophy further shows us that free will is a property deriving

[3] Necessarily determined *in sensu composito;* but not *in sensu diviso.* See *supra,* p. 273, n. 1.
[4] *Bulletin de la Société française de Philosophie,* meeting of February 26, 1903.—Bergson adds: "and the creation of which I speak is wholly in the *progress* by which these reasons *have become determining.*" To tell the truth, this *progress* is the (instantaneous) act of free will itself, and not the flow of becoming.
[5] Garrigou-Lagrange, *op. cit.,* p. 50.

from our very nature as beings endowed with intelligence: so that those who deny our *specific difference* must also deny our freedom. So also that free- dom is not the absurd power of choosing without motive or in spite of motive, but the power of choosing according to reason; in the words of Saint Thomas quoted above: *vis electiva mediorum servato ordine finis,* the power of choosing the means while the ordination to the end—to the ultimate end, in short—remains fixed. For every creature this signifies: the power of obeying the eternal Law without being necessitated to do so. From which it follows that we are at the lowest degree among free beings, because in our choice (even with regard to the natural order taken in itself), we can only too greatly deviate from our true ultimate goal. For the power of choosing evil, of preferring apparent good to real good, far from being an essential attribute of freedom as such, is only a sign of the imperfection of all created freedom, and especially of the weakness and infirmity of human freedom.

What is essential to freedom is the power to act or to not act, to produce or withhold one's action. The scholastics called that freedom the *freedom of exercise* (or again—practically speaking the two terms coincide,—*freedom of the contradictories*), because in it we have the choice between acting and not acting, loving and not loving. They called *freedom of specification* the freedom which no longer bears solely on the positing of the act but on its nature, or in other words consists in choosing between contrary things, as between loving and hating. This freedom generally accompanies the first, but not always (we can will neither evil *in its very character* of evil, nor what is essentially incompatible with the appetite for good in general, for example, non-being *in its very character* of non-being), and it is not at all necessary in order that there should be freedom; for the fact that I can hate does not at all increase the mastery I have over my act of loving or not loving.

Because no created intelligence is Truth itself and because no creature is the rule of its own acting, freedom of specification extends in every creature (considered in its nature, with the exception of the privileges to which the supernatural order can admit it) to the point of being able to choose evil: which still assumes an absence—a voluntary absence—of practical consideration. If, *in a wholly improper sense,* one calls "ignorance" the fact of thus averting his gaze from the rule, one can say that in this wholly improper sense *omnis peccans est ignorans,* which does not prevent the possibility of sinning in full realization of what one is doing. For the lack of practical consideration in question (*ignoring*) is in no way an ignorance in the proper sense of the word (*being ignorant of*); it is consistent with a perfect knowledge and without any ignorance. And it is the will which is the cause of this practical lack of consideration. While the intellect sees clearly (in a *speculative-practical* judgment) what the law is and what the true good, it is the will which *bends at its pleasure*[1] practical judgment, freely guiding and arresting deliberation. It is thus responsible for the final practical judgment, the one which is not only examined, weighed, tried, but which is formally made, and which is necessarily followed by action.

But the higher the intellect is raised in perfection, the more freedom to choose evil is restrained in extent (and augmented in gravity). Thus it is that, according to Saint Thomas Aquinas,[2] angels can fall in instituting for their good (that is, the good that they prefer and on which they settle) a thing good in itself (their own greatness) insofar as it is willed *in a manner and by an impulse both disordered*—and which they know to be disordered: for that, no shadow of ignorance (properly so-called) or of error in intellect is required; bad will alone suffices. But they cannot fall, as men can, in instituting for their good a thing *bad in itself:* because, for that, bad will no doubt suffices, but on condition that some error or ignorance (properly so-called) be produced in the intellect; there, in fact, is an *object* to judge, and in order to prefer a thing bad in itself I must judge it good for myself, or deceive myself about it—which is inconsistent with the perfection of the angelic intellect. Last of all, at the highest degree of spiritual perfection, immediately joined to increase light, the blessed, made fast to good by the bea-

---

[1] "Absolute loquendo de determinatione intellectus, dicendum simpliciter est quod voluntas determinat intellectum ad judicandum alterum oppositorum faciendum; sed diversimode in bonis et malis. Quia cum neutrum oppositorum habet rationem mali moraliter, *voluntas ex se sola flectit judicium quo vult*; ad alterum vero oppositorum moraliter malum, *voluntas ipsa flectit judicium*, sed non nisi concurrente ad hanc flexionem aliquo alio defectu intellectus, saltem non consideratione omnium considerandorum, quae sufficit ad hoc quod *omis malus ignorans sit*, ut de peccato angeli dictum fuit." Cajetan, in I^{am} II^{ae}, q. 77, a. 2, n^o iv.—Not forgetting that the *lack of consideration* of which Cajetan is speaking is itself voluntary.

I may add that in quoting Socrates' phrase: *omnis peccans est ignorans*, Cajetan does not distinguish sufficiently between ignorance properly so-called (*to be ignorant of*) and voluntary non-consideration (*to ignore*) which does not imply any imperfection whatsoever in the intellect (except perhaps—and this is the mark of all created intellect—the dependence with regard to the will as exercised, hence the possibility of *turning aside one's glance* under the action of the will). Cajetan considered voluntary non-consideration a defect incompatible with the perfection of the angelic intellect in the natural order. From this we have the doctrine upheld by the great Thomistic commentators (cf. Cajetan, *loc. cit.*; John of Saint Thomas, *Curs. theol., De Angelis*, t. IV, disp. xxiii, a. 1; *Salmantic.*, t. IV, disp. ix), of the impeccability of the angel in the natural order, if he had been created in the state of pure nature. I am breaking away from this doctrine which I had followed in the first edition of the present work, but which seems to me on the one hand to detract from the teaching of Saint Thomas on the peccability of any intelligent creature considered in its sole nature—and on the other hand to fail to recognize the sovereign freedom with which the pure spirit chooses evil, without any light in the world being able to turn it aside by convincing it of ignorance or of error, pointing out to it that it is mistaken: for it is ignorant of nothing and commits no error of judgment, knows perfectly that it constitutes its good in a bad act and renders itself bad, and rises up against the order established by the subsisting Truth —without having to find an excuse or ask for mercy—simply because it *prefers* this. In the moment of its falling you cannot find any fault in its intellect; you can teach it nothing. It wills to be bad, that's all there is to it; although knowing obviously that it should will its own greatness in measure, it wills it out of measure. (New footnote, for the present edition.)

[2] Cf. *Sum. theol.*, I, p. 63, a. 1, *ad* 3; *de malo*, q. 16, a. 2 and 3.

tific vision, absolutely cannot sin. Their freedom of specification subsists for choosing between things that are good, not for choosing between good and evil—which cannot be called a diminution of that freedom, evil being nothing positive, being only a privation. As to their freedom of exercise, it remains whole. Except for the beatific vision itself and beatific love itself, all the good they do, therefore all they do, they do freely. From the fact that the intellect judges in all evidence that a certain act is purely and simply evil, it does not follow in fact that the contrary act is purely and simply good; for, being particular, it is not absolute Good. It always has therefore at one and the same time, ineluctably, a value of good and of non-good, and the will, in willing this good, acts freely, in full mastery of its act. It is only before the divine Essence, intuitively known as the plenitude of all good, that all freedom disappears, the freedom of exercise as well as the freedom of specification.[1] Then, in the light of that blessed vision, our will finally satisfied, will be impelled towards God with all its weight, although perfectly vitally and spontaneously; it will plunge into Him, strike Him like a thunderbolt, in an infinite necessity of loving without end the infinite Love.

[1] *Sum. theol.*, Iᵃ, q. 82, a. 2.

Chapter Twelve

THE NEW PHILOSOPHY

The Bergsonian doctrine opens up a *new era* in the history of knowledge, Bergsonian philosophy renews human thought. Since there have been men, and men who can think, human intellect cuts out, carves up, immobilizes; and if fugitive intuitions have enabled a small number of thinkers to glimpse something of the truth, the brutal concept, with its geometrical aspect and its mania for cutting up, has always put to flight this fluctuating, elusive truth. The discovery of duration, luckily, teaches us to dilate ourselves by intuition, to found philosophy on a method this time really positive, to apprehend life and movement in themselves, and Bergson's philosophy will gradually lead humanity, by an "exchange of impressions,"[1] to transcend itself in order to fuse again into the whole. That, or just about that, is what Bergsonians full of ardour (but certainly less discreet than their master) are busy spreading in our minds. We are not without reason for questioning these claims.

What is new in Bergsonian philosophy is the pure becoming of Heraclitus, that river in which one never bathes twice because one drowns in it the first time, and which after having received a few tributaries from Schopenhauer and Schelling, now threatens to inundate us. What is new is also the perpetual refusal to recognize the intellect and being, and an invincible aversion, so curiously manifested by William James, for analytical concepts, for that great malefactor Socrates, for Aristotle, in short for the natural metaphysics of the human mind, which these Bergsonian philosophers look upon as the illusion *par excellence* and strive to relegate to the *Greek antiquities,* without understanding to what intention, to what providential preparation Greek thought responded.

An anti-intellectualist philosophy cannot form *disciples* properly speaking, for a disciple is one whose *intellect,* set in action by a doctrine received, thinks it anew on its own account; *ideas* alone are communicated; impres-

[1] *Creative Evolution,* p. 192.

sions, sensations and intuitive sympathies can only be individual. Bergsonism can therefore have only propagators more or less faithful to the "current of thought" of their master and who repeat more or less well the metaphors they have learned.

It would be very unfair to impute to Bergson all that is said in his name. We may nevertheless wonder whether we do not find a normal development of certain aspects of his doctrine, either in the religious conceptions of Le Roy, who considers the idea of a first cause to be an "idol of deduction," or in that sort of happy cheerfulness with which William James boasts of his "inner catastrophe," and declares that "for my own part, I finally found myself compelled to *give up the logic,* fairly, squarely and irrevocably,"[1] an affirmation he would never otherwise have dared to enunciate "without the confidence," as he said, "which being able to lean on Bergson's authority gives me";[2] or in Jean Weber's sad efforts at paradox, already so out-of-date, when he wrote: "Morality, in taking its position on the terrain where immediate and living invention continually gushes forth, in posing as the most insolent encroachment of the world of intellect upon spontaneity, was destined to be constantly contradicted by that undeniable reality of dynamism and creation which our activity is [. . .]. Against these moralities of ideas we shall outline the morality, or rather the *amorality of the fact* [. . .]. We call good that which has triumphed [. . .]. Success, provided it be implacable and cruel, provided the vanquished is well vanquished, destroyed, hopelessly annihilated, success justifies everything [. . .]. The sinner who repents [. . .] was unworthy to sin, etc."[3]

As to the possible exaggerated statements of Bergsonism, we shall allude to only one of them here, because of the philosophical lesson it provides.— When we hear futurist painters asseverating: "They persist in painting the immobile, the frozen and all the static states of nature [. . .] With absolutely futuristic points of view we, on the contrary, seek a style expressing movement, which has never been tried before.—Far from basing our work upon the example of the Greeks and the Ancients, we never cease to exalt individual intuition."[4]—"The gesture we wish to reproduce on canvas will no longer be a *fixed instant* of universal dynamism. It will be nothing short of *dynamic sensation* itself. For everything moves, everything runs, everything is rapidly transformed [. . .]. Thus it is that a running horse has not four

[1] *A Pluralistic Universe,* p. 212.

[2] *Ibid.,* p. 215.

[3] *Rev. de Métaph. et de Mor.,* 1894, pp. 549–560.

[4] *Déclaration* by Messrs. Puccioni, Carrà, Russolo, Balla and Severini, in the foreword of the catalogue of their exposition at Bernheim's (February 1912), p. 2.—My very good friend, Gino Severini, who is indeed a most honest and scrupulous artist, and whose horizon has greatly broadened since then, will pardon this allusion to his early struggles. Moreover, it was here a question of the theories of the futurists rather than of their painting, which should naturally be judged on another plane.

feet but twenty, and their movements are triangular. . . .—Space no longer exists. In fact, the cobblestone, drenched under the rain, by the brilliance of the street lights seems to recede and grow immensely hollow, as deep as the center of the earth [. . .]. Our bodies enter the sofas on which we sit, and the sofas enter into us. The bus springs forward into the houses it passes and in their turn the houses rush at the bus and fuse with it,"*—when the simple public hear the futurists express themselves with such felicitous grace, why are they more joyously surprised than when they hear Le Roy say that the principle of non-contradiction is not as universal and necessary as was thought, that axioms and categories, everything in fact becomes, everything evolves; or Bergson declare that there are changes but not things which change, that movement does not imply a mobile, and that the real is pure becoming? Because the futurist ideology offends sense perception and the testimony of our eyes. Whereas Bergsonian philosophy offends intelligence and ruins the principles of reason.

This philosophy, considered as a metaphysical system, is in short a philosophy of a moment. It has tackled the philosophical problem in terms of mechanicism, the problem of the world in terms of Spencerian evolutionism, the problem of the soul in terms of psycho-physical parallelism, the problem of freedom in terms of associationist psychology. And in order to refute these errors it has chosen to abandon being and the intellect. But being is the only thing that endures.

It is even probable that the greater the present vogue for Bergsonism is, the keener will be the reaction—and the more unjust. For no one should forget that at a particularly difficult period Bergson was the only one among the wise ones of this world victoriously to attack agnosticism, Kantianism, and the silly, narrow positivism which reigned unchallenged. In so doing, whatever he may have said of the intellect, he has served intelligence and truth. And many who have come out of the darkness of official atheism owe this to him and to the desire for truth that permeates and animates his teaching. Therefore, even if a just defence of intellectual and metaphysical values requires criticism of Bergsonism—and Catholic philosophers, especially Garrigou-Lagrange[1] and de Tonquédec,[2] have not failed to make such a defence —nevertheless the bitter zeal and deliberate disparagement in Julien Benda's book are intolerable.[3]

* Ibid., pp. 16–19.

[1] Le Sens Commun, la Philosophie de l'être et les formules dogmatiques (Paris, Beauchesne, 1909; 3rd. edition, Desclée-de-Brouwer); and the works by the same author already quoted.

[2] Dieu dans l'Évolution Creatrice (Beauchesne, 1913); Études, articles already quoted; La Notion de vérité dans la philosophie nouvelle (Beauchesne, 1908). Cf. the well-documented article by Leslie J. Walker (Revue de Philosophie, Sept.–Oct., 1911) on "Évolutionisme dans la théorie de la connaissance et de la vérité."

[3] Le Bergsonisme ou une philosophie de la mobilité (Paris, Mercure de France, 1912).

Few philosophers devote to the composition of their works as scrupulous a consciousness and as patient a labour as Bergson, and from this point of view his work represents an enormous effort. But the subtlety and penetration of his thought, his love for truth, the quest for reality immediately perceived, the feeling for things of the soul, his esteem for the spontaneous and the living, the desire for a truly disinterested philosophy in true conformity with the real, truly plunged into the absolute, all these gifts which so completely predisposed Bergson to understand and love Christian philosophy also show us the powerlessness of human effort to attain its noblest end when from the outset it has fallen short of some primordial condition assigned by reality. "He that is a searcher of majesty shall be overwhelmed by glory."[1] What shall be said of philosophers who wish to reach truth by despising intellect, and find something better than the light which enlightens every man coming into this world? It is not the overwhelming power of glory, it is the fascination of change without substance which will end the adventure.

[1] *Proverbs*, xxv, 27.

THIRD SECTION

THE TWO BERGSONISMS

Chapter Thirteen

BERGSONISM OF FACT AND BERGSONISM
OF INTENTION

It is a fact of current observation that the doctrine of a philosopher often has a quite different significance according to whether one studies it in disciples or tries to understand its genesis in the mind of the master. This fact is not always imputable to the lack of intelligence in the disciples, to the methodical and mechanical use of formulae which they have not thought out for themselves; it sometimes requires a more profound interpretation. For the doctrine of a philosopher, as soon as it is expressed and systematized, takes on a character of objectivity, impersonality, universality, which definitively separates it from the intellectual tendencies, the desires, the inner convictions and also from the hesitations and anxieties, in short, from the individual history of him who conceived it. It has left, so to speak, the atmosphere and the milieu in which it was born, henceforth to make its way alone in the world. From then on it can no longer be judged except in its relation to immutable and universal truth, and that is how its essential theses and intrinsic meaning will be determined. On the other hand, if it were given us to divine it in the mind where it was formed and nourished we should doubtless see it take shape along very different lines, and it is on the basis of the spiritual activity of the philosopher, of the special difficulties he had to surmount, of the errors in which he at first found himself involved and against which he directed his efforts,—in short, of the most intimate aspirations of his mind and heart that we must judge it and determine its principal aspects as well as its profound tendencies. All these things, it is true, are particular, contingent and perishable. They will die with him whose history they relate: *exibit spiritus ejus, et revertetur in terram suam.* That is why they cannot directly serve either pure science or the universal good of men's minds. On the other hand they have an absorbing interest for us when we seek to discern the real affinities of a richly endowed intelligence, and its actual tendencies.

If we take this point of view and try to interpret Bergson's thought, albeit

285

in a wholly hypothetical and schematic fashion,—to claim anything more would be over-bold—taking care to use the indications he gives us in his work itself and in additional explanatory sources such as his letters to de Tonquédec[1] or his lectures at Oxford,[2] or again his lecture on the soul and the body,[3] we shall doubtless be led to conclusions very much like the following. The early intellectual formation and early studies of Bergson followed rather closely upon the official triumph, celebrated in the 60's and 70's, of atheism and materialism in European thought. Intellectual pride and so-called positive science were then in the full blaze of their glory. Under the influence of Comte, Littré, Renan, everything was expected from the future of science and the reign of the scientists. Berthelot was shining in the first rays of that apotheosis. Darwin was explaining the origin of the species and the descent of man; Spencer was integrating the universe, Taine was demonstrating the mechanics of the intellect, Cournot had sketched the synthesis of all the sciences. How could one help but abandon oneself to this dizziness of human wisdom, to this "mechanistic intoxication," as Bergson later said? It is therefore reasonable to believe that Bergson was initiated into philosophy by an exclusively scientific culture and that it was to the problems of physico-mathematical mechanicism that he first turned his attention.

But no doubt he soon perceived the inanity of mechanicism; he saw that mathematical physics, far from getting to the bottom of all reality, merely gives us a more or less arbitrary image constructed on measurement relations and that so-called scientific positivism is only a crude agglomeration of more or less unconscious metaphysical prejudices, and that so enormous an illusion must implicate the responsibility of the whole of modern philosophy and even perhaps have its deeper causes in certain general errors into which the human intellect naturally runs the risk of falling. Thus led almost forcibly to seek the reality unrecognized by mechanicism,—not, it is true, in the philosophy of being (the taste for experiments, the *taste of the sense,* which saturates our age, inspires many minds even today with an invincible prejudicial distrust of this philosophy)—but in an order of facts which does not admit of mathematical methods, Bergson had to approach the study of psychology. Then he was to recognize, by a more profound study of experimental data, the radical insufficiency of the ideas our scholars ordinarily form of the relations between the physical and the moral. He was to conclude successively against "psycho-physical parallelism" and in favour of the reality

---

[1] *Études,* February 20, 1912. J. de Tonquédec, *M. Bergson est-il Moniste?*

[2] *La Perception du Changement,* lectures given at the University of Oxford May 26 and 27, 1911, London, Henry Frowde, pp. 36–37. ("The Perception of Change," in *Creative Mind,* pp. 153–186.)

[3] Lecture given as one of those organized by the review *Foi et Vie* and published in that review (December 1912 and January 1913); reproduced in *L'Énergie spirituelle,* pp. 31–63.

of free will, the distinction between spirit and matter, the existence of a difference "of nature" between man and animals, a certain substantiality of the soul and even perhaps its immortality; and thus, finally, he was to arrive at problems of general metaphysics and almost of theodicy, probably inclining toward the recognition of a personal God and allowing gradually to come to light the religious anxieties and the needs of the spiritual life of a soul instinctively inclined to contemplation, but whose intellectual advance had been made, up to then, on merely scientific soil.

Such, in a way, would be the curve formed by Bergson's thought, and perhaps the points emphasized in this very brief sketch indicate, with regard to the individual data mentioned above, the essential aspects of the Bergsonian doctrine. Perhaps the meaning of this doctrine, interpreted subjectively, seen "from within," is in conformity with such a spiritual direction, with such an orientation, made constantly more definite, toward the light.

Is it necessary to recall how different the significance of Bergsonism is from the other point of view, from the wholly objective point of view of the doctrine judged in itself, perceived "from without" as far as the mind which conceived it is concerned, but "from within" with regard to its intrinsic philosophical value?[1] Let us but indicate here that, in order to avoid mechanism, Bergson resolves to sacrifice the intellect and to sacrifice being; that he contradictorily identifies substance and movement, making of time that flows the very stuff of things, and that he denies reason an authentic power of attaining the true (outside the realm of mathematical physics); that he thus in spite of himself destroys truth at its root and that the very spiritual theses he wishes to restore lose both their solidity and their proper significance in his doctrine. For freedom is confused with contingency or with spontaneity; the unity of the human compound is endangered without the essential distinction between body and soul being established; man, contrary to what Bergson thinks he is proving, can differ only in degree from the other vertebrates, the immortality of the soul is only a sort of physical perpetuation of the vital impulse; there is no creation, properly so-called, no real distinction between bodies, no absolute difference between God and the world; divine nature and the divine attributes become empty words. In general, only the words are kept, their intellectual content is dissipated, replaced by fleeting images. To what cause are we to ascribe this nihilism which most certainly runs against the intentions of the philosopher himself? It seems that Bergson has too readily accepted the conclusion of modern philosophy, granting its assertion that intellect tends of itself toward mechanism and that metaphysical knowledge is only a mirage; that he has thus deprived himself of both the indispensable organ and the indispensable technique, and that henceforth

---

[1] See moreover the first and second sections.

he could only gropingly advance toward the light which he loved, of which he had the presentiment, but which he did not see. This would explain the strangely contingent character of his doctrine, which seems to have at the most crucial moments a choice between opposite directions: might it not have turned toward explicit monism as easily as toward a dualism more apparent moreover than real? toward a metaphysics of creation properly so-called as easily as toward a theory of hypostasized evolution? toward an avowed pantheism as easily as toward a theism which, at that, is but slightly based on reason? However that may be, the essential theses of Bergsonism and its real significance, the metaphysical principles which fix it in the universe of thought, are in only too manifest and irreducible opposition to the verities of the *philosophia perennis.*

And yet, be it noted, if we were to return to the point of view mentioned at the beginning of this chapter, if we were to try to envisage the Bergsonian doctrine, not in itself but in relation to the particular and contingent conditions of its conception, then these objectively fundamental principles would appear rather as consequences, as external necessities, as servitudes so to speak, to which the philosopher is forced to resign himself; and the principles of the doctrine, from this point of view, would be found rather in a very clear intuition of the vanity of mechanicist materialism and in a persevering tendency toward the philosophy of life and the spirit. Thus one is led to distinguish two Bergsonisms, a Bergsonism of fact and a Bergsonism of intention, not absolutely incompatible (at least as long as the second remains as a simple intention), but truly different and, in reality, contrary in meaning, for the first tends to tear down what the second desires to build up.

Chapter Fourteen

BERGSONISM OF INTENTION
AND THOMISM

Certainly few systems are as contrary in their principles and in their essential results as Bergsonian mobilism and scholastic doctrine. It is nevertheless not difficult to perceive strange points of agreement between these two philosophies to the extent that many of Bergson's theses might be presented as refractions, and (with no desire on our part to qualify their value in using the word) as quite unexpected *deformations* of certain Thomist theses. It would be impossible to make them coincide with Thomism or to make them Thomist without completely recasting them. And yet they sketch, in a confusion of discordances, *something* of what is found fully affirmed in Thomism; flitting and disjointed images perceived through intelligible fluids of capricious densities . . . We can indicate here only some of these fugitive analogies and these contrasts.

Let us admit for the moment that the criticism of the idea of 'nothingness'[1] bears in fact, as Bergson insists, only on being as Spinoza conceives it.[2] Does it not then amount to recognizing the infinite difference which separates being *a se* from being by participation, and the absurdity of seeking a cause for the One Whose essence is His very act of existing? It thus implies the necessity of admitting a transcendent cause for everything whose being is merely a participated being. But in this case the criticism of the idea of 'nothingness,' it seems useless to point out, would have to undergo strange modifications.

Bergson takes care, at the beginning of *Creative Evolution,* to note the purely hypothetical character of the transformist theory. He accepted it only because of a kind of scientific scruple and because no other language, in the

---

[1] Cf. *Creative Evolution,* pp. 275–299.—*Études,* no. quoted, pp. 515–516.

[2] But it seems, let us note once more, that for the author of *Creative Evolution,* any philosopher who does not think as a Bergsonian is obliged to think like Spinoza, so that this concession is more apparent than real.

present state of science, seemed to him to be more appropriate. Let us suppose then that common sense,—happening to notice that no one can give what he has not,—and that science, understanding that infinitely small variations can never accumulate and preserve themselves in such a way as to create a new type and that sudden harmonic variations, if they could, (according to the capacities of nature) go beyond the limits of the (real) species, would have destroyed any possibility of a systematic classification of living organisms,—agree to reject, I do not say any evolutionist hypothesis, I say at least that of a descent in which the creative influx of the first Cause would not specially intervene. To tell the truth, we cannot imagine what would then become of creative evolution, the genesis of intelligence, the genesis of matter, etc. We perceive only the necessity for bringing back to the simple plane of *history*—which does not make superfluous but *supposes* natures and essences —the genealogical relationship of living forms and for admitting a transcendent and creative Intelligence, immutable in itself and the supreme cause of all evolution as well as of being of things, and of whose simplicity the multiplicity and movement of created nature are only a faint image. It seems also that the "vital impulse," considered at least within the limits of a specific phylum (a real species) could no longer be anything but a sort of defective metaphor for designating the sóul, the substantial form,—the first principle of being and of action,—of living bodies; while this pure distension, interruption, deficiency which, according to Bergson, constitutes extensive matter would become another defective metaphor for designating matter properly so-called, the principle of pure passivity.

If we now go on to the criticism of the concept and of analysis, and if we forcibly reduce it to a criticism of a certain perverse use of the concept and of analysis, it becomes, as we pointed out above,[1] perfectly consonant with the principles of traditional philosophy. Yet in this case we shall indeed have to abandon without regret the very foundations of Bergsonian anti-intellectualism.

Bergson affirms that there is no place in psychology for quantity and for number. In so far as this thesis tells against associationism and those who treat states of consciousness as material magnitudes, it is in full accord with the doctrine of Saint Thomas, who tells us that spiritual things do not follow either the law of mathematical number or of quantity properly so-called. But Saint Thomas adds that we must recognize, even for pure spirits, a transcendental multiplicity and a quantity of virtue (intensive quantity, qualitative *intention* and *diminution*), which have nothing in common with space;[2]

---

[1] See above, *supra*, pp. 102–104 and 136–138.

[2] *Summa theol.*, I^a, q. 48, a. 4; I^a II^ae, q. 52, a. 2; II^a II^ae, q. 24, a. 5; cf. the dissertations of the theologians *De augmento habitum* (John of Saint Thomas, *Curs. theol. de Passionibus et Habitibus*, *Vivès*, t. VI, disp. xiii, a. 5, 6 and 7; Salmenti censes, t. XII, tract. XIX, disp. v and vi).

while in Bergsonian philosophy, all real distinction, all determinate quality, all augmentation or diminution of intensity finally disappear from the soul whose fluid continuity henceforth completely eludes the intellect.

To try to make the whole of reality enter into the frameworks of a mathematical knowledge is, for Bergson as for Saint Thomas, perfectly meaningless. But for the former mathematical knowledge is the very type toward which intellect tends; on the contrary, Saint Thomas tells us, that mathematical knowledge cannot fully satisfy intellect, for it gives us only one *aspect* of things, even of material things, which it studies neither in their efficient cause nor in their being;* the achieved type of science is metaphysics, not mathematics.

Bergson insists upon the fact that there is novelty in the world, and that a universal mathematics capable of foreseeing the state of any part of the universe at any moment whatsoever is, even for a superhuman spirit, a pure figment of the imagination. That is an eminently Thomistic thesis; for the future is not *ready-made* in the present; created causes have indeed an activity proper, all change implies the birth or disappearance of something real, and in all substantial change a really new form is "educed" (or drawn) from the passive potentiality of matter.[1] As to the foreseeing of futures, there is in things to come, not to mention events which may depend on free will, a whole region of radical contingency into which the eyes of the Angels themselves cannot penetrate.[2]—Which does not in the least mean that there is only becoming, or that becoming is incompatible with the law of causality, or that it is false that future things,—necessary, contingent or free,—are all naked before the eternal regard of God, Who knows not only created effects in their created causes (where free acts cannot be known in advance), but Who sees all things in His own essence and in His decrees, such as they are in themselves and in their "presentness."

Now here is perhaps a more unexpected point at which they meet: the scholastics agree with Bergson in admitting a certain *connaturality* between human intellect and material things. But for Bergson human intellect is

---

* Cf. *Summa theol.*, Iᵃ, q. 44, a. 1, *ad* 3.

1 The theory of the *eduction* of substantial forms under the action of efficient cause in no way signifies that these forms exist ready made ahead of time, are already virtually outlined in matter. That is a misconception absolutely incompatible with the notion of *passive potentiality* and with the notion of *primary matter;* but it is one that is only too frequently met with among modern philosophers (and in Bergson himself) when they speak of Aristotle. Substantial forms are no more "prefigured," "ready-made ahead of time" in matter than an accidental form, as that of a statue for example, is "prefigured" in the marble before the sculptor's action.—Let us also note that *what is* properly and what, in substantial transformations, is properly engendered, produced, is the new *compound* (since matter and substantial form are not properly *beings,* but only *principles* of being).—Save for the human soul, which is a substance, and which is *made out of nothing,* created, to state it properly. See *supra,* pp. 244–246.

2 Cf. *Summa theol.*, Iᵃ, q. 57, a. 3. Cf. *supra,* pp. 50–51.

only an instrument manufactured by evolution in order to permit man to act upon inert matter and manipulate solids, and is naturally incapable of understanding life. Whereas for Saint Thomas the intellect is an immaterial power, ordered, as intellect, to being itself, and to the extent that it is human, to the being of material things. If it can know spiritual natures only by analogy, it nevertheless tends of itself to know them, and if the things whose essential principles it can attain are those in which form is united to a material principle, the most perfect type of these things is found in life, not in the inorganic. So that philosophy, if it is faithful to the intellect, will orient itself, not toward geometry, but toward the life supreme.[3]

It is because of this innate adaptation of the human intellect to compound natures that we transfer to spiritual things names borrowed first from corporal things; that our intellect understands nothing actually without turning toward sense-images; and that all sorts of images of sensible and spatial things always subtend the work of human thought.—This, however, does not mean that the idea of space vitiates all our judgments and that, on the other hand, the philosopher has to make it his duty to use images rather than ideas!

Bergson, like the scholastics, thinks that the perception of sensible qualities really gives us something of the objects. But the scholastics blame him for making separate bodies immediately melt into a "universal interaction" where the consciousness of the subject runs the similar risk of drowning.

For Bergson, as for Saint Thomas, knowledge, if it attains the absolute, must be a vital act which establishes a sympathy, a communication, a real assimilation between the object and the subject. But he ascribes this act to an intuition foreign to intellect, contrary to our nature, an intuition which absorbs the spirit in the materiality of the object. Saint Thomas on the contrary teaches that by intellectual perception it is the object itself which, thanks to "abstraction," being present in the understanding, makes it produce like a common fruit of life the mental word (*verbum mentis*) and thus finds itself assimilated to the immateriality of intelligence. The latter then *becomes* the object in a perfectly vital way.

Like the scholastics[1] Bergson wishes to restore the authority of common sense and of spontaneous consciousness. He also seeks exactly to evaluate what credit should be given to rational knowledge and to find the proper balance between the pride and the despair of human reason. But what he especially succeeds in doing is equally to endanger rational knowledge and common sense: neither will ever admit that change is being. He cuts the mind into two parts, imputing a natural tendency toward illusion, that is to say toward

---

[3] The philosophy of nature is thus oriented first of all toward the life of the human being and the human soul; metaphysics toward the divine life of creative Intelligence.

[1] Cf. R. Garrigou-Lagrange, *Le Sens commun, la Philosophie de l'être et les Formules dogmatiques;* Kleutgen, *la Philosophie scolastique,* t. I, iii, chap. i, ii.

the disorder of the mind, to the "intellect," while he fixes no limit to the ambitions of "intuition."—How much more discreet and how much wiser is the teaching of the scholastics! For them, since the intellect is a participated resemblance of the increate Light and since the apprehension of truth is the very reason for the human being's organization, it is not surprising that man should reach by instinct, by the spontaneous play of his native faculties, the knowledge of the principal verities which technical reflection establishes for its part scientifically, with greater perfection but more laboriously. There is nothing in the mind, just as there is nothing in the world, which tends of its own accord toward evil. The faculty by which we know the being of things is one; it cannot be divided. Ordered to the universal, it is pre-eminently the quality which marks a difference in nature between man and brute. Proportioned to the being of man, bound up with the functioning of a multiplicity of inferior faculties and, as it were, blinded when upon it falls the brilliance of the most luminous truths, it occupies the lowest degree among intelligences; but by nature it tends toward its good, toward truth. Discursive, forced by its very imperfection to go forward step by step, its horizon is limited; it is subject to error, anything can cause it to fall. And finally, deprived by the original Fall, of the free gifts which sustained it in rectitude, bewildered by the concupiscence which wounds the soul in which it resides, weakened, enslaved, condemned to suffering, it is exposed by the disorder which has been in our nature since the time of Adam, to illusions, lapses and perversions a great deal worse than might have occurred in the state of pure nature, but always accidental. Thus it is that an unimaginable grandeur and misery meet in it without destroying its unity. Efforts contrary to nature can only plunge it into darkness, but it is fit to receive the divine consummation of grace which makes it capable of a supernatural activity and leads it, over and beyond time, to the beatific vision.

And last of all, even the Bergsonian theory of duration presents from a certain aspect scholastic affinities. It is in fact easy to see that this *duration* is nothing but the passing from being in potency to being in act. It is in this movement, in this passing, that Bergson tries to install his *intuition;* perfectly well aware that if philosophy posits everything as in act, it condemns itself to insuperable contradictions, he nevertheless refuses,—perhaps because it is of a conceptual order,—the key to all metaphysics, the Aristotelian distinction between potency and act. That being the case, he clearly recognizes the irreducible reality of becoming and movement, but confuses movement with essence and reduces everything to nothingness by this supreme contradiction.

We thought we discerned in Bergson's philosophy two different aspects which might be called Bergsonism of fact and Bergsonism of intention. The first, (alone important if we consider the doctrine in itself and in its metaphysical principles, and if we examine where it takes those minds who abandon themselves to its inner logic), leads to an art of approaching the truth as if in a dream-state paid for by a sort of intellectual nihilism. We do not doubt that this is quite contrary to the philosopher's intentions and to the natural aspirations, the original impulse of his thought. If we try to divine the intellectual genesis of Bergsonian philosophy, not only does it present itself as an effort to avoid the empty formulae of modern dogmatism and to reconstruct a spiritualist metaphysic; but, in addition, most of its theses appear in a way to be attempts (attempts it is true, which soon swerve out of line) at Thomist affirmations. The final reason for this is no doubt explained by the fact that Bergsonian philosophy operates with the intellect not according to its proper and properly speculative mode, but according, as it were, to the rather poetic mode which becomes it when it immerses itself in imaginative activity to produce a whole world of forms; thus employed in philosophy, the intellect obtains a sense imitation of intellection, a sort of extraordinarily refined *cogitative* which cannot grasp the truth but which perceives its fleeting shadow. However that may be, if ever one tried to isolate and liberate this *Bergsonism of intention* we are now discussing, it seems very likely, according to all the indications we have been able to single out, that if it became actual it would release and order its potencies in the great wisdom of Thomas Aquinas.

Chapter Fifteen

AT THE LIMITS OF PHILOSOPHY

If it is true that Bergson's attention is henceforth to bear more and more upon theodicy (after having passed perhaps through the stages of ethics), one might well wonder toward what solutions he will prefer to direct himself. Judging by the slight indications he has given us as to his intentions we may assume that he will seek above all to restore the great affirmations of spiritualist philosophy; but judging by the objective principles of his doctrine it is to be feared that these affirmations will find themselves "restored" on such shaky foundations that they will soon be engulfed in the old Heraclitean torrent. It is not that we can foresee the doctrines of so rich and supple a mind as we can those of an *a priori* reasoner who automatically draws from his theory an indefinite number of conclusions. It is only that no one can avoid the consequences of the metaphysical first principles of a doctrine.

The questions concerning divine things occupy in philosophy, from this point of view, a dangerously privileged position. On the one hand, they are at the limit and the summit of our knowledge; so that if there is in our knowledge any principle of illusion, any basic metaphysical error, it is impossible for them not to be vitiated in a very special and, if one may say so, a very eminent way. On the other hand, they bear upon the source and the sovereignly primary reason of all being; so that if a philosopher really presupposes atheism, the knowledge he will have of being, constituting itself in the lack of what assures the reality and order of things, will not avoid lack of balance and illusion. There is no contradiction in thus placing the knowledge of God at the crown and the base of our knowledge; for it is at the crown with the absolute certitude of *science,* and it is at the base with the absolute certitude (but in an imperfect mode) of *common sense.* In its exploration of the truth, philosophical knowledge is at no time obliged to have recourse to the authority of common sense as to a demonstrative principle (that is what the Scots did not see); but the certitudes of common sense constitute for the activities of philosophical thought a truly indispensable atmosphere because the particular investigations of the philosopher, in order to maintain a perfect balance, need to be related to the general system of great truths naturally perceived by common sense, which are in our knowledge a very simple projection, as it were, of the very order of things. And by the same token, since it is the same intelligence which knows spontaneously by common sense and methodically by philosophical knowledge, if we begin by warping it so much that it doubts what is easiest, how can it help going astray in what is most difficult? So, to sweep away the certitudes of common sense in the name of science is just about as reasonable as to abandon the use of one's eyes because one has a telescope. From this point of view, a good many philosophical systems seem like the frenzy of savants.

In any case, let us simply remember here that according to the testimony of the Fathers of the Church and of the theologians, if science (the science *par excellence,* metaphysics) in order to demonstrate by its technical procedure the existence of God, has to begin by a sort of methodical doubt, common sense on the contrary, spontaneous reason, *le bon sens,* whatever you wish to call it, naturally adheres with such strength to that truth that we cannot really doubt it without doing violence to a testimony present within us; this spontaneous knowledge is not intuitive, but it is truly a *dowry of nature,* it is produced ἐμφύτως καὶ ἀδιδάκτως in the mind of man, at the mere sight of creation, and with the ordinary assistance that God gives us in the order of nature.[1]

Bergson is no doubt far from professing atheism: has he not written that his criticism of the idea of "nothingness" held only against Spinoza and that even in *Creative Evolution* he thought he had established the existence of a God creative and transcendent?[2] But we cannot forget that this philosophy developed and that it constituted its principles in that ignorance, or that real doubt, of the existence of God which already supposes a dimming of the light within us and an act of consent to the greatest deviation of human knowledge. Now, by the progress of scientific reflection it brushes atheism aside; but the false principles it adopted still remain in it. In order to end in a consistent theodicy it would have to renew itself from first to last. Such a transformation is highly improbable; for there is no reason why the problems of theodicy should be more likely than any others to make Bergson change the foundations of his system.

---

1 Cf. Kleutgen, *Theologie der Vorzeit,* t. II, pp. 33 ff.; Clement of Alexandria, *Strom.,* V, chap. xvi; Saint Thomas, *Opusc. LXX sup. Boet. de Trin.:* "Dei cognitio nobis innata dicitur esse, inquantum per principia nobis innata de facili percipere possumus Deum esse." For that, although it is a question of a purely natural knowledge, "requiritur tamen divina operatio; praeter operationem enim qua Deus naturas rerum instituit, singulis formas et virtutes proprias tribuens, quibus possent suas operationes exercere, operatur etiam in rebus opera providentiae, omnium rerum virtutes ad actus proprios dirigendo et movendo."

2 *Études,* n⁰ quoted, pp. 515–516.

In an altogether different manner however,—assuming that the philosopher is, to the end, heedful to reason,—everything might be called into question again.

For we are at a unique moment in the development of a doctrine. Attacking the study of divine things the philosopher arrives at the limit of philosophy. He becomes anxious to know God, and the relations of man to God. But reason demands—and Bergson is faithful to this method—that before coming to a decision on a question we should first surround ourselves with all the accounts, all the inquiries, all the positive documents which can enlighten us. Now, if God has spoken, are we going to disregard His testimony and neglect such a *document? Deum nemo vidit unquam: unigenitus Filius, qui est in sinu Patris, ipse enarravit.*[1]

It is, of course, understood that solely by its own power human reason is capable of recognizing both the existence of God and several of the verities concerning Him. But if a very small number of these truths are easily accessible to spontaneous reason, others can be for it an occasion for errors that are just as easy; and for reflective reason, which wishes methodically to scrutinize the causes of things and which tends to systematize everything, all these truths are very difficult to attain and very difficult to preserve intact. How can we help fearing to go astray when error is so easy? And why should a philosopher not have many more fears than anyone else? Does he not know the sad story of the many ways in which simple and sane common sense can be impaired by ideological cultivation? Is he ever sure that the long habit of a certain system as well as the inevitable friction due to many different kinds of errors has not caused a distortion or attenuation of the natural vigour of his reason? Does he not himself in fact, especially if he approaches these supreme problems only in a roundabout way, know better than anyone else the hesitation of his thought? If God has told us about Himself it is indispensable for us to have recourse to His testimony, even for the problems which philosophy is capable—but at what risk!—of solving by itself alone.

I know, of course, that in doing this the philosopher must cast off his professional attitude and that *long pedant's gown* in which we picture Aristotle and Plato. But as a matter of fact it is no longer a question of philosophizing. It is a question of living or dying. *Prius vivere.* You glimpse the existence of a personal God. It is not the God of the learned; it is a living and active God; it is the God of the whole man. Can you continue to deal with Him as a theorist does with an idea, and not as a man with his Lord? There are secrets which He alone can reveal. You yourself are one of these secrets. You would know your end and the means to attain it if you knew these secrets. But you

---

[1] "No man hath ever seen God: the only begotten Son, who is in the bosom of the Father, he hath declared him." *St. John,* I, 18.

will only know them if it pleases God to reveal them Himself.—Truly, philosophers play a strange game. They know very well that one thing alone counts, and that all their medley of subtle discussions relates to one single question: why are we born on this earth? And they also know that they will never be able to answer it. Nevertheless they continue sedately to amuse themselves. Do they not see that people come to them from all points of the compass, not with a desire to partake of their subtlety but because they hope to receive from them one word of life? If they have such words why do they not cry them from the housetops, asking their disciples to give, if necessary, their very blood for them? If they have no such words why do they allow people to believe they will receive from them something which they cannot give? For mercy's sake, if ever God has spoken, if in some place in the world, were it on the gibbet of one crucified, He has sealed His truth, tell us; that is what you must teach. Or are you indeed masters in Israël only to be ignorant of these things? The moment it is a question of divine things and our salvation, the question to be answered first is the one which comes before everything else: is there a Revelation?

Thus it is that reason leads the philosopher to a living person greater than himself, Whose name is ineffable. And certainly, once having reached this point he will be able to learn enough to renew his science from top to bottom. But will the philosopher follow reason to the very end?

One thing is evident, we cannot find God without God, and God reveals Himself only to those who seek Him, not through a certain curiosity of the intellect, but with their whole heart, and as the sovereignly desirable good of their whole being. That at least is true of the knowledge of things divine as procured by the first theological virtue. A philosopher or an historian may, therefore, by an impeccable apologetic demonstration, conclude with certainty in favour of the reality of the fact of Revelation. If, in addition, grace does not come to move his heart he will forever remain incapable of making an act of faith. How could it be otherwise since the gift of faith is an essentially supernatural gift? That is why the demonstration by reason alone of the fact of revelation is useful and desirable only to the extent that it disposes the soul to receive the action of sanctifying grace.

Such a demonstration, moreover, rarely takes place by the forces of nature alone, and without at least some actual grace assisting the work of the mind. That is a fact worthy of retaining our attention. Among all the reasons one may advance for it, we shall mention only the following. The most general cause of philosophical errors consists, it seems, in a certain inversion of the order of the intellect to its goal, an inversion by which the intellect, instead of tending to conform to the real, tends, as far as it can, to conform the real to itself. It will not therefore admit any other realities than those it already knows. It challenges any proof other than those to which it is accustomed, it declares all things explainable solely by the data it already possesses. And thus it reduces the immensity of truth to a narrow region containing the already-known. This vice, to which the wise men of this world only too easily fall a prey, can only with great difficulty be avoided in matters directly accessible to human knowledge. If it were not so, would there be so many materialists, idealists, sensualists, critical philosophers, positivists, solipsists and scienticists? With greater reason then, if some day some exceptional *datum* requires us to admit, not this or that demonstrable truth, but a whole order of truths absolutely undemonstrable in themselves, is it likely that the poor intellect laden with human knowledge will have the strength to assent and that it will resist the temptation to believe that its knowledge is the measure of being, and that what man knows is all that is, or in other words, that there can be no other reality than nature? Not only can we not of ourselves have access to supernatural reality, but it is also utterly improbable that erudite reason, the reason of philosophers and savants, should by its own resources avoid the absurd presupposition of the impossibility of a properly supernatural order of things. In other words, from the real we naturally conclude the possible, and we take advantage of this to deny the possibility of what we have not experienced. So long as faith does not bring us into contact with the reality of the supernatural world, as does the sense with the material world, our intellect continues stupidly to deny the very possibility of such a world.

Consequently, any demonstration of the fact of Revelation will break against the iron wall of this prejudice, and only when liberated by grace will reason be in condition to recognize the whole scope of apologetic demonstration. Hence we can understand why this demonstration so rarely occurs, in fact, by natural forces alone.

The vice we are referring to here is nothing else than a certain self-sufficiency or pride of intellect; it flaunts itself now-a-days with an excessive impudence in people who call themselves intellectuals and who candidly reject, with a careless scorn, all that does not conform to the science of the laboratory or the university. And it is at its highest pitch in some fanatical positivists who have become really incapable of understanding anything but material systems made up of parts which are bound together mechanically. But when metaphysicians brush aside *a priori* the possibility of the supernatural order and of Revelation, and refuse with easy consciences and simply because they are philosophers to ask themselves seriously whether, yes or no, the Son of God came to proclaim the truth and die for us, they fall into the very same error, they yield to the same pride, they too presuppose and affirm implicitly the omniscience of their minds. That indeed for the wise men of this world is a sort of *philosophical veil* comparable to the terrible *velamen* that Saint

Paul saw on the faces of the Doctors of the Law. For a philosopher to turn to primary Truth, he, like any man, must not only triumph over his personal pride,—he must also tear off this blinding veil and triumph over the natural pride, if one may call it that, from which philosophy is suffering.

Hence, in all natural and human probability, there is no reason to think that any philosopher will ever undertake to follow reason to the point we have indicated.

And yet, it is not that truth hides itself so deeply or that the light is difficult to see. If the philosopher would stop poring over dry dust, if he would only raise his head, he would see an immense city of living stones, illuminating the whole horizon with its rays, a city whose brilliance resembles nothing seen on this earth. For twenty centuries, or rather, since Adam's day, the Church has been proclaiming the same doctrine and proving her supernatural mission by constantly producing miracles and constantly giving birth to saints. She teaches us today as of old, *sicut potestatem habens*. She promises men eternal life and joy beginning here below. There is not a syllable of the symbol of her faith which does not stream with the blood of martyrs, and she gives such love to those who live in her truth that their most burning desire is to die for her. Most certainly it would not be very difficult to verify the evidence of such an extraordinary testimony. And if it happened that one were to understand, in making that study, that He alone Who created intelligence can illuminate intelligence, it would not be very difficult to turn to this living God Whose existence one divines and Who, according to what the Catholic doctors affirm, always answers the prayer of men when it is humble, persevering, and when it asks for a thing that is useful for salvation. That would be less complicated and more profitable than piling up files of folk-lore and *völkerpsychologie,* or scrutinizing what is pathological and subconscious in "religious experience," or looking into dead documents and asking one's way of ten thousand blind men.

Whosoever asks shall receive, Christ says; whosoever seeks shall find, and to whomsoever knocks it shall be opened. But why, then, do so many philosophers not seek as they should? Probably because they insist on being the first to seek. In reality, it is not we who seek first; the one who knocks, and to whom the door is opened, is first He Who stands at the door of our heart: *ecce sto ad ostium, et pulso.* Without the initial gift of divine grace no one can ask, or seek, or knock;—no one can aspire to hide in the light and *to climb to the peak of supreme humility.* And thus, in a way, they alone seek who have already found.

SECOND PART

ESSAY OF APPRECIATION

Chapter Sixteen

THE METAPHYSICS OF BERGSON

The very title of this chapter raises a question and requires some sort of justification. Bergson was a born metaphysician; how otherwise could he have been a great philosopher and a great renovator of the mind? But would Bergson himself have been willing to say that he undertook a metaphysical life-work or that he propounded a metaphysical system for his contemporaries? I do not think so. In this there is both an indication of Bergson's admirable modesty—not, indeed, unaware of its own quality—and an effect of that unbounded, scrupulous *conscience* and extraordinarily lucid *consciousness* (I use both words—a psychological *consciousness,* awareness, of himself and a meticulous scientific *conscience*) by reason of which he held himself strictly within the results which he believed he was justified in expecting from his method, which is an experiential or *empirical* method, utilizing indeed the most intelligent and the most refined of empiricisms, but still at root empirical.

Here we are at the very outset, before we have even made a real beginning, at the heart of the matter. The whole is in every part, especially for a philosophy of a vital-organic and, as it were, biological variety (this, be it noted in passing, makes Bergson and Aristotle neighbors): we cannot take up one problem without all the others being also present. Let us hope, despite this, that we may develop the present discussion without going into everything at the same time and not without parcelling out our ideas in some suitably ordered sequence.

In the days when I, in company with the little group associated with Charles Péguy and Georges Sorel, enthusiastically followed Bergson's lectures at the Collège de France, what we looked for was the revelation of a new metaphysics, and it was that which the lecturer himself seemed to promise us.

This was not the case, in reality. Bergson did not give us that metaphysics; he never intended to do so. And for many among us that was a very vivid disappointment; it seemed to us that a promise on which we relied had not been kept.

When we look back on all this today, distance casts a new light on things. When Bergson revived the worth and dignity of metaphysics in the minds of his listeners, minds engaged to their sorrow by agnosticism or materialism, when he said, with an unforgettable emphasis, to those minds brought up in the most depressing pseudo-scientific relativism, "it is in the *absolute* that we live and move and have our being,"[1] it was enough that he should thus awaken in them a desire for metaphysics, the metaphysical *eros:* that was accomplishment enough. And nothing is perhaps more moving than that species of detachment with which he freely let that desire, once aroused, travel its own road, in the minds of everyone, and lead some to a metaphysics which was not his metaphysics, which was even directly opposed to his metaphysics, until there should be, on deeper terms, relating not so much to philosophic conceptualization as to the spiritual directives of philosophy, new meetings of the mind.

If Bergsonian philosophy never completely avowed the metaphysics it involved, and which it could have brought forth into the light of day, if it remained much more rigidly linked to the science of phenomena, and more dependent on the latter than its lively reaction against the pseudo-metaphysics of scientism would have led one to suppose, it was because that very reaction had been managed from its outset by a radical empiricism. It is with the very weapons of anti-metaphysical science—with experience, but an *experience* incomparably more true and more searching—that Bergson sought to overcome the false cult of scientific experience, the mechanistic and determinist experimentalism which a philosophy of vulgar simplification claimed to be necessary for modern science. In this way he hoped for the possibility of a philosophic method (to use his own words) "rigorously drawn from experience (internal and external)," and which "does not allow the assertion of a conclusion that in any way whatever goes beyond the empirical considerations on which it is based."[2] Here is a singularly bold declaration of integral empiricism.

Determined to remain rigidly faithful to the method thus defined, it would seem that Bergson was progressively drawn to foreswear the metaphysical in order more and more to fall back on the experimental. For one thing, what he expected from his philosophy was not the elaboration of a metaphysics which would be placed on a level in the scale of knowledge higher than experimental knowledge (thus, indeed, he objected when his philosophy was compared with metaphysical doctrines so elaborated and so *placed*); what he expected from his philosophy was that it make fertile the experi-

---

[1] These words were spoken by Bergson in his lectures at the Collège de France.
[2] Letter to the Reverend Father de Tonquédec (June 12, 1911), *Études,* 20 février 1912, p. 515.

mental sciences and that it even arouse the latter (especially the biological sciences) to certain new directions. For another thing (but I postpone discussion of this to my next chapter) he was to move not so much in the direction of a metaphysics as in the direction of a philosophy of morals and religion, precisely because there only could he find the experiential knowledge which he needed to follow, in accordance with the method he had once and for all adopted, the upward movement of his enquiries.

Yet it is clear that there is a metaphysics implied in Bergsonism. And even if it were only in the nature of *excursuses*, of what one might call marginal trials, Bergson could not but from time to time give his explicit attention to the principles of that metaphysics. It is with that metaphysics, in an attempt to extricate it as a whole and examine its value, that we shall here be concerned.

THE INTUITION OF DURATION

It is well to indicate first certain elements relating to the genesis of the Bergsonian metaphysics. What is truly central and primary in that genesis is the deepening of the sense of *duration*.

Let us recall the passage where Bergson himself supplies us with important and precise indications of the history of his thought. "In my opinion," he wrote to Harald Höffding, "any summary of my views will deform them as a whole and will, by that very fact, expose them to a host of objections, if it does not take as its starting point, and if it does not continually revert to, what I consider the very center of the doctrine: the intuition of duration. The representation of a multiplicity of 'reciprocal penetration,' altogether different from numerical multiplicity—the representation of a heterogeneous, qualitative, creative duration—was my point of departure, and the point to which I have constantly returned. It requires of the mind a very great effort, the breaking of many frames of reference, something like a new way of thinking (for that which is immediate is far from being that which is the easiest to perceive); but once you have attained that representation and possessed it in its *simple* form (which must not be confused with a reconstruction by concepts), you feel obliged to shift your point of view on reality; you see that the greatest difficulties have arisen from the fact that philosophers have always put time and space on the same line: you see that the greater number of those difficulties are eased or dispelled."[1]

Arising above all from a close study of modern science and modern physics, and perhaps brought about—if we are prone to believe certain evidences thereof—by the examination of the arguments of the Eleatics against movement, what, in this, has been the central discovery of Bergson? I am not

---

[1] Letter to Harald Höffding (in Höffding, *La Philosophie de Bergson*, Paris, Alcan, 1916, pp. 160–161).

thinking at the moment of the Bergsonian *theory* of duration, nor of the Bergsonian *theory* of the intuition of duration. I am thinking of that kernel of *genuine intellectual intuition* which was for Bergson a discovery of duration.

In discussing the central intuition from whence proceed the great philosophical doctrines and the intermediary "image" between the absolute simplicity of that intuition and the complexity of its conceptual interpretations, Bergson writes: "What first of all characterizes that image is the power of *negation* it carries in it. Confronted with currently accepted ideas, with theses which seemed self-evident, with assertions which had until then passed muster as scientific, it whispers in the philosopher's ear, *impossible!* Impossible even though data and reasoning would appear to urge you to believe that it is possible and real and sure. Impossible because a certain experience, confused perhaps but decisive, speaks to you by my voice; impossible because it is incompatible with the data that are alleged and the reasons given, and because therefore these data are wrongly observed, those reasonings false. . . . Later on [the philosopher] will be able to vary in what he affirms; he will not vary in what he denies. And if he varies in what he affirms, it will again be by virtue of the power of negation immanent in the intuition or in its image."[2]

Thus, according to Bergson himself, his basal intuition of duration above all carried with it a negation. And of what sort was that negation—so powerful and invincible? Real time *is not* the spatialized time of our physics; and this is true indeed, for the various times of the physicist are mathematical entities which are built up on complex patterns of spatio-temporal measurements, and which are doubtless based on real time, but are not that time. The latter is in the ontological, not the mathematical, order. And the negation in question goes much further. Not only is real time *not* the spatialized time of physico-mathematics; motion is *not* a scattering of positions succeeding and replacing each other; reality is *not* reducible to reconstruction worked out after the event, reality is *not* a reiteration of identical happenings, reality is *not* that concatenation of immobilities and of ready-made elements, without internal ontological substance or propensity or internal power of expansion, conceived by the mechanist.

Still there is not merely a negation, however strong, however important, however fruitful, in the intuition Bergson has had of duration. There is also a positive content in that intuition. (Herein I still do not accept that intuition in the conceptual form in which Bergson has thought it; but, by an abstractional procedure which I am well aware is not devoid of a certain presumption, I try to rediscover this intuition in so far as it has been an authen-

2 "L'Intuition Philosophique," *Revue de Métaphysique et de Morale*, 1911, pp. 810–811. (*La Pensée et le Mouvant*, Paris, 1934, pp. 138–139.)

tic intellectual intuition—in other words, within the very peripheries where, I believe, it evinces truth.) The positive content, then, of the experience under discussion seems to me to relate to the internal progress of the life of the psyche, or the lived movement, wherein, on a level deeper than that of consciousness our psychic states are fused in a potential multiplicity which is one nevertheless, and by which we feel that we are moving forward through time—that we endure while we change in a way which is really unfragmented, and yet which enriches us qualitatively and triumphs over the inertia of matter.

Here indeed is an experience of the concrete reality of *duration,* of *existence continuing itself* of our deep *psychic life,* in which is enfolded, implicitly present, the irreducible metaphysical value of the act of being. Let us have confidence in the light of metaphysical abstraction, let us not fear the extreme purification which abstractive or eidetic intuition involves, and which does not attenuate but rather concentrates into an absolutely crucial simplicity that which is most important in the real and that which before everything makes the real manifest. This experience of the lived duration of the soul will transfigure itself, will open out directly not only on duration, but on *existence,* or rather upon the actual *esse* in its pure consistence and its intelligible amplitude, will become the metaphysical intuition of this act: *to be.* This further step Bergson did not take. With all this intuition of psychic duration, faultless to the extent that it involved an authentic intellectual intuition, he did not himself grasp all the ontological content with which it was, and despite all would continue to be, pregnant; he did not express to himself that actuality and that generosity of being, and that creative abundance which permeates action and movement (and which indeed derives from the cause of being)—in short, everything ontological which his intuition in fact attained in the experience of psychic duration. On the contrary, he at once conceptualized his intuition in the *notion,* in the idea (to my mind equivocal and misleading) of that which it is proper to call, in an historical and systematic sense, *Bergsonian duration.*

INTUITION AND CONCEPTUALIZATION

Here we are face to face with a great—and a forbidding—mystery of intellectual life. There is no intuition *per modum cognitionis,* there is no intellectual intuition without concepts and conceptualization. And yet the intuition can be true and fruitful (indeed it is, to the extent that it is truly intuition, infallibly true and fruitful) and the conceptualization in which it finds expression and in which it takes place can be mistaken and illusory.

How can this be? Let us first of all remember that the intelligence sees by and in the concepts which it, in a living way, produces from its own depths. Everything in the way of concepts and ideal constructions that the intelligence—ceaselessly leading its insatiable hunger for reality over the whole extent of exterior and interior experience, the whole extent of truths already acquired, perpetually on the *hunt for essences,* as Aristotle put it—causes to surge up in itself is only to serve that *sense of being* which is indeed the deepest thing in the intelligence, and to achieve an intuitive discernment which is the act itself of the intelligence. In those matchless moments of *intellectual discovery,* wherein we seize for the first time upon a pulsing, intelligible reality in the seemingly infinite abundance of its possibilities for expansion, and wherein we feel rising and confirming itself in our deepest beings that intellectual word which makes such reality manifest, we then know well what the intuitive power of the intelligence is, and that it is exerted by means of concepts.

True enough, but then we shape that intellectual word as the ultimate term of all the immense equipment of conceptual tools, of the universe of ideas and images already dwelling within us, which results from the years and years of the workings of knowledge to which we have yielded ourselves from the first wakening of reflection in our mind. If there is some serious lack, or if there are warpings and distortions in that universe; in other words, if the doctrinal equipment with which we are already supplied admits of errors and deficiencies, the effort of the mind through which the intelligence —by virtue of the active light which is within it—suddenly extricates from experience and from the accumulation of data and from all sensory contacts the freshness, murmuring with life, of some new countenance of the real . . . it touches that countenance, grasps it, looks upon it; the intelligence has brought it forth out of things; with it the intelligence ends its act of intellection, for it is things that that act seeks out; it does not stop at signs or statements . . . well then, the effort of the mind which achieves an authentic (and to that extent infallible) intuition will thus only reach reality by and in signs which, being produced and patterned under the ægis of a pre-existing equipment encumbered with errors and deficiencies, will ill express that intuition and will express it in statements more or less erroneous—sometimes seriously, irremediably erroneous. This will be the case as long, at least, as our general scheme of concepts has not been recast, perhaps by virtue of that very intuition and the ruptures it produces.

At the heart of every great philosophic system there is thus a very simple and yet inexhaustible insight—Bergson has singled it out in a celebrated passage—which on some occasion has overwhelmed the mind with its certitude. With every great philosopher and every great thinker there is a central intuition which in itself does not mislead. But that intuition can be conceptualized, and in fact in a great number of cases is conceptualized, in a mistaken, perhaps even pernicious, doctrine. So long as he remains bound to his own ideas, the philosopher himself cannot effectuate discernment in this matter; yet some day a proper discernment must be effectuated. How grand a dramatic spectacle is this! Here we have an intuitive certitude through which the real suddenly yields itself to the mind, through which the real and the mind suddenly enjoy a mutual ecstasy; and here is at the same time and in the same event, since all this cannot take place without a conceptualization drawn from our invested capital, the risk of deceiving oneself more or less seriously and of jeopardizing an entire, well-tested system of statements held as true by the sages. To avoid this risk, will the mind turn away from the real which offers itself, away from being for an instant overtaken by an aspect which had never before been manifest to the mind? That is impossible. The mind knows that its first duty is not to sin against the light. It must subject to the most careful verification its conceptual equipment, but it cannot prevent itself from rushing toward being. No matter what the price. It is required of the mind not to fall into error, but first of all, it is required of the mind that it *see*.

THE BERGSONIAN CONCEPTUALIZATION OF DURATION

But let us cease from this digression and return to the idea, the notion of Bergsonian duration. I have said that in my judgment it is an illusory notion.

Why and how? We were considering, a while back, the primarily *negative* signification of the intuition. Well, the Bergsonian notion denies *more* than does the intuition; it stretches that negation beyond the proper content of the intuition. The Bergsonian notion of duration does not merely say that real time is not the spatialized time of our physics, that change is not a scattering of positions succeeding each other, that movement is *non-divided, undivided,* that is to say *one* in act and of such nature that if it be divided, its own proper quality together with its unity is thereby suppressed (in this sense Aristotle went so far as to say that 6 is different from *3 plus 3*). Even more—and this is what is false—the Bergsonian idea would have movement be *non-divisible, indivisible,* and such that no parts in it can be distinguished from each other, even were they potential as in all *continua*. And it would have time not be *something* of change or of movement, *distinct* from change itself and *distinct* from the subject of change—indeed, the uninterrupted flux of the impermanence of change. Real time is that, it is this flux of impermanence, which is to say that it is that which is the least substantial in the world. And yet the Bergsonian notion of duration would not have it be that.

And what does this notion do in its *positive* aspect? It makes of time something substantial; it seems indissolubly to lump together in one same idea-image the idea of substance and the idea of time and the idea of psychic flow and multiplicity, all this making that "snowball which gets bigger as it moves forward" of which Bergson has so often spoken.

Instead of directing itself toward being and instead of opening out into the metaphysical intuition of being, as the nature of things requires, the Bergsonian experience of duration, in brief, took a wrong direction to conceptualize itself—while at the same time, in so far as it is experience, it continued, without saying so, to pulse with all the ontological content discussed above. Bergsonian experience of duration, then, has conceptually opened out into an unstable and fleeting notion of *time* as *substitute for being,* of *time* as primary stuff of the real and specificating object of metaphysics, of *time* as first object not, of course, of the intelligence, in the sense in which Aristotle said that being is the first object of the intelligence, but of that twisting of the intelligence back onto itself which would have it recover the virtualities of instinct and which is called Bergsonian intuition and which for Bergson replaces the intelligence as a power vitally apprehending the real, despite the fact that he himself momentarily considered calling it itself "intelligence."

A METAPHYSICS OF MODERN PHYSICS

To press the discussion further, we can note that metaphysics—the science which is wisdom, the highest sort of knowledge which human thought can attain—from its beginning constituted itself as transcending time. It was born when the intelligence of the philosophers lifted its head above the flood of succession. But from the very moment when the physico-mathematical method permitted the setting up of a science of phenomena *as such,* with the condition that concepts shall be resolved only within the *measurable* and *sensible* and the rôle of the ontological be reduced to the construction of "explanatory" ideal entities (*entia rationis*), intended to sustain a tissue of mathematical law-structures unifying phenomena, from that moment one can say that thought, coming back to the world of the senses, took up its abode in time. It required three centuries and the Kantian revolution to make men see what had happened.

What then is to become of metaphysics? If it is faithful to itself and to what is, metaphysics will transcend the science of phenomena as it transcends time, and it will at the same time recognize that that science, from the very fact that it consists in an *empiriological* or *empiriomathematical* analysis of the real, is autonomous with regard to the analyses of an ontological order to which philosophy proceeds—precisely because science does not itself contain, hidden away in it, a philosophy.

But if one denies to metaphysics that transcendence and that autonomy with regard to science and yet would wish to set up a metaphysics, one's only recourse is to seek out that metaphysics not at a level above that of the world appropriate to the mathematization of the sensible, but in its own depths. It will be necessary to seek within the physico-mathematical tissue a metaphysical substance, a stuff with which the physico-mathematical cognition of nature is unconsciously pregnant.

But where dwells this physico-mathematical cognition if not in the flux itself? What does it strive to organize through its formulas if not the relational stabilities which it isolates in the very flow of sensible becoming? Bergson's stroke of genius has been to see that if phenomenal science itself enfolds and hides, on its own level and in its formal object, a metaphysical stuff, that stuff can only be time. It is in time that we must immerse ourselves in order to find a knowledge which shall no longer have for its direct goal the necessary and the universal, but the flux itself of the singular and the contingent, pure movement considered as the very substance of things. All this presupposes, as Bergson perfectly well saw, the absolute superseding of the concept and a total inversion of the natural movement of the intelligence. In this same *time,* in which physics dwells without wishing to ponder its reality (for physics is indeed well satisfied with its mathematical substitute) and which physics translates into spatial symbols and the reality of which mechanicism suppresses, in this *time* metaphysics will fasten upon the absolute itself, which is invention and creation.

Much more basically dependent on modern physics than the immanent Cause of Spinoza, which substantialized the mechanistic explanations of a still youthful phenomenal science, Bergsonian duration achieves in metaphysics the very soul of pure empiricism or of pure experimentalism, of which modern physics has become aware as it progressed and with which it approaches reality in order to explain it. The last pages of *Creative Evolution* are supremely significant in this connection. "It seems then," writes Bergson, "that parallel to this physics [modern], a second type of knowledge should have set itself up. . . . It is to the inwardness of becoming that it would have transported us by an effort of sympathy. . . . If [this knowledge] were to succeed, it is reality itself which it would clasp in a final embrace."[1] And again, "An experience of this type is not a non-temporal experience. It merely seeks, beyond spatialized time wherein we believe we see continual rearrangements of parts, the concrete duration wherein ceaselessly operates a radical recasting of the whole."[2] And again, "The more one reflects upon it, the more one will find that this conception of metaphysics is that which modern science suggests."[3] "Thus understood," he finally says, "philosophy is not only the return of the mind to itself, the coincidence of the human consciousness with the living principle from whence it emanates, an establishment of contact with the creative effort. Philosophy is the deepening of becoming in general,

[1] *L'Évolution Créatrice,* Paris, Alcan, 1909, pp. 370–371 (*Creative Evolution,* New York, Holt, 1911, pp. 342–343).
[2] *Ibid.,* Paris Ed., p. 392; New York Ed., p. 363.
[3] *Ibid.,* Paris Ed., p. 371; New York Ed., p. 343.

the true evolutionism, and hence the true continuation of science."[1] In short, and properly speaking, metaphysics consists in "seeing in time a progressive growth of the absolute";[2] it is summed up in the affirmation that *time is creator.*

Such, it seems to me, considering what is most basic about it, has been the genesis of the Bergsonian metaphysics, and at the same time these considerations have already indicated a few of its essential characteristics.

BERGSONIAN IRRATIONALISM

It is from *this,* from this fundamental discovery (and, in truth, as we have seen, ambivalent discovery) which Bergson thought he had made concerning duration that issues as a secondary (if inevitable) characteristic the *irrationalism* of the Bergsonian philosophy. The irrationalism is secondary, not primary. It is as though involuntary; I should even say that it goes against his grain. And that creates a fundamental difference between Bergson's thought and a thought by first and deliberate intention inimical to the intelligence, like the thinking of Klages.[3] Still the Bergsonian philosophy is an irrationalist philosophy: Irrationalism is the ransom set by the errors we discussed a few pages back in the conceptualization of the fruitful realities toward which moved, in so far as it was a genuine intellectual intuition, Bergson's original intuition.

For one thing no labour of metaphysical reflection, properly so called, had preceded this intuition and prepared the conceptual equipment which it was to use. There was no metaphysics of being nor of the intelligence, and no previously worked out critique of knowledge (the first chapter of *Matière et Mémoire* clearly shows that at that time Bergson believed he could still do without a choice between the idealist conception and the realist conception of knowledge; later on he was freely to assert that if he must choose between two *isms,* as he put it, it is realism he would choose, and with no hesitation.) From the great metaphysical tradition of humanity, it is only through Plotinus that Bergson received the λόγος σπερμάτικος—a *logos* singularly precious, indeed, and which perhaps was to go further than philosophy. Bergson's original training was entirely scientific, or rather scientistic; it was

---

[1] *Ibid.,* Paris Ed., p. 399; New York Ed., pp. 369–370.

[2] *Ibid.,* Paris Ed., p. 372; New York Ed., p. 344.

[3] "You are perfectly right," Bergson wrote to Jacques Chevalier, "in saying that all the philosophy I have expounded since my first *Essay* affirms, against Kant, the possibility of a supra-sensible intuition. Taking the word 'intelligence' in the very broad meaning given it by Kant, I could call 'intellectual' the intuition I speak of. But I should prefer to designate it as 'supra-intellectual,' because I believed I must restrict the sense of the word 'intelligence,' and because I reserve this name for the set of discursive faculties of the mind, originally destined to think of matter. *Intuition bears toward spirit.*" (April 28, 1920. Letter published in the book *Bergson,* by Jacques Chevalier.)

from Spencer that he emanated. And that very fact renders more moving for us, and even more deserving of gratitude the work he has done for the rediscovery of the spirit. But this also explains certain deficiencies in that work.

Then again (and this is only another aspect of the same consideration, this also was a legacy of the modern philosophic tradition, unrectified by a sane metaphysics of knowledge) the one and only sure recourse to which thought might have access was in Bergson's eyes, and was exclusively to remain, *experience*. Faced with the contradiction and the fluctuations of abstract knowledge, experience alone (as though it itself were not inevitably indicated in abstract knowledge)—experience alone in his eyes had any philosophic value. Hence if experience—an experience more profound than the experience of the laboratory sciences—seems to admit me to the presence of a *creative time* and a *change which is substance* and a duration which is a kind of *pure act in becoming,* well then, let logic and the principle of identity and all the rational requirements of the intelligence perish as they must. All that is secondary from the point of view of the truth which I hold. This kind of desperate energy whereby the intelligence tears itself to pieces and prefers to deny its most vital law and its very existence rather than loosen its grip, rather than let go the truth which a deficient conceptualization causes the intelligence to hold badly, but to hold onto for dear life—we find this desperate energy in several of those philosophers who today call themselves existentialists, in Heidegger, for example, and in Berdyaev. It was for this that William James expressed his gratitude to Bergson with charming frankness, when he thanked Bergson for having helped him to liberate himself once and for all from logic. Such deliverances are scarcely more profitable than an immersion in the river of Heraclitus, in which one does not bathe twice, for one drowns the first time one tries it. For Bergsonism, the continuous duration of life escapes all logic, and cannot accommodate itself to the principle of non-contradiction; from this it follows, as has been said, that "the method made necessary by that density proper to the things of the soul can only be entirely *irrational.*"[1]

That assertion is taken from one of the best statements yet made of Bergsonism from the point of view of Bergson, and it has the merit of leaving no doubt in the reader's mind on this point of capital importance.

One of the results of this actual irrationalism, and one of its expressions, indeed its specific and systematic expression, is the Bergsonian theory of the *intelligence,* essentially incapable of understanding life, capable only of knowing matter and making geometry, and the Bergsonian theory of *intuition.* Here we have that which in Bergsonism plays the rôle of a metaphysics of

[1] Vladimir Jankélévitch, "Prolégomènes au Bergsonisme," *Revue de Métaphysique et de Morale,* Oct.–Dec., 1928, p. 42 (later published as a book).

knowledge. These are well-known portions of the teaching of Bergson on which it does not seem to me that there is any need to elaborate here.

On the subject of the theory of intuition, a theory which, as Bergson wrote Höffding, occurred to him later than the theory of duration, I shall point out only one thing.[1] An intuition which requires a kind of violent recovery, through an effort contrary to our nature, of the instinctive virtualities spaced out along the course of zoological evolution; an intuition "which prolongs, develops, and carries over into thought whatever remains of instinct in man,[2] which buries us in concrete perception in order to deepen and broaden it, which is, thanks to the instrumentality of the will, an expansion of the perception of the senses and the consciousness,[3] a painful effort wherein "the faculty of *seeing*, bending and twisting back on itself" should no longer be "but one with the act of *willing*"[4]—such an intuition it seems very difficult effectively to consider as a *supra-intellectual* intuition. I am nevertheless convinced that if the Bergsonian conceptualization here requires criticism, it still expresses in a deficient way views which are profoundly true on the supremely vital act of the intellect, on that which in the intellect is the most genuinely intellectual and is more valid than the reason. However questionable may be the Bergsonian intuition, as Bergson describes it, true intellection, that is to say intellectual intuition, often slips into it on the sly. It is the intelligence which gives value to all this, even though Bergson objects to the intelligence. (And I fully realize that he uses the word intelligence in a sense other than that commonly given it. Yet it is precisely the intelligence in its common meaning that he thus seeks to make suspect.)

THE BERGSONIAN CRITIQUE OF THE IDEA OF NOTHINGNESS

As I have said in a preceding part of this book (for I am taking for granted the permission of repeating myself when I deem it necessary) three theories supply us with the metaphysical backgrounds of or the metaphysical keys to Bergsonism. These are the Bergsonian critique of the idea of nothingness, the Bergsonian theory of change, the Bergsonian critique of the possible.

If what I said at the outset concerning Bergson's position with respect to metaphysics is just, it will be understood that these three theories appear in his work as tentatives for projects, or as sketches (as though seen through a window open for a moment and then quickly closed) for what could be the

---

[1] Cf. *Introduction à la Métaphysique* (*The Introduction to a New Philosophy*, translated by Sidney Littman; John W. Luce & Co., Boston, 1912) later reprinted in *La Pensée et le Mouvant* (Chapter VI); *L'Évolution Créatrice*, notably p. 192 (New York Ed., pp. 176–177) and p. 290 (New York Ed., p. 268); "L'Intuition Philosophique," (*Revue de Métaphysique et de Morale*, Novembre, 1911, notably pp. 89 and 827), later reprinted in *La Pensée et le Mouvant*, Chapter IV.

[2] Letter to Harald Höffding (see p. 305), p. 163.

[3] "La Perception du changement," p. 8 (*La Pensée et le Mouvant*, Chapter V, p. 169).

[4] *L'Évolution Créatrice*, p. 258 (New York Ed., p. 237).

bases of a Bergsonian metaphysic, rather than as essays intended to supply the foundations of a doctrine properly so called. Yet I am convinced that Bergson has set down in these three theories ideas to which he attached the greatest importance and which he has worked out very thoroughly and very carefully. The critique of the idea of nothingness may be found in *Creative Evolution*. The theory of change appears in two lectures given at Oxford in 1911 on the *Perception of Change*. The critique of the possible was made at an Oxford philosophical conference in 1920, and was developed in an article published in a Swedish review, *Nordisk Tidskrift*, in 1930. This article and the 1911 lectures were gathered together in 1934 in Bergson's most recently published volume, *La Pensée et le Mouvant*.

First of all a few words concerning the critique of the idea of nothingness.[1] Bergson therein upholds the thesis that the idea of absolute nothingness, the idea of the nothingness of the whole being, is a *pseudo-idea,* which we never really *think.* Since the understanding as such is able to perceive or record only *presences,* not *absences,* to think the nothingness of a thing is to posit the reality of another thing, of a thing which drives the first from existence, and which replaces it. "The unreality of a thing consists in its being driven out by other things." If negation appears in our formulas, it is only through extra-intellectual motives, affective or social, by reason of which—for example, to anticipate someone else's possible mistake—we fix our attention on the reality replaced or driven out, of which we then say that it *is not,* while leaving indeterminate the reality that replaces or drives out, of which we are effectively thinking but thinking without concern. The fact is that we think only the *plenum,* and that to picture to oneself the nothingness of a thing is in truth to depict another thing which drives the first away and takes its place. It follows that to think absolute nothingness implies a contradiction.

This singular thesis is justified only by an original misunderstanding: it is obvious that one will strive in vain to picture nothingness to oneself; one will not succeed. But the idea of nothingness is not a representation of nothingness, it is a *negative idea:* its content is not a "nothingness" which one would picture as something (on that score indeed one can picture the nothingness of a thing only as its expulsion by another). The content of the idea of nothingness is *being* affected by the sign of the negative; it is *non-being.* The proper activity of the intelligence suffices for the shaping of this idea. And as it is only the idea of being, but of being indicated as denied, the idea of the nothingness of a thing in no way consists in the replacement of that thing by another which would drive it out. From this it follows that the idea of absolute nothingness, which means purely and simply the expulsion of all things —but not by other things which would replace those expelled—in no way implies a contradiction, in no sense is a pseudo-idea.

---

[1] *Ibid.,* Paris Ed., pp. 298–323; New York Ed., pp. 275–299.

But *why* did Bergson set up this critique, in our opinion fallacious, of the idea of nothingness?

In his thinking it was a question of struggling against the temptation of Spinozism, a temptation natural to each philosopher. "Scarcely had he begun to philosophize" when the philosopher asks, *"Why is there such a thing as being?"* And this question implies, says Bergson, the supposition that nothingness is before being, that being is "spread over nothingness as on a carpet." If we admit that question, we can answer it only by granting, with Spinoza, a being as cause of itself which is alone capable of "conquering non-existence" and which "plants itself in eternity even as logic plants itself"[1] and which will cause to perish all effective causality, all contingency and all freedom in things, these being but the endless unrolling of this hypostasized logic. But this question is only a pseudo-problem (we have just seen how Bergson believes that he has demonstrated this); the problem should not be posed at all, and the Spinozist reply is as illusory as that which provoked it.

Yet Bergson, in his desire to strike at Spinozism, strikes a blow at all metaphysics. If his critique is justified, the idea of a Being existing through itself, of the *Ipsum esse subsistens,* the idea of the divine aseity is a mere pseudo-idea and a *hypostasierung* of logic, as is Spinoza's idea of substance, *causa sui.* For it is the idea of the contingency of things, the idea that they could not-be, in other words the idea of the possibility of the nothingness of things, which compels the mind to conceive that Being and its necessity. And even that idea of the possibility of nothingness would be a pseudo-idea.

We have seen that it is nothing of the sort. And the idea of the Being-by-itself is in no sense the substantiation of logic and of logical necessity. It relates rather to a pre-eminently real necessity, to the infinite necessity by virtue of which there exists a Being so rich and superabundant and independent that its very essence is its act of existing, of knowing, and of loving.

But for Bergson the question *Why do things exist?* constitutes a pseudo-problem and rests on a pseudo-idea. As a result the classic distinction between the necessary and the contingent is definitively a pseudo-distinction, and that *which is not necessary* posits itself through itself. Thus we perceive in a rapid flash of enlightenment why a Bergsonian theodicy, a rational demonstration of the existence of God in the Bergsonian system, is not possible. It is by another road that, for Bergson, this existence will be attained. Bergsonian metaphysics, following its own line of approach, arrives at the admission that God, prime source of the creative spurting forth, probably exists as a supremely concentrated duration and life; it cannot demonstrate that such exists. And it cannot determine whether this God, who exists *in fact,* is or is not necessary in Himself, and infinitely necessary *by right.*

---

[1] *Ibid.*

THE BERGSONIAN DOCTRINE OF CHANGE

Did not the critique of the idea of nothingness have somewhat the character of an argument *ad hominem?* In any case was it not above all intended to sweep the premises clear—following a method dear to Bergson—of one of those pseudo-problems by means of which, a little too easily perhaps, he frees philosophy of many an embarrassment? Let us now consider the Bergsonian doctrine of change. It has a much stronger positive value and makes us enter far more deeply into the intimacies of Bergsonian metaphysics. But it shows us also what sort of positive virtualities were contained in the critique of the idea of nothingness.

Let us look carefully at a few specially significant passages in the "Perception of Change." *"There are changes, but there are underneath the change no things which change: change has no need of a support. There are movements, but there is no inert or invariable object which moves:*[1] *movement does not imply a mobile."*

Doubtless the utilitarian preoccupations of the sense of sight have accustomed us to chop movement up into successive positions, so that "movement would seem added onto the mobile as an accident." "But we shall have less difficulty in perceiving movement and change as independent realities if we turn to the sense of hearing. Listen to a melody, permit yourself to be cradled in its embrace: do you not have a sharp perception of a movement which is not attached to anything mobile, of *change without anything that changes? That change is enough; it is the thing itself."* [Italics mine, here and in the following quotation.] "Once we have abstracted these spatial images, there remains *change—pure, self-sufficient, and in no way divided, in no way attached to a 'thing' which changes."*

"Let us, then, revert to the sense of sight. Meditating upon it more closely, we perceive that even here movement requires no vehicle, nor change a substance . . ." "But in no way is the *substantiality* of change as visible, as touchable, as in the realm of the inner life . . ." "Thus whether it is a question of the inner or the outer, of us or of things, reality is mobility itself. That is what I meant when I said that there is change, but that there are no things which change."

"Confronted with the spectacle of this universal mobility, some of us will be seized with dizziness. Such minds are accustomed to *terra firma* . . . They think that if everything is in passage, nothing exists, and that if reality is mobility, it no longer exists at the moment when one thinks it—it escapes the mind. The material world, they say, is going to dissolve, and the mind is going to drown in the torrential flux of things. Let them be at rest! Change,

---

[1] The words "inert, invariable" were added by Bergson in the second edition of his lecture. See in this connection p. 318, n. 1.

if only they will look it in the face, without any interposed veil, will soon seem to them as that which in all the world is most substantial and most enduring."[1]

Otherwise stated, and to turn again and ever to Bergson's own words, *if change is not everything, it is nothing*;[2] it is not only *real*, but *constitutive of the reality*,[3] it is the *very substance of things*.[4]

The Bergsonian metaphysics is then indeed the metaphysics of pure change. In my opinion there has not been enough emphasis placed on the central importance for the whole Bergsonian philosophy of the metaphysical doctrine which I have just summarized. That doctrine supplies us with a key to Bergsonian philosophy. We are here confronted with one of the most determined and one of the boldest attempts ever made to drive out being and replace it with becoming—not indeed after the fashion of Hegel's panlogism; on the contrary, after the fashion of an integral empiricism. Yet two things are clear: in the first place, if it is true that being is the connatural object of the intelligence and that it constitutes, if I may put it so, the climate in which the intelligence thinks what it thinks, this metaphysics of pure change must be considered as not thinkable. For to say that change is the very substance of things is to say that things change inasmuch as they are and in so far as they are. And therefore in so far as they are they cease to be what they are, they leave their being, they no longer are what they are but are something else. Secondly, in order to try to think this, it is necessary to find something better than the intelligence, or to turn the intelligence against itself, and in any case to deny, as did Heraclitus of old, the principle of noncontradiction.

This doctrine of pure change at the same time affords us useful insight into certain implications of Bergsonian intuition, which here is seen to be clearly "anti-intellectualist," as it does likewise into certain implications of Bergsonian duration. Bergsonian duration is nothing else but time. "Real duration," Bergson writes, "is that which has always been called *time*, but time perceived as indivisible";[5] it is an *indivisible* time and one in which *the past endures*. "The conservation of the past in the present is nothing more than the indivisibility of change."[6] "It suffices that we convince ourselves once for all," we read once more, "that reality is change, that change is indivisible, and

---

1 *La Pensée et le Mouvant*, pp. 185–189. It is to be noted that, according to the views of Thomas Aquinas, substance is not an "inert" object; on the contrary it is the very root of action. Substance is *"invariable" in itself*, that is to say in so far as it is the primal being of a thing. But substance varies, substance moves—through accidents, which are *its* secondary being, and are not at all things superimposed upon another thing.

2 *Ibid.*, p. 183.

3 *Ibid.*, p. 190.

4 *Ibid.*, p. 197.

5 *Ibid.*, p. 188.

6 *Ibid.*, p. 196.

that in an indivisible change, the past is one with the present."[3] In short, "it is a question of a present which endures."[4] Those few phrases show us the altogether characteristic metaphysical content of Bergsonian duration.

Furthermore Bergson explains to us that all the difficulties raised by philosophers over the problem of substance and the problem of movement "sprang from our closing our eyes to the indivisibility of change." And he adds, "If change, which is evidently constitutive of all our experience, is the fleeting and elusive thing about which the majority of philosophers have spoken, if one sees in it only a scattering of positions which replace other positions, we are forced into re-establishing continuity between these positions by means of an artificial bond. . . ." It is thus, he thinks, that the figment of a substance distinct from change was born. "Let us try on the contrary," he continues, "to perceive change as it is, in its natural indivisibility. We see that it is the *substance itself of things.*"[5]

These statements seem to me highly significant. I point out again that here we pass over from the true assertion that change and movement are *undivided* into the erroneous assertion that they are *indivisible,* and that Bergson attacks with equal vigour two altogether different conceptions: the conception of motion as a *scattering of positions which replace positions,* which is a very false concept against which Aristotle and the best philosophers have not failed to make objection, and the conception of motion as that *"fleeting and elusive thing about which the majority of philosophers have spoken."*[1] And they did well so to speak, for that is exactly what motion is. Since, moreover, motion is that, it follows that the being to which our intellect at once tends when it thinks things, the being which by itself exercises existence, and the notion of which, far from being the notion of a bond between positions of change, is *anterior* to the notion of change—it surely follows that *substance* must be really distinct from movement and from change: it is *substance* which changes; change is not *substance.*

But that which I should like above all to emphasize is the bond which unites the thesis of the substantiality of change to that of creative time. We must understand this last expression as being rigorously meant. We are dealing with a time that is properly creative; motion is the absolute, and that absolute grows of itself, it creates and creates itself as it unfolds; "following the new conception through to the end" we come, says Bergson in *Creative Evolution,* "to see *in time a progressive growth of the absolute.*"[2]

And finally why should this be stated if it is not that Bergson expressed and conceptualized in the notion of time, not in that of being, an intuition which,

[3] *Ibid.,* p. 196.
[4] *Ibid.,* p. 192.
[5] *Ibid.,* pp. 196–197.
[1] *Ibid.,* p. 196.
[2] See p. 312, n. 2.

aiming at the concrete duration of the psychic life, attained—through that duration and in it—that deeper reality which is *being itself* and substantial *existence* and the very *activity* thanks to which, through the motion of the first cause, being still superabounds. To tell us what he saw, Bergson should have said *being;* he said *time.*

The result is that we are to "see in time a progressive growth of the absolute."[1] This amounts to saying that change precedes being and that becoming exists by itself, enjoys *aseity* as well as creative power. Contingency and becoming, change and diversity posit themselves. Posit time, and things make themselves. Or rather they make themselves through an expansion of the creative being, that is to say of the pure creative act, which we have lumped together with things, with their being and with their changing, in the same ambiguous notion, which improperly transcribes a true intuition by causing it to speak falsely. The *intentions* of Bergsonism are fundamentally opposed to every form whatever of pantheism; yet one cannot see how a certain pantheism is not in line with the internal logic of those concepts through which in fact the Bergsonian system finds expression.

Yet on the other hand, if change is *indivisible,* and if consequently one cannot distinguish in its parts which succeed one another—of which one has disappeared when another begins to exist—if the past, the past as such, continues to exist and "preserves itself of itself, automatically,"[2] we must say, inasmuch as we also say that the past passes, we must say that *that which no longer is, still is.* In a memory that is true indeed. For the memory no longer is. But in things? Again as always we come up against the principle of noncontradiction, and we have to undertake to break through it in order not to be ourselves broken by it.

THE BERGSONIAN CRITIQUE OF THE POSSIBLE

It is possible to go even more deeply into the metaphysical roots of Bergsonism. One then comes to the denial of the *possible,* in the sense of a real possible, or of potentiality—a denial already involved, in truth, by the critique of the idea of nothingness.

Were things *possible* before they existed? No, Bergson replies. It is an illusion to think so. The possible does not precede the act.

Now he undertakes to prove this thesis by an analysis of the psychological and cognitional function of the idea of a real possibility. But from the very outset he misunderstands that idea. He takes real possibility to be a *virtual or ideal pre-existence,* that is *an image of tomorrow* already provided in things today, and in which there lacks only the act to exist; in short, he takes real

[1] *Ibid.*
[2] *La Pensée et le Mouvant,* p. 193.

possibility to be something actual lacking only existence—a notion of the possible which is indeed scandalous for an Aristotelian or a Thomist!

Once supplied with such a pseudo-idea of the possible or of potentiality, it is simple enough to explain that here is only a pseudo-idea, and that it springs from a *retrospection,* from a projection which we extend into the past at the instant when *that which was not yet* comes to exist. At that specific moment, says Bergson, and at that moment only, at the moment when it is, the new thing is thought as *having been* possible. Thus in fact it begins *to have been* possible only at the moment when it *is.*

In this so subtle an argument let us let the philosopher himself speak. "At the foundation of the doctrines which fail to recognize the radical novelty of each moment of evolution, there are many mistakes, many errors. Above all there is the idea that the possible is *less* than the real and that, for this reason, the possibility of things precedes their existence . . . If we put to one side closed systems, subject to purely mathematical laws, able to be isolated because duration does not bite into them; if we consider the whole of concrete reality, or merely the world of life, and even more the world of consciousness, we find that there is *more,* and not *less,* in the possibility of each of successive positions than there is in their reality. For the possible is only the real with an added act of the mind which casts back into the past the image of the real once it has been produced." A work of art *will have been,* but actually *is* not, possible. "As reality step by step creates itself, unforeseeable and new, its image is reflected behind it in the indefinite past. Thus reality is at all times found to have been possible. But it is at that precise moment that it begins always to have been possible. And this is why I said that its possibility, which does not precede its reality, will have preceded it once reality appears. The possible, then, is a mirage of the present in the past . . . The idea, immanent in the greater part of philosophic systems and natural to the human mind, of possibles which realize themselves by acquiring existence, is, therefore, pure illusion. One might as well claim that flesh-and-blood man springs from the materialization of his image perceived in a mirror. . . . Is it not . . . absurd . . . to suppose that the future designs itself in advance, that possibility existed prior to reality?" "There is an effective stirring of unforeseeable moments." "One has to take one's stand: it is the real which makes itself possible, and not the possible which becomes real."[1] It would be impossible to state in more absolute fashion that everything is in act (*in actu*) at the same time that everything is becoming.

Here the fundamental error, as we pointed out a moment ago, relates to the nature of the *possible,* which is considered as something actual by one remove, and which at once, unless we deny becoming, can only be ideal, and

---

[1] *Ibid.,* pp. 126–33.

retrospectively indicated by a future perfect. In reality what happens in change at a given moment in no sense existed in the preceding moment as something *already actual* but not yet made manifest; what is to be is in no way *already realized* under any form whatever. Yet what a subject becomes, not being a simple extrinsic qualification, must affect the subject in its being: but cannot affect it as regards what it already is (that is, in act), because what it already is, it is; that it does not become. Therefore the new qualitative endowment affects the subject, and is drawn from it, as though from a kind of capital fund or an ontological fertility which is in no way reducible to any being in act, and which actuality from all sides invests and sustains in the being, but which in itself is absolutely non-actual, not realized, is pure determinability—in a word, potentiality. This is real possibility, and wherever there is change and becoming, it necessarily precedes whatever new actuations the subject receives. If, moreover, it is quite true that the possible is recognized after the event, after it is realized, it is precisely because potentiality—being nothing that may be uttered, for everything which may be uttered is in act— is purely *ad actum,* and is knowable only through act.

It is indeed the mark of that which is created—of that which can increase, acquire, undergo, of that which depends on another—to bear in its inner inwardness this metaphysical unevenness, which is completely levelled off only in the Being itself subsisting, in Being which can become nothing, because it is supereminently everything. In everything which is not God, reality is the realization of a possible.

For Bergson, on the contrary, what things become they of course were not, but before becoming so, they already were everything that they could be. From the very fact of their being actual, they pass over into another actuality. It is sufficient for things to be, and to be in act,—I mean in their continuity with the effusive actuality whence emanates that universal *élan,*—in order for them to become other. Here we are confronted with a "new method of thinking" which consists in the full and entire substitution of the verb *change* for the verb *be.* Here is an affirmation of *pure actuality,* not of Parmenidean being, or of Spinozist substance, but of *movement* itself and of becoming. "We have only," as wrote M. Jankélévitch, "to make a transposition in order to pass from the impassible universe of Spinoza to the qualified universe of Bergson."[1] Let us not say "transposition"; the word does not seem to me quite appropriate; let us rather say "reversal." In its metaphysical significance, Bergsonism gives the appearance of being a Spinozism reversed.

Whence it comes to pass that certain interpreters of Bergsonism, particularly the philosopher I have just quoted, themselves aflame with the same fire as enflamed Spinoza, evoke Bergson in the Spinozist sense. It is essentially important, says M. Jankélévitch, to refuse to allow oneself to be drawn into

[1] *Ibid.,* p. 95.

the shadows of virtuality; all must be in clarity and in act. And he continues: "From the very moment when the shadow of the possible invades the universe, giving rise to the illusory optics of finality, of (possible) disorder and of indifference, the idea occurs to us that perhaps things might have been other than they are," and that idea gives birth in us to the wonder which affects "fanatics" confronted with the spectacle of the world.

I do not at all believe that Bergson would be inclined to yield to the fanaticism of Spinoza and of his present-day disciples. On the contrary he holds his own philosophy to be determinedly anti-Spinozist. And it is not *substance*—on the contrary, it is *change*—which for him is *pure actuality*. But in such cases one can say that extremes meet.

Even though he frontally opposes Spinoza, Bergson has in common with him one major premise of absolutely primordial importance—the denial of potentiality in things. For Bergsonian metaphysics, and here we touch on basic questions which order the destiny of a philosophy, everything is pure act—pure act in perpetual growth, radical recasting and constant motion of the ever new. Here was matter from which could be drawn a whole system of atheist metaphysics. Yet we know that it is not at all in this direction that Bergson chose to go. Far from it! He chose to affirm a personal God, as well as the spiritual nature of the soul and free will. The question is to find out whether his metaphysics helped him in this, or whether in a certain sense in this he himself triumphed over his metaphysics, and whether, between very different and even opposite possibilities of development (here once more the possible holds us in pursuit!), it was not extra-philosophic factors which made him decide.

THE UNFORESEEABLENESS OF BECOMING

The root motive for Bergson's elaboration of his critique of potentiality is, I believe, his desire to safeguard the unforeseeableness of becoming, not only the absolute unforeseeableness of free acts and the relative unforeseeableness of contingent happenings in the course of nature, but also what he calls the "radical unforeseeableness" of every moment in the universe. This feeling for *unforeseeableness,* as I have just observed, can lead a philosopher into excesses and errors. In itself it is a highly philosophic feeling and one which we should not let lie quiescent within us. I have explained that when it is understood in its exact meaning, the Aristotelian idea of potentiality, far from threatening, in fact justifies this feeling of unforeseeableness. Certain too elementary expositions of theodicy might seem to compromise it. In reality the God of Saint Thomas safeguards as much as the God of Bergson the unforeseeableness of concrete becoming. If He knows all things from all eternity, and the feather which tomorrow will fall from the wing of a certain bird, it is not because the history of the world is only the unfolding of a *ready-made scenario.* It is, on the contrary, that all the moments of the whole of time are present for the divine Eternity, who sees in its own instant, and hence always, everything creatures do, have done, will do in the very instant that it *happens,* and hence in an eternal freshness of life and newness.

If, as I have indicated at the beginning, Bergson did not desire to erect a whole system of metaphysics, his metaphysics is nevertheless one of the most profound, most penetrating, and most audacious of our time. The critical discussion thereof I have endeavoured to conduct in this chapter is in homage to his greatness. For the errors for which one is justified in reproaching him could only take shape as the ultimate, logical consequences of the projection, in a field of conceptualization unhappily altogether empiricist and nominalist, of intuitions and of truths which touch at the very roots of things.

Chapter Seventeen

THE BERGSONIAN PHILOSOPHY OF
MORALITY AND RELIGION

A BOOK LONG AWAITED

Bergson's *Creative Evolution* appeared in 1907; twenty-five years later, in 1932, Bergson published his *Two Sources of Morality and Religion*. This book was not only the result of a long and patient labour of meditation performed with that scientific conscience and that care in the accumulation and verification of data and documents which Bergson's method exacts in so high a degree; it was also a victory over serious illness, and is one of the purest and most moving of available testimonies to the life of the spirit.

We had all for a long time been aware that Bergson was preparing a moral philosophy and that he even intended to enter upon questions of theodicy.[1] What would this morals, this theodicy be? A few disciples had chanced some timid anticipatory essays, inevitably rather thin, and tending in different directions, and even more extremist in their conclusions inasmuch as the internal directive principle, the principle of vital equilibrium, was lacking.

Others wondered whether indeed an ethics could ever arise from a philosophy which, despite its irrationalism, seemed as if it were settled in the slightly disdainful coolness of pure speculation, and as if it were rather scornful of practical human affairs (in fact no one was less a pragmatist than Bergson).

During this entire time, Bergson laboured in silence. He was reading, he was building up for himself a vast historical, ethnological and sociological documentation; he was meditating the history of humanity. He was reading the great spiritual writers—those we call mystics. Already in 1906 he spoke to me of Saint Theresa of Avila, and said to me that in his opinion the philoso-

---

[1] As to theodicy, very few indications were to be found in the first books of Bergson. He wrote to Höffding, in 1912: "That problem [of God], I have not really touched in my works; I believe it to be inseparable from moral problems, in the study of which I have been absorbed for some years; and the few lines of *Creative Evolution* you are alluding to have been placed here only as a stepping-stone." He also wrote to another friend that his critique of the idea of nothingness was only an objection directed against Spinoza, and that even in *Creative Evolution* he aimed at portraying the existence of a transcending and creative God. (*Cf.* the review *Études*, February 20, 1912.)

phers would do well to become a little more mystical, and the mystics a little more philosophical. Mystic. Perhaps that word bothers some people; yet after all we must call things by their right names. Thirty years ago in France, the word "mystic" stirred up all sorts of reactions of mistrust and uneasiness; one could not hear it spoken without immediately being on one's guard against an eventual invasion of fanaticism and hysteria. What is the situation in regard to this in the New World? I do not know. With us, in any case, a more careful observation of reality has caused these parasitical connotations to fall by the wayside, and now we understand better and better that the more or less pathological counterfeits of the mystical life are doubtless numerous, but that the true mystics are the wisest of men and the best witnesses for the spirit. Bergson himself has had a great deal to do with this change.

I was saying, then, that for a long time he had been reading the mystics. But I must at once emphasize that he did not read them with that curiosity of the collector, of the hobbyist in rare plants or exotic butterflies, which is sometimes displayed in regard to them by certain historians who are firmly determined to be on guard against them, to look down at them, to prevent the questions they have raised from entering their hearts. He read the mystics as one consults witnesses, eager himself for any traces of the spiritual he might find in this sad world, and perfectly prepared to allow any evidence of it, no matter how cumbrous and unsettling it might be, to exert on him its full weight. The mystics are dangerous beings. We have heard that often enough. Inevitably and from the beginning there is a betrayal of yourself in your manner of reading them. As you read, and by the way you read, they judge you.

Bergson read them humbly, and with love.

THE BASIC THEME OF THE TWO SOURCES

One fine day, without any notices in the press, without informing any one not even the author's closest friends, after twenty-five years of anticipation, the work was published. A classic from the day it appeared, it smashed the narrow framework of the rationalist, idealist and sociologist ethics, or pseudo-ethics; it outlined an ethics which does not shut man in on himself, but reveals and respects in him (and in this the title of the book is remarkably appropriate) the well-springs of moral experience and of moral life. He affirmed in magnificent language, and with a new emphasis, that humanity and life can be loved effectually only in Him who is the Principle of humanity and life; he recognized, if not the absolute truth of Christianity, on which he withheld judgment, at least the unique value and the transcendence of the fact of Christianity.

I shall not set forth in detail the contents of the *Two Sources of Morality and Religion;* that would take up too much space. We know, on the other hand, that Bergson's thought constantly progressed until his death, but he did not publish any statement concerning his more recent views. I shall restrict myself to the *Two Sources* and to a rapid résumé of its essential theses.

I should like at once to point out for one thing that Bergson herein brought us something profoundly new in relation to his previous work, what I would call an unforeseen spiritual substance—unforeseeable he doubtless would himself say—unforeseen because it stemmed from the very root of his own inner life; and for another that he has ordered and organized that spiritual substance in a logical whole which in itself seems on the contrary to bring us very little that is new and to be merely the expected and foreseen projection of themes already elaborated in *Creative Evolution. Intuition* and *conceptualization*—we know how significant and at times dramatic is the contrast between them in many philosophies, but especially in Bergsonism.

The fundamental theme of the *Two Sources* is the distinction and opposition between that which in moral life proceeds from *pressure* and that which proceeds from *attraction.* Pressure comes from social formations, and from that law of fear to which the individual is subject with regard to those rules of life imposed by the group and intended to assure its preservation, and which seeks only to turn to the routine and ferocious automatism of matter.

Attraction comes from the call of superior souls who commune with the *élan* of the spirit, and who penetrate into that infinitely open world of freedom and love, which transcends psychological and social mechanisms; *attraction* comes from the *call of the hero,* and from the propulsive force of the emotion which at once invading the soul, makes it free, because it awakens the soul to its most secret inner vitality. To the law of *pressure* and the law of *attraction* are linked two quite separate forms of morality: *closed* morality which, to put it briefly, is that of social conformism, and *open* morality, which is that of holiness.

A similar distinction must be made according to Bergson concerning religion: on one side we would have *static religion,* of which the beliefs of primitive peoples offer us a typical example, and which corresponds to the somewhat biological necessities implied by the conservation and historical movement of social groupings on the surface of the earth. By virtue of these necessities, a myth-making function must develop as a defensive reaction of nature against the dissolving power of the intelligence, in particular against the representation by the intelligence of the inevitability of death, and against the representation by the intelligence of a discouraging margin of contingency between initiative taken and desired effect.

This gives Bergson the opportunity to incorporate, while placing them on their proper level and criticizing their excessive pretentions, modern works on ethnology and sociology which relate to primitive mentality, magic, totemism, and mythology.

On the other hand we have *dynamic religion,* which is above all a vocation to the mystical life. In his chapter on dynamic religion, Bergson studies Greek mysticism, Oriental mysticism, the Prophets of Israel, Christian mysticism; and at the conclusion of this study he considers himself justified in saying that Christian mysticism alone has reached real achievement.

And it is the experience of the mystics which leads him to the existence of God. This existence, which his previous philosophic speculation on the *élan vital* and on the primary centre of movement wherefrom it springs made possible of conjecture, now compels unconditioned acceptance. How? By witness of those who have experience of things divine. We must believe the mystics about God, as we do the physicists about matter; both are competent, they both know whereof they speak.

In the last chapter of his book, to which he gave the title "Mechanics and Mysticism," Bergson, as if eager to add his testimony, offers us his ideas on many of the questions, in the cultural, social, and moral orders, which today torment humanity. The connection between this chapter and those that precede it is not very strong. But the author's concern to provide us, in the twilight of his life, with the warnings of a wholly free and wholly disinterested wisdom is only the more significant and moving. I shall not have space here to discuss this chapter.

I shall only point out that, taking the opposite view to a very wide-spread and superficial opinion, Bergson asserts that *mechanics* and *mysticism,* far from being opposites by nature, attract each other and require the completion of the one by the other. "Man will rise above earthly things," Bergson writes, "only if a powerful equipment supplies him with the requisite fulcrum. . . . In other words, the mystical summons up the mechanical. . . ." And, on the other hand, "We must add that the body, now larger, calls for a bigger soul, and that mechanism should mean mysticism. . . . Machinery will find its true vocation again; it will render services in proportion to its power, only if mankind, which it has bowed still lower to the earth, can succeed, through it, in standing erect and looking heavenwards."[1]

TWO POINTS OF VIEW

In order to try to appraise the latest developments of Bergsonian thought as they appear in the *Two Sources* one can take two vastly differing points of view, look at things from two widely different perspectives: the perspective of conceptualization and of doctrinal construction, of philosophy as a system; and the perspective of intentions and guiding intuitions, of philosophy as a spirit. We shall begin with the first. From that point of view it would be

---

[1] *Les Deux Sources de la Morale et de la Religion,* Paris, 7ᵉ Ed., Alcan, 1932, pp. 334–335; *The Two Sources of Morality and Religion* (Tr. by R. A. Audra and C. Brereton), New York, Holt, 1935, pp. 298–299.

fruitless to hide the fact that Bergson's ideas on morals and religion call for serious reservations in spite of the great truths on which they cast light.

The metaphysical apparatus of Bergsonism is responsible for this. The "ontological gap" and radical empiricism which wound this metaphysics have often and rightly been pointed out, especially in connection with the *Two Sources*. That serene elevation of thought, that scrupulous concern for the integral testimony of experience, that happy and powerful subtlety which we admire in Bergson—all this cannot avail as a complete remedy for such doctrinal deficiencies. Moreover, I must limit myself to the statements contained in the *Two Sources*. I am aware that Bergson did not express in these statements many thoughts he considered at this time to be private opinions (he wished his friends to read "between the lines"); I also know that his constantly alive effort of discovery did not stop at the *Two Sources* and continued progressing, above all in the religious field. But in this philosophical discussion I am allowed to take into account only those points of doctrine which Bergson offered to us in his books.

Considering in itself the system of interpretation proposed by Bergson in the *Two Sources,* one might ask whether his attempt to discover and comprehend the spiritual in its highest forms, to the extent that that attempt is bound up with the system of ideas propounded in *Creative Evolution,* does not, despite everything, amount to a reduction of the spiritual to the biological. I mean a biological itself made so transcendent that it is conceived as the creative source of all worlds, but which ever remains biological, in so far as the word relates to those levels of life, above all characterized by the organic and the psychic, on which life manifests itself in the animation of matter, and on which consequently immanent activity is bound up with conditions of transitive action and of productivity. Of course it is true enough that outside the world of grace and of supernatural life, man's spirituality never transcends what is biological except in a more or less imperfect fashion.

Let us at once try to develop precisely a few aspects, first of the Bergsonian conception of morality; second, of the Bergsonian conception of religion; and third, of the Bergsonian conception of the mystical life.

THE BERGSONIAN THEORY OF MORALITY

It has been justly observed that in matters of moral philosophy there exist two possible attitudes: one, which we may call *idealist,* being purely reflexive, refuses to distinguish between the speculative order and the practical order; it makes moral life the fundamental element, and if I may put it so, the very vitality of all thought; it moreover recognizes no other thought but human thought, which it calls Thought, with a capital T. The other attitude we might call *cosmic;* focussed upon being, it acknowledges that man is *situated* in a universe which spreads beyond him in every direction, and sees in the moral life of man a particular case in universal life, made specific within this universal life by the existence of free will.

The attitude of the ethics of Saint Thomas Aquinas is a cosmic attitude; that of Bergsonian ethics is also cosmic. And we cannot insist enough upon the importance of the renewal which modern thought thus owes to Bergson. He has recognized the dependence of moral philosophy with regard to metaphysics and the philosophy of nature, and has linked to a philosophy of the universe the destinies of the philosophy of human action. He thus delivers us from the last surviving attraction of Kantianism, and rediscovers the great philosophic tradition of humanity.

An ethics of the cosmic type cannot possibly dispense with a system of the world; the universe of freedom presupposes the universe of nature and fulfills a wish of the latter: I must know where I am and who I am, before knowing, and in order to know, what I should do. All that is fundamentally true; on all that Bergson and Saint Thomas are at one. But it is immediately obvious that the problem now shifts ground and relates to the validity of that metaphysics and system of the world proposed for our consideration. Is the world, as Bergson believes, a creative evolution? Or is it, as Saint Thomas believes, a hierarchy of growing perfections? Is man's intellect capable of attaining being, and does it consequently possess a power of regulation over life and action so that, as Saint Thomas Aquinas puts it, reason is the proximate rule of human acts? Or indeed is that which keeps man in contact with reality, with the dynamic *élan* that constitutes the secret of the real, is that, as Bergsonism would have it, a sort of instinct, as it were a vital inspiration, which runs through us from the depths of our souls, an instinct which emotion, above all, is apt to stir into action, to awaken? In each case, clearly enough, the edifice of ethics will be differently constructed. We are grateful to Bergson for having founded his ethics in a metaphysics; but we must note that that metaphysics is the metaphysics of the *élan vital,* and that the metaphysics of the *élan vital* does not take into account many essential truths.

Bergsonian ethics carries on and completes the fundamental theme of Bergsonian metaphysics: life is essentially a creative dynamism, but one which advances only under the burden of a dead weight, the obstacle constantly created by habit, by the "slipping back," which *is* matter. Thus, from our very first moral experience we feel ourselves caught between two dependencies: on the one hand a dependency with regard to the social disciplines which put pressure on us and which appear to us interior, because they have become habit; on the other hand a dependency with regard to the universal *élan* of life, which draws us on when we yield to the hero's call. We are inhabited: pressure and aspiration are both natural energies which are in us without being of us. Here we have, in the case of social pressure, an *obligation* to which Bergson seems to ascribe only a sort of physical meaning;

in the case of liberating aspiration, an *emotion*, resembling grace, whether natural or supernatural, itself conceived as an irresistible attraction, a victorious allurement.

In all this, and in the restitution of a certain profound *docility*, as an essential element of moral life, we find precious truths. But what of morality itself? What shall we consider the specific task of morality? It has vanished into thin air. Reduced to its essential work, and especially if it is considered in its basic natural structures, morality is a very humbly human thing, and not brilliant or glorious—rough and resolute, patient, prudent, argumentative, hard-working. For that poor devil, a rational being, it is a question of finding his way as best he can along the paths of happiness, using as he must a certain little light which places him above the whole bodily world, and thanks to which he is in a position to choose freely, to select for himself his own happiness, to say yes or no to whatever guides and hawkers offer to show him the way. It is a matter of taking oneself in hand by means of reason and freedom. And to what end? In order to decide that it is reasonable to obey a Law one has not made. What weariness! It is a thankless task to take oneself in hand, when one is as uninteresting a thing to look upon as is a man. And it is thankless to put freedom into use, especially when it is, in the last analysis, to do what Someone else wills. All this is a work of man, a work of reason and of thwarted freedom. How can we wonder that in a sense it seems to be volatilized by an *irrationalist* philosophy, for which the intelligence is good only to make tools, which teaches that the motives for acting come only after the decision to act has been taken, which does not succeed in conceiving free will except as a very high peak of vital spontaneity? The most captivating thing about Bergsonian ethics is precisely that morality, in the strictest sense of the word, has been eliminated from it. In it, man is caught between being something *social,* infra-rational, and something *mystical,* supra-rational.

Truth to tell, he is torn between the two, and when he becomes conscious of this, he will perhaps regret the absence of morality's exacting effort, but effort toward autonomy. Bergson does not leave us any means of choosing between the service of society and the call of the hero, between piety which imitates and fervour which invents. A kind of Manichæan cleavage is here the price paid for a thoroughly empiricist conception, in which to act can only be to yield to a force. Only reason, which is the principle of a moral universe distinct at once from social obedience and mystical impulse, can recognize, in dependence on the laws proper to that universe, the internal hierarchy which subordinates the social entity to the mystical and at the same time reconciles them with each other. But to posit that subordination and that reconciliation is to get away from Bergsonism.

If I had space here to delve deeply into things, I should have to recall at this point the central importance for ethics of the notion of *end;* since the human being is ordered to a certain end by the nature of things and by his ontological structure, ethics and the human will are dependent upon *another,* whom they should welcome, and are involved in the great cosmic play of being. But it is reason that knows that end—reason, and the will which accepts it freely and which freely chooses the means of attaining it. Thus the universe of morality is a universe of freedom, founded on the universe of nature. A cosmic type of morality we indeed must have, but on condition that reason and freedom are at the heart of the cosmic. Now the idea of end—the idea on which all this depends—is absent from Bergsonian morality as from Bergsonian metaphysics; that gap is the inevitable result of Bergsonian irrationalism.

One might say that for a philosophy of being, which is the philosophy of Saint Thomas, the temper of ethics is *cosmic rational;* for Bergson, it is *cosmic irrational.* Here everything for Bergson springs from a creative *élan* which ceaselessly pushes forward universal life; and moral generosity, the particular work of the hero of the moral life, is only the furthest and highest apex of that *élan* of universal life, which pushes on from degree to degree in the midst of so many set-backs. There is not, finally, any distinct order which constitutes the proper order of morality. But for Saint Thomas, for the philosophy of being, the order of the moral life is the order of the practical reason guiding the freedom of the human being to the true end of that being; and this order constitutes a *specific and autonomous* order in the bosom of universal metaphysical order, and yet founded upon it. And God, who is the Head and the Principle of universal order and universal life and who thus has no opposite and whom nothing resists, is also, Himself, the Principle of being, the Head and the Principle of that specific and autonomous order which is the moral order, and of that specific life which is the moral life, wherein man can offer his own refusal to the divine Will. If reason is the rule of human acts, it is so to the extent to which it is a participation in that eternal law which is creative wisdom itself.

Here then, all things considered, we have, for Bergsonism, an ethics of the creative *élan* or of creative evolution which preserves, I dare say, all of morals except morality itself; we have, for a philosophy of being, an ethics of creative wisdom, which in securing the specificity of morality, nevertheless recognizes its biological roots and social conditioning and makes the social disciplines a part of morality in so far as they are in conformity with reason; and, on the other hand, leaves morality open to the transcendent demands, to the most profound purifications and the highest regulations of the mystical life.

THE BERGSONIAN THEORY OF RELIGION

So is it also with the Bergsonian theory of religion. Bergson has admirably appraised, that is to say he has reduced to very modest proportions, the ambitious speculations of the sociological school on primitive mentality. In particular he calls attention to the fact that the thought of primitive man obeys the same laws as our own, under altogether different conditions and therefore with quite different results. I cannot resist quoting two pages here— pages which serve as a perfect example of the good nature with which the wisdom of metaphysicians on occasion permits itself to smile:

"Let us take for instance one of the most interesting chapters in M. Lévy-Bruhl's books, the one dealing with the first impressions produced on primitive man by our fire-arms, our writing, our books, in a word by everything we have to give him. We find this impression disconcerting at first. We should indeed be tempted to attribute it to a mentality different from our own. But the more we banish from our minds the science we have gradually, almost unconsciously, acquired, the more natural the 'primitive' explanation appears. Here we have people before whom a traveller opens a book, and who are told that the book gives information. They conclude that the book speaks, and that by putting it to their ear they will hear a sound. But to look for anything else in a man unacquainted with our civilization would be to expect from him an intelligence far greater than that of most of us, greater even than exceptional intelligence, greater even than genius: it would mean wanting him to re-invent the art of writing. For if he could imagine the possibility of depicting words on a sheet of paper he would possess the principle of alphabetic, or more generally of phonetic, writing; he would straightway have reached a point which civilized man has reached only by a long accumulation of the efforts of a great number of exceptional men. Let us not then speak of minds different from our own. Let us simply say that they are ignorant of what we have learnt.

"There are also, we added, cases where ignorance is coupled with an aversion to effort. Those would be the ones grouped by M. Lévy-Bruhl under the title of 'ingratitude of the sick.' Primitive men who have been treated by European doctors are not in any way grateful; nay, more, they expect payment from the doctor, as if it were they who had done him a service. But having no notion of our medical science, no idea that it is a science coupled with an art, seeing moreover that the doctor is far from always curing his patient, and finally considering that he certainly gives his time and his trouble, how can they help thinking that the doctor has some interest, unknown to them, in what he does? And why, instead of striving to shake off their ignorance, should they not adopt quite naturally the interpretation which first occurs to their minds, and from which they can profit? I put this question to the author of *La Mentalité primitive*, and I shall evoke a recollection, a very ancient one, though scarcely older than our old friendship. I was a little boy and I had bad teeth. There was nothing for it but to take me now and again to the dentist, who at once showed no mercy to the offending tooth; he pulled it out relentlessly. Between you and me, it hardly hurt at all, for the teeth in question would have come out of their own accord; but I was no sooner seated in the dentist's chair than I set up a blood-curdling yell, for the principle of the thing. My family at last found out a way to make me keep quiet. The dentist, taking care to make a noise about it, would drop a fifty-centime piece into the glass from which I was to rinse my mouth (ascepticism was unknown in those far-off days), the purchasing-power of this sum being at that time ten sticks of barley sugar. I must have been six or seven, and was no stupider than most boys. I was certainly capable of guessing that this was a put-up job between the dentist and my family to bribe me into silence, and that they conspired together for my particular good. But it would have needed a slight effort to think, and I preferred not to make it, perhaps from laziness, perhaps so as not to change my attitude towards a man against whom my tooth was indeed bared. So I simply went on not thinking, and the idea I was bound to form of the dentist then stood out automatically in my mind in letters of fire. Clearly he was a man who loved drawing teeth, and he was even ready to pay for this the sum of half a franc."[1]

Thus can "primitive mentality" be found in civilized man. The data to be found in today's newspapers would allow me to illustrate that assertion with examples not quite so innocent as that of young Bergson's tooth.

But let us come back to the theory of religion. In my opinion what spoils the Bergsonian theory of *static religion*, despite his many profound observations, is his refusal to discern in it the natural energy of human reason, as it operates in the midst of those incoherences and contradictions which Bergson so well analyzes, and which relate to a mental universe bathed and inundated by the waters of the imagination; the obscure natural workings of the metaphysical intelligence, the natural pursuit of and feeling for the absolute are thus disregarded. Instead of that, religion in its primitive and strongly socialized forms, the religion Bergson calls static, together with the myth-making function which is linked to it, seems to him like a defensive reaction against the dangers of the intelligence.

The embarrassment caused by these fascinating theories is like that caused by the aphorisms of genius. Consider such an aphorism; you may well ex-

---

[1] *Ibid.*, Paris Ed., pp. 158–160; New York Ed., pp. 139–141. Quoted by permission of Henry Holt and Co.

press a truth equally profound by saying just the opposite. For instance, selecting as samples a few of the most celebrated aphorisms of classical French literature: *One can face neither the sun nor death without flinching. Man is a thinking blade of grass. Genius is patience long drawn out.* Well, suppose I say: *One can face unflinchingly the sun and death?* Or: *Man is* NOT *a thinking blade of grass?* Or: *Genius is impatience long drawn out?* It seems to me these aphorisms are as good as the first. Bergson thinks that the intelligence discourages and that it inspires fear, and that the myth-making function, translating great biological instincts, is necessary to give man heart to live. On the other hand one may think that the spectacle of life is indeed depressing—"You have multiplied men," says the psalmist, "but you have not multiplied joy,"—and that intelligence, with its primordial metaphysical certainties, inspires one with the courage to live, and that the myth-making function is a kind of refraction in the realm of the imagination of the intellect's practical encouragements. After all, it would be quite possible for both these ways of thinking to be true at the same time.

However that may be, it is ever the same process of severing and opposing (to use a word certainly too strong, one could call it Manichæan) that, for Bergson, separates static religion, religion in its inferior forms, socialized and materialized, from dynamic religion, open to the universality of the spirit. That which might constitute the unity of both, that is to say the ontological value, now hidden, now exposed, of certain perceptions and certain beliefs, disappears in both the one and the other.

For even as regards dynamic religion the logical implications of the Bergsonian distrust of intelligence tend to attenuate that objective content of knowledge, those properly intellectual data whose supra-rational value one cannot affirm without at the same time affirming the rational values they envelop. It is the entire domain of *truth* communicated to man by the formulas and the assertions of faith which finds itself thus disregarded. As a matter of fact, if this is the case, it is so because in the philosophical order itself Bergson began by failing to recognize the value of *metaphysical reason,* properly so called. Against the heritage of this reason he continues to raise criticisms most unjust, and the picture that he draws of the ideas of Plato and Aristotle is distorted by the nominalistic and irrationalistic prejudices of his own metaphysics.

THE BERGSONIAN THEORY OF THE MYSTICAL LIFE

Let us go on to what Bergson tells us of the mystics in the *Two Sources.* If one considers things less from the point of view of the spirit whose instinct he followed than from the point of view of the doctrinal conceptualization he proposes, one is compelled here also to make certain reservations.

When the mystics say that they are united to their Principle as to the life of their life, they do not think they are welcoming some vital *élan* or some anonymous creative effort. They already know the name of the One to whom they cling: they already know—by the faith they have in common with all those who have received the revealed Word—who is this God, and what are His designs upon men.

The question of knowing whether the principle to which the mystics are bound is the transcendent cause of all things[1] seemed, in the *Two Sources,* secondary to Bergson. The mystics themselves are not uninterested in that question; they answer it with a definite affirmative. They testify (and on this point it seems to me that Bergson's book at least leaves us in an equivocal state) that their will and their soul are impelled not toward the joy of a creative urge definitively free of all end, but on the contrary toward an infinite end, and that the prodigious energy which moves them has meaning and existence only as it carries them on to that final end wherein they shall be established in a ceaseless life.

They testify (and it is the whole problem of the validity of dogma that they thus set and that they resolve—a problem which Bergson, wishing to remain purely a philosopher, has not set, but one to which I do not see how one can give appropriate answer if one accepts his basic criticism of the concept and of conceptual formulas) ... the mystics testify that their experience of divine things has living faith as its proximate and proportioned principle, and that if that experience is obscure and is obtained by love, it is nevertheless a supreme knowledge, since the intelligence is nourished in this notknowing by its most noble Object.

Finally, to come to the problem of action and of contemplation, the mystics testify that if contemplation overflows into action, still it is not precise to write—I criticize the expression more than the thought; I shall come back to that in a moment—it is at least ambiguous to write as did Bergson that the final state for contemplation is to *spoil itself in action* and in an *irresistible urge which casts the soul into the most vast undertakings.*

FROM THE POINT OF VIEW OF THE SPIRIT
AND OF DIRECTIVE INTUITIONS

We have been considering, from the point of view of conceptualization and doctrinal construction or of philosophy as a system, some important matters contained in the *Two Sources,* and on that score we have been obliged to make several criticisms. Everything changes its aspect if we change the point of view to one of philosophy as *spirit,* of directive intentions and intuitions. In such case we may give ourselves the joy of admiration, pure and simple.

There is nothing more moving, nothing which in a sense better bears wit-

[1] *Ibid.,* Paris Ed., pp. 256, 269, 281; New York Ed., pp. 228, 239, 250.

ness to the transcendence of the spirit, than to see an untiringly courageous thought, in spite of its philosophical equipment and by virtue of fidelity to the light within, follow a pure spiritual trajectory and thus come to the very doors at whose threshold all philosophy stops short (but which Bergson himself was to pass through some years later).[1]

I indicated a moment ago the reservations which concern for correct doctrine obliges us to make with regard to the general interpretation that Bergson proposes for the mystical life. As a matter of fact, the delinquencies I have pointed out in that interpretation show above all that philosophy *alone* is not enough in these matters. To the extent that philosophy, in its desire to use merely philosophical means, believes that it should not explicitly consider the reality of grace and the mystery of the Cross—in other words, to the extent that philosophy believes it should refuse to enter into continuity with theology in its treatment of such matters—to that extent philosophy will remain unable to reach in their specific causes the things of mystical life, with whatever good faith the philosopher honours them. And what pure philosopher has ever studied all those things with greater good faith, with a more humble and generous love, than Henri Bergson?

It is high time to indicate the gratitude we owe him for the admirable pages he has devoted to the mystics, pages which reveal a marvellously faithful and loving attention with regard to realities felt as present and efficacious. Bergson here reduces to nothingness the indigent constructions of vulgar phenomenalist psychology; and if one bears in mind the anti-mystical prejudices to which I alluded at the beginning of this chapter, one cannot help thinking that Bergson offers the mystics fine compensation when he dwells upon the *intellectual robustness* of these souls, who attained a life in some fashion superhuman. Let us take a look at his own words. I quote some pages from the *Two Sources:*

"We may therefore conclude that neither in Greece nor in ancient India was there complete mysticism, in the one case because the impetus was not strong enough, in the other case because it was thwarted by material conditions or by too narrow an intellectual frame. It is its appearance at a given moment that enables us to follow in retrospect its preparatory phases, just as the volcano, bursting into activity, explains a long series of earthquakes in the past.

[1] Mme. Henri Bergson has made public part of her late husband's will, dated February 8, 1937. Here are a few sentences from this document: "My reflections have led me closer and closer to Catholicism, in which I see the complete fulfillment of Judaism. I would have become a convert had I not seen in preparation for years the formidable wave of antisemitism which is to break upon the world. I wanted to remain among those who tomorrow will be persecuted. But I hope that a Catholic priest will consent, if the Cardinal Archbishop of Paris authorizes it, to come to say prayers at my funeral." A priest did in fact fulfill this wish. Henri Bergson died on January 4, 1941.

"For the complete mysticism is that of the great Christian mystics. . . .

"When we grasp that such is the culminating point of the inner evolution of the great mystics, we can but wonder how they could ever have been classed with the mentally diseased. True, we live in a condition of unstable equilibrium; normal health of mind, as, indeed, of body, is not easily defined. Yet there is an exceptional, deep-rooted mental healthiness, which is readily recognizable. It is expressed in the bent for action, the faculty of adapting and re-adapting oneself to circumstances, in firmness combined with suppleness, in the prophetic discernment of what is possible and what is not, in the spirit of simplicity which triumphs over complication, in a word, in supreme good sense. Is not this exactly what we find in the above-named mystics? And might they not provide us with the very definition of intellectual vigour?

"If they have been judged otherwise, it is because of the abnormal states which are, with them, the prelude to the ultimate transformation. They talk of their visions, their ecstasies, their raptures. These are phenomena which also occur in sick people and which are part of their malady. An important work has lately appeared on ecstasy regarded as a psycho-asthenic manifestation. But there exist morbid states which are imitations of healthy states; the latter are none the less healthy, and the former morbid. A lunatic may think he is an emperor; he will systematically introduce a Napoleonic touch into his gestures, his words, his acts, and therein lies his madness: does this in any way reflect upon Napoleon?

"In just the same way it is possible to parody mysticism, and the result will be mystic insanity: does it follow that mysticism is insanity? Yet there is no denying that ecstasies, visions, raptures, are abnormal states, and that it is difficult to distinguish between the abnormal and the morbid. And such indeed has been the opinion of the great mystics themselves. They have been the first to warn their disciples against visions which are quite likely to be pure hallucinations. And they generally regarded their own visions, when they had any, as of secondary importance, as wayside incidents; they had to go beyond them, leaving raptures and ecstasies far behind, to reach the goal, which was identification of the human will with the divine will. The truth is that these abnormal states resembling morbid states, and sometimes doubtless very much akin to them, are easily comprehensible, if we only stop to think what a shock to the soul is the passing from the static to the dynamic, from the closed to the open, from everyday life to mystic life. . . .

"We cannot upset the regular relation of the conscious to the unconscious without running a risk. So we must not be surprised if nervous disturbances and mysticism sometimes go together; we find the same disturbances in other forms of genius, notably in musicians. They have to be regarded as merely accidental. The former have no more to do with mystical inspiration than the latter with musical.

"Shaken to its depths by the current which is about to sweep it forward, the soul ceases to revolve around itself and escapes for a moment from the law which demands that the species and the individual should condition one another. It stops, as though to listen to a voice calling. Then it lets itself go, straight onward. It does not directly perceive the force that moves it, but it feels an indefinable presence, or divines it through a symbolic vision. Then comes a boundless joy, an all-absorbing ecstasy or an enthralling rapture: God is there, and the soul is in God. Mystery is no more. Problems vanish, darkness is dispelled; everything is flooded with light. But for how long? An imperceptible anxiety, hovering above the ecstasy, descends and clings to it like its shadow. This anxiety alone would suffice, even without the phases which are to come, to distinguish true and complete mysticism from what was in bygone days its anticipated imitation or preparation. For it shows that the soul of the great mystic does not stop at ecstasy, as at the end of a journey. The ecstasy is indeed rest, if you like, but as though at a station, where the engine is still under steam, the onward movement becoming a vibration until it is time to race forward again.

"Let us put it more clearly: however close the union with God may be, it could be final only if it were total. Gone, doubtless, is the distance between the thought and the object of the thought, since the problems which measured and indeed constituted the gap have disappeared. Gone the radical separation between him who loves and him who is beloved: God is there, and joy is boundless. But though the soul becomes, in thought and feeling, absorbed in God, something of it remains outside; that something is the will, whence the soul's action, if it acted, would quite naturally proceed. Its life, then, is not yet divine. The soul is aware of this, hence its vague disquietude, hence the agitation in repose which is the striking feature of what we call complete mysticism: it means that the impetus has acquired the momentum to go further, that ecstasy affects indeed the ability to see and to feel, but that there is, besides, the will, which itself has to find its way back to God. When this agitation has grown to the extent of displacing everything else, the ecstasy has died out, the soul finds itself alone again, and sometimes desolate. Accustomed for a time to a dazzling light, it is now left blindly groping in the gloom. It does not realize the profound metamorphosis which is going on obscurely within it. It feels that it has lost much; it does not yet know that this was in order to gain all.

"Such is the 'darkest night,' of which the great mystics have spoken, and which is perhaps the most significant thing, in any case the most instructive, in Christian mysticism. The final phase, characteristic of great mysticism, is imminent. To analyze this ultimate preparation is impossible, for the mystics themselves have barely had a glimpse of its mechanism. Let us confine ourselves to suggesting that a machine of wonderfully tempered steel, built for some extraordinary feat, might be in a somewhat similar state if it became conscious of itself as it was being put together. Its parts being one by one subjected to the severest tests, some of them rejected and replaced by others, it would have a feeling of something lacking here and there, and of pain all over. But this entirely superficial distress would only have to be intensified in order to pass into the hope and expectation of a marvellous instrument. The mystic soul yearns to become this instrument. It throws off anything in its substance that is not pure enough, not flexible and strong enough, to be turned to some use by God. . . . *Now* it is God who is acting through the soul, in the soul; the union is total, therefore final. . . .

"A calm exaltation of all its faculties makes it see things on a vast scale only, and, in spite of its own weakness, produce only what can be mightily wrought. Above all, it sees things simply, and this simplicity, which is equally striking in the words it uses and the conduct it follows, guides it through complications which it apparently does not even perceive. An innate knowledge, or rather an acquired ignorance, suggests to it straightway the step to be taken, the decisive act, the unanswerable word. Yet effort remains indispensable, endurance and perseverance likewise. But they come of themselves, they develop of their own accord, in a soul acting and acted upon, whose liberty coincides with the divine activity. They represent a vast expenditure of energy, but this energy is supplied as it is required, for the superabundance of vitality which it demands flows from a spring which is the very source of life. And now the visions are left far behind: the divinity could not manifest itself from without to a soul henceforth replete with its essence. Nothing remains to distinguish such a man outwardly from the men about him. He alone realizes the change which has raised him to the rank of *adjutores Dei,* 'patients' in respect to God, agents in respect to man. In this elevation he feels no pride. On the contrary, great is his humility. How could he be aught but humble, when there has been made manifest to him, in mute colloquy, alone with The Alone, through an emotion in which his whole soul seemed to be absorbed, what we may call the divine humility? . . .

"The love which consumes him is no longer simply the love of man for God, it is the love of God for all men. Through God, in the strength of God, he loves all mankind with a divine love. This is not the fraternity enjoined on us by the philosophers in the name of reason, on the principle that all men share by birth in one rational essence: so noble an ideal cannot but command our respect; we may strive to the best of our ability to put it into practice, if it be not too irksome for the individual and the community; we shall never attach ourselves to it passionately. Or, if we do, it will be because we have breathed in some nook or corner of our civilization the intoxicating fragrance left there by mysticism. Would the philosophers themselves have laid down so confidently the principle, so little in keeping with every-day experience, of an equal participation of all men in a higher essence, if there had not been mystics to embrace all humanity in one simple indivisible love? This is not, then, that fraternity which started as an idea, whence an ideal has been erected. Neither is it the intensification of an innate sympathy of man for man. Indeed we may ask ourselves whether such an instinct ever existed elsewhere than in the imagination of philosophers, where it was devised for reasons of symmetry. With family, country, humanity appearing as wider and wider circles, they thought that man must naturally love humanity as he loves his country and his family, whereas in reality the family group and the social group are the only ones ordained by nature, the only ones corresponding to instincts, and the social instinct would be far more likely to prompt societies to struggle against one another than to unite to make up humanity. The utmost we can say is that family and social feeling may chance to overflow and to operate beyond its natural frontiers, with a kind of luxury value; it will never go very far. The mystic love of humanity is a very different thing. It is not the extension of an instinct, it does not originate in an idea. It is neither of the senses nor of the mind. It is of both, implicitly, and is effectively much more. For such a love lies at the very root of feeling and reason, as of all other things. Coinciding with God's love for His handiwork, a love which has been the source of everything, it would yield up, to anyone who knew how to question it, the secret of creation. It is even more metaphysical than moral in its essence. What it wants to do, with God's help, is to complete the creation of the human species. . . .[1]

"In reality," again adds Bergson, "the task of the great mystic is to effect a radical transformation of humanity by setting an example."[2] And what was it that Saint Paul said? It is our task to complete that which is lacking (as far as application, not merit, is concerned) of the sufferings of the Saviour—in other words to continue the work of redemption in time as His instruments—to the point, as said Saint John of the Cross, "of quitting one's skin and all the rest for Him." That is why Christians receive baptism: and not in order to thank God for not being like other men, even like that publican. . . .

Short of making an analysis through *inherent proper causes,* which theological instruments alone permit, by informing a philosopher of the realities which are grace, the theological virtues, and the gifts of the Holy Spirit, it is impossible to discuss the mystical experience with more depth and with

1 *Ibid.,* Paris Ed., pp. 242–251; New York Ed., 216–223. Quoted by permission of Henry Holt and Co.

2 *Ibid.,* Paris Ed., p. 256; New York Ed., p. 228,

a more intense, farsighted sympathy than does the author of *Two Sources*. Perhaps theologians themselves might find in the pages quoted above matter fit for instruction. We can see, on the other hand, that if at certain times in other passages which I do not here reproduce the conceptual expression may call for reservations, the spirit which animates all this study of Bergson's can only elicit our admiration. And even as Bergson seemed to subordinate contemplation to activity and to vast undertakings, his thought really had quite a different meaning. During one of our last conversations I questioned him in this matter. He answered that it was not in his mind to assert any primacy of action over contemplation. He meant simply to say that the contemplation of the perfect mystics is a contemplation of love which, because it essentially implies the giving of self, requires an overflow into action, in accordance with the obligations and the opportunities of the moment; and that this overflowing, when it takes place, gives testimony to the full transformation of the human soul, regarding the will as well as the powers of knowledge.

If Bergsonian theodicy is evidently very deficient in the order of demonstration and rational knowledge, or rather, is inexistent in so far as it is rational, nevertheless that humility by which the philosopher in all this *believes* those who have journeyed into the realm of things divine, and who have returned from it, is not only a great testimony to the internal hierarchy of wisdoms, it also insures him against the risk of errors from which it might have been particularly difficult for his philosophical conceptualization by itself to escape. He henceforth knows with certainty that God exists, and that He is personal, and that He is freely creative. If the dangers of pantheism are in my opinion inherent in the Bergsonian metaphysics, Bergson himself has deliberately made his choice against pantheism. He has asked the mystics to instruct him; they have not led him astray. They have taught him the great secret, which the Gospels revealed, even though in a sense it be accessible to natural reason. What the testimony of the mystics clearly tells us, writes Bergson, is that "divine love is not something of God, it is God himself."[1]

I have just said that in a sense reason alone could have discovered the truth that God is Love—the highest truth to which the reason of itself can attain. True, but the reason did not do so. It required the help of those positive historic contributions which the Judæo-Christian tradition calls revelation. If the revelation of the divine Name to Moses, *I am who I am,* taught the reason from above what the reason itself could have known but did not know how to discover, by how much stronger reason is this true of the revelation made to Saint John: *God is love.* Let me point this out: if you consider

---

[1] *Ibid.,* Paris Ed., p. 270; New York Ed., p. 240.

the relation between the creature and God, then to say that God not only should be loved, but that He loves, and I mean with the madness proper to love, that there can be relations of friendship, of loving forgiveness, of a common life, of shared happiness, between the creature and God—all that implies the supernatural order of grace and of charity. Both this supernatural truth, and this experience, help the reason to understand the meaning of that same word, God is love, in so far as it asserts that in God to love is the same as to exist, which is a truth of the natural order. It is the most resplendent sign of divine glory, as our reason can attain it, that love, which presupposes intelligence and which is above all an overflowing, an ultimate superabundance of the life of spiritual living beings, should be in God identical with the very essence and the very existence of God. In that sense Love is His Name above all names: it is His Gospel Name.

The mystics have taught Henri Bergson this name, causing him at one bound to outstrip his whole philosophy. If the philosopher "attaches himself to mystical experience," he writes, "Creation will appear to him as God undertaking to create creators, that He may have, besides Himself, beings worthy of His love."* Let us say, rather: to create gods, transformed in God by love and in love, and then we rejoin Saint Paul and Saint John of the Cross.

Given the very special method here followed by Bergson; that is to say, given that, in order to philosophize on divine things, he consulted the experience of mystics, it is not astonishing that certain echoes of a properly supernatural order which spring from the living faith of his instructors should have passed over into his philosophy. One can thus understand that, whatever may be the insufficiencies of his theory of dynamic religion, what matters most to the Christian is nevertheless there. When, in connection with the coming of Christianity, he says, in his own special phraseology, "The essence of the new religion was to be the spreading of mysticism,"[1] or again, "In this sense religion is to mysticism what vulgarization is to science,"[2] what does he affirm if not the central truth which Saint Thomas sets forth in the following terms: "The new law, at least that which is principal in it, is not a written law, but is infused in the heart, because it is the law of the new covenant. What is above all important in the law of the new covenant, and that in which lies *all its power,* is the grace of the Holy Spirit which is given by living faith. . . ."[3] From whence it follows that without love I am nothing, as Saint Paul says, and that the perfection of charity, the union which transforms the soul in God, is *of precept,* not indeed as a thing imme-

* *Ibid.,* Paris Ed., p. 273; New York Ed., p. 243.
1 *Ibid.,* Paris Ed., p. 255; New York Ed., p. 227.
2 *Ibid.*
3 *Sum. theol.,* I–II, 106, 1.

diately to be realized, but as a goal toward which to strive, each in accordance with his condition.

I have pointed out that the system developed in the *Two Sources* with regard to static morality and dynamic morality retains all of morals except
morality itself.

This formula, doubtless too severe, must obviously be understood as applying to the strictly rational and human content of ethics, and it relates to
Bergsonian conceptualization. In considering on the other hand the spiritual
intentions of the doctrine, one must grant that it brings us very precious enlightenment on the subject of the conditions, the environment, the social orchestration of morality, and also concerning its internal dynamism.

For one thing, it puts us on our guard against the enormous amount of
deliberate or unconscious imitation, of routine, of social reflexes, and of social
conformity which threaten the moral life within us. For another it warns us
that in fact, in concrete reality, moral life loses all truly transforming value
in us if it is not infused with a call and a vocation, with an *élan* and a desire,
with an insatiable desire, with a mad desire, and for what, if not for holiness?
Because what Bergson terms the call of the hero is very evidently the call of
the saint. In thus having the moral fastened to the supramoral, that is to say
the divine, in having the law appendant to love and freedom, Bergson saves
morality.

AFTER TWENTY-SEVEN YEARS

My first published work was a severe criticism of Bergsonism. It appeared
late in 1913.[1] The last chapter of this book was called "The Two Bergsonisms"; I there distinguished what I called the *Bergsonism of fact*, which I
criticized, from what I called the *Bergsonism of intention*, which I believed
to be orientated toward Thomistic wisdom.

I take the liberty of quoting here some lines from this chapter. With great
temerity I addressed myself, as it were, to Bergson, and I said: "You glimpse
the existence of a personal God. It is not the God of the learned; it is a living
and active God, it is the God of the whole man. Can you continue to deal
with him as a theorist does with an idea, and not as a man with his Lord?
There are secrets which He alone can reveal. You yourself are one of these
secrets. You would know your end and the means to attain it if you knew
these secrets. But you will only know them if it pleases God to reveal them
Himself. Truly, philosophers play a strange game. They know very well that
one thing alone counts, and that all their medley of subtle discussions relates

---

[1] *La Philosophie Bergsonienne, Études Critiques*, Paris, Rivière, 1913. Seconde édition revue
et corrigée, et augmentée d'une préface de 86 pages, Paris, Téqui, 1930. [*First Part* of the present
volume. The chapter to which I am referring here is the *Third Section* of this First Part.]

to one single question: why are we born on this earth? And they also know that they will never be able to answer it. Nevertheless they continue sedately to amuse themselves. Do they not see that people come to them from all points of the compass, not with a desire to partake of their subtlety but because they hope to receive from them one word of life? If they have such words, why do they not cry them from the housetops, asking their disciples to give, if necessary, their very blood for them? If they have no such words, why do they allow people to believe they will receive from them something which they cannot give? For mercy's sake, if ever God has spoken, if in some place in the world, were it on the gibbet of one crucified, He has sealed His truth, tell us; that is what you must teach. Or are you indeed masters in Israel only to be ignorant of these things?"

How then, after so many years, can I fail to see in the last developments of Bergson's philosophy an answer to the anxious questions I then raised?

This master, who freed in me my metaphysical desire, and whose doctrine I had in turn criticized—through love of the truth, as he well knew—this master was generous enough not to hold these criticisms against me although they touched what is most dear to a philosopher, his idea. He wrote some years ago that, though having but little acquaintance with Saint Thomas, each time he met with one of his texts along the way, he had found himself in agreement with him; and that he was gladly willing to have his philosophy placed in the same stream as flowed from Saint Thomas. I do not cite this with some ludicrous idea of annexing Bergson to Thomism. But rather because he himself was perfectly willing to think that I had not been wrong in saying that his philosophy contained certain as yet undeveloped virtualities, and because it thus happened that as last we met one another as it were halfway, each having journeyed unwittingly in such a manner as to approach the other: he, toward those who alone represent without betraying it the faith to which I belong, I toward a comprehension, a little less deficient, of the human task of those who seek without yet having found.

Charles Du Bos once spoke of the kind of euphoria to which an intelligence *too felicitous in being right* is in danger of abandoning itself. Twenty-seven years ago I well knew that it was not myself, but the long tradition of wisdom of which Saint Thomas is the great Doctor, that was in the right as against the metaphysical system of Bergson. But I did not yet know that even if one is never too much in the right, this is nevertheless (as I said in the Preface to the French second edition)[2] so great a privilege, and so undeserved, that it is always appropriate to apologize for it. It is a courtesy which must be offered to truth.

[2] See *supra*, p. 12.

APPENDIX

MARGINAL NOTES ON ARISTOTLE

I have considered that it might be useful to reproduce here two notes on Aristotle's philosophy. The first concerns the work of O. Hamelin and the doctoral thesis of Jacques Chevalier;[1] the second relates to an already ancient controversy, but one in which questions of historical and speculative order of permanent interest are involved. It consists of two articles[2] that I have combined in a single text and from which I have eliminated certain polemical passages written in answer to a number of rather too heated attacks and on which I do not care to insist since, in spite of my disagreement with Chevalier regarding Aristotle, Descartes and Bergson, in other respects I have for him only cordial sentiments.

I

TWO BOOKS ON ARISTOTLE

Among the works published in recent years on ancient philosophy, two studies devoted to Aristotle are particularly worthy of our attention: the one, entitled *le Système d'Aristote*, is the series of lectures delivered on the Stagirite by the late-lamented Mr. Hamelin and edited, like the *Système de Descartes,* by some of his faithful followers; the other is the thesis written by Jacques Chevalier on *la Notion du nécessaire chez Aristote*. I have no intention here of following these two studies in detail; I only wish, while pointing out their interest, to present a few general reflections with regard to them.

Hamelin's book is commendable for its scientific probity. It is a fine example of careful, patient, historical reconstruction based on excellent source material and critical research by one who has a thorough comprehension of his subject. It marks a very notable progress over the massively incomprehensive erudition of Zeller, already strongly criticized in Germany by Brentano and corrected in these lectures on a good many important points. It elucidates in a most satisfactory manner a great many questions of detail; one might say that the first five chapters especially, devoted to the life and writings of the philosopher, or again the chapter on modal syllogisms, are little masterpieces.

But can we say that this work fully lives up to its title and brings to life before our eyes *Aristotle's system?* I hardly think so. Through a defect that Hamelin would doubtless have corrected had he lived long enough to put the final touches to his work, its parts are unevenly balanced: the importance of logic and problems

1 *Revue universelle,* November 1, 1921.
2 *Les Lettres,* April 1920 and March 1922.

in logic is certainly very great in Aristotle's work, and Hamelin was right in giving them an important place in his lectures; but in comparison the attention given to the problems of natural philosophy seems rather limited; the ethics has been sacrificed entirely, and, what matters most, the metaphysics has been cut down and schematized to excess. The picture we are thus given of the system is very incomplete and unsatisfactory; it leaves in the background what might best enable us to appreciate both the vigorously experimental realism and the profound metaphysical unity of Aristotle's doctrine. That is doubtless why this very conscientious work, so interesting to the specialist, often produces a painful impression of archeological reconstruction.

That is not the most serious objection, for Hamelin, in spite of all his care to be exact, has distorted the philosopher's thought on several important points.

As Aristotle teaches on the one hand that the object of knowledge is the conceptual and hence universal element of things and on the other hand that only the individual exists in reality, Hamelin is quite right in asserting that it would be "too unjust and too unintelligent" to accuse him bluntly here of contradiction and to claim that for him, as for Kant, "what is known is not real, and what is real is not known." He himself, however, sees only an ill-digested Platonic heritage, where what we have in fact is a fundamental enunciation of the nature of our knowledge and of our mind (the direct object of our knowledge is universal). He discovers only a powerful effort to adjust disparate elements thanks to a laborious compromise—provisional, like all compromises, and ultimately useless—where Aristotle, having made certain of his grasp of things and of the mind, rises in the most conscious and logical fashion to the unity of a superior point of view. In short he admits in the philosopher's thought an irreducible conflict between two incompatible tendencies, a "conceptual" or "universalist" tendency which would explain things by the most general and the hollowest of logical universals and which would manifest itself especially in the theory of knowledge—and a "realist" or experimental tendency, much more fundamentally Aristotelian, but insufficiently developed by Aristotle, which would place in the individual, along with sovereign reality, the sovereign value of intelligibility and which would manifest itself especially in the theory of being. In my opinion Hamelin misses the central intuition which constitutes precisely the most characteristic and original feature of the doctrine he is explaining.

What might be called the *system of internal conflict* is a commonplace procedure of the "historical method" and an infallible recipe used by those who turn out theses at the Sorbonne: a procedure universal in its application, long-since patented by the historian-critics of Christian origins. In philosophy it leads the student to judge the interest of a doctrine by the original contradictions it is supposed to embrace and to show the thinker on whom he is expending his efforts as being occupied in fitting together as best he may incompatible principles or data, and finally being overcome in spite of all his ingenuity. This procedure, which recognizes only tendencies contending with one another in the author and achieving contingent compromises among themselves, has all the more chance of succeeding the less vigorously the thinker to whom it is applied is possessed by the object. It has, furthermore, the advantage of saving the historian a great deal of intellectual effort and, at the same time, of enhancing his powers of judgment, for it is a fine thing not to be taken in by the great men and to be able to reveal the "seams" in their thought (as the Abbé Durantel did recently with regard to Saint Thomas). But Hamelin was certainly insensible to such advantages. How then does it happen that a man of his mental powers could have allowed himself to be caught in the system of internal conflict, even though in his use of it he shows more restraint than many other writers? I imagine that in his case he was a victim of his idealist fad and, more generally, of that insufficient elaboration of the theory of knowledge from which, in spite of the arrogant claims of the Kantians, it must be admitted, the whole of modern philosophy suffers.

It seems, and here we touch the heart of the debate, that modern philosophy always has been and still remains secretly tormented by a double-faced prejudice whose distant origin might be sought in the two capital errors of decadent scholasticism: the Scotist theory of individuation and Ockhamist nominalism.

In the universal ideas which make up human science it sees nothing but impoverished schemata enframing a certain number of individual cases. On the other hand, it is more or less consciously persuaded that essences or natures are complete as such only in the individual, with the result that all knowledge by the universal is fundamentally inadequate and that to know the essence of a thing in its integrity, it would be necessary to know that thing in its basic individuality, in that singularity which the Thomists, after Aristotle, declare to be "ineffable." It would require a lengthy technical study to follow along the course of the history of modern thought the effects of this double prejudice, which affirms itself in Spinoza to a radical extreme that is truly magnificent. It is in any case clear that a critic convinced, as Hamelin was, 1) that the universal is an "inert residue," a "dead residue," 2) that we must seek in what Aristotle calls 'form' the root of individuality and "treat the individual as a final species,"—is not in condition to grasp the essential spirit of Aristotle. He finds himself condemned from the outset, in spite of the most loyal effort of comprehension, to pull Aristotelian ideas in the direction of an idealist monism completely at variance with their true significance; to blame Aristotle for not having admitted like the Platonists of the Alexandrian school,—and Leibnitz later,—an idea for each individual; in short, to accuse of incoherence a doctrine which makes of God, the supreme Individual, a pure form and which, contrariwise, explains corporal individuals by matter. As though an absence of external symmetry—of that external symmetry which played so many shabby tricks on a Kant—was equal to an absence of internal logic and could in no circumstance be required by the real. "The weak point, by no means demanded by the logic of the doctrine, is the theory of individuality," writes Hamelin. One might as well declare that the keystone of an edifice is by no means demanded by the logic of that edifice.

To tell the truth, we are here faced with one of the most delicate problems of metaphysics and logic, that old problem of the universal and of individuation which preoccupied the ancients to such an extent, and in which modern philosophy is more than ever involved. (If only it would make up its mind to face it!) Developing the fundamental principles of Aristotelian philosophy, Saint Thomas and his great disciples taught that essence—the object of pure intelligence—is found complete as such not in the individual but in specific nature, although it cannot exist outside of the mind except in individuals, which it is for the senses to perceive directly in their singular existence. Thus they affirmed the existence and the value of the sensible singular (from which we draw our ideas by abstraction, and in which all physical science must be verified, and upon which art and prudence work), but they also affirmed that our science, far from being obligated to penetrate the individuality of things, is constructed with the universal, the sole direct object of our intelligence. An intellectual but indirect knowledge of the individual is possible by a return upon the senses or by an affective inclination, but this knowledge cannot deserve the name of science, that is to say of "perfect" knowledge in the order of intellectuality. And no doubt a science which, knowing the universal, would apply not only to individual things, but would descend at the same time to the intimate nature of individuality, would be—angelic or divine science—more perfect than ours. Nevertheless our human science, which transcends the individual, is a true science whereas a perception limited exclusively to the individual is only the most imperfect degree of knowledge, the purely sensitive knowledge of animal life.

On the other hand, the ancients taught that to be universal, that is, communicable to more than one, and consequently to have what logicians call an "extension" embracing a plurality of individuals, is for the object of our ideas a logical property which pre-supposes a more profound property, namely: the property of being a certain "quiddity," a certain type of intelligible being expressible by a definition and endowed with a multitude of notes necessarily linked together, and consequently of having what the logicians call a certain "comprehension" or "connotation." Therefore, if they took into account the extension of concepts (and they were obliged to do so since it is one of their properties), it was always by referring it to this essential content, to this intelligible type, rich and full, whose communicability it merely indicates. They would never have taken it for the capacity of a simple "class" in which individuals would supposedly be arranged like matches in a box (a conception of extension which certain modern theoricians attribute to them—Hamelin himself, in fact, in his strange criticisms of the Aristotelian syllogism,—and whose real source is in Leibnitz, Euler and, more profoundly, in nominalist logic).

All this perfectly coherent doctrine of the concept elaborated by the best scholastics is already in Aristotle but apparently not quite explicitly enough since Hamelin,—who sees indications of it in him and who quite consciously quotes several unmistakable passages from the text and points out their importance,— was unable to define it in its unity. Those who are fond of subtle and invaluable elucidations can consult the preamble to Cajetan's commentary on the *de Ente et Essentia,* in which are distinguished the *abstractio totalis,* which defines the universal under the simple aspect of generality, and the *abstractio formalis,* which defines it under the aspect, much more essential to science, of typical and determining formality. They will then see that the ancients with a shrewdness of which we have scarcely any idea, have gone deeply into the questions which concern the concept, and to which the logicians of our day are forced, not always successfully, to return; as an example of this we can take the distinction between the concept and the idea that Goblot has brought into fashion and which, as it is, must be regarded as faulty, although Chevalier does not hesitate to rely upon it. They will also understand that the principles of Aristotle include no latent logicism, no tendency to take the simple logical arrangement of concepts in their order of increasing generality as the philosophical or scientific explanation of things, which is an explanation by causes and by essence. It is not in the categories of the logician, but in specific nature (*species specialissima*) that the sciences find the means of perfecting themselves; and if metaphysics works with the most universal intelligible—being insofar as it is being—it is not because this intelligible is a supreme genus (being, in fact, is not a genus), it is because, as an "analogous" and transcendental intelligible, it imbibes all reality and because it corresponds to such a high degree of abstraction that its supreme analogue can exist outside of all matter, as happens in the sovereign individuality of God.

The whole doctrinal network that we have only been able to indicate imperfectly here enables the mind, thanks to the vast labour of the scholastic tradition, to grasp Aristotle's thought in its living unity. If one fails to understand it, not only will one break that unity, but will also fail to recognize certain of the most characteristic aspects of Aristotelianism: the theory of potentiality and of matter, of substantial form, of the soul (which will be confused for example with habit or the aptitude for functioning), the theory of sensation, of abstraction, of intellect. Such misapprehensions are to be found in Hamelin's work, but only sporadically.

In Chevalier's thesis, although it is a scholarly work, it must be confessed that they are more generalized and more serious, probably because Chevalier is not content, as Hamelin was, to aim at simple historical description, but cherishes the loftier ambition, a more dangerous one, however, of proposing a systematic interpretation of Aristotle's philosophy and even of the whole movement of Hellenic thought.

For such an undertaking it is important carefully to choose one's point of view; and it is to be feared that the one adopted by Chevalier has been chosen in response to preoccupations and influences that savour too much of the contemporary. Whether this be so or not, we find ourselves obliged to assume that he shares the double-faced prejudice already mentioned,—and others too perhaps,—in explaining how it is that a man of so distinguished a mind, so steeped in modern scholarship, both English and German, and whose remarkable qualities of balance and clarity are shown by certain pages (in particular the appendix of the thesis we are discussing) can suddenly find himself,—when he reaches the centre of his subject, and first of all Plato (of whom he presents an interpretation that is very *up to the minute* but very arbitrary and already attacked by several recent works, e.g. those of Soulhié), and especially when he reaches Aristotle,—prevented from taking advantage of an historical *status quaestionis* excellent in spots, and from understanding the true significance and scope of that philosophy of science which, as he rightly points out following Hamelin, is above all a doctrine of intelligible necessity.

Fascinated by the dramatic conflict which supposedly brings to grips Aristotle the logician and "analyst" and Aristotle the observer and "finalist," and which shows him as a victim of a deplorable fate forced to sacrifice, turn and turn about and indefatigably, reality to logic and logic to reality (after so many alternating sacrifices how can there be any logic or reality left, alas!) it seems that Jacques Chevalier cannot realize that for the true Aristotle necessity in science and contingency in the world are equally safeguarded without either reality or logic having to suffer any harm.[1] And this is so because, for the true Aristotle intelligible necessity is one of forms or of universal quiddities disengaged by abstraction from empirical reality and consequently regulating in things, absolutely, everything that belongs to their essence but not the detail of their individual actions and reactions. Thus it is that the *laws of nature* are necessary ("hypothetically necessary" as the scholastics say), but that the *course of terrestrial events* is not. In other words it seems that Chevalier reasons as though everything that is must according to the fundamental tendencies of Aristotle and "all the Greeks," fall within the certitudes of knowledge, as though the proposition *"there is no knowledge* save that of the necessary" was equivalent to: *"only* the necessary *exists,"* which makes the Aristotelian world—if Aristotle were logical to the end—a world of pure necessity.

In reality, the notion of a knowledge existing alone in the absolute without being the knowledge of some specific person, of God or of man, and which would be exhaustive of all being is a modern invention absolutely opposed to the spirit of Aristotle. Aristotle wished to construct the theory of *our knowledge* (as Hamelin, whose lectures Chevalier must have followed, so well expresses it: "Aristotle considers that knowledge is the work of the individual or at least that it is made in the individual and cannot be detached from him, unless by abstraction. It is therefore human knowledge,—and to the extent that it is human,—that is the object of his logic."), and according to him human knowledge is very far from exhausting all the real. There is a whole domain reserved for simple statements of fact, for opinion, for the probable and particularly, in the practical order, for art and prudence,—which by nature baffles the infallible certitudes of scientific demonstration and anticipation. This is the immense domain of the singular, of the contingent, of the fortuitous which, in fact, for him is characteristic of the sublunary world and which is founded on the potentiality and the matter of which corruptible beings are compounded. It is the domain of our free will as well, which is also founded on the fact that all particular goods that we can wish for are mixed with potentiality. The Christian Doctors explicitly link this double domain to the sovereign liberty of creative will and teach that the knowledge of God is exhaustive of all being and extends to the individual and to the contingent because it is the cause of things. They thus bring Aristotle's thought to a point of perfection that he himself was unable to attain,—but in doing so have only to actualize its virtualities along its own line without distorting or falsifying it.

The profound harmony of this whole Chevalier may later perceive,—we hope so, at least,—when the progress born of reflection will have rid him of certain preconceived ideas. For the moment he fails to understand it and finds himself forced to explain as superadded fragments, foreign to the essential spirit of the system and forcibly imposed by that demon, the concrete, which in spite of everything

---

[1] On this point see my study "Philosophie et Science expérimentale," published in the second *Cahier de Philosophie de la nature* (Vrin, 1929).

torments Aristotle and makes him sacrifice logic just in time, all those many clear affirmations in which the philosopher teaches the reality of the individual and of contingency. Sometimes he even goes so far as to declare,—not without reserving for himself the possibility of saying the contrary elsewhere, in virtue of the system of internal conflict which enables one to impute to the author studied all possible vacillations and contradictions,—that according to Aristotle, or at least according to his basic tendencies, "there can be no knowledge, *and no reality,* outside of general essence," that "God is perhaps the only individual Who exists," that "there is only one true individuality, which is God"; that Aristotle, having by a "concession to the real," scarcely introduced matter "into the narrow circle of analytical necessity," when he "immediately bends all his efforts to reduce the contingent to the necessary and the individual to the species." In short, for him "the individual is real only through the species," just as for "the Greeks" "the individual . . . *is* only in the measure that it is general and immutable," the individual being "absorbed in the *cosmos*" as he is "submerged in the city." ("In the order of being," says Hamelin, "Aristotle thinks first of all, and very decidedly, with the ancients, that being is the individual.") Chevalier declares further that "Aristotle sees in the conditions of science the conditions of the real," and that he starts "from the same initial postulate" as Plato, "from the same identification of being and concept." Such assertions will make those whose minds have been formed by Aristotle's teaching rub their eyes. Being thus mistaken about the very foundation of the doctrine, it is not surprising that Chevalier should enunciate on several particular points a series of daring propositions which it would take too long to enumerate here (matter is an incomplete form; it is also, says Rodier—an expositor famous in the Sorbonne,—"a sort of will and tendency endowed with an activity proper"! Aristotle's point of view leaves no place for liberty, etc.).

Finally, taking from the Stagirite whatever constitutes his philosophical personality and neglecting all that is implied by that recognition of being in potency which was the philosopher's own source of pride because it definitively freed thought of the absolute intellectualism of a Parmenides, he takes it into his head to make Aristotle a sort of Hegel in spite of himself and to show him as the prisoner of *panlogism* and *pantheism* on the strength of his most fundamental principles, without, it seems, being in the least surprised that such a doctrine could have been adopted by the one whom the Church looks upon as its Doctor *par excellence;* for in fact, we can suppose that Thomas Aquinas corrected Aristotle as much as we like, but no matter how much one corrects a doctrine one cannot take away its fundamental principles.

But then! Chevalier considers that Aristotle formed a false idea of intelligibility and that he should "have recognized in contingency, which is the effect of final determination [relative to an end], the proper character of rational necessity or of the intelligible," in short, he should have assimilated intelligible reality "to the power of a will inserting itself into the temporal production of effects."

This way of improving the Philosopher would have appeared strange to the Angel of the Schoolmen. However that may be, and to get back to the simple resemblance value of the portrait presented to us, it is to be feared that to those who on their own account have studied the works of the original, Chevalier's Aristotle will seem much less close to reality than the brilliant historical variations developed by Bergson at the end of *Creative Evolution*.

But I hear the reader who has had the courage to follow me thus far ask himself in his innocence: how can we admit that an author who is crammed with knowledge, documents, intelligence and good will be mistaken about a philosopher such as Aristotle, almost all of whose scientific works we have and whose commentators are countless? Ah! That is the question I should like to have dealt with today and which, everything considered, I shall refrain from attacking, for I should run the risk of being drawn into it more deeply than I intend to venture. Let it suffice to note that the most conscientious reading is not enough, that one has to extract from the texts a spiritual something no doubt contained in them, but in scarcely as material a way as the art of the painter in the brush he moves or as thought in the sonorous waves of the voice; and that in order to do this the assistance of a tradition which on one hand forms and disciplines ourselves, on the other makes us realize the organic development and living fruits of the principles of a doctrine, is perhaps not altogether useless.

II

VARIOUS QUESTIONS

I.—ARISTOTELIAN CONTROVERSIES

1. *God and the world.—a*) Did Aristotle *deny* the knowledge of God with respect to the world? It is claimed that this negation is to be found in the text of the Metaphysics (lib. XII, c.9) where the Philosopher, seeking to determine the formal object of divine intellect, 1) remarks that it is better not to know than to know[1] certain inferior things, 2) from this infers the general law that the nobility of the act of thought depends upon the nobility of the object thought, and 3) concludes that the sole object of intellection which can cause the sovereign nobility of divine intellection, is God Himself: hence it follows that God thinks Himself and that in Him intelligence and intellection and the object of intellection are one and the same thing.

This text means, as Saint Thomas teaches, that the divine intellect must have an object which is its perfection, and that this object can only be the divine essence. It does not mean that God does not know things other than Himself, it signifies only that He does not know them as the formal term on which His intellection fixes itself. Saint Thomas proceeds along precisely the same lines to demonstrate his great thesis that God's only formal object is His own essence and that He knows things *not in themselves,* but *in His essence* and *His light,* where all is life. Similarly, Saint Augustine teaches that God knows nothing outside Himself; even the lowest things He knows, He knows by His essence, and that is why in Him all knowledge is at the same time knowledge of Himself. In order to believe that

---

[1] "It is better, in fact, not to see certain things." This statement is sometimes given for the *conclusion* of Aristotle. In reality he invokes it only to explain one of his *premises,* namely that the dignity of the act of intellection depends on the dignity of the object considered by the intellect. The *conclusion* of the reasoning is: "it is Himself [God] Who is His subject of intellection, αὐτὸν ἄρα νοεῖ (Cf. Arist. *Meta.*, XII, 9, 1074 b 34).

Aristotle's reasoning concludes purely and simply in the negation of divine knowledge with regard to things, one would have to have that disinterestedness about philosophy that is to be deplored in so many modern historians and critics. I cannot resist the desire to quote in a footnote, for the pleasure of those who delight in the purple patches of metaphysics, the page in which Saint Thomas explains the text in question, and even shows that it *necessarily includes,*—far from denying,— the consequence that God knows all things.[2]

Does not Aristotle himself upbraid Empedocles for the fact that in his doctrine (which will have it that like knows like), God could not know discord, "thus blessed God would have less wisdom than other beings"? "Διὸ καὶ συμβαίνει αὐτῷ τὸν εὐδαιμονέστατον θεὸν ἧττον φρόνιμον εἶναι τῶν ἄλλων· οὐ γὰρ γνωρίζει τὰ στοιχεῖα πάντα· τὸ γὰρ νεῖκος οὐκ ἔχει, ἡ δὲ γνῶσις τοῦ ὁμοίου τῷ ὁμοίῳ." (*Metaphysics*, III, 4, 1000b 2–6.) The same argument is found again in the *de Anima*: "συμβαίνει δ' Ἐμπεδοκλεῖ γε καὶ ἀφρονέστατον εἶναι τὸν θεὸν· μονὸς γὰρ τῶν στοιχείων ἕν οὐ γνωρίζει, τὸ νεῖκος, τὰ δὲ θνητὰ πάντα· ἐκ πάντων γὰρ ἕκαστον." (*De Anima*, I, 5, 410b 4–7.) Thus Aristotle expressly declares that all that mortals know, God must also know; otherwise He would be less wise than they. Upon which our modern historians repeat undismayed that the God of Aristotle does not know the world.

b) Did Aristotle *deny* the efficient causality of God with regard to the world? On this point it is customary to invoke[1] the text of the Metaphysics, lib. XII, c. 7,

2 "Considerandum est autem quod Philosophus intendit ostendere, quod Deus non intelligit aliud, sed seipsum, inquantum intellectum est perfectio intelligentis, et ejus, quod est intelligere. Manifestum est autem quod nihil aliud sic potest intelligi a Deo, quod sit perfectio intellectus ejus. Nec tamen sequitur quod omnia alia a se sint ei ignota; nam intelligendo se, intelligit omnia alia.

Quod sic patet. Cum enim ipse sit ipsum suum intelligere, ipsum autem est dignissimum et potentissimum, necesse est quod suum intelligere sit perfectissimum; perfectissime ergo intelligit seipsum. Quanto autem aliquod principium perfectius intelligitur, tanto magis intelligitur in eo effectus ejus: nam principiata continentur in virtute principii. Cum igitur a primo principio, quod est Deus, dependeat caelum et tota natura, ut dictum est, patet, quod Deus cognoscendo seipsum, omnia cognoscit.

Nec vilitas alicujus rei intellectae derogat dignitati. Non enim intelligere actu aliquod indignissimum est fugiendum, nisi inquantum intellectus in eo sistit, et dum illud actu intelligit, retrahitur a dignioribus intelligendis. Si enim intelligendo aliquod dignissimum etiam vilia intelligantur, vilitas intellectorum intelligentiae nobilitatem non tollit." (*Comm. in Metaph.*, lib. XII, c.q., lectio II).

Saint Thomas sets forth the same doctrine in his *Summa theol.*, I, q. 14, a. 2, 4, 5 and 6.— Notice that all modern commentators cannot be reproached for failing to understand this point. Brentano and Rolfes, for example, have clearly recognized that the God of Aristotle has the knowledge of things.

1 The texts sometimes quoted from the *Nicomachean Ethics*, X, 8, and from the *de Caelo*, II, 12, if taken in their exact meaning refuse God *formally transitive* causal activity only, for it implies some imperfection in the subject acting, and supposes that it acts toward an aim or a good it does not already have. Brentano quite rightly points out in this regard: "Zu beachten ist besonders, dass Aristoteles in der Nikomachischen Ethik, nachdem er im zehnten Buche, Kap. 7 und 8, erklärt hat, das theoretische Leben sei das beste, als das dem Leben Gottes ähnlichste, der nicht ein poietisches oder praktisches, sondern nur ein theoretisches Leben führe, sogleich im folgenden (neunten) Kapitel (1179 a 22) und mit deutlicher Beziehung auf die soeben gegebenen Erörterungen erklärt, das die Götter den dem theoretischen Leben sich Ergebenden und so das

where it says that God *"movet sicut appetibile et intelligibile,"* and *"ut amatum,"*[2] to conclude that according to Aristotle God acts only as final cause and that the Philosopher denies the Primary Mover efficient causality. But this text bears solely on the manner in which the spirit which moves the first heaven is itself moved by God,—by love of God contemplated eternally, "ut assimilet se ei in causando, et explicet in actum id quod est virtute in primo movente." (S. Thomas, *Comment.,* lect. 7.) It says that God moves this spirit as a final cause. It does not say that God can act only as a final cause, and that He did not make things.

How could Aristotle teach that the primary being has not efficient causality when he affirms (*Meta.,* lib. II [I min.], c. 2) that in no genus of causality can one proceed to the infinite in the series of causes, but that in every genus of causality (and therefore in the genus of efficient causality) there is a first cause? Need we recall that for him (*Meta.* XI, 7) God is the first principle of all things, πρώτη καὶ κυριωτάτη ἀρχή (1064b 1), the first immobile mover (*Phys.* VIII, 6, 258 b 10) because sovereignly in act and active (*Meta.* XII, 6, 1071 b 17-20; 7, 1072 b 14— 1073 a 13), endowed with an infinite power because He moves throughout an infinite time (*Phys.* VIII, 10), as a purely immaterial agent (*ibid.*)?[3] God is the

ihnen Verwandte Pflegenden gewiss eine besoners liebevolle Fürsorge zuwenden und ihnen sum Lohne Wohlthaten erweisen weden (ἀντευποιεῖν), so dass auch aus diesem Grunde das kontemplative Leben das glückseligste sei. Unmöglich konnte er dies thun, wenn das frührer Gesagte einem Sinn hatte, der jede Fürsorge und jede Werkthatigkeit der Gottheit ausschloss." (*Arist. Lehre vom Ursprung des menschl. Geistes,* p. 29, note.)

Some think that Aristotle is loathe to attribute to the primary mover efficient causality because "according to him, all contact implies reciprocity, that is to say, passion at the same time as action." Permit me to refer them to O. Hamelin (*Système d'Aristote,* p. 330), who rightly points out that for Aristotle "the agent must always be in contact with the patient, *but the obverse is not true"* when it is a question of an immaterial contact (*De gen. et corr.,* I, 6, 323 a 31-33; 7, 324 b 13). The primary mover then is in contact with heaven without its being in contact with him. Those who know (cf. *La Notion du Nécessaire chez Aristote,* p. 166, note 1), these passages from the *De Generatione* should use them in order exactly to understand the passages from the *Physics* wrongly invoked in a contrary sense; these texts (Phys. III, 2, 202 a 7; VIII 10, 266 b 28; VII a, beginning) show 1) that *reciprocal* contact implies passion in the agent; 2) that a *contact* between the world and God is necessary in order that God should move heaven as efficient cause. But they do not say that this contact is reciprocal: on the contrary, it cannot be reciprocal, God being purely immaterial. It is enough that *the world should have God in contact with it,* without itself being in contact with Him, as the texts of the *De Generatione* formally indicate.

2 "Κινεῖ δὲ ὧδε τὸ ὀρεκτὸν καὶ τὸ νοητόν [κινεῖ οὐ κινούμενον] τούτων τὰ πρῶτα τὰ αὐτά." (*Métaph.,* XII, 7, 1072 a 26-27); "κινεῖ δὲ (τὸ οὗ ἕνεκα) ὡς ἐρώμενον· κινούμενον δὲ τ' ἄλλα κινῖε." (*Ibid.,* 1072 b 3-4).

3 And therefore by His intellect and His will, as Saint Thomas is to explain *in Phys.,* lib. VIII, lect. 21. As Saint Thomas established against Averroës, Aristotle, in demonstrating here that a movement of an infinite duration cannot be explained by the *infinite* motor virtue of a *corporal and extensive* primary mover, at the same time demonstrates that such a movement requires the *infinite* motor virtue of an incorporal and inextensive primary mover (Cf. in *Metaphys.,* lib. XII, lect. 7 and 8).

There is moreover no difficulty in conceiving that God moves as an object of love and as an end the spirit which moves the first heaven, and that at the same time He acts as motor cause, communicating to that mind the motor power with which that spirit moves the first heaven.

In the way in which he conceived the causality of the pure Act passing through the divine spheres of the celestial bodies, so that the uniform and invariable gradually descended in the scale to the variable and the changing, in short, in his figuration of a hopelessly classical uni-

Governor and Head of the universe ("the world refuses to be governed badly, . . . one ruler let there be," *Meta.* XII, 10, 1076 a 3-5); and being in the soul as He is in the universe, He is in the soul the principle of movement, the principle which sets in motion the activity of reason (*Eth. Eud.* VII, 14).[1] And so the contemplative life being the one which most closely approaches the divine life, and the sage being therefore the best-loved of the gods, he is in return favoured by them in a special way (*Eth. Nic.*, lib. X, c. 9, 1179 a 22-32);[2] and it is through "certain divine causes" that he has received from nature the good fortune to become an upright man (*Ibid.*, c. 10, 1179 b 20-23). This general doctrinal position is absolutely incompatible with the idea of a God deprived of efficient causal power.

But there is more. Let us omit the texts where he declares that God does nothing in vain (*De Coelo*, I, 4, 271 a 33: "God and nature create nothing that has not its use"), or that we must admit a primary intelligence which is the cause of all the universe because the world cannot have happened by chance (*Phys.* II, 6; VIII, 5), and come to book II [1 min.] of the *Metaphysics*, chapter I, 993 b 28, where he states the law that "the principles of things which always exist [that is to say, celestial bodies] must be supremely true; for their truth is eternal, *and they have no cause of their being but are the cause of other things,* and it is with truth as it is with being." These supreme principles or causes are, as the whole of Aristotle's *Metaphysics* shows, the primary cause and the ultimate end. Aristotle therefore expressly affirms here, *Philosophus hic expresse dicit,* declares Saint Thomas in his Commentary (lect. 2), that celestial bodies depend on the primary cause not only as to their movement, but *as to their very being.* Saint Thomas quotes this text in the *Summa theologica,* Ia, q. 44, a. I, speaking of creation, which he deduces immediately from Aristotle's metaphysical principles; he comes back to it in his commentary on book VI of the *Metaphysics,* cap. 1, 1026 a 17 (lect. 1), where Aristotle sets forth that the most immobile and most immaterial causes (the most "separate" from matter) are the object of the "primary philosophy" or "theology,"—"eternal causes *par excellence,*" "*since they are the cause of divine things manifested before our eyes,*" that is to say the celestial bodies themselves.[3] To which Saint Thomas

verse presided over by the King of the gods rather than created by an infinitely mysterious and yet paternal All-powerful, Aristotle reveals a spiritual *tonality* profoundly foreign to Christian conceptions. But that is quite another question from that of knowing whether he intended to deprive God of all other causality than final causality. He did not intend to refuse Him either motor causality properly so-called, or efficient and productive causality.

[1] "As in the universe, so in the soul, God moves everything. For in a sense the divine element in us moves everything. The starting-point of reasoning is not reasoning, but something greater. What, then, could be greater even than knowledge and intellect but God?" *Eud. Eth.,* VII, 14, 1248 a. 26-29 (tr. J. Solomon).

[2] Cf. *supra,* p. 357, n. 1. Brentano interprets this text much more correctly than does Rodier.

[3] The Greek text: "αἴτια τοῖς φανεροῖς τῶν θείων," is much clearer than the Latin translation Saint Thomas used, and which refers to another reading: *hae namque causae manifestis sensibilium sunt.* It expressly designates celestial bodies.

If Aristotle here says "causes" or "principles" in the plural, it is 1) because he is speaking in general, not having as yet determined the nature of these supreme causes or established the unity of the primary mover (which he will not do until the twelfth book of his *Metaphysics*); 2) because there are *two* causalities to consider in the unity of the primary mover: He is *efficient cause* and *final cause.*

adds: *Ex hoc autem apparet manifeste falsitas opinionis illorum, qui posuerunt Aristotelem sensisse, quod Deus non sit causa substantiae caeli, sed solum motus ejus.*[2]

Thus, if Aristotle did not insist upon the causality of the Supreme Principle as the cause of being as much as on His causality as primary mover, *he did not deny* that causality, and, in this text from the second book of the *Metaphysics,* he even *expressly indicated* that he admitted it. He has also expressly affirmed the efficient causality of the primary mover, as Hamelin acknowledges (*op. cit.,* p. 410, n. 1) in the *de Generatione et Corruptione* I, 3, 318 a 1, sq.: οὔσης δ'αἰτίας μὲν ὅθεν τὴν ἀρχὴν εἶναι φαμεν τῆς κινήσεως . . . (This passage concerns the perpetuity of generation which depends partly on matter, partly on the efficient and motor cause which, immobile itself, eternally moves the heavens. Aristotle there affirms the existence of a first cause which is immobile and impassible in the order of efficient causality itself; cf. *ibid.,* 7, 324 a 30, 32, 35; a4, 12; lec. 7 and 20 of Saint Thomas). One would be very wrong to allow oneself here to be impressed by Zeller whose perspicacity does not equal his erudition. In his controversy with Zeller on this subject, Brentano won an undeniable victory,[3] and if we are looking for authorities, he tells us that Trendelenburg,[4] in a letter written sometime before his death, expressed himself as being in full accord with him.

c) Did Aristotle *deny* creation, that is, the causation of things *ex nihilo?* The creation of the world follows so necessarily from his principles that in the *De Potentia* (written between 1259 and 1263) Saint Thomas concedes that he and Plato too for that matter, knew creation.[5] Some years later, however, when he was writing the *Prima Pars* and when in that admirable article 2 of question 44, so

[2] The last chapters of book I and the first chapter of book II of the *de Coelo* do not contradict this doctrine. In them Aristotle is trying to show only that heaven had no beginning and that it is not subject either to generation or to corruption. (On the question of the eternity of the world, Aristotle would have been irreproachable had he contented himself with denying that one could demonstrate that the world began in time. But he claims to *prove* that the world had no beginning. Therein lies one of his gravest errors,—which, however, does not of itself touch the problem of divine causality with regard to the world. For, even though the world had not begun in time, the problem: from whence comes its being? would always arise.)

[3] For the Brentano-Zeller controversy in general see, against Zeller (*Philosophie der Griechen,* 2nd. ed., 1862, II, 2), Franz Brentano, *Die Psychologie des Aristoteles,* 1867 (appendix "von dem Wirken, insbesondere dem schöpferischen Wirken des aristotelischen Gottes"). Zeller's answer in the 3rd. edition of his book (1879, pp. 369 ff.). Brentano's reply in his study *Ueber den Creatianismus des Aristoteles* (Akad. der Wissensch. zu Wien, philosoph.-hist. Klasse, CI. I. Bd. I. Heft, 1882). Zeller's reply *Ueber die Lehre des Aristoteles von der Ewigkeit des Geistes* (Akad. den Wissensch. zu Berlin, 1882, Bd XLIX); published since then in the *Kleine Schriften* by Zeller. Brentano's reply *Offener Brief an Herrn Professor Dr. Eduard Zeller,* Leipzig, 1883; and finally *Aristoteles Lehre vom Ursprung des menschlichen Geistes,* 1911.

A similar controversy brought to grips Stöckl, *die Ideenlehre und Schöpfungstheorie bei Plato, Aristoteles und dem hl. Thomas* ("Katholik," June and August 1884) and Rolfes, *Ein Beitrag zur Wurdigung der aristotelischen Gotteslehre (ibid.,* November, 1884). Stöckl's reply, *Die Ideenlehre und Schöpfungstheorie bei Aristoteles noch einmal (ibid.,* December 1884). Cf. Rolfes, *die aristotelische Auffassung vom Verhältnisse Gottes zur Welt und zum Menschen,* Berlin, 1892.

[4] *Aristoteles Lehre vom Ursprung des menschlichen Geistes,* p. 28.

[5] *De Potentia,* q. III, a. 5.

remarkable for its nobility and balance, he was summing up the progressive movement of ancient thought, he did not classify Plato and Aristotle among those who have risen to the idea that primary matter was produced by God.

For in reality Greek thought did not arrive at the explicit concept of creation. But to say that Aristotle did not expressly conceive or affirm creation, is not to say that he denied it. Saint Thomas has no difficulty in pointing out against Averroës (*Comment. in Physic.*, I, VIII, lect. 2) that the negation of creation is neither in the thought nor in the general doctrinal line of Aristotle, *non est secundum intentionem Aristotelis;* and on this point the only state of mind that should be attributed to the Philosopher is ignorance and suspension of judgment: he stops short, as though suddenly rendered powerless, before a conclusion that, by all his metaphysical principles, he however affirms virtually. A deficiency sufficient to show the infirmity of human reason, but which does not permit one to say that Aristotle, properly speaking, was *mistaken* on this point.

2. *The immortality of the soul.*—Did Aristotle *deny* the personal immortality of the human soul? *No*, answers Saint Thomas most unequivocally. And I believe that one would find it difficult to say just where Aristotle declares that the νοῦς *is not individual*. We take the liberty of summing up the principal utterances in this discussion.

a) Aristotle affirms the spirituality and immortality of the intellect, of the νοῦς which is "free of all corporal composition"(ἀμιγής) and "separate" (χωριστὸς)(*de Anima*, III, 4, 429 a 11, 18),—which comes from without (θύραθεν)into the human embryo and which is "divine" (θεῖον) (*de Gen. Anim.*, II, 3, 736 b),*—and which survives the body (ὕστερον ὑπομένει) (*Meta.*, XII, 3, 1070 a 26). The last two texts (*de Gen. Anim.; Meta.*) refer to intellect purely and simply so-called, the first (*de Anima*) refers incontestably to what, in scholastic language, we call the *"intellectus possibilis,"* since there the text shows that it is a question of the part of the soul which, before knowing, is all intelligibles in potency, and which becomes all things by knowing.[1] (Cf. S. Thomas, lect. 7.)

The *"intellectus agens"* is also incorporal and separate (*de Anima*, III, 430 a).[2]

---

* "Λείπεται δὲ τὸν νοῦν μόνον θύραθεν ἐπεισιέναι καὶ θεῖον εἶναι μονον· οὐθὲν γὰρ αὐτοῦ τῆ ἐνεργείᾳ κοινωνεῖ σωματικὴ ἐνεργεία." *De Gener. Anim.*, II, 3, 736 b 25. Cf. Trendelenburg, *Comm. in de Anima*, p. 175: "Quorsum tandem divina haec in naturali rerum ordine origo, si revera intellectus sensibus contineretur? Ipsam igitur humanam mentem tanquam reliquis majorem Aristoteles segregavit et divinitus genuit."

[1] In the Aristotelian school the *intellectus agens* which is a sort of light of our intellect determining it to produce acts of thought is distinguished from the *intellectus possibilis* determined to produce acts of thought by the light of the active agent (which imprints on the possible intellect the abstract intelligibles of images); this *intellectus possibilis*, which is the faculty in which intellectual knowledge happens—a faculty to which Aristotle's school applied the name of νοῦς παθητικός used by him only once and perhaps in a somewhat different sense—is characterized by Aristotle (*de Anima* III, 5, 430 a) as made to *become all things* through knowledge. On Aristotle's use of the *expressions* themselves νοῦς ποιητικός and παθητικὸς νοῦς see *infra*, p. 364, n. 1.

[2] To establish it Aristotle reasons *a fortiori*. The intellect agent is *all the more* certain of having these properties because the possible intellect, which is less noble (because patient) already has them.

b) Whether it is a question of the *intellectus possibilis* or of the *intellectus agens*, the word "separate" does not mean separate *from the soul*, but separate *from matter*, as Saint Thomas shows indisputably against Averroës and against Avicenna, since the very operation of thinking (which depends on the *intellectus possibilis*) and that of abstraction (which depends on the *intellectus agens*) are personal operations of each human individual. Aristotle moreover affirms that the possible intellect and the intellect agent are *in the soul*, and therefore parts of it,[3] and calls the νοῦς *separate* only because it has no corporal organ like the sense. "Mirum est autem quomodo tam leviter erraverunt, ex hoc quod intellectus est separatus, cum ex littera sua hujus rei habeatur intellectus. Dicit enim separatus intellectus, quia non habet organum sicut sensus." (St. Thomas, *in de Anima*, lib. III, lect. 7. Cf. lect. 10, and the opus c. *De unitate intellectus.*)

Intellect—immaterial and immortal—is therefore *personal* to every man, and a part (μόριον) of his soul. Hence the immortality of intellect can only be the immortality of the soul itself, an evidently personal soul since it is the "substantial form" of each individual person.

Cf. *Meta.*, lib. XII, c. 3, 1070 a 26, where Aristotle says incidentally that among the forms not each soul, μὴ πᾶσα ψυχή, but only the νοῦς can subsist after the corruption of the compound.[1] This text is of great importance for of itself it shows clearly that the immortality of the *nous* is indeed the immortality of the soul (*psyché*) and is indeed personal. In fact, 1) he ranks the *nous* among the formal causes and explicitly assimilates it to a category of *soul* (human soul); 2) he says that the *nous* survives the body and yet, in the capacity of formal cause (formal causes do not pre-exist the compound, 1070 a 22), *it is not pre-existent to the body*. From these two points of view, as Saint Thomas points out (lect. 3), the *nous* manifestly appears as unable to be a "separate substance," and as necessarily personal.

Cf. also *Meta.*, lib. VI, c. 1, 1026 a, where Aristotle says that it is for natural philosophy (*Physica*) to study the soul, *at least the soul that cannot* exist without matter, thereby clearly meaning that there is another sort of soul (*psyché*) capable of existing without matter.[2]

---

[3] "Est etiam praedicta positio (Arabum) contra Aristotelis intentionem, qui expresse dixit has differentias duas, scilicet intellectum agentem et intellectum possibilem, esse in anima: ex quo expresse dat intelligere quod sint partes animae, vel potentiae, et non aliquae substantiae separatae." (Saint Thomas, *in de Anima*, lib. III, lect. 10.)

[1] "Si autem posterius aliquid manet, perscrutandum est. In quibusdam enim nihil prohibet, ut si est anima talis, non omnis sed intellectus, οἷον εἰ ἡ ψυχὴ τοιοῦτον, μὴ πᾶσα, ἀλλ' ὁ νοῦς. The particle εἰ by no means implies a real doubt in Aristotle's thought. He expresses himself thus each time that he incidentally comes across a theory to which he alludes or that he takes up without treating it *ex professo.*

[2] Note also that from the first chapter of the *de Anima*, the Philosopher orients his enquiry toward the question of knowing whether there is not a certain soul (*psyché*) which is immaterial (*separated from matter*, and therefore immortal).

When he says that the *nous* alone is immortal, this signifies not that the *intellect* is the only immortal part of the soul, but that the *intellective soul* alone is immortal as against other souls (souls of plants and of animals without reason).

Saint Thomas likewise uses the word *intellectus* in the sense of intellective soul, when he says, for example: "intellectus est humani corporis forma." (I[a], q. 76, a. 1.)

Is it necessary to insist further on the *individual* or *personal* character of the *nous?* It follows clearly from the *Nicomachean Ethics*, X, 7 (cf. I, 1–7), that intelligence, whose highest operation attaining the highest object constitutes our subjective beatitude, is indeed *something of the soul,* an *individual* intelligence and not an intelligence common to all men. *Each one,* says Aristotle, is *principally* what he is by the principal part of himself, that is, *by the intellect* (1178 a 1–8). Similarly, what Aristotle says (*Periherm.,* c. 9 and *Eth. Nic.,* III, 7, VII, 7) about human free will clearly indicates that being personal, it presupposes a personal intelligence. The famous definition of the soul given in book II, c.2, 414 a 12–13, of the *De Anima,* "id quo primo *intelligimus,* sentimus et vivimus, τοῦτο ᾧ ζῶμεν καὶ αἰσθανόμεθα καὶ διανοούμεθα πρώτως," implies that the intellectual operation is a personal operation, since it has as its *first principle* the same individual soul by which we live and feel. And this personal operation is that of the incorruptible intellect: let us recall here (and this is very important) the *order* of the propositions in the *De Anima.* Before distinguishing the active intellect from the possible intellect, Aristotle established (III, 4) that the intellect (and here it is undeniably above all a question of the *possible intellect,* by which we think and reason,[1] which is all the intelligibles *in potency,* which is first of all a *tabula rasa*), is *incorporal* and *separate* from matter—therefore incorruptible.

Finally, let us point out the passage from the *De Generatione Animalium* (II, 6, 744b 22), which Philopo misunderstood, where Aristotle says that the νοῦς which comes from without (θύραθεν), once introduced into the embryo, regulates the growth (αὔξησις) of the tissues previously formed by nature (φύσις); "just, therefore, as the *nous,* having come from without, observes this distribution of wise steward to operate the growth (of tissue), so nature works it in their production, composing on the one hand the flesh and the sensory organs out of the purest matter, on the other hand the bones, nerves and hair from the scraps. . . ."[2] The *nous* is therefore taken in the sense of *intellective soul* or of *substantial form* of the human organism, and it is certainly personal. In my opinion this text from the *De Generatione Animalium,* too little known it seems, is of first class importance in the present discussion.

To tell the truth, Aristotle's position on the individuality of the *nous* is one of those about which there should be no dispute, and there is absolutely no doubt that the interpretation of the Arabs has distorted the philosopher's thought on the subject. As Kaufmann points out,[3] there is reason for noting "that the best-known modern Aristotelians in Germany—Trendelenburg in his commentary on περὶ ψυχῆς, Brentano in his *Psychologie des Aristoteles,* Hertling in *Materie und Form*—on this point all come to a result which fully conforms with the result at which Thomas Aquinas arrived with his limited philological means." It is de-

---

[1] Whereas the active intellect which determines the possible intellect to know, does not know itself.

[2] "Καθάπερ οὖν εἰς τὴν αὔξησιν ὁ θύραθεν ταῦτα ποιεῖ νοῦς· οὕτως ἐν τοῖς γινομένοις αὐτοῖς ἡ φύσις ἐκ μὲν τῆς καθαρωτάτης ὕλης σάρκας καὶ τῶν ἄλλων αἰσθητηρίων τὰ σώματα συνίστησιν, ἐκ δὲ τῶν περιττωμάτων ὀστᾶ καὶ νεῦρα καὶ τρίχας." De Gener. Animalium, II, 6, 744 b 22 ff.

[3] N. Kaufmann, *Die teleologische Naturphilosophie des Aristoteles,* Paderborn, 1893, p. 101, note.

plorable that French university criticism maintains an obstinate attitude of lazy incomprehension on this point, due perhaps to the undeserved influence of Rodier. It is regrettable to note the weakness of the pages (386–387) where O. Hamelin deals with the *nous*.

On the other hand, personality is not constituted by memory, as Bergson's disciples run the risk of thinking, but by the metaphysical *subsistence* of the soul, which memory presupposes, so that speaking absolutely, there might be personal immortality without memory. And does not the soul of an infant dead before or at the moment of birth, in whose mind no idea and no intellectual memory can have been awakened, enjoy personal immortality?

c) There remain to be explained the last lines of chapter 5, book III of the *de Anima*, where Aristotle, after having said that the separate intellect χωρισθείς alone is immortal and eternal (ἀθάνατον καὶ ἀΐδιον), declares that the *pathetikos nous* is perishable. Saint Thomas in his commentary (lect. 10) explains that as the "separate intellect" designates all the intellective part of the soul (since the intellect which becomes all things, and which will later be called the *intellectus possibilis*—Aristotle has established this in chapter 4—is separate from matter like the *intellectus agens*), the expression *pathetikos nous* cannot refer to the *intellectus possibilis*, but only to the organic faculties (memory and imagination) which insofar as they have some participation in the life of reason can be called *intellectus passivus*. One could also, and perhaps more probably, in this case take the *pathetikos nous* for the *intellectus possibilis* itself, but insofar as it necessarily makes use of the imagination in order to think (for we do not think without turning to images): taken thus in fact, it is corrupted at death, in the sense that as the body is destroyed, and the imagination can henceforth not be exerted, it can no longer (at least according to the natural mode by which it acts here below) produce any intellectual act. Saint Thomas suggests this interpretation in the *Summa theologica*.[1] Granted, the passage is obscure and difficult. But is it reasonable to depend upon an obscure text to invalidate an assemblage of clearly established evidence? In any case the only "clear and decisive" thing here is that the corruptible *pathetikos nous* of the *de Anima*, III, 5, *cannot* designate "the possible intellect" taken in itself, *since previously, in chapter 4, Aristotle demonstrated the incorruptibility of the latter.*

[1] *Sum. theol.*, Iᵃ, q. 89, a. 1, ad 1: with regard to another passage of the *de Anima* (I, 5). It should be noted that the expression *nous pathetikos* is met with only once in Aristotle, in the passage we are dealing with here. Where later the expression *intellectus possibilis* will be employed, Aristotle says simply *intellect*. It is quite possible that in the passage in question he meant the expression *pathetikos nous*, not in the sense of *intellectus possibilis*, but in the sense of *intellectus passivus* indicated by Saint Thomas, whose interpretation thus appears to be much more likely. Let us add, in confirming the interpretation given by Saint Thomas, according to which the *pathetikos nous* is the imagination or the sensitive memory insofar as it serves the intelligence, that the adjective *pathetikos*, in the other passages where Aristotle uses it, designates the sensitive part of the soul. "Τῷ παθητικῷ μορίῳ [τῆς ψυχῆς] (συμφέρον ἐστιν) ἄρχεσθαι ὑπὸ τοῦ νοῦ." (*Polit.* I, 5, 1 254 b 8; cf. III, 15, 1 286 a 18.)

(As to the expression *nous poietikos*, it is not Aristotle's own; it was introduced by Alexander of Aphrodisia. It is the theory of the active agent, not the name itself, that is found in Aristotle.)

d) In what after that concerns memory, it cannot be denied that for Aristotle the sensitive memory perishes with the body; as to the intellectual memory, the guardian of acquired knowledge, he says nothing about its survival. And how, the one being an organic faculty, the other using organic faculties like so many instruments, could they still exert themselves naturally after the separation of the soul and the body? The question was enough to embarrass the philosopher. Aristotle here, as on all problems which concern the conditions of life of the separate soul, maintains a prudent, a too prudent expectant attitude. Nevertheless, when Saint Thomas teaches the existence of the intellectual memory as distinct from the sensitive memory, and as causing the separate soul to preserve the knowledge acquired here below, he is only making explicit a doctrine implicitly contained in Aristotle's psychology (for knowledge, which is a *habitus* of the intellect, is preserved, once it is acquired), and already touched upon by him when he says that "the soul, not the whole soul, but the intellective part, is the *place of forms, τόπος εἰδῶν*" (*de Anima,* III, 4, 429 a 28. It is to this expression of Aristotle's that Saint Thomas refers, *Sum. theol.,* Ia, 79, 6 and 7). If Aristotle does not speak more explicitly about intellectual memory it is because it is not a special faculty, it is only the intellect itself insofar as it preserves the intelligible forms and acquired knowledge (cf. *Sum. theol.,* Ia, q. 79, a. 6 and 7; q. 89, a. 5 and 6). Consequently Saint Thomas teaches that in regard to the thing known (abstract and universal) its object is not the *past qua past.* "Si vero de ratione memoriae sit, quod ejus objectum sit praeteritum, ut praeteritum, memoria in parte intellectiva non erit, sed sensitiva tantum, quae est apprehensiva particularium: praeteritum enim, ut praeteritum, cum significet esse sub determinato tempore, ad conditionem particularis pertinet." (Ia, q. 79, a. 6.) Nevertheless as far as the knowing activity itself is concerned (not the known object) this does not prevent the intellectual memory from bearing on the past as such because our acts of intelligence are individual realities and localized in time, and at the same time immaterial realities, therefore knowable to the intellect in their very singularity.[1] Neither does it prevent the separate soul from keeping the memory of the singular individuals and events of which it has formed indirect and reflex ideas here below (cf. JOHN OF SAINT THOMAS, *Curs. phil.,* III P., p. X, a. 4, p. 477 of Vivès; *Sum. theol.,* Ia, 89, 4). In this case it makes use of its intellectual *habitus* according to another mode than the mode of the here below (*Sum. theol.,* Ia, 89, 6), without needing to exercise its sensitive faculties; and if it is deprived of the actual exercise of the *species* of the sensitive memory, it can always bring into use the ideas of the singular that it had formed indirectly by returning upon these *species*.[2]

---

[1] *Sum. theol.,* Iᵃ, q. 79, a. 6, ad 2: "Et ideo, sicut intelligit seipsum intellectus, quamvis ipse sit quidam singularis intellectus; ita intelligit suum intelligere quod est singularis actus, vel in praeterito, vel in praesenti, vel in futuro existens. Sic igitur salvatur rato memoriae quantum ad hoc quod est praeteritorum in intellectu, secundum quod intelligit se prius intellexisse, non autem secundum quod intelligit praeteritum prout est hic et nunc."

[2] If it is true that the *species* of the sensitive memory, once acquired thanks to the activity of the animate organ, and while preserved in the compound (*Sum. theol.,* Iᵃ, q. 79, a. 6, *ad* 1), are preserved *principally* in the faculty of the soul itself, we may believe that these *species* remain *radicaliter* in the separate soul like the sensitive faculty itself, and will resume life when the soul is once more joined to the body.

As to the word (ἀΐδιος) used by Aristotle to characterize the νοῦς (*De Anima.*, III, 5, 430 a 23) and which is sometimes insisted upon, it can just as well mean simply *without end*, as mean "eternal" in the strict sense of the word; Chevalier is fully aware of this. Cf. BRENTANO, *Aristoteles Lehre vom Ursprung des menschlichen Geistes*, pp. 44, 68. The text of the *Metaphysics* mentioned above (XII, 3, 1070 a 22-26) furthermore clearly shows that the *nous* is not pre-existent to the body. That is why we must conclude with Saint Thomas: "Dicitur autem perpetua, non quod semper fuerit, sed quod semper erit. Unde Philosophus dicit in duodecimo *Metaphysicorum,* quod formam nunquam est ante materiam, sed posterius remanet anima, non omnis, sed intellectus" (*in de Anima,* lib. III, lect. 10).

And finally the οὐ μνημονεύομεν of the *de Anima,* III, 5, 430, a 24, and the οὔτε μνημονεύει οὔτε φιλεῖ of I, 4, 408 b 28, by no means signify that the intellect is not personal, but only that by the lesion or destruction of the bodily organ, the sensitive faculties and consequently the intellect itself which uses them (τὸ νοεῖν δὴ καὶ τὸ θεωρεῖν μαραίνεται ἄλλου τινὸς ἔσω φθειρομένου, I, 4, 408 b 24), can no longer exert themselves. "Sine hac autem parte animae corporali intellectus nihil intelligit. Non enim intelligit aliquid sine phantasmate, ut infra dicetur. Et ideo destructo corpore non remanet in anima separata scientia rerum secundum eumdem modum, quo modo intelligit. Sed quomodo tunc intelligat, non est praesentis intentionis discutere." (Saint THOMAS, *in de Anima,* lib. III, lect. 10; cf. lib. I, lect. 10). Brentano adds—which explains the use of present tense: οὐ μνημονεύομεν, οὔτε μνημονεύει—that in these passages Aristotle does not have in view the nonpreservation *post mortem* of memories or acquired knowledge, but rather the obstacles which during this life befall memory and the intellect itself, from some indisposition of the organ. "Hier spricht Aristoteles von nichts anderem als von der bekannten Tatsache, dass eine bereits erworbene Erkenntnis uns oft wieder verloren geht, und bringt sie mit der Inkorruptibilität seines Nus in Einklang."[1]

e) These long discussions may seem tedious. They are dedicated to those readers who desire to study Aristotle directly, with the necessary attention and without any prejudices, in the original texts. I consider, moreover, that if these texts have been subjected to such long and obstinate efforts on the part of a negativist exegesis, it is particularly important not to be over-impressed with this exegesis, but to try to grasp in its full authentic meaning the thought of the prince of philosophers. That, without any shadow of a doubt, was what Saint Thomas felt. Wherever he touches upon the most controversial of the Aristotelian problems,—on the problem of the *nous*, in his commentary on the *De Anima*, in the *De Veritate*, in the *Summa theologica*, in the *Contra Gentes*, in the quaestiones disputatae *De Anima*, in the *De unitate intellectus*,—he comes to Aristotle's defense on this point.

The critics who think that Aristotle "without any possible doubt denied personal immortality," and who claim to be in agreement on this point "with all those who know Aristotle" probably have not consulted either the Angelic Doctor, or Silvester Maurus, or Julius Pacius, who after all appear to know Aristotle, or, if we must quote more modern authors, the *Psychologie des Aristoteles* by Franz Bren-

[1] F. Brentano, *Aristoteles Lehre vom Ursprung des menschlichen Geistes*, Leipzig, 1911, p. 10; cf. *Psychologie des Aristoteles*, pp. 206 ff., 209.

tano, or his *Aristoteles Lehre vom Ursprung des menschlichen Geistes,* in which this remarkable authority on Aristotle is bold enough to maintain, with a profusion of demonstrations, that Aristotle believed in the *creation,* by divine power, of the individual and immortal intellect of every human being.[1]

That Aristotle, as John of Saint Thomas expressed it, suffered perplexity on this question of immortality (especially because of his theory of the eternity of the world, from which it must have followed that separate souls are infinite in number,—*unde valde opprimebatur*), we grant without hesitation. Therefore, the principal question here is not to know whether he explicitly defined and set forth the thesis of the personal immortality of the human soul. Abiding by the exactitude of Saint Thomas's interpretation it is enough to say that, urged on by the internal logic of his principles, Aristotle (as we have already shown), taught in an implicit and virtual way,—positing the reasons which establish it,—and several times clearly hinted at that immortality.

3. *The commentaries of Saint Thomas.* We have reproduced above the teachings of Saint Thomas commenting on Aristotle. I am not unaware that for most moderns these teachings are not acceptable, on the one hand because most of the moderns are attached to a *material* mode of interpretation which was not that of Saint Thomas; on the other hand because Saint Thomas, being a Christian, *must have,* so they think, pulled the texts of the philosopher in the direction of Christianity (a way of looking at things which leaves Christian critics, if they wish to be considered "scientific" and not be suspected of partiality, the only resource of perseveringly coming to the same conclusions as the non-Christians).[2]

1 In my opinion Brentano goes to a certain extreme in sustaining the thesis of Aristotle's *creatianism,* in the sense that (as appears by the word itself), he does not sufficiently bring out the point that one should not regard as a conclusion *explicitly* posited by Aristotle what is merely contained *implicitly* in his philosophy. Brentano is right in affirming along with Brandis and Trendelenburg that the origin of the *nous* is divine. But that this divine origin was truly conceived as a *creation* by the Philosopher, remains very doubtful. Since his metaphysical principles moreover absolutely hinder him from conceiving it as a pantheistic emanation, it must be concluded that his explicit thought remained indefinite on this point.

2 One cannot deny moreover that Saint Thomas occasionally gave a kindly interpretation of the Philosopher,—"pluries glossat Aristotelem ut Philosophum, non ut Aristotelem," as Cajetan very prettily puts it (in ii–ii, q. 172, a. 4, *ad* 4),—not at all because of his being carried away in spite of himself by his Christian tendencies (such a hypothesis is absurd for anyone who knows how scrupulous Saint Thomas was to observe scientific objectivity), but because of the exigencies of his office as Commentator, as he conceived it, which consisted in throwing the maximum amount of light on the text explained.

Yet the accidental errors Saint Thomas might have thus committed are only the price one pays for a *formal* method of interpretation, which consists in re-thinking with the greatest possible coherence, an author's philosophy while assuming as far as possible the hypothesis that the author was an intelligent being. Such a method, if it risks failure to take into account certain contingent circumstances (race, milieu, etc.) which materially condition a doctrine, and the attribution of too much logic, precision and self-consciousness to the author himself, is the only one, however, which leaves any hope of attaining or at least approaching the truth; whereas the material method of interpretation so often practised in our day, on the contrary leads infallibly to error.

Let me add that Cajetan, in uttering the expression mentioned above, was certainly not thinking of the interpretations where Saint Thomas, in his commentaries, expressly declares (as in

May we nevertheless be permitted to remark that being under the absolute necessity of "interpreting" the texts of Aristotle if we wish to be intelligent about them and act as men, not as card-indices, there is *a priori* just the chance that the "interpretation" of the loftiest mind and the purest regard may be the truest "interpretation." There is therefore *a priori* a chance that the interpretation of a genius as powerful, as limpid, as submissive to the real, as profoundly impartial and objective as Saint Thomas, should be truer than that of Averroës or Avicenna, or of Pomponazzi, or of Scaliger, or of Bonitz, Ravaisson, Zeller, Trendelenburg, Gomperz, Rodier, or of any other scholar.

The objection is raised that Saint Thomas's authority as an Aristotelian commentator is diminished because Saint Thomas "read Aristotle in a Latin translation," and because his purpose was to extract from Aristotle a "manual of philosophy adapted to the Christian dogma."

Let us confess that this objection is rather slight. And notice that Saint Thomas's *commentaries* on the works of Aristotle have as little resemblance as possible to a manual of philosophy, and still less to an *adaptation,* but are in fact an exegesis or formal elucidation, which is quite another thing.

In Germany, where Aristotelian criticism is less backward than in France, Franz Brentano professed that one finds in "the penetrating commentaries of Thomas Aquinas, many more exact interpretations than in later authors" however "paradoxical" might be, in the eyes of modern critics, the idea of asking "a scholastic with no knowledge of Greek to teach us how to understand Aristotle."[1] Must we then go to an author whose worth is certainly great, and who has exerted a useful influence on contemporary German philosophy, but who has broken with the Church, in order to find a little justice with regard to these commentaries by Saint Thomas, so moderate, so objective, so *free* from passion and prejudice, which so many of our Catholic scholars regard with such haughty disdain?

Let them try the experiment, however! Crammed with the prejudices of formal instruction, they will doubtless first of all be surprised by some of these commentaries, and tempted to find them tendencious. But if they deal with each of the assertions, each of the philosopher's words, with the attentive consideration and extreme care demanded by such a work, and if they take into consideration the context, the movement of the thought in each particular case as well as the articulations of the doctrine as a whole, they will be astonished to see that the closer one sticks to the letter of Aristotle, the more one is forced to agree with the majority of Saint Thomas's interpretations. They will thus be led to a better appreciation of the distance which separates the Aristotelian εἶδος from the Platonic Idea; they will stop thinking that a philosopher who insists as energetically as does Aristotle on the individuality of the *substantia prima* tends to reabsorb the individual in the species; and they will stop seeking a theory of immortality in the con-

the case of questions under discussion here) that he is setting forth the thought of the Philosopher. He merely had in view certain glosses sometimes found in the *Summa* on points of detail, for example (this was the one which occasioned his remark) on the point of knowing whether the power of divination with regard to dreams is given to the best men.

[1] F. Brentano, *Aristoteles Lehre* . . ., p. 1.—On these commentaries of Saint Thomas, see Grabmann's study in *Mittelalterliches Geistesleben,* Munich, 1926.

clusion of the *de Generatione et Corruptione,* where Aristotle, explaining the singular theory of the perpetuity of generations in the sublunary world, says that animals and men cannot by generation endlessly return upon themselves uniformly except according to the identity of the species, not according to numerical or individual identity (which seems rather evident).

"This digression was not without its use," as Bergson often said in his courses at the Collège de France I remember so well. Let us put aside certain remarks I should like to have developed on the absolute need for a living and spiritual *tradition* (*spiritus vivificat*) for the interpretation of any *writing,* even a purely human one, a need nowhere more manifest than in the case of the texts of Aristotle or Saint Thomas. What we especially wish to note is that, as far as Aristotle's errors are concerned, the essential question bears much less on the particular conclusions that the Philosopher himself did or did not formulate, than on the *foundations* and *principles* of his doctrine; much less on the "human subject" Aristotle than on the intellectual "formality" Aristotelianism. Let us assume that Nicomachus's son made the "enormous mistakes" imputed to him,—he did not really make them, but he did make a good many other more or less serious mistakes (who denied it? Could it by chance be myself? Where then have I denied it?). If all those errors are only materially and accidentally in his doctrine, if they are imputable to his self, not to his principles, what importance have they for us today; how do they affect the "*present* worth of Aristotle"?

We judge the tree by its fruits. By ITS fruits, no doubt, and not by the fruits of foreign growths mingled for a time with its boughs. Just as a philosopher like Descartes (or like Bergson) can fail to see the mistakes which derive from his principles and can even affirm conclusions which are materially true but which are jeopardized by these principles, so a philosopher like Aristotle can fail to see the truths which follow from his principles, and even affirm false conclusions which are incompatible with them. The human subject is so feeble in relation to things of the intelligence that in general several centuries are needed for a philosophical doctrine to develop its logical consequences, divesting itself of the accidental characteristics which the circumstances of its historical genesis had implanted in it in the beginning.

Only in the mind of Saint Thomas Aquinas did Aristotle's doctrine bear its purest fruit. Not only did Saint Thomas correct and give depth to Aristotle, but he also transfigured him, by bringing him into the superior light of the faith and theology. But, as he always remained strictly faithful to all Aristotle's principles it may be said that he is much more purely Aristotelian than Aristotle himself.

Let us then judge Aristotelianism by its real fruits. We shall then understand that the demonstration of those philosophical verities which have the greatest importance for us depends upon the principles posited by the Greek thinker, and we shall perhaps admire instead of trying to ignore the providential provision which decreed the peaceful encounter of human effort starting from below, but rising toward the true,—and which, in the whole of the ancient world *succeeded*[1] only in

[1] I do not mean thereby to insinuate that the philosophical thought of the other peoples of antiquity, especially that of India, should be regarded as sterile or negligible and should

Greece,—with the divine truth revealed from on high. Perhaps we shall also understand that since truth can conform only to truth, it is absolutely impossible that a philosophy which is not true either in its foundations or its roots, or in all the formal principles which make up its life as a spiritual organism, will ever find "its Saint Thomas."

The principles of the eternal metaphysics to which the name of Aristotle has remained attached, are the only ones upon which one can unshakably found the great truths of Christian philosophy, in particular, the personal immortality of the human soul, which depends upon its *immateriality,* itself invincibly proven by the immateriality of the intellective operation; the creation of the world *ex nihilo,* a necessary conclusion from the principles stated by Aristotle on the primacy of the Act and on causality; the absolute distinction of God and the world, which Aristotle, by the doctrine of the pure Act, has absolutely established.

"A system," we are told, "is judged by its attitude on this question on which all the rest depends: the question of personal immortality and the personal God," or in other words, is judged by its *conclusions about the highest objects.* Nothing is truer if these conclusions are considered *formally,* insofar as they necessarily derive from the fundamental principles of the system. Nothing is more erroneous if these conclusions are considered *materially,* according as they are professed in fact by the philosopher who, for all sorts of reasons, does not pursue his own principles more than half way or makes personal convictions of a different origin co-exist with them. As proof of this we have the example of Descartes and that of Aristotle, both having been encouraged, one in his affirmations, the other in his reservations concerning these ultimate objects, by their moral atmosphere, which in the one case was Christian, in the other Greek. But the moral atmosphere of a philosopher is quite another thing from his intellectual principles. I like to think that as the Aristotelian idea of science (there is science only of the necessary) passed as a whole over into Saint Thomas's system, and there developed all its consequences without at all compromising personal immortality it will be granted that this idea does not involve as logically perhaps as some people have thought the negation of personal immortality. As to the formula: "to make of the conditions of intelligibility the conditions of reality," if it simply means: to admit that all being is intelligible to the very extent that it is (*ens et verum convertuntur*), one can scarcely see how it would not force itself on any philosophy which does not give up thinking;[1] and if it means more than that and contains the charge of absolute

simply be rejected. I only mean to indicate that no matter how lofty and how profound that thought may have been, and whatever may be the truths it discovered, it did not end as it did with Aristotle, in a rational system whose principles permitted the mind to be applied in an endless progression to the comprehension of the whole of reality without any falsification. It is in the light of the Aristotelio-Thomist principles that the doctrines of the Vedanta, in order to be saved, must be understood and carried to their point of perfection.

[1] We are told that it is not to be imputed to Aristotle in this sense. The formula "every being is intelligible to the very extent that it is" expresses a capital truth, but it says quite the contrary to what Aristotle thought! And yet Aristotle was the man who wrote it: ἕκαστον ὡς ἔχει τοῦ εἶναι, οὕτω καὶ τῆς ἀληθείας. A thing has truth to the extent that it has being." *Met.,* II (I min.), I, 993 b 29.—According to this are we to understand that what Aristotle is taken to task for is to have thought that the conditions of intelligibility, that is to say what is proper to a thing known *insofar as known* (the logical conditions of abstraction and universality, for example) are

intellectualism, it is easy to see how it applies to Parmenides, to Spinoza, to Hegel, but we cannot see how it can be applied to a philosophy whose characteristic is precisely that of recognizing in things a principle (matter) *not intelligible in itself:* ἡ δ' ὕλη ἄγνωστος καθ' αὑτήν. (*Meta.,* VII, 10, 1036 a 8).

But no! According to some *"in the principles of Aristotle also,* there is something rotten." Either, therefore, Saint Thomas did not take over the principles of Aristotle, as has always been believed up to the present, or is there something rotten in his principles *also?* The assertion just alluded to is the more serious because they take the trouble to tell us just what "that something rotten is"; it is the famous proposition: *"there is no science except of the necessary and the general."* Now that is one of the Aristotelian propositions to which Saint Thomas adheres, as it happens, with the greatest firmness and constancy, and which he makes one of the essential principles of his philosophy.

What then? is it enough to say that Saint Thomas is a Christian, and that he bases "his belief" on the singular facts which are "the facts of revelation"? It is not a question of Saint Thomas's faith, but of his philosophy; and the principle: *there is no science except of the necessary and the general* is as clear and as fundamental in Saint Thomas as in Aristotle.[1]

As to the value of the singular in the domain of knowledge, Aristotle never denied it. It is fairly well-known that sense knowledge, which plays an absolutely fundamental rôle in the Aristotelian doctrine—since all our knowledge has its origin in sense perception—has the singular as its proper object; and in addition, the intellect itself can think only by turning toward phantasms (*De Anima,* III, 7), toward the representations of individual things.

I know perfectly well that most modern historians of philosophy seem to have rather imperfectly "realized" the idea of matter[2] and perhaps the idea of poten-

the same as the conditions of reality (the condition of singularity, for example)? We should then be right in reproving this proposition: but Aristotle expressly and at long length reproved it himself. His whole logic is constructed on the contradictory of this proposition.

If God, for Aristotle, is the "thought which thinks itself," it is because He is *pure act,* and therefore the *Living Being par excellence,* and because sovereign life is the act of sovereign intellect. Saint Thomas teaches the same doctrine. Furthermore, eminent theologians (John of Saint Thomas, Gonet, Billuart . . .) are known to make *subsisting Intellection* the formal constitutive (according to our way of conceiving) of the divine nature; and those who see this formal constitutive in *Being by itself* base themselves *precisely* upon the Aristotelian notion of the *pure act.*

1 *"Intellectus noster, per se loquendo, singularia non cognoscit, sed universalia tantum"* (*De Verit.,* q. 2, a. 5 and 6; *Sum. theol.,* I, q. 14, a. 11, ad 1).—*"Scientia non est nisi de necessariis"* (*De Verit.,* q. 2, a. 12). *"Illud quod scitur a nobis, oportet esse necessarium, etiam secundum quod in se est."* (*Sum. theol.,* I, q. 14, a. 13, ad 3.)

Then again, let us not forget that Aristotle, when he theorizes about knowledge and declares that it bears only on the καθόλου and the ἀναγκαῖον, is speaking only of human knowledge, which presupposes abstraction. "It is human knowledge, insofar as it is human, that is the object of his logic," wrote Hamelin (*Système d'Aristote,* p. 94), refuting in advance Chevalier's idea of Aristotle's *panlogism* and *necessitarism.* "Would Aristotle," he said further, "have absorbed logic in metaphysics and conceived logic as the science of thought necessary insofar as it was identical with being, in a word, very much like the Hegelians who define it as the science of pure idea? . . . Even though Prantl tried to find a conception of this kind in Aristotle, we may state that it is not Aristotelian." (*Ibid.,* pp. 93–94.)

2 In his thesis (p. 176) Chevalier declares after Rodier (*Ann. philos.,* 1909, p. 11) that

tiality as well, which are the two main articles of Aristotle's doctrine, but I cannot help being struck with astonishment, *stupor ingens*, at the tranquillity with which they present to us, as being bent on absorbing all reality in form, on refusing the contingent the right to exist, on denying the real existence of the singular, a philosopher who not only constantly affirms that the singular alone exists in reality,[1] that human will is the free cause of its acts,[2] that the presence of the contingent and the fortuitous is the characteristic proper of our sublunary world,[3] that what strictly speaking exists (in the world of bodies), is the compound (σύνολον) of matter and form, and not form alone,[4]—but who also makes of these affirmations the main axes of his system. He for whom "being insofar as it is being" is the object of that supreme knowledge which is divine and which man cannot fully possess because of his nature *in bondage in so many ways*,[5] he who declares that the highest intelligible realities are to our intellect as the light of the sun to the eyes of the owl,[6] and who finds more joy obscurely and imperfectly knowing divine things than in knowing perfectly the things proportionate to our minds,[7]—are we to think that he was not turned toward being, and that he defined being by human intelligibility? If Aristotle goes to the supreme realities with a less vehement impulse than Thomas Aquinas who had not only knowledge but also charity, and who knows that it is better here below to love God than to know Him, if a certain narrowness is his from the fact that he is only a philosopher and moves solely in the domain of pure reason, he does nevertheless affirm the primacy of reality with a vigour that no philosopher has equalled, he is the founder (that is, not the inventor but the first great architect) of the *philosophy of being*, and it is for this that we love him.

II.—ON THE NATURAL KNOWLEDGE OF GOD BY REASON

Can it be said that human reason as long as it had not received the light of the Mosaic and Christian revelation did not in fact know the true God (according as He can be attained by reason apart from the revealed mysteries) because it did not rise to the explicit notion of God the creator?

Listen to Saint Paul speaking of the pagans (*Rom.* I, 19–22): "*Quod notum est Dei, manifestum est in illis. Deus enim illis manifestavit. Invisibilia enim ipsius, a creatura mundi, per ea, quae facta sunt, intellecta conspiciuntur: sempiternaque*

matter is "*a sort of will and tendency with an activity proper.*" More generally he seems to forget that if, for Aristotle, matter is "a lesser being, an imperfect being," it is no less *real* for all that.

[1] Cf. *Cat.*, 5, 3 b 10; 4 a 10; *Met.*, VII, 16, 1040 b 26; *Anal. post.*, I, II, 77 a 5, etc. Chevalier will allow me to point out to him, in this regard, that *second substances* are not accidents (*Notion du nécessaire chez Aristote*, p. 121), but that they are opposed to *primary substances* as the universal is to the singular, as man in general is to Peter (*Cat.*, 5, 2 a 11; cf. *Met.*, VII, 3, 1029 a 1) and exist outside the mind only in the singular.

[2] *Periherm.*, c. 9; *Nic. Eth.*, III, 7, etc.

[3] *Periherm.*, c. 9; *Phys.*, II, c. 4 to 6; *Met.*, V, 30; IX, 3, 1047 a 20–24; *De Gener. et corrupt.*, II, 11, 337 b 5–9.

[4] *De Anima*, I, 1, 403 a 29-b 19; *Met.*, VII, 3, 8, 11 (1037 a 26); VIII, 6, etc.

[5] *Met.*, I, 2, 982 b 29.

[6] *Met.*, II [I min], 1, 993, b 10.

[7] *De part. anim.*, I, 5.

ejus virtus, et divinitas: ita ut sint inexcusabiles. Quia cum cognovissent Deum, non sicut Deum glorificaverunt." They *have known* God, says the Apostle. ("It is scarcely necessary, I think," says Kleutgen in this regard, "to point out that Scripture is not speaking here of any supreme cause in particular, but of the true and living God Who created heaven and earth and inscribed His law in the heart of man.")[1] The invisible perfections of God, His eternal power and virtue, *have been made visible* since the creation of the world. God *has made* them *manifest* unto them. If they are inexcusable, it is because they *have known* God and have not glorified Him.

Now what do the Fathers of the Church say? "They distinguished," writes Kleutgen,[2] "the knowledge of God one obtains by means of learned research from the knowledge born spontaneously in every man at the mere spectacle of creation. They call this latter knowledge a *testimony* that God has given of Himself to the soul in creating it, a *dowery of nature*, an *infused knowledge*, inherent in every man without previous instruction, a knowledge which in a way is born of itself at the same time that reason develops and which can be lacking only in the man deprived of the use of reason or a victim of the vices which have corrupted the nature with which God created him. And when the Fathers of the Church unanimously testify in this connection that this knowledge is really found and affirmed in all men, we understand the importance of this testimony, when we think that they lived in the midst of pagan peoples. Dealing with this subject in another work,[3] we took as our authority a great many Fathers of the Greek and Latin Churches. No mention was made, however, of an ecclesiastical writer who particularly deserves to be heard upon this question. *Clement of Alexandria* was perfectly well acquainted with the life and customs of the pagans of his time, and very well versed in all their literature. Now, in order to prove that all men know naturally and without instruction (ἐμφύτως καὶ ἀδιδάκτως) not only the existence but also the Providence of God, he shows by the texts of a great number of pagan authors that Greek philosophers were not alone in attributing providence to the invisible, unique, all-powerful God, the infinitely wise Cause of all goodness and all beauty Whom they had recognized; but that this same knowledge, although less developed, is spread through all classes of human society and in the peoples of all regions."

Saint Paul and the Fathers of the Church therefore affirm that pagan people not only *could have known*, but in fact even really *did know* the true God by reason.

And what can we conclude from that?—A human reason which would formally *deny* that God created the world, would not know the true God. But a human reason which has an idea of God (a philosophical idea or a common sense idea) in which the idea of creative power is *implicitly* contained, and yet which does not succeed in explicitly defining this idea, knows, perhaps imperfectly, but knows the true God, the creative God. Thus it is that He was known by the ancient peoples, and their philosophers, and Aristotle in particular.

---

[1] Kleutgen, *La philosophie scolastique exposée et défendue,* t. I, p. 437.

[2] *Ibid.,* p. 438.

[3] *Theologie der Vorzeit.*

III.—THE CONDEMNATIONS OF ARISTOTELIANISM IN THE MIDDLE AGES

a) The works of Aristotle first came to us in Latin-Arabic translations, accompanied by the *commenta* of Arabian interpreters. It is first of all because of the errors taught by the Arabs (and of which Albert the Great and Saint Thomas were to vindicate Aristotle) that these works were censured. Is it because of unbelieving commentators that the books of Descartes, Malebranche and many other modern philosophers have been put on the index? Think, however, of the prestige Descartes' philosophy boasted; it presented itself to the public of the seventeenth century as a much more decidedly theistic and spiritual system than is apparent today in any other contemporary philosophy. In spite of the decrees of the Sorbonne and the University councils, in spite of official "persecutions" (or because of them, for restraining measures succeed only if the "clerics" also, the philosophers and theologians, do their duty of enlightening men's minds and defending truth), the great minds of Gallican France took no notice of the condemnations incurred by Descartes and Malebranche. The future has shown whether Rome had the wrong view of things.

b) The censures brought against Aristotle's natural philosophy (and metaphysics) in 1210 by a council of the province of Sens meeting at Paris, and renewed in 1215 in the statute granted the University of Paris by the legate Robert de Courçon, were valid only for the University of Paris. And they forbade the use of Aristotle's books only in public or private lectures, each master "in private and for his own personal use," writes Msgr. Chollet,[1] "could read these books, study them, and write commentaries upon them."

The statute in question was confirmed in 1231 by Gregory IX, but, although in principle maintaining the old prohibition, the Pope declared that it would be only provisory, that is, valid until Aristotle's books had been submitted to examination and expurgated. At the same time he commissioned three masters in Paris, William of Auxerre, Simon of Authie and Stephen of Provins, to make this attempt at revision, which moreover was not at all successful. Later, in 1255, the Faculty of Arts did however inscribe on its programme the teaching of Aristotle practically unexpurgated, as it was then available. The Averroïst current was forming in Paris at about that time.[2] Disturbed by this grave danger, Urban IV in 1263 renewed the prohibition of 1231.

It is a question in this case of a statute concerning university studies: the prohibitions with which it condemns Aristotle are the sign of a very lively suspicion (justified by the advantage the Arabs and Averroïsts derived from works very difficult to understand and never tackled without the help of commentators). They are not at all comparable to an interdiction by the Index, which is valid for the universal Church and forbids all those who have no special authorization to read the forbidden work. Let us remember that in 1229 the University of Toulouse, founded and organized under the high patronage of the pontifical legate, sought to attract

---

[1] Dictionnaire de Théologie (Vacant-Mangenot), article *Aristotélisme de la Scolastique.* Cf. Forget, Report to the scientific Congress of Catholics, Brussels, 1894.

[2] Mandonnet, *Siger de Brabant,* t. I, pp. 18–26.

students to its rosters by luring them with the advantage of hearing there the inter-pretations of books banned at Paris: *Libros naturales qui fuerunt Parisius prohibiti poterunt illic audire qui volunt naturae sinum medullitus perscrutari,** and that at the time when Urban IV renews the prohibitions of 1231 and 1215 for Paris, we find at his court and under his encouragement, William of Moerbeke translating, and Saint Thomas Aquinas commenting on Aristotle's treatises.

The papacy has never denounced the Aristotelian doctrine as essentially linked up with errors incompatible with the faith. It only *applied the brakes* with pru-dence and energy until the Arabo-Aristotelian invasion, bearing along with it so many confused and pernicious elements, could be canalized, and become adapted to integration in Christian thought. Thanks to Saint Thomas that great work succeeded. The fact remains that the doctrines of Siger de Brabant show us "along what paths Aristotle, commented by Averroës, was capable of leading a philosopher who called himself a Christian, when the Church had departed from its severity with regard to the Stagirite."[1]

IV.—DESCARTES ON ARISTOTLE

Shall we not ask Descartes what to think about Aristotle? Perhaps he will give us a more objective and more scientific interpretation than Saint Thomas's. "Be-tween Plato and Aristotle," writes the father of modern philosophy, "there was no difference except that the first, following in the footsteps of his master Socrates, artlessly confessed that he had not yet been able to find anything certain, and con-tented himself with writing the things which seemed to him to be probable, imagining for that purpose some principles by which he attempted to give an ex-planation of the other things; whereas Aristotle was less frank; and although he had been his disciple for twenty years and had no other principles than his, he en-tirely changed the fashion of delivering them and proposed them as true and as-sured, although there is no evidence that he ever considered them as such."[2]—Note carefully that it is the scholastics who give a distorted image of modern philoso-phers and of Aristotle himself.

V.—CONCLUSION

In conclusion, I propose the following remarks: we are told that the Aristotle of Saint Thomas is not the Aristotle of history, and that he "is irreproachable." The Aristotle of history, the damnable Aristotle, is the Aristotle of the scholars. But that Aristotle is certainly dead, if indeed he ever lived, since the Aristotle to whom the disciples of Saint Thomas refer is not the Aristotle of history (of whom they are in ignorance as every one knows), and is precisely none other than the ficti-tious Aristotle, the "irreproachable" Aristotle of Saint Thomas.

What danger then can this irreproachable Aristotle cause Christian thought to run? Is it fair to denounce in him those errors of which the Angel of the School-

---

* In 1245, Innocent IV extended the prohibition to Toulouse, in the form established by Gregory IX in 1231. (Cf. de Wulf, *Hist. de la Phil. médiévale*, 1924, t. I, p. 236.)

1 Mandonnet, *op. cit.*, p. 18.

2 Preface to the French translation of *Principia Philosophiae*.

men so thoroughly relieved him? I am very much afraid that our despisers of Aristotle may find themselves, in truth,—some without wishing to do so and through an incomplete knowledge of Saint Thomas's doctrine, others by intention, and as a result of a deliberate aversion for the Doctor communis[1]—striking their blows not only against the Aristotle of history, but against the irreproachable Aristotle of Saint Thomas, and therefore against Saint Thomas himself.

Do our scholars insist on "throwing the Aristotle of history to the lions"? We are very glad to let them have THEIR *Aristotle of history. And as to the truly historical Aristotle (to the extent that he is accessible), if we defend his doctrines and his metaphysical principles against interpretations which in our view are pure misapprehensions, we know by other considerations what his errors were, his deficiencies, and the strictly terrestrial orientation of a wisdom which the grace of Christ had not yet delivered. He is not the one to whom we shall confide our soul. He interests us much less, moreover,—being only an historical personage,—than the intemporal substance, which alone is really important, of the truths with which he enriched the common patrimony. Under Saint Thomas's leadership, we reject in short, and as cheerfully as he, the Aristotle of the Arabs and the philosophical naturalism of the Averroïsts of the Middle Ages, as well as the Aristotle of the political naturalism of our day. Will it be granted on the other hand that we must follow Aristotle only to the extent, but to the full extent, that Saint Thomas Aquinas is Aristotelian? That is the only question worth more than an hour's pain, and it is all we ask. But certainly that can lead us very far.*

We shall have to say it once again: Saint Thomas is much freer and more original with regard to Aristotle than is often thought. With an "angelic" vigour he has rectified and really transfigured his doctrine, deepening and purifying it in the speculative order, creating entirely new and absolutely fundamental syntheses, like the theory of essence and existence; and completely recasting that same doctrine, by changing its spirit and practical orientation in the moral order, where the eternal destinies of the soul subordinate to themselves the conditions of our right existence here below, where human life hangs on a supernatural final end that Aristotle did not know, and is perfected by the grace of Christ, under the primacy of charity. But in all this work of integration, of correction, and of transfiguration, in which Plato has his place as well as Aristotle, and in which Saint Paul and Saint Augustine JUDGE *Plato and Aristotle, Saint Thomas, in order to go beyond Aristotle, has constantly used Aristotle as a perpetual philosophical* INSTRUMENT, *giving evidence,—not with regard to Aristotle, but with regard to the truths that Aristotle had recognized,—of that incomparable filial docility, of that chaste fear which is quite the contrary of servile docility, and which genius alone, and a perfect freedom of mind, is capable of; and following with a fidelity more complete and more rigorous than that of Aristotle himself the exigencies and internal logic of Aristotelian principles, of all the Aristotelian metaphysical principles. That is why we have written that* Saint Thomas is much more purely Aristotelian than Aristotle, *that is to say, since apparently a commentary is needed here, that the essential and specific principles which constitute the very life of Aristotelian philosophy are found in Saint Thomas in a much purer state than in Aristotle.*

[1] I am not thinking of Jacques Chevalier in this case.

This assertion may seem harsh to those who consider the distinction between the per se *and the* per accidens *to be an affair of supererogation. They see in it a "convenient" and gratuitous opinion whose principle would allow one to attribute to a proposition any meaning at all, and arbitrarily to approve or condemn "any system whatever." They do not realize that in talking that way they are destroying philosophy itself, which begins with the discernment of what is essential and what is not. Nor can the history of philosophy escape that law, if it is not a pure phenomenism (and it should then give up any search for intelligibility). It may be said that the necessity of separating the* per se *from the* per accidens *is painful and tiring, and that in a practical sense this distinction is difficult to handle. Granted! We shall have to resign ourselves to the risk of a headache. One cannot challenge that distinction without suicide. As to the opinion we have expressed on Saint Thomas in relation to Aristotle, any one who, on his own account, penetrates into Saint Thomas's thought will, I believe, easily verify its correctness.*

BIBLIOGRAPHY[1]

Essai sur les Données immédiates de la Conscience (Alcan, 1889).
  Translated under the title *Time and Free Will, an Essay on the Immediate Data of Consciousness*, by F. L. Pogson, M.A. (London, George Allen & Co.;) New York, The Macmillan Co., 1913.
  Cf. *Bulletin de la Société française de Philosophie*, meeting of February 26, 1903.
  Bulletin de la Société française de Philosophie, Philosophical Vocabulary, articles "Immédiat," "Intuition," "Liberté," etc. (Published since in the *Vocabulaire* by A. Lalande.)

Matière et Mémoire, essai sur la relation du corps à l'esprit (Alcan, 1896). Translated under the title *Matter and Memory*, by Nancy Margaret Paul and W. Scott Palmer (London, Swan, Sonnenschein & Co.; New York, The Macmillan Co., 1911).
  Cf. *Bulletin de la Société française de Philosophie*, meeting of May 2, 1901 (*Le Parallélisme psycho-physique et la Métaphysique positive*).
  Le Paralogisme psycho-physiologique (*Revue de Métaphysique et de Morale*, November 1904). Since published in *l'Énergie spirituelle*.
  l'Ame et le corps, Lecture given under the auspices of the review *Foi et Vie*, and published in *Foi et Vie*, December 16, 1912, and January 1, 1913. (Since published in *l'Énergie spirituelle*.)

Introduction à la Métaphysique (*Revue de Métaphysique et de Morale*, January 1903. Translated as Chapter VI (pp. 187–237) in *The Creative Mind*, by Mabelle L. Andison, New York, Philosophical Library, 1946.

L'Évolution Créatrice (Alcan, 1907).
  Translated under the title *Creative Evolution*, by Arthur Mitchell, Ph.D., New York, Henry Holt & Co., 1911.
  Cf. *L'Évolution Créatrice*, Bergson's answer to M. Le Dantec (*Revue du Mois*, September 10, 1907).
  Lettres de M. Bergson au R. P. de Tonquédec, published in *Études*, February 20, 1912.
  Lettre à Édouard Le Roy, in *Une philosophie nouvelle*, by Éd. Le Roy, Alcan, 1912.

---

[1] In this bibliography, which does not claim to be absolutely exhaustive but in which I believe I have indicated all that is essential, I have tried to group according to the affinity of the subjects dealt with, the main works and shorter articles of Bergson.

Lettre à Harald Höffding, in *La philosophie de Bergson*, by H. Höffding, Alcan, 1916.

Lettre à J. Chevalier, in *Bergson*, by J. Chevalier, Plon, 1926.

La Perception du Changement, Lectures given at the University of Oxford, May 26 and 27, 1911 (London, Henry Frowde, 1911).
Cf. *Réponse à M. W. D. Pitkin* (*Journal of Philosophy, Psychology, and Scientific Methods*, July 7, 1910).
Life and Consciousness (*Hibbert Journal*, October 1911).

L'Intuition philosophique, Lecture given at the international Congress of Philosophy at Bologne (*Revue de Métaphysique et de Morale*, November 1911.) Translated as Chapter IV in *Creative Mind*, pp. 126–152. Edited separately, Helleu and Sargent, 1928.

Address to the Oxford Meeting of 1920 (*Rev. de Mét. et de Mor.*, 1921, pp. 100–103).

L'Énergie spirituelle (Alcan, 1919).

Durée et simultanéité (Alcan, 1922; 2nd ed., 1923).

Extraits de Lucrèce (Delagrave, 1884).

La politesse, Speech at the closing exercises of the lycée of Clermont-Ferrand, August 5, 1885.

Quid Aristoteles de loco senserit, Alcan, 1889.

Le Bon Sens et les Études classiques, Speech given at the closing exercises of the 'Concours général,' July 30, 1895.

Le Rire, essai sur la signification du comique (Alcan, 1900).

Note sur les origines psychologiques de notre croyance à la loi de causalité, Library of the international Congress of Philosophy of 1900, vol. 1.

Le Rêve (*Bulletin de l'Institut psychologique international*, May 1901; *Revue scientifique*, June 8, 1902). (Since published in *l'Énergie spirituelle*.)

L'Effort intellectuel (*Revue philosophique*, January 1902). (Since published in *l'Énergie spirituelle*.)

Notice sur la vie et les œuvres de M. Félix Ravaisson-Mollien (Séances et travaux de l'Académie des Sciences morales et politiques, 1904). Translated as Chapter IX (pp. 261–300) of *Creative Mind*.

Lettre to the director of the *Revue philosophique* on the subject of Ward and James, 1905.

Rapport sur le concours pour le prix Bordin, ayant pour sujet Maine de Biran et sa place dans la philosophie moderne, Report of Séances et travaux de l'Académie des Sciences morales et politiques, Picard, 1906, vol. I.

Le souvenir du présent et la fausse reconnaissance (Revue philosophique, December 1908). (Since published in *l'Énergie spirituelle.*)

Introduction to the French translation of *Pragmatism* by William James, Alcan, 1911 (published by the *Journal des Débats* of April 25, 1911, under the title: *Vérité et Réalité*).

INDEX